Mental Illness in Popular Culture

Mental Illness in Popular Culture

Sharon Packer, MD, Editor

PRAEGER™

An Imprint of ABC-CLIO, LLC

Santa Barbara, California • Denver, Colorado

Library of Congress Cataloging-in-Publication Data

Name: Packer, Sharon, editor.
Title: Mental illness in popular culture / Sharon Packer, editor.
Description: Santa Barbara, California : Praeger, [2017] | Includes
    bibliographical references and index.
Identifiers: LCCN 2017002831 (print) | LCCN 2017005700 (ebook) |
    ISBN 9781440843884 (alk. paper) | ISBN 9781440843891 (EISBN)
Subjects: | MESH: Mental Disorders | Mentally Ill Persons | Motion Pictures
    as Topic | Television | Literature | Music
Classification: LCC RC454 (print) | LCC RC454 (ebook) | NLM WM 49 |
    DDC 616.89—dc23
LC record available at https://lccn.loc.gov/2017002831

ISBN: 978-1-4408-4388-4
EISBN: 978-1-4408-4389-1

21 20 19 18 17   1 2 3 4 5

This book is also available as an eBook.

Praeger
An Imprint of ABC-CLIO, LLC

ABC-CLIO, LLC
130 Cremona Drive, P.O. Box 1911
Santa Barbara, California 93116-1911
www.abc-clio.com

This book is printed on acid-free paper ∞
Manufactured in the United States of America

Contents

Introduction

Sharon Packer, MD

How times change. The more things change, the more they stay the same.

Each of those seemingly contradictory statements apply to our topic of mental illness in popular culture.

Fifty years ago, in 1966, legendary songwriters saluted the psychotic state. The Rolling Stones sang about "My 19th Nervous Breakdown." *Rolling Stone* magazine described Mick Jagger and Keith Richard's song as "a lyrical breakthrough, with references to drugs and therapy."[1] The song peaked at No. 2 on the *Billboard* Hot 100.[2] The Stones performed the song on *The Ed Sullivan Show*, the Sunday night TV show that catapulted up-and-coming entertainers to stardom.[3]

"They're Coming to Take Me Away, Ha-Haaa!" by Napoleon XIV (Jerry Samuels) also made it to the *Billboard* Hot 100 in that very same year: 1966. "They're Coming to Take Me Away, Ha-Haaa!" reached No. 3 by week 3, but plummeted after two New York Top 40 music radio stations banned the song, fearing that it might offend the mentally ill. The ban inspired teen protests and arguably boosted the song's profile and prestige. The commotion made it even more memorable. Many of today's baby boomers can still recite the lyrics they heard as teens in 1966.

In 1966, and throughout the early 1970s, society vacillated in its attitudes toward "mental illness"—as evidenced by the polarized reactions to Jerry Samuels's novelty song about the "funny farm" and "men in white coats." On one hand, counterculture/youth culture valorized psychotic states, as happened during the romantic era, when artist Francisco Goya (1746–1828) inadvertently started the trend as his career as a court portrait painter neared its end. Goya's chronic lead poisoning (related to lead-based white paint) led to visions, deafness, and tremor. His mental state declining, his imagery changed from prim and proper to dark and diabolical.

Psychedelic drugs of the 1960s and 1970s replicated psychotic perceptions and were sought after because of those very qualities—although Sandoz Laboratories intended those research drugs to treat schizophrenia or at least illuminate the mechanisms behind this severe mental illness. Drugs that since became known as "psychotomimetics" (because they mimic psychosis) took center stage in the countercultural circus. Only a small percentage of the American public used LSD (5 percent, per Lee and Shlain's book, *Acid Dreams: The CIA, LSD and the Sixties Rebellion*[4]), yet LSD-like imagery saturated the media, inspiring posters, graphic art, even fashion, as well as so-called psychedelic music. Stories about psychologists-turned-"high priests" of LSD were told and retold[5]—but in 1966, Sandoz recalled the LSD it had supplied to medical researchers and withdrew its formal support of once-serious studies that got out of control and created chaos (as well as cultural change and a permanent place in popular cultural history).[6] Still, per the reigning counterculture's ethos, psychosis was aspired to, not avoided or stigmatized as it is today.

In 1966, cult films proclaimed the counterculture's preference for psychotic states over ordinary activities of daily life and certainly instead of wartime activities. Alan Bates starred in a Scottish film (*King of Hearts*) about a World War I soldier sent to disarm a bomb left by the German army. Everyone in the town has fled except for jubilant asylum inmates, whose incarceration has sheltered them from the goings-on in the "real world." Instead, they celebrate daily life and dance through the streets. One calls herself "Columbine," adopting the name of a flower (like the "flower children" of the era). The soldier falls in love with her and opts for the delusional world of asylum inmates over the "insanity" of those who wage war on the outside. As the film ends, he arrives at the asylum gate, without clothes but with a birdcage in hand, waiting to enter the asylum. Philipe de Broca's *King of Hearts* (1966) remains a cult classic to this day, a vestige of the antiwar movement and an endorsement of the value of retreating from the "real world" of sanity, in favor of pursuing more pleasant alternative realities and avoiding war's conflicts and conflagrations.

As the years passed, *King of Hearts* retained its loyal following and evoked fond memories of a bygone youth culture, but critics of *King of Hearts* have since denounced the film's stereotyped portrayal of the asylum's inmates. They claim that their childlike insouciance and cheerfulness are, well, childlike and thereby do a disservice to persons with mental illness. Let me point out that critics exist to criticize and so it should be no surprise that some critics damned this lighthearted comedy almost as vigorously as mental health advocacy groups condemn slashers for their unkind portrayals of psychiatric patients.

Those *King of Hearts* asylum inmates are far removed from movies' violent mental patients that invoke the ire of present-day detractors of mass media. Some argue that the overrepresentation of psychotic characters in cinema misrepresents the majority of persons who seek treatment for mental illness. And many Americans do indeed seek treatment for various mental woes—20 percent of the population currently gets prescriptions for psychotropic medications and some 25 percent will receive a diagnosis of mental illness at some point in their lifetimes. Only a small minority of those persons suffer from serious mental illness such as schizophrenia or bipolar I disorder, the latter of which may include psychotic features as well as mood swings. Depression is much, much more common than mania, and even persons with "manic-depression" (now known as bipolar disorder) typically spend far more time in the depressed phase than in flamboyant, attention-grabbing, hyperbolic manic episodes. Statistics aside, the manic phase of bipolar disorder gets much more screen time than the decidedly more prevalent depressed phase.

There are good reasons why we do not see many movies about depression as a stand-alone condition (unless it ends with suicide). Depressive states do not make for interesting movies. Depressed persons sleep more, move little, talk less, and hardly socialize at all (although some depressives pace endlessly and aimlessly). For cinema that depends upon visuals and dialogue, the dramatic manic phase of bipolar disorder is far, far more interesting. Perhaps a skilled writer could do justice to depression—and many have succeeded over the centuries—but movies can be boring (unless, perhaps, they are Bergman's or "art cinema"). Kierkegaard's brooding journals, several of Dostoyevsky novels, even Goethe's *Sorrows of Young Werther* captured the spirit of sadness and suicide, and remain classics to this day. More recent works, many by women writers, have eloquently translated dark feelings into words. Even more recently, poignant graphic novels and memoirs wed image and word, with powerful effect and to public acclaim.

However, novels, poems, and memoirs, even when illustrated, do not share the persuasive power of the moving image. And so cinema bears the brunt of the criticism about mass media, even if the film is based on a previously-published novel that tackled the very same topics.

There is no denying that slashers portrayed psychosis (and Down syndrome) as scary and dangerous. Slashers peaked in popularity in the late 1970s, and continued through the early 1980s and even longer, in modified form. In hindsight, slashers began in earnest with Hitchcock's *Psycho* (1960). Norman Bates is not identified as a mental patient until the film ends, when a psychiatrist explains the origins of his bizarre behavior.

Until that moment, his obsession with taxidermy and his mother's clothes, his social awkwardness and isolation, and his escalating arguments with an unseen "mother" suggest that something is seriously amiss.

Did the entertainment industry set out to degrade and devalue persons with mental illness when it released unsavory portrayals of persons with psychosis?[7] I doubt it. Do Hollywood films about mental illness compare to Nazi-era films such as *Jud Suß* (1940), which spread vicious anti-Semitic propaganda and reified racial discrimination policies outlined by the Nuremburg Laws of 1933? Highly, highly, highly unlikely. Are Hollywood filmmakers diverting their resources to advocate Nazi-style extermination of "mental defectives," chronically mentally ill persons, or "incurable alcoholics," as occurred during the Third Reich's formal T4 program?[8] Not by a long shot, on all counts—although one might expect to find (non-existent) crossovers, given the vitriolic allegations made against the movie industry and against the media in general.

I am more inclined to turn to economic determinism to explain the proliferation of such films at certain points in time. After one slasher proved profitable and popular, it led to another and another, since success breeds success. Soon enough, an entire genre emerged. Perhaps *Psycho* launched this trend, and perhaps Hitchcock's masterpiece reflected society's unease about releasing more institutionalized patients in the mid-1950s, after the antipsychotic medication Thorazine became available in the United States and made it possible to move previously incurable patients from locked wards to open communities. Or perhaps *Psycho's* commercial and critical success simply reflected Hitchcock's mastery of his art and nothing but. Or both.

As to why the public appreciates these themes enough to patronize movie houses (in the days before TV reruns of first-run films, video releases, or pay-per-view broadcasts), I would consider the unquantifiable contribution of "schadenfreude." Schadenfreude refers to the enjoyment experienced when learning of someone else's failures or misfortunes—not because of the spectator's sadistic streak but because of the sense of relief that comes from learning that someone else—and not oneself—suffers from an affliction that strikes a certain percentage of the population. Even the German-speaking psychoanalysts could not coin an adequate English term for this common reaction and retained the German word. This is a very primitive, visceral reaction that is almost biblical in nature. It reminds us of myths about the angel of death or the grim reaper who must capture a set number of souls, but can stop their "harvesting" after meeting their quota. Knowing that someone else besides ourselves has incurred some miserable fate that is known to afflict a certain percentage of the population assures us—the spectators—that our own number is not yet up.

How to explain the rise of slasher franchises two decades later? It is plausible that unique social and medical conditions of the early 1980s, when AIDS emerged, encouraged the slashers' proliferation in that era. AIDS connected the dots between sex and death (once known in psycho-analytic lore as "Eros and Thanatos"). Slasher victims were typically sexually free young women who got their come-uppance and implicitly "merited" death sentences as retribution for their sexual "sins." This recurring meme seemed so much more real after AIDS emerged.

These patterns in film genres repeat themselves. For instance, in 1975, Steven Spielberg's *Jaws* became a big-budget, high-grossing blockbuster film. The unexpected success of *Jaws* inspired more movies about "natural evil," often action-adventure-oriented and special effects-laden—not because the filmmakers harbored unspoken (or even unconscious) anti-shark attitudes, and probably not because directors or producers or actors were "working through" traumatic childhood swimming memories left over from summer camp or because someone on set wanted to taunt someone with shark phobias. More likely, someone saw possibilities of future box office success with *Jaws* look-alikes and knockoffs. (Admittedly, *Jaws* did change popular attitudes toward oceans and made many people fearful of swimming in unenclosed spaces.)

The big screen may bear the brunt of these antimedia attacks, but television shows' attitudes toward persons with mental illness has not gone unnoticed. An article in *U.S. News* predictably condemned television, citing scholars that claim that "mental illness is misrepresented in the media," in that "mental illnesses are all severe—or all alike" [on the small screen].[9] Quoting Diefenbach's research, the author complains that "depression only accounted for 7 percent of the psychiatric disorders shown on TV. However, 12 percent of the characters suffered from some form of psychosis—experiencing delusions or voices, or losing touch with reality" . . . [but] "In reality, depression is much more common than mental disorders such as schizophrenia and bipolar disorder. . . . The real-world relationship is going to be that depression outnumbers the family of psychotic disorders by about 6 or 7 to one." Yet on TV, "the most extreme cases—and the rarest disorders—tend to be disproportionately represented."

In a way, I am surprised that the author is surprised. For this should not be so surprising, if we compare representations of mental illness on television to representations of medical illness on TV. Since the early days of television, medical dramas, soap operas and occasional comedies have enjoyed prime time spots. Many such shows became household words (think *Ben Casey, Dr. Kildare, Quincy, House,* or *ER*). Yet how many of those family doctors and ER doctors or neurosurgeons or pathologists (in the case of *Quincy*) diagnose only mundane medical woes? Few, if any, even though medical care is replete with mundane care, as attested by the oft-quoted medical expression, "when you hear hoofbeats, don't look for zebras" (implying that hoofbeats herald the arrival of ordinary horses much more often, so look for ordinary illnesses first).

In my experience as a medical student rotating through general surgery at a private lakefront hospital in Chicago (intended to offset the rigors of rotations at Cook County Hospital), I mostly scrubbed on hernias or hemorrhoids. Rotations on surgical "specialty services" might have offered more intriguing possibilities, but death-defying heart transplants or heroic separation of Siamese twins were all but nonexistent. Yes, occasional GSWs (gunshot wounds) or stabbings arrived at the emergency room, but all in all, most surgeries performed outside of major trauma centers did not make for interesting dinnertime conversations, either for the doctors or the medical students (though possibly for the patients and their families). Can you imagine a medical show that showcases the day-to-day OR schedule of a community hospital—instead of interesting and unusual cases that make it to prime-time TV? Where would Quincy or House be, were it not for the so-called zebras they diagnose?

Much the same could be said for pediatrics rotations at the university hospital that treated inner city residents, farmers, and their families who traveled from all over Illinois, as well as children requiring specialized hematology, cardiology, or nephrology services. Apart from the fact that children develop different diseases than adults, the pediatrics ER and clinic visits were predictable and revolved around mundane medical care. Only very, very rarely do checks for nuchal (neck) rigidity require spinal taps to rule out the uncommon meningitis case. Can you imagine a medical show filled with repeated ear inspections, sore throat swabs, and temperature-taking, rather than rare leukemias that require bone marrow transplants from reluctant, missing, even imprisoned relatives (some of whom might need presidential pardons or prison furloughs so they can donate life-saving cells)?[10] Children on medical shows may suffer from uncommon brain cancers, sickle cell crises, or status epilepticus, or need transfusions that their parents' religion prevents—but those life-threatening cases constitute a tiny percentage of consultations compared to the vast numbers of earaches, sore throats, and benign bellyaches.

Given these precedents, why would anyone expect ordinary yet common psychiatric symptoms—such as anxiety—to merit more attention than hernias and hemorrhoids accrue on ER shows? Perhaps our expectations of representations of psychiatric conditions are higher, since "mental cases" occur on a continuum with "the human condition," and force us to distinguish ordinary suffering related to life's unfair blows (or even life's expected losses) from diagnosable and distinctive disorders that deserve diagnoses as "mental illness." Humans have good reason for concern about the so-called human condition that intrigued philosophers and poets throughout history, long before such suffering fell under the rubric of "mental illness." To be fair, I should add that it is not always easy to distinguish pathological reactions to extreme stress or loss from "ordinary" or expected reactions, as demonstrated by the heated debates about labeling grief following bereavement as major depressive disorder or about conflating "shyness" with a diagnosable and (pharmacologically treatable) social anxiety disorder.[11]

Some of those who blame movies and mass media for stigmatizing mental illness also claim that such negative portrayals deter persons who need treatment from seeking treatment. Critics make eloquent arguments and present persuasive data, but without necessarily contemplating the contribution of direct-to-consumer (DTC) pharmaceutical advertising. DTC ads became legal in the US in 1985, but skyrocketed after 1997, when the FDA further loosened its rules on television "infomercials." Previously, advertising psychiatric medications had been discouraged but was not officially outlawed.

DTC ads do not necessarily tout a product—some merely supply information about symptoms and recommend consultations with doctors.[12] Sources such as *The New England Journal of Medicine* note that such ads can prevent underprescription of medications while they also encourage overutilization.[13] Think of them as dandruff commercials from the 1950s, which showed the hapless dandruff sufferer—who never suspected his dandruff—brushing off specks of skin from the shoulders of his dark suit, as others looked on with expressions of scorn and disgust. Those ads aimed to increase awareness of dandruff, for starters, as much as they sought to sell special shampoos. Similarly, DTC pharmaceutical ads try to convince viewers that they suffer from new conditions before they push new products to treat those conditions.

We know that DTC ads drive up health care costs, and increase demand for expensive brand name medications in lieu of less costly generics, yet we do not fully understand their impact on attitudes toward mental illness, among the public or professionals, except for the fact that those ubiquitous ads sell prescription medications. A 2016 *Medscape* article[14] that summarizes a research study from *The Journal of Clinical Psychiatry*

(September 2016) is more cautionary and adds more specific data. It notes that psychiatric medications represented 20 percent of the most advertised drugs between 2014–2015 and were 10 percent of the 100 top-selling drugs.

To date, only the United States and New Zealand permit pharmaceutical ads targeted directly to consumers (as opposed to health care professionals or hospitals). In the wake of this advertising trend, more and more consumers are exposed to DTC advertising imagery and are presumably influenced by those ads—for why else would pharmaceutical manufacturers invest their stockholders' money in such pricey propaganda? Those ads that began on TV commercials now pop up on social media, in Internet searches, on personal mobile devices as well as computers. As most of us know by now, a Google search for a symptom, a click on a medication ad, or a visit to a manufacturer's Web site guarantees a barrage of ads for products promising to treat the symptoms—or the disease complex that the symptoms suggest. Ads for competitors' products appear instantaneously and without provocation. Were Andy Warhol alive today, he might be painting repeat images of bouncing, smiling antidepressant pills instead of Campbell's soup cans.

Ads for psychopharmaceuticals remind viewers that they need treatment, often for conditions that they never knew they had before an unsolicited ad flashed on their cell phone screens. (Some ads target specific demographics that are likely to use such products or choose audiences with online purchasing histories that correlate with histories of other persons who purchased their products.) Very often, medications that were developed for psychosis or schizophrenia are marketed as "depression adjuncts," to be prescribed to persons whose mental distress is far-removed from such serious psychosis. Some of the most profitable medications on the market started out as powerful antipsychotic agents. The overwhelming majority of those medications are prescribed in doctors' offices (and not even in psychiatrists' offices, since primary care physicians or nurse practitioners prescribe about 85 percent of psychiatric medications).

Clearly, it is not in the interest of those powerful marketers to stigmatize their potential market and push it away, especially after they invest millions (or more) of advertising dollars. In contrast, it is in their interest to convince their audience that psychiatric symptoms, be they major or minor, can be—and should be—treated with their products. Pharmaceutical ads are not so new—they abounded in the days of patent medications. Displays of those compelling—and often amusing—graphics abound on Pinterest and other social media sites. Patent medications went by the wayside long before television made its way to most American homes and long, long before the advent of computers and mobile devices. Over-the-counter nonprescription medication advertising remains a fixture on television commercials, although many were revised or eliminated as regulations tightened. (Think of early Geritol commercials, which promised to pep up iron-deficient geriatric consumers—without disclosing the high alcohol content of the vitamin and mineral tonic hawked by smiling grey-haired male models.)

When we consider how many advertising dollars are spent on these pharmaceutical ads, and how profitable pharmaceutical sales can be in the United States, we must wonder why so many lobbying groups (some of which are funded by pharma) protest so loudly. If Dr. Jonas Salk, inventor of the polio vaccine, were making these allegations, we might take them at face value, for the altruistic and high-minded Salk refused to patent his discovery because he believed that protecting public health and preventing infantile paralysis overrode the importance of profits. However, most present-day practitioners and Big Pharma boards of directors are far-removed from Dr. Salk. We would be foolish to believe that pharma-funded lobbying groups have only the public good in mind when they protest "misrepresentations" of mental illness in media.

In short, entertainment-oriented mass media is not America's only exposure to mental illness. Moreover, not all entertainment denigrates persons with mental illness. Some media romanticizes mental illness or portrays patients as super-powered or extra-talented. Many media representations of mental illness celebrate the accomplishments of persons with mental illness and recognize that some of the most enduring contributions to culture were made by persons who were formally or retrospectively diagnosed with mental illness: Poe, Van Gogh, Cobain, Goya. Outsider artists and "autists" (autistic artists) gained currency in the 20th and 21st centuries, so much so that prestigious Ivy League art schools train MFA students to emulate such "raw art."

Unlike residents of Nazi Germany, the imaginary inhabitants of *1984*, members of the armed forces, or persons remanded to rehab for DWIs (driving while intoxicated) or other drug offenses, no adult in America is forced to view specific films or TV shows. We can choose our entertainment. With trailers, teasers, and reviews so easily accessible through apps or the Internet, no one needs to walk into a movie theater or turn on a TV show without some awareness of what is to come. Even though films and broadcast media are persuasive, and some films have been shown to change attitudes, it is likely that persons who deliberately choose to watch negative depictions of persons with mental illness already have preset notions about mental illness and are seeking to validate their views. That said, our choice of entertainment often functions as a Rorschach test, and tells us what we want to see. It is not propaganda.

In other words, the "hypodermic needle" model of media influence is not necessarily correct, even if it is touted so often as to make it appear accurate. The hypodermic needle model references the belief that "behaviors [or attitudes] are essentially injected into hapless consumers," as psychologist Christopher Ferguson, Ph.D., explains in the November 24, 2016 *Psychiatric Times* edition and in other publications as well. Focusing largely on media-mediated aggression more than on attitudes, Ferguson elaborates on newer theoretical models such as Self-Determination Theory and Mood Management theory. Such models contradict the more moralistic models that assume that imitation of behavior or attitudes is "automatic, universal, and purposeless." That is not to say that some films are *not* persuasive; the anti-ECT attitudes adopted by medical students after a single viewing of *One Flew Over the Cuckoo's Nest* have been well-documented by social psychologists and others. Yet let me point out that Milos Forman's film about mistreatment in a mental hospital *did not* make spectators think less of the patients under Nurse Ratched's charge. Rather, *Cuckoo's Nest* made medical students (and the public) mistrust the mental hospital staff. The viewers commiserated with the mental patients/inmates and presumably identified with those who were victimized and subjected to punitive (rather than curative) electroconvulsive therapy.

We can argue these points back and forth indefinitely, but arriving at a consensus, as if this were a jury trial, is not the point of this collection. We do not seek a totalizing explanation of all representations of mental illness in media or pop culture. Just the opposite. We emphasize pop culture's pluralism, and include chapters by scholars with diverse points of view and from varied academic backgrounds. We deliberately avoid knee-jerk, antipopular culture reactions. While it may be politically correct to blame pop culture for almost anything, such claims are not necessarily factually correct.

This single volume does not cover all the many fascinating topics relevant to this theme—that venture would require a multivolume encyclopedia at minimum. To my regret, we do not have as many chapters on music or musicians as I had wished, so it is my hope that my own musical references at the start of this introduction will offer some recompense for this admitted shortcoming. The topic of popular music and mental illness is vast, and has been a subject of study since ancient times. In the Hebrew Bible, David soothed the soul of the paranoid King Saul by playing his harp, while the Greeks linked music to wine, debauchery, and altered states of consciousness (anticipating the 1960s adage about "sex, drugs, and rock and roll").

At this point, I must mention other aspects of mental health that are intentionally not included in this volume, such as substance use disorders. Even though substance use disorders are listed as psychiatric disorders in the American Psychiatry Association's *DSM-5* (*Diagnostic and Statistical Manual of Mental Disorders*, 5th edition), essays exclusively related to the representation of substance use disorders in popular culture were culled out, not because substance use is not important or relevant, but, contrarily, because it is so very important and so prevalent as to merit many separate studies. In a few instances, essays address substance use disorders that are comorbid (that coexist) with other mental illness, to emphasize the difficulty of determining which is the cause and which is the effect, or which is the chicken or the egg.

Dementia (such as Alzheimer's Disease or Huntington's Disease) is also excluded from this collection, even though the dementias that impair cognition and memory are classified as psychiatric or behavioral disorders in both the *DSM-5* and in the ICD-10 (International Classification of Disease). Again, this circumscribed and specialized topic, which falls on the threshold of psychiatry and neurology, deserves a separate study to do it justice and to consider our society's evolving attitudes toward aging, memory, intelligence, and behavioral disinhibition. We find thoughtful treatments of this topic in a wide range of movies, from *Memento* (2000), to *Rise of the Planet of the Apes* (2011), to *Still Alice* (2014). Outsider art by older persons, some of whom have suffered strokes or other age-related neurological illness, is equally important and has been given attention in museum shows and folk art exhibitions and deserves more attention.

Similarly, developmental disorders or intellectual disability (formerly known as "mental retardation") that begin in childhood are not subjects of our study, even though persons with cognitive limitations commonly show behavioral changes that require psychiatric intervention. Considering that some films featuring persons with such disorders, such as *Charly* (1968) or *Rainman* (1988), remain among the most beloved or best-known films of all times, this topic is also ripe for a thorough review in a more specialized collection.

Yet another unfortunate omission from this volume is essays on pop cultural representations of children's mental illness, found most notably in *The Exorcist* (1973) and elsewhere. Debates about the proper diagnosis and treatment of childhood behavioral disorders are legion, and engage parents, teachers, pediatricians, child psychiatrists and psychologists, the courts, and CPS (child protective services), for starters. Literary and filmic depictions of bizarre behavior in children invite almost as much discussion as currently contested—but increasingly used—psychopharmaceutical approaches to treating such behavior. (Once-popular long-term hospitalizations, residential schools, "wilderness programs," or even "juvie" (juvenile hall) for delinquent children have caused contention as well, but pharmaceutical approaches, often untested and used "off-label" for children, have taken center stage in 21st century debates.)

Edited collections by Markus P.J. Bohlmann and Sean Moreland (*Monstrous Children and Childish Monsters: Essays on Cinema's Holy Terrors*, McFarland 2015) covers one slant of this broad topic, and includes my own essay about Ritalin prescriptions for MBD (minimal brain dysfunction)/proto-ADHD diagnoses in *The Exorcist* (1973) ("Demon Drugs or Demon Children: Take Your Pick"). Amazon's book listings show several academic publications about diametrically different media memes regarding children. Since we were all once children, each of us is qualified in one way or another to opine on the topic of children and aberrant behavior.

Another issue that this collection does not address, and for which I offer no apologies, is the topic of "madness" (as opposed to mental illness), and for very good reasons. This book specifically covers mental illness, although allusions to madness seep into some sociologically-oriented essays which conflate madness and mental illness. Again, that omission does not imply that madness is not significant, but simply that madness and mental illness carry very different connotations. "Madness" is a descriptive bestowed by society—not by organized medicine or mental health professionals. "Madness" is shorthand for behaviors or perceptions that fall grievously outside of a given society's social norms. What one society deems "mad" and therefore undesirable may be esteemed in another society, making the study of madness the purview of the anthropologist, if not also the psychiatrist.

Mental illness, in contrast, denotes disorders that are identified as illness and are diagnosed as pathological by medical or psychiatric practitioners. Mental illness is a medical/mental health rubric whereas madness is a sociological construct. In our contemporary American society, the medical/mental health establishment decides who is mad and who is not and then translates those behaviors or perceptions or cognitions into DSM terms. In that case, the American Psychiatric Association (which publishes *DSM*) substitutes for the "elders" of less complicated societies and spells out its views in published and often revised volumes. The American Psychological Society, comprised of non-medically trained psychologists, comments on such controversies as well. At times, there is no consensus, and in those cases the *DSM* is revised once again, after several years of careful study.[15]

Importantly, please note that mental illness is not synonymous with insanity, even though the two can be conflated and (incorrectly) used interchangeably. "Insanity" is a legal term, not a clinical term. The courts of law determine who is sane and who is insane, and who can be held criminally culpable for their unlawful actions, be lawfully deprived of freedom of movement (e.g., confined to a psychiatric ward), or denied financial independence (e.g., deprived of the right to execute a valid will), or the right to self-determination (e.g., refusal of medical treatment) because such persons lack mental capacity for safe decision making. The courts typically seek psychiatric opinions to make these legal—rather than clinical—decisions.

What does this book include? Divided into five parts this book covers movies; television; popular literature, encompassing novels, poetry, and memoirs; the visual arts, such as fine art, video games, comics, and graphic novels; and popular music, addressing lyrics and musicians' lives. Some of the essays reference multiple media, such as a filmic adaptation of a memoir, a video game adaptation of a story, or characters that were originally in comics.[16]

With roughly 20 percent of U.S. citizens taking psychotropic prescriptions or carrying a psychiatric diagnosis, and with many times that number having friends, family members, co-workers or colleagues who use psychiatric services, this topic is relevant to far more individuals than many people would admit. Mental illness is on the radar for almost everyone, and so is pertinent to society overall, given that discussions about mental illness invariably follow the adverse events that society has witnessed in recent years.

The uptick in mass shootings in schools, on military bases, in workplaces, on public transportation, or at large public gatherings casts a harsher light on mental illness, especially since some perpetrators carry mental illness diagnoses at the time they commit their acts, while some have shown symptoms that went undiagnosed or untreated.[17] Discussions typically focus on mass shootings, even though mass shootings account for only a tiny percentage of firearm-related deaths. Debates about rights to carry arms—or denial of that constitutional right to persons with histories of mental illness—typically follow these events and turn discussions into political battlefields, with antigun activists typically waging war against gun rights groups. Multiple murders that *do not* involve firearms (such as drowning one's children) do not follow the patterns of mass shootings and often involve family members, and so tap into other fears.

Persons with serious mental illness are admittedly three to four times more likely to commit violent crimes, and the concomitant use of intoxicants increases that likelihood, as per a 2016 article in *JAMA* (*Journal of the American Medical Association*),[18] but most people with mental illness are not violent and are more likely to be victims of crimes rather than perpetrators.

While politically or religiously motivated terrorists make headlines, and claim lives or cripple their victims (and incite terror), for most of us, those terrorists are "others" who are distinct from us and deserve the attention of law enforcement agencies. In contrast, the mentally ill live among us (for the most part), perhaps even in our own homes or in the house down the block. Mentally ill persons attend our children's schools (and sometimes also teach in them). Seriously mentally ill persons attend colleges in greater numbers than ever before. They visit churches, synagogues, mosques, temple picnics, and yard sales like anyone else. For the most part, persons with mental illness are invisible to others, unless they self-identify. In a way, their ability to pass in a crowd compounds society's fear that they will act out erratically, without warning, to do us harm.[19]

Mentally ill offenders leave us wondering who is "mad" and who is "bad," and when and if illness exonerates otherwise unpardonable behavior. These questions linger in our consciousness and increase interest in these issues. Popular culture offers a forum for playing and replaying these events, and for deliberating difficult decisions that are both moral and medical. Some psychiatric physicians see such pop culture as an avenue for peaceful public interchange of opinions and for challenging our preconceptions, sometimes by presenting provocative imagery that demands response. Other mental health professionals and advocates point a finger at pop culture for sensationalizing and stigmatizing mental illness, perpetuating stereotypes, and capitalizing on the increased anxiety that follows attacks mentioned above.[20]

In the end, I leave it to readers to make their own decisions, if they feel compelled to make any overarching decisions on such matters at all. Unfortunately, the once-popular arguments about genius and madness that intrigued the Romantics and neo-Romantics of later generations do not seem as compelling as contemporary arguments about violence and illness, but those deliberations may offer some respite from less pleasant realities of real life today. Then again, psychologist and scholar Louis Sass offers an alternative explanation and posits that madness defines modernity and that psychotic perceptions are intertwined with the zeitgeist of the 20th century—so it should be no surprise that the 21st century seems so off-kilter.[21]

Notes

1. "100 Greatest Rolling Stones Songs," accessed online November 13, 2016, www.rollingstone.com.

2. Billboard, www.billboard.com, March 19, 1966, accessed online November 20, 2016, www.billboard.com.

3. The legacy of Mick Jagger's and Keith Richard's song lives on. "My 19th Nervous Breakdown" was used in Adam Sandler's spoof on *Anger Management* (2003), in Stephen King's *Dark Tower* series (1982–2012), and in a short-lived TV medical drama, *Miami Medical* (2010); my thanks to Harold Benson, PhD, professor emeritus, for his exegesis of these lyrics.

4. Martin A. Lee and Bruce Shlain, *Acid Dreams: The CIA, LSD and the Sixties Rebellion* (New York: Grove Press, 1994).

5. Articles about bankers who sought shamanic hallucinogens graced the front page of coffee-table "family magazines" as early as 1957, well before the start of the 1960s. See R. Gordon Wasson, "Seeking the Magic Mushroom," *Life*, May 12, 1957.

6. Albert Hofmann, *LSD: My Problem Child* (New York: McGraw-Hill, 1980); Sharon Packer, "Drugs and the Summer of Love: A Summer Fling, not a Lasting Romance," in *Pop Culture Universe*, Eternal Questions Series (ABC-Clio, Fall 2012).

7. For harsh criticism of depictions of mental illness in horror movies and elsewhere, see Otto F. Wahl, *Media Madness: Public Images of Mental Illness* (New Brunswick, NJ: Rutgers University Press, 1995). Less emotive accounts appear in Jacqueline Noll Zimmerman, *People Like Ourselves: Portrayals of Mental Illness in the Movies* (Lantham, MD: Scarecrow Press, 2003); David J. Robinson, *Reel Psychiatry: Movie Portrayals of Psychiatric Conditions* (Port Huron, MI: Rapid Psychler Press, 2003); and Danny Wedding, Mary Ann Boyd, and Ryan M. Niemiec, *Movies and Mental Illness: Using Films to Understand Psychopathology*, 3rd rev. ed. (Cambridge, MA: Hogrefe Publishing, 2010). For approaches that view madness in movies as metaphors or as historical artifacts, see Fernando Espi Forcen, *Demons, Monsters and Psychopaths* (New York: CRC Press, 2017); Sharon Packer, *Cinema's Sinister Psychiatrists* (Jefferson, NC: McFarland, 2012); or Sharon Packer, *Movies and the Modern Psyche* (Westport, CT: Praeger, 2007).

8. See Rael D. Stone, "Nazi Euthanasia of the Mentally Ill at Hadamar," *American Journal of Psychiatry* 2006 (163:27). Gas chambers originally built for Operation T4 were subsequently repurposed to annihilate Jews and Gypsies. The Nazis halted the gassing of mentally and physically handicapped persons in response to international protests and interventions by clergymen. In effect, those gas chambers served as SS training grounds for the Final Solution.

9. Kirstin Fawcett, "How Mental Illness is Misrepresented in the Media," *U.S. News & World Report*, April 16, 2015, accessed online November, 16 2016, http://health.usnews.com/health-news/health-wellness/articles/2015/04/16/how-mental-illness-is-misrepresented-in-the-media.

10. *The Blacklist*, a 2016 television drama about government agents and their personal and professional intrigues, uses a similar ploy in a hospital scene.

11. Freud's 1917 essay "On Mourning and Melancholia" explains how persons suffering from melancholia (today's equivalent of major depressive disorder) behave as if in mourning. Even though much of Freud's work has been contested over the decades, this essay remains a classic and is relevant (yet often overlooked) to this day.

12. Ishmael Bradley, "DTC Advertising, and Its History with the FDA," Kevinmd.com, September 18, 2016 (reprinted on Doximity), accessed online November 16, 2016.

13. Julie M. Donahue et al., "A Decade of Direct-to-Consumer Advertising of Prescription Drugs," *New England Journal of Medicine*, August 2007; Bryan C. Liang and Timothy Mackey, "Direct-to-Consumer Advertising with Interactive Internet Media," *JAMA* 305, no. 8 (2011): 824–5; Jeremy A Greene and Elizabeth Watkins, "The Vernacular of Risk-Rethinking Direct-to-Consumer Advertising of Pharmaceutical," *New England Journal of Medicine* 373 (2015): 1087–9.

14. Pauline Anderson, "Direct-to-Consumer Ads Boost Psychiatric Drug Use," *Medscape Medical News*, September 19, 2016, accessed online November 20, 2016.

15. Allen Frances, MD, chair of the *DSM-IV* Task Force, eloquently explains the complicated reasoning behind these processes in his book *Saving Normal* (New York: Morrow, 2013).

16. Thanks to George Higham, BFA, for his cover art depicting the musical scales, film reels, TV and video game monitors, writers' plumes, and artists' palettes that suggest the wide range of pop culture covered in this book.

17. Michael S. Rosenwald, "Most Mass Shooters Aren't Mentally Ill. So Why Push Better Treatment as the Answer?" *Washington Post*, May 18, 2016, accessed online November 20, 2016.

18. Seena Fazel et al., "Triggers for Violent Criminality in Patients with Psychotic Disorders," *JAMA Psychiatry* 73, no. 8 (2016): 796–803.

19. Aaron Levin, "Media Cling to Stigmatizing Portrayals of Mental Illness," *Psychiatric News*, December 16, 2011.

20. Otto F. Wahl, *Media Madness: Public Images of Mental Illness* (New Brunswick, NJ: Rutgers University Press, 2001).

21. Louis A. Sass, *Madness and Modernity: Insanity in Light of Modern Art, Literature and Thought* (New York: Basic Books, 1992).

PART I

Cinema: The Big Screen

CHAPTER ONE

Psychoanalytic Renditions and Film Noir Traditions

Rosa JH Berland

The psychological thriller, born of the 20th-century genre of cinema, film noir, remains one of the most popular forms of entertainment. It is a constant in the yearly movie repertoire. With its roots in early 20th-century German and Austrian literary and visual expressionism, the theatrical productions of Max Reinhardt, and the study of the mind by Sigmund Freud, classic film noir and its many subgenres remain one of the most important forms of pictorial modernism.

In fact, film noir is perhaps the most enduring narratival model for the telling of popular culture's mythologies of mental illness, whether autobiographical, fictive, or even allegorical. References to mental illness in noir abound, explicitly as motifs of psychiatric troubles and psychoanalysis. Noir shows psychiatric treatments, such as hypnosis or asylums; the almost mystical phenomena of amnesia; persons with presumptive mental illness, such as sadists or murderers; those with psychosomatic illness or sexual neurosis; and, finally, the idea of gas lighting. All this makes for a grandly dramatic narrative of betrayal, horror, tragedy, and perhaps redemption.[1] This essay considers ways in which mental illness is depicted in a microcosm of popular films, classified variously as proto-noir, classic noir, or neo-noir.

While critical definitions of film noir seem constantly mutable, the term traditionally refers to the classic Hollywood films of 1940–1959. Writer James Naremore has made a convincing case for the way in which the enduring genre of film noir can be seen in parallel to the typology of Anglo-American literature, a phenomenon described as "a national canon of blood melodrama."[2] Nevertheless, while noir is considered a product of American ingenuity, it is in fact a cross-pollination of the Hollywood film industry and the influence, both conceptual and ideological, of two groups of expatriate German and Central European filmmakers.[3] In the resulting body of cinema, there are clear connections to the early-20th-century literary, artistic, and theatrical movement, expressionism. Additionally, their films, like expressionism itself, reflected the influence of Nietzsche and Freud, particularly Freud's concept of the unknowable, dark, chaotic id. For many expressionists, the metaphorical or allegorical power of the unconscious, the criminal, and the perverse gave voice to their own psychological disturbances, or alternately enhanced public perception of their legitimacy and lack of regard for bourgeois values. A major feature of expressionist art consisted of challenging conventional notions, including the accepted definitions of contemporary psychology. Some expressionists eschewed pathologizing views, insisting that what may appear as mental illness could be a connection to otherworldly, mystical insight. These classic films relate to popular culture of their time, and are expressive of a particular zeitgeist, namely mid-century wartime and postwar angst. This sensibility is personified in characters who are deeply troubled, trapped, or deceived by other deeply troubled, manipulative, or criminal enemies and are themselves sometimes duplicitous, criminal, and/or psychologically disturbed. Overall, the films share a pictorial language intended to create feelings of disorientation, loneliness, and entrapment. Specifically, narratival tactics include time ellipse, first person voice-over narratives, and flashbacks. Visual devices often include stylized scenery, low-key interior lighting, chiaroscuro, deep shadows, and the use of neo-Gothic and dark, urban settings.[4] As such, film noir is inescapably connected to ideas of mental illness; the often-disturbed and morally corrupt protagonists seem to be in a fragmented, unreal-seeming world where events follow no discernible order. French, German, and English films also feature unknown or hidden worlds, gothic horror, criminal psychology, and ominous plots, as in Alfred Hitchcock's thriller *Notorious* (1946), *Les Diaboliques* (1955) by Henri-Georges Clouzot, and *Breathless* (1960) by Jean-Luc Godard.

The unifying factor is not entirely an external event or temptation, but rather the internal struggle of the antihero. Often the protagonists of British and American film noir resist moral corruption, which they discover all around them; they are deeply unsettled and sometimes operate as morally ambiguous agents in a morally corrupt world—often while moving toward justice. An abiding interest in criminality is seen in both Anglo-American high culture and pulp fiction of the 1920s. With its roots in the disjointed frenzy of expressionist art, dance, and theatre, noir metamorphosed into a form that assimilated the American penchant for crime novels and the popular fantasy of the gangster. Films such as *The Night of the Hunter* (1955) delight in the dark underside of humanity and a fascination with the split and divided self.[5] This fusion is seen clearly in American films such as *Double Indemnity* (1944), *Mildred Pierce* (1945), *Scarlet Street* (1945) and later neo-film noir science fiction *Blade Runner* (1982). Francis Ford Coppola's *Rumble Fish* (1983) also uses disarticulated dream sequences and haunting urban landscapes. Alfred Hitchcock's *Spellbound* (1945) is especially interesting, since it has almost every film noir element: the femme fatal, the nefarious villain, the psychiatrist, the asylum, and the victim of amnesia. Hitchcock's irreverent interpretation of both the field of psychiatry and the state of the mentally ill makes for an entertaining film, although it is well known that Hitchcock had little use for psychiatry in general. Ingrid Bergman plays a psychiatrist who falls in love with an amnesiac man who cannot remember his name but introduces himself as the new asylum director upon arrival. Yet the intended director was murdered in the interim. She uses psychoanalysis to identify the true murderer: the aging asylum head (Leo G. Carroll) who faces replacement by a younger rival. Hitchcock's cinematography connects to the visual arts via a surrealistic hallucinatory sequence designed by Salvador Dali.

A certain horror exists within all film noir manifestations, as the audience is locked into the often-skewed perspective of a single character, using flashbacks to show two worlds, that of the mind and mental realm versus the physical world. The style and imagery suggest alternate realities, with memories fractured by trauma. The real, lived experience of the other (women, homosexuals, non-Western people or culture, or the mentally ill) is transformed into a symbolic construction. These constructions are either morbidly romantic and/or distorted in a voyeuristic, if not nightmarish, pattern.[6] Noir extends the transformation of Romanticism to a nihilistic reflection of the traumatic experience of war and an increasing interest in the unconscious. The connection to expressionism lies both in the undermining of the commonplace and in the formal use of visual devices such as chiaroscuro, oblique and geometric angles, dramatic lighting effects, and a sense of encroaching sky or oppressive interior space. These motifs evoke a sense of entrapment, danger, and a crisis of the mind. It is not important to the filmmakers that these visions are accurate depictions of the experience of madness or mental unrest, although there is a deliberate psychological effect. However, the connection of such effects to psychoanalysis (or pseudopsychology) is at best tenuous, for the various forms of science of the mind seem interchangeable. Characters are often given spurious diagnoses, heavily inscribed by stereotypes of madness, criminality, and gender roles. Nevertheless, the spectacle of madness is a currency too omnipresent to ignore, and despite the many psychological fallacies, there is considerable artistic value in many of the films. This value lies in their power of evoking a kind of haptic experience of illness, even when plot and character interaction reduce the protagonists to caricatures. Many of the films share a disjuncture of plot, a nihilistic tone, and an interest in the psychiatric and the criminal. Formally, these productions also share an expressionist aesthetic—the use of visual devices to evoke not only the despair and crisis of postwar life, but also an echo of the realms of a constructed idea of mental illness, often in turn associated with criminality. This space, primarily nocturnal, is interspersed with visual and narrative evocations of deception and claustrophobia. It is populated with uneasy combinations of authority figures, liminal heroes, and wayward women. Fate in the most fluid sense of the word is a current that runs throughout, often laid out as a force of evil, and disarray or loss, in the language of a paranoiac.

Through all the complex and theoretical analyses of noir runs one primary thread: the idea that the genre acts as a mirror for sociopolitical anxieties. These fears are artistically cloaked in pictorial and theatrical language, and often deeply inflected by the language of psychiatry, however distilled, or used in a reductive or allegorical way. It should also be noted that popular understanding of psychiatry and mental illness seems mysteriously fluid. Critics often point out the inaccuracy of the way films depict doctors, patients, disorders, and treatments. Nevertheless, this brings me to an important point, that renditions of mental illness in film represent another type of despair: a malaise, anxiety, postwar trauma, sense of difference and otherness. This crisis of meaning includes narratives about power struggles, with underlying issues of gender, sexuality, violence, and ideas of the other. If a character or villain is particularly garish and sadistic or murderous or raving, she or he is sufficiently so to allow the audience to disengage from the character and instead pay close attention to the psychologically informed plotline that "explains" or dissects the cause of such madness. Much of the recent critical literature on the import of film noir focuses on its symbolic representation of a postwar gender crisis in America. Dr. Scott Snyder notes that the femme fatale is a means to lead the male protagonist and she is often depicted as suffering from a range of Cluster B psychopathology that includes anti-social, narcissistic, and histrionic traits:

> The type of character pathology personified in the femme fatale may be viewed as representative of certain misogynistic conceptualizations of the women of the time. Concurrently, these screen women may have helped to create a certain cultural image for some real-life women of the 1940s and 1950s as reflected in the areas of fashion and style, personality, and social status. "Bidirectional" causality is therefore noted in regards to the relationship between femme fatales and behavioral manifestations of Cluster B disorders in society.[7]

However, because noir is also a genre of the imagined world, the fantastic, the hallucinogenic, and the paranoiac, it is inherently ambiguous and constantly expansive—whether its focus is on the hard-boiled detective, the femme fatale, or the beleaguered tragic hero. Whether set in middle America or a haunted urban cityscape, noir occupies a place of dreams, fate, and descent into madness and criminality. It is a truly imagined space. In the fictive space that seems to function as fantasy, projecting an idea of illusory control over trauma, or as a device to separate oneself from the possibility into madness (e.g. ascribing a villain's descent to a trauma so outlandish it could never happen to the spectator), we see the imprint of cultural notions of normalcy throughout.

The homicidal woman represents the unsettling of the normal or "well" person whose demons are reflected in the new nomenclature for film noir and its various subgenres. A woman may have been driven mad by deceptive family members, or she suffers from amnesia, or is herself unwieldy, without the trappings of domesticity. Or she may be an agent of her own powerful sexuality, which is considered deviant because it fails to acquiesce to a patriarchal perspective or socially acceptable arrangements, such as marriage and/or monogamy. Many works in the film noir genre position female protagonists as deviants, characterized by sexual expressiveness, which is in turn paired or equated with sociopathic and violent tendencies. *Tender Is the Night* (1962)—which was based on F. Scott Fitzgerald's novel about his wife Zelda's psychosis and institutionalization—redirects the female character into a normative pattern. Alternatively, *Three Faces of Eve* (1957) is an explicit rendering of the various archetypes of femininity.[8] Many critics see such dialogues as a reflection of dominant social or cultural anxiety about gendered divisions of power after World War II.[9] The condition of postwar America is viewed as a space of chaos, where the most destructive and terrible parts of humanity lurk behind visages and facades, a sort of haunting or possession. In turn, many of the films map out the idea of the antihero who has been transformed into this destructive force through traumatic events or self-destructive tendencies. The enduring story of quelling the "other"—whose nonnormative behavior is often shown as a mental illness—serves to reinforce power structures. Specifically, we see the way in which female characters are often associated with deadly sexuality. Thus emerges the classic paradigm: the femme fatale, whose uncontrolled sexuality is characterized not only as a mental break but also as a threat to society. Interestingly, some critics have seen this figure as heroic, for she rejects the dominant rules of power and sexual expression. Lacking a moral character, however, she is often a villain of high glamour and appeal, although clearly insane. After all, the lack of morality in the femme fatale indicates something beyond mere weakness—it is a lack of normality or even an illness. Feminine sexuality and mental illness—and estrangement from socially circumscribed gender roles—are central to much critical analysis of noir.[10]

In *Sleep My Love* (1948), the lead female character, Alison Courtland, experiences the familiar malady, amnesia. She seeks psychiatric help at her husband's request, but in fact the psychiatrist is not a real doctor, but rather part of the nefarious husband's plan to drive his wife to insanity and suicide so he can inherit her money. She is merely a plaything in this scenario. The fetishization of the female psychiatric patient is a long-standing rubric. As depicted in noir, mental illness involves weakness, loss of control, and victimhood, often creating a gateway into a sort of gothic horror.[11] While many feminist critics see women in this genre as reflections of male fantasy, founded in Freudian theory, others have pointed out that the audience for this narrative of rebellion is much more multifaceted, and taps into fantasies of the immoral, oversexualized female character. Often using extreme or even sadistic measures to achieve power or control, this figure apparently appeals to both men and women.[12]

On the other hand, Janet Walker has argued that films such as *Three Faces of Eve* present "female roles that correspond to the limited range of roles offered in the socio-historical context of post war America."[13] Similarly, *Tender Is the Night* shows how the patient is led back to her feminine role, her normalcy, by the guiding doctor. Any diversion from this path is an expression of her deviance, if not illness. The conflation of a kind of distorted homosexuality with criminality is another strange thread of neo-noir, reflected most deviously in the sensational movie from 1992, *Single White Female*. Here deviance has a face, that of Jennifer Jason Leigh as Hedy, the immoral villain who develops an unhealthy obsession with

Allie (Bridget Fonda). Depicted as an almost farcically mentally disturbed murdering lesbian, Hedy seduces and murders Allie's fiancé. The story is poorly wrapped up in a pseudopsychiatric explanation: that Hedy had a twin whom she was trying to replace by taking over Allie. Here, as in many noir movies, the flashback ostensibly provides evidence that this is a psychiatric case, although the only real value of the flashback is to produce a voyeuristic thrill. As such, otherness (as in case of the lesbian killer) is meant to thrill, titillate, and shock. At the same time, it reinforces the idea that such extravagant criminality is confined to someone else's sphere, and we are disinterested viewers.

Since the 1940s, film noir has served as a conceptual and stylistic framework for much of popular century filmmaking, and the considerable number of creative directors, actors, and technical styles weave into an equal number of variations of plots, narratives, characters, and depictions of psychiatric disorders. The critical language used to frame the protagonists in the various types of noir are of interest. For example, John Grant calls the elements of noir "symptoms," a term that places the characters in the realm of psychiatry and medicine.[14] Thus, film noir is positioned as a reflection of cultural anxieties. Among the primary symptoms are nihilist attitudes, plotlines that rely on the power of a femme fatale, visions of a downward spiral into loss of control, hallucinations, paranoia, flashbacks, and even confinement in asylums.

Moreover, the presence of psychiatrists or psychologists, whether nefarious or helpful, cannot be ignored and reflects an interest in psychology, analysis, and psychiatry in mid-century America, including the work of. Even when a film does not feature psychoanalysis, the language of psychoanalytic pseudoscience persists and underscores the visual disjuncture noir inherits from expressionism. We see many metaphors in some films. Specifically, the mentally ill or disturbed characters of noir are so representative of the average man that they become a metaphor for the postwar human condition, rather than an absolute representation of mental illness per se. Their narrative is an allegory for a universal crisis of the mind and spirit. Film noir psychiatrists demonstrate varying personalities; at times, they are Delphic-like beings, oracles of truth and stability. Or they might represent a nefarious force. They variably seem to be detectives, prison guards, or spiritual guides.

Noir filmmakers used these imaginary constructs of mental illness, hallucination, and criminality to develop highly stylized nightmarish scenes, narratives, and the impression of imprisonment within the disturbed mind. The fact that so many protagonists of film noir seem to find happiness only to descend into violence or experience loss, not only reflects the idea of fate and misfortune that underlies so many noir narratives, but is also a language familiar to those who suffer from mental illness. The onset of a psychological breakdown often comes in waves, as a destructive force, leveling any achievement or semblance of normalcy, alienating loved ones, collapsing educational or work opportunities. This suffering, personified in the hero-antihero, is a paradigm of the reality of those plagued by mental illness and all its injurious fallouts. Mental torture is within not only the unconscious or the Freudian model of the troubled mind, but is also real in the world experience, capable of bringing down the edifices of human achievement, social systems, and relationships through violence and despotism.

At the same time, some mental imbalance or suffering may become a force to produce extraordinary intellectual and artistic ideas, creativity, personal charisma, and sexual allure. Still, in these films, just as in so much American popular culture, the crazed or the mentally ill are metaphors for evil, strangeness, and the abnormal, so that the real, lived experience of suffering is secondary. Perhaps, in the end, rather than telling the true story of the experience of living with mental illness, noir does little more than expressing our culture's fears of the larger forces that remake the map of humanity.

Notes

1. For further discussion of this metaphorical and modernist spectacle of madness, refer to Marlisa Santos, *The Dark Mirror: Psychiatry and Film Noir* (Lanham, MD: Rowman & Littlefield Publishers, 2010).

2. J. Naremore introduced the idea of the connections between film noir and Anglo-American literature in his article "High Modernism and Blood Melodrama: The Case of Graham Greene," *Iris* 21 (1996), *Special Issue on European Precursors of Film Noir*. As well, Geoff Mayer notes that in contemporary coverage these films were often referred to as melodramas, with additional qualifiers or adjectival phrases (rather than diagnosis) such as neurosis, psychiatric, psychological. Mayer refers to Steve Neal's extensive survey of American trade journals (1938–1960), "Melo-Talk: On the Meaning and Use of the Term 'Melodrama' in the American Trade Press," *The Velvet Light Trap* 32 (Fall 1993): 66–89; Geoff Mayer and Brian McDonnell, *Encyclopedia of Film Noir* (Westport, CT: Greenwood Press, 2000), 8–11.

3. The first group arrived in the 1920s during the Weimar period (1919–1933). Expressionist films of this era include *The Student of Prague* (1913), *The Golem* (1915), *The Cabinet of Dr. Caligari* (1919), *Nosferatu* (1922), *The Last Laugh* (1924), *Metropolis* (1926), *Sunrise* (1927) and the sound film *M* (1930). The second wave of German directors came in the 1930s as a reaction to the rise of the Nazi Reich.

4. Annette Kuhn and Guy Westwell, *A Dictionary of Film Studies* (Oxford: Oxford University Press, 2012).

5. Lotte Eisner, beginning with *The Cabinet of Dr. Caligari*, not only provides an interesting analysis of visual devices, but also connects the genre to motifs seen in German Romanticism, expressionist literature, and cinema; *The Haunted Screen, Expressionism in the German Cinema and Expressionism and the Influence of Max Reinhardt* (Berkeley: University of California Press, 1965). Another important model was Oskar Kokoschka's famous 1908 play *Mörder, Hoffnung der Frauen*, a black drama about seemingly mad rituals of mating and murder. The play would become a visual, emotional, and thematic model for German expressionist theatre, and in turn for film noir's stylistic tendencies. Theatrically, models include Reinhardt's productions such as Hugo von Hofmannsthal's *Elektra* (1903). See also Jill Scott's analysis of gender roles in theatre and other art forms after Freud in *Elektra after Freud, Myth, and Culture* (Ithaca: Cornell University Press, 2005).

6. Modern artists such as Oskar Kokoschka, Max Beckmann, Otto Dix, and Richard Gerstl adopted the trope of the troubled mind to express their own sense of alienation. It should be mentioned that, in fact, for the most part the embodiment of these is a device and is used either stylistically or allegorically; in part. film noir follows this model.

7. See Dr. Scott Snyder's article "Personality Disorders and the *Film Noir* Femme Fatale." *Journal of Criminal Justice and Popular Culture* 8, no. 3 (2000): 155–168.

8. Janet Walker, "Couching Resistance: Women, Film, and Postwar Psychoanalytic Psychiatry," in *Psychoanalysis and Cinema*, ed. E. Ann Kaplan (London: AFI and Routledge, 1990), 143–44.

9. The post–World War II crisis of gender identity is often associated with the depiction of the aberrant female who seeks to define herself or rejects traditional feminine roles, a reflection of the problem of women returning to the domestic sphere after their wartime role as primary contributors to the public workforce. See W.H. Chafe, "World War II as a Pivotal Experience for American Women," in *Women and War: The Changing Status of American Women from the 1930s to the 1950s*, M. Diedrich and Fisher Hornung, eds. (New York: Berg Publishing, 1990), 21–34.

10. Bram Dijkstra discusses the idea of feminine "perversity" in depth in the context of visual art in his critical texts *Evil Sisters: The Threat of Feminine Sexuality in Twentieth Century Culture* (New York: Henry Holt, 1996) and in *Idols of Perversity, Fantasies of Feminine Evil in Fin de siècle Culture* (New York: Oxford University Press, 1986).

11. See Didi Huberman's incisive analysis of the moral and cultural image of the female patient in *Invention of Hysteria: Charcot and the Photographic Iconography of the Salpêtrière* (Boston: MIT Press, 2003); Asti Hustvedt, *Medical Muses: Hysteria in Nineteenth Century Paris* (New York: W. W. Norton, 2011); Paul Coates, *The Gorgon's Gaze: German Cinema, Expressionism, and the Image of Horror* (New York: Cambridge University Press, 1991). Late 20th-century films reflecting the myth of the mentally ill femme fatale, as well as the legacy of expressionism and

film noir include *The Kiss of the Spider Woman* (1985), *Paperhouse* (1988), and *Jacob's Ladder* (1990), among many others.

12. The critical interpretation of fantasy is varied: Tania Modelski argues that the struggle between men and women or women and society as depicted in film noir expresses the difficulty of normalizing or conforming to restrictive roles and expectations. See Introduction, Kaplan (1990), 2.

13. See Walker, 153.

14. See John Grant, Introduction, *A Comprehensive Encyclopedia of Film Noir: The Essential Reference Guide* (Milwaukee: Lime Light Editions, 2013); refer to Santos (2010).

CHAPTER TWO

The Meme of Escaped (Male) Mental Patients in American Horror Films

Jeffrey Bullins

It is a dark, rainy night. A single car drives along a winding country road. Its destination is an asylum for the criminally insane. Dr. Loomis is traveling there to oversee the transfer of a dangerous, violent patient, Michael Myers, described by Loomis as "evil, pure evil." This setting is the second scene in John Carpenter's 1978 film *Halloween*. Produced on a low budget, it has become one of the most successful independent films of all time and introduced the iconic masked killer, Michael Myers. Likewise, its style and themes are conventions within the horror genre and it is an example of the "slasher" subgenre, movies that feature killers stalking babysitters, campers, sorority girls, and so on.[1]

These stalking killers are also tied together via another horror genre meme: mental illness. Myers escapes from the asylum in *Halloween*, Jason's mother speaks in her son's voice in *Friday the 13th* (dir. Sean Cunningham, 1980), and Norman Bates channels his mother in *Psycho* (dir. Alfred Hitchcock, 1960). Historically, the horror genre is full of antagonists who are presented or described as mentally ill. The implication of the ills' danger is inescapable, and when asked if Myers should ever be released from the asylum, Dr. Loomis replies, "Never, never, never."

According to Dr. Loomis's learned assessment, there is no hope for Myers's rehabilitation. Eventually, Loomis murders Michael to save society from Michael's evil, not because the psychiatrist is psychopathic, like Michael, and not because he belongs to the same class of sinister cinema psychiatrists immortalized by Drs. Caligari and Mabuse.[2]

Halloween spawned seven sequels, a remake, and a remake sequel. The *Friday the 13th* series is another long-standing franchise featuring the mentally unstable Jason. *Psycho* had three sequels, a remake, and the recent television program *Bates Motel*. It seems audiences have a fascination with these types of characters, though most would likely be unable to determine if the behavior exhibited by these characters is plausible. Nonetheless, using insanity to explain why a character is exhibiting extreme antisocial behavior is a favorite device of the horror genre, which accomplishes its goal of fear with the audience frightfully pondering, "Could this *actually* happen!?"[3]

Where mental illness is historically used in horror films to simplify the reason for an antagonist, contemporary horror films are moving away from the simplistic "insane masked psychopath" meme and exploring the origins of these killers. With these characters, focus is often put on a past trauma that has caused their illness, thus explaining abnormality in psychodynamic terms and potentially garnering sympathy or personal identification from the viewer. Of course, these characters are still antagonists, but are now presented contextually.

Instead of beginning with Myers's escape from a mental hospital, the 2007 remake of *Halloween* (dir. Rob Zombie) features a lengthy backstory detailing his troubled childhood. Contemporary horror films' inclusion of back-story allows the audience insight and understanding about their antagonists. Though it does not justify his actions, perhaps the killer is not simply "pure evil," but has been driven to this behavior by past trauma. This chapter contains an analysis of these two contrasting ways in which the horror genre presents mental illness: the known killer vs. the masked. Discussion follows on how the evolution of mental illness representation in the horror genre moved from the inherent, unexplained evilness of *Halloween*'s (1978) masked "Shape," and *Black Christmas*'s (dir. Bob Clark, 1974) unseen Billy to the explicit elucidation of both in their 21st-century remakes.

While mentally ill antagonists are obviously a mainstay in horror, early genre films from the 1930s featured mostly supernatural threats such as vampires, mummies, and wolfmen. Though during this time the trope of the "mad" scientist was developed with characters such as Drs. Caligari and Frankenstein creating external monstrous threats. The "madness" that explains their behavior also sets a precedent for later negative representations of mental illness.

The theme of external threats continued into the 1950s with Cold War–era, atomic-age "creature features" such as *Them!* (dir. Gordon Douglas, 1954) and *The Blob* (dir. Irvin Yeaworth 1958). With 1960's *Psycho*, however, a shift occurs in the genre from external, fantastic antagonism to internal threats. *Psycho* is considered a classic within the horror genre and with it emerges mental illness as a prevalent device in the horror genre. Instead of a "mad scientist" creating an antagonist, the "madman" is the antagonist. The extreme popularity of *Psycho* caused a trend of followers such as *Homicidal* (dir. William Castle, 1961), *Paranoiac* (dir. Freddie Francis, 1963), *Maniac* (dir. Michael Carreras 1963), and *Hysteria* (dir. Freddie Francis, 1965).

Otto Wahl notes that this time was a turning point where we see "psychotic killers who are not merely scientists gone mad, who kill repeatedly, and whose murders are accounted for almost solely by their insanity."[4] Thus, mental illness becomes the primary identifier for these villains. Andrew Tudor also points to the statistic that the vast majority of films featuring psychotics, over 90 percent, were released after 1960.[5] The appearance of psychotics on screen in the 1960s directly correlates to the "slasher" killer of the 1970s, an antagonist also commonly identified based upon his/her mental illness.

Psycho and its contemporaries therefore mark a change from how mental illness or psychosis is presented onscreen. "If the 'madman' (or mad scientist) occupies a different universe, the psychotic is firmly in this one."[6] After all, the character of Norman Bates, as well as *The Texas Chainsaw Massacre's* (dir. Tobe Hooper, 1974) Leatherface, is allegedly based on the actual serial killer Ed Gein. Basing a fictional character on reality may add to the fright factor of a horror film, but it perpetuates incorrect perceptions of mental illness. Hal Arkowitz states that the mentally ill are actually only responsible for three to five percent of violent crime.[7] Likewise, Rob Whitley claimed in a 2011 study at the Douglas Institute that the mentally ill are actually more likely to be a victim rather than a perpetrator of violent crime.[8] Yet most genre films would imply that the asylum walls are all that is protecting the public from rampaging killers.

Throughout the genre's history, horror films have depicted characters with mental illness in various manners, but two contrasting archetypes are especially notable due to their transformation over the past 30 years: the known killer and the one who is faceless. *Psycho's* Bates is an example of this first type of mentally ill antagonist. He is neither a shadowy figure nor does he wear a mask. Though we see the face of this character from the point of his introduction, Bates is indeed only exposed as mentally ill at the climax of the film. Other notable villains with a face are *Silence of the Lamb*'s (dir. Jonathan Demme, 1991) Hannibal Lecter, *The Cell*'s (dir. Tarsem Singh, 2000) Carl Stargher, and *American Psycho*'s (dir. Mary Harron, 2000) Patrick Bateman.

The "slasher" subgenre holds a large number of the second classification of characters: faceless killers. These films feature literally masked killers and seem unconcerned with any personal identification. *Halloween*'s Michael Myers, described as simply being "pure evil," is a principal example. Also included would be *Friday the 13th*'s Jason Voorhees, *Black Christmas*'s (1974) Billy, *The Texas Chainsaw Massacre*'s Leatherface, and many others all the way through the *Scream* (dir. Wes Craven, 1996) and *I Know What You Did Last Summer* (dir. Jim Gillespie, 1997) franchises of the late 1990s. In the early 21st century, we also see remakes of *Halloween, Friday the 13th, Black Christmas*, and *Texas Chainsaw*. What separates the masked killers of the 1970s and 1980s, though, from their contemporary versions is the inclusion of backstory and, in most cases, a revealed face. Previously "faceless" killers are now exposed and explained.

Where the original *Halloween* was content to have Myers as an "evil" escaped mental patient, the 2007 remake attempts to show *why* he was there in the first place. The famous point-of-view opening of the original, in which Myers kills his sister, does not extrapolate as to why he did it; the fact he was just born "evil" is enough. *Black Christmas*'s Billy breaks into a sorority house and starts killing indiscriminately. It isn't until the 2006 remake that he is determined to be an escaped mental patient. Many early slasher films seem content to use the "insanity" excuse for their killers, with contemporary versions giving further explanation and thus allowing the audience the opportunity to identify with a previously "inhuman" character. Mental illness is thus the explanation as to why violent characters act the way they do, even though this lacks any realistic evidence.

The introduction and evolution of the mentally ill killer appears to be a product not only of cultural and social changes of the time, but also psychological research and the public's awareness of it. The majority of the viewing public is most likely aware of but unfamiliar with the realities of mental illness. Like fictional portrayals, sensationalized media coverage of real-world events can influence the public's opinion of it. In discussing tragic events such as a mass shooting at Virginia Tech and an attempt on the life of an Arizona congresswoman, Arkowitz states, "These events and the accompanying media coverage have probably fed the public's perception that most profoundly mentally ill people are violent. Surveys show that 60 to 80 percent of the public believes that those diagnosed with schizophrenia, in particular, are likely to commit violent acts."[9] Likewise, the tragic shooting at Sandy Hook Elementary School on December 14, 2012, sparked discussions on not just gun control but about the mentally ill, the effectiveness of their treatment, and efforts to make sure they do not have access to firearms. This latter point again suggesting that it is not a matter of if, but when, a mentally ill individual will commit a violent act.

Just as a juicy headline attracts readers, the horror genre is also cashing in on the public's misguided view of mental illness. Horror is, of course, not the only genre that features stories about mental illness or is set in mental hospitals, but it has historically treated mental illness as almost exclusively negative. The evil, escaped mental patient is an easy go-to for an antagonist, so much so that, in the case of films such as *Halloween* (1978), *The Driller Killer* (dir. Abel Ferrara, 1979), and *When a Stranger Calls* (dir. Fred Walton, 1979), further explanation or backstory may not be necessary. Wahl states, "Along with the notion that mentally disordered characters are fundamentally evil rather than ill, there is also the frequent suggestion that those with mental illnesses do not get better with treatment—and thus they remain violent and dangerous."[10]

While films in other genres may attempt to depict mental illness in a more positive way than horror, their impact with regard to public opinion may be no better. A study by George Domino into reactions by college students to *One Flew Over the Cuckoo's Nest* (dir. Milos Forman, 1975) revealed those who had seen the film had more negative opinions about mental illness than those who had not seen it. Further, students who then watched a documentary with a more realistic portrayal of mental illness claimed their opinions of it became even more negative. Referencing this study, Priscilla March notes, "non-stigmatizing information does not counteract the effects of dramatic portrayals of the violent as mentally ill."[11]

These negative opinions do not stop at the doorway to the movie theater, but translate directly to the real world. In an extensive study by Wahl on the stigma of mental illness, the effectiveness of positive portrayals is questioned by stating, "The media's coverage of mental illness and policies affecting people with these illnesses are still largely stigmatizing and discriminatory."[12] What follows is daily discrimination targeted towards the mentally ill. In the same study, one patient recounts taking her son to see the Nickelodeon children's movie *Good Burger* (dir. Brian Robbins, 1997). As innocuous as the film may seem, she was surprised and upset by a scene in the middle of the film that had the characters going to "Demented Hills Asylum" where patients were hyperbolically abnormal. While humor at the expense of mental illness may seem harmless to some, this patient was genuinely offended and worried if the depiction of mental illness in the film would influence her son's opinion of her. As long as opinions and representations of mental illness continue to be misguided, it follows that films will exploit them to meet their ends: horror to frighten or comedy to amuse.

A 1984 study by the National Institute of Mental Health (NIMH) determined that "thirty to forty million Americans, in any given six-month period, will be suffering from a diagnosable mental disorder and that, over the course of a lifetime, one out of every five citizens in this country will experience a significant mental illness."[13] That NIMH study was completed over 30 years ago. Since that time, prescriptions for psychotropic medications have soared, so much so that antipsychotic medications number among the most popular and profitable medications on the market.[14] Mental illness is something, therefore, that could affect any range of persons. The potential for mental illness in anyone is what feeds the horror genre's convention of the psychopathic killer. He is at once an external, malignant force and an internal representation. Contemporary horror films subsequently mix these two by providing previously masked antagonists with faces, backstories, and identifiability.

By the time *Halloween* was released in 1978, identification with the antagonist was not readily apparent, nor was it part of the film's focus. From the beginning of the film, we understand that Myers is an evil, external force. He is a faceless killer, escaped from the mental hospital. There is very little to which the audience can connect. Therefore, the viewer instead must side with Dr. Loomis and accept the fact that Myers is evil. This is not the case in the 2007 remake where Myers is given a face and close to an hour's worth of backstory. Here one sees a turn towards a method of characterization that humanizes and gives a face to the antagonist.

In his discussion of the original and remade *Halloween* movies, Andrew Nelson makes the claim that Myers is presented as a fantastic, unexplainable force in the original but in the remake is demystified using "pop psychology." He goes on to state that in the remake Myers "rather than being an entity. . . is a character."[15] Thus, Myers is given a face both literally and figuratively. Instead of having to accept him as simply "evil," we are now given reasons as to why he behaves as he does. Likewise, in films such as *Silence of the Lambs*, *The Cell*, and *Texas Chainsaw Massacre: The Beginning* (dir. Jonathan Liebesman, 2006), the conventional theme of "early trauma and horrific child abuse creates a monstrous adult"[16] is evident. However, just because an audience is given reasons as to why an antagonist exhibits extreme antisocial behavior does not mean that its opinion of mental illness is improved.

Like *Halloween*, the remake of *Black Christmas* (dir. Glen Morgan, 2006) gives extensive backstory to the killer. In the 1974 original, the antagonist, Billy, is unseen through the majority of the film, though there is extensive use of point-of-view (POV) shots. The opening of the film features a POV of Billy climbing into the attic of a sorority house, where he will go on to terrorize and kill the residents. This is the only introduction to the killer that the audience gets. Like Myers, he is faceless, and though we know that he is a person, he maintains externality due to his anonymity. 2006's *Black Christmas* gives a full backstory to Billy. He is an escaped mental patient who is returning to his childhood home where he endured trauma and abuse. Like *Halloween* (2007), the audience is shown traumatizing events from the antagonist's childhood. Billy suffers from untreated jaundice that causes his skin to appear yellow and is kept in the attic. While there, he sires his sister-daughter with whom he later teams up in order to terrorize the coeds. Though the convention of adding backstory here is similar to that of *Halloween*, adding the elements of physical deformity and incest seems to distance the audience from an otherwise more identifiable character. Here we see an antagonist whose actions are explained, but who remains alienated from the viewer. Similar to Loomis's attitude toward Myers at the beginning of the original *Halloween*, Billy is to be locked up in an asylum with no hope of release. While in the remake of *Halloween* the audience sees Myers attempt rehabilitation and therapy, Billy merely waits for his opportunity to escape his hospital and begin killing.

The addition of the element of Billy's physical abnormality follows a trend observed by Wahl in which "those with mental illnesses are recognizably different from others in both manner and appearance, they stand out as deviant and bizarre."[17] While it would be difficult to try and determine if a person is mentally ill by just examining their appearance, the suggestion of physical change due to mental illness adds to the otherness of the character. While Myers's and *Friday the 13th*'s Jason's faces are obscured by masks, it is still understood that they hide physical deformities. Likewise, in the 1978 film, Dr. Loomis, in speaking of meeting Myers, claims that he had "the blackest eyes. The devil's eyes. . . .What was living behind that boy's eyes was purely and simply evil." In the remake Dr. Loomis states dramatically, "These are the eyes of a psychopath."

Suggesting that mental abnormalities may manifest as physical allows the viewer the comfort of knowing they are not like the character on screen. Thus a contradiction appears between giving the audience knowledge and understanding of the character, but at the same time using physical difference as a separator. Tudor comments, "The typical threat, that of psychosis, is internal—generated within human beings—although in other respects the psychotic's relation to his or her victims is much the same as that of any externally threatening monster."[18]

It is noteworthy that the examples above concern *male* escapees from mental institutions, largely because men are overrepresented in such tropes about escaped mental patients and also because males in general are perceived to be more lethal than females, making their threats all the more ominous. Films such as *Fatal Attraction* (dir. Adrien Lyne, 1987) temporarily deflected attention onto temporarily psychotic female assailants, such as Glenn Close's portrayal of Beth, a jilted book editor who pursues her one-night stand with a vengeance. In spite of her imbalance, Beth is not fully psychotic—she functions well enough in the real world to hold an impressive position at a publishing company. Before the action starts, she lives in a world that is far away from the institutions inhabited by incarcerated killers like Michael Myers.

Wahl notes, "Films about mentally ill villains provide the fear, suspense, and sometimes dramatic special effects necessary to engage paying audiences."[19] Though simplistic categorization of antagonists as "evil" has changed via backstory extrapolation, mental illness remains an explanation for their behavior. One must remember that these sensationalized depictions of mental illness are used to fill those theater seats, and as long as misconceptions continue, then the meme of the escaped mental patient will persist in the horror film.

Notes

1. See related studies in Jeffrey Bullins, "Know Your Killer: Changing Portrayals of Psychosis in Horror Films," in *A History of Evil in American Popular Culture: What Hannibal Lecter, Steven King and Zombies Reveal about America* (Santa Barbara, CA: ABC-CLIO, 2014). Editors Sharon Packer and Jody Pennington focus on the evilness of Michael Myers, whereas this essay focuses on the stereotyped portrayals of male escaped mental patients in movies.

2. Sharon Packer, *Cinema's Sinister Psychiatrists* (Jefferson, NC: McFarland, 2012).

3. Other studies such as Patricia Owen's "Portrayals of Schizophrenia by Entertainment Media: A Content Analysis of Contemporary Movies" featured in the *Psychiatric Services* 2012 journal have used empirical data to determine that stereotypes of the mentally ill are rampant in film and television, and that these stereotypes contribute to negative opinions. However, beyond identifying this issue, less has been said about the underlying reasons as to why this persists and how to combat it. Much research from the mental health community tends to focus on psychiatric issues and their prevalence in media, but do not consider

factors from a media studies perspective such as historical film conventions, audience's expectations and receptions, and industry economics.

4. Otto Wahl, *Media Madness* (New Brunswick, NJ: Rutgers University Press, 1995), 56.

5. Andrew Tudor, *Monsters and Mad Scientists: A Cultural History of the Horror Movie* (Cambridge, MA: Basil Blackwell, 1989), 20.

6. James Marriott, *Horror Films* (London: Virgin Books, 2004), 83.

7. Hal Arkowitz, "Deranged and Dangerous?" *Scientific American Mind* 22 (2011): 3, accessed November 15, 2011, https://www.scientificamerican.com/article/deranged-and-dangerous/.

8. Rob Whitley, "Myths of Madness: Media Representations of Mental Illness," last modified January 13, 2012, http://www.youtube.com/user/recoverymentalhealth, 8:55.

9. Arkowitz, "Deranged and Dangerous," 1.

10. Wahl, *Media Madness*, 76.

11. Priscilla March, "Ethical Responses to Media Depictions of Mental Illness," *Journal of Humanistic Counseling, Education and Development* (1999): 70–79, 70.

12. Otto Wahl, *Telling Is Risky Business* (New Brunswick, NJ: Rutgers University Press, 1999), x.

13. Wahl, *Media Madness*, 47.

14. Allen Francis, *Saving Normal* (New York: William Morrow, 2013).

15. Andrew Nelson, "Traumatic Childhood Now Included," in *American Horror Film*, ed. Steffen Hantke (Jackson: University Press of Mississippi, 2010), 107.

16. Nelson, "Traumatic Childhood," 126.

17. Wahl, *Media Madness*, 37.

18. Tudor, *Monsters and Mad Scientists*, 10.

19. Wahl, *Media Madness*, 58.

CHAPTER THREE

Filming Hallucinations for *A Beautiful Mind, Black Swan, Spider,* and *Take Shelter*

Jocelyn Dupont

This chapter deals with the representation of hallucinations and delusional universes in a selection of four contemporary American films. They are, in chronological order: *A Beautiful Mind* (dir. Ron Howard, 2001), *Spider* (dir. David Cronenberg, 2002), *Black Swan* (dir. Darren Aronofsky, 2010), and *Take Shelter* (dir. Jeff Nichols, 2011). In the following pages, I intend to discuss strategies of narrative deception and manipulation in the context of the feature film, thus attempting to investigate the so far little-studied notion of delusional or "mad" narration in film. What triggered the composition of this article are two general observations that can be made about the seventh art and that seem to have held true for nearly as long as it has existed.

The first is an almost inbred tendency of the movies, at least since Georges Méliès, to lean towards the spectacular and the disruptive. It is a well-known fact that many character-based fiction films—not to say almost all—especially those from Hollywood, privilege extreme psychological states rather than serene ones. Explosions of violence, profound personal crises, and fits of all kinds have long been the stuff film drama is made of. The same goes for insanity versus sanity. As Jason Horsley observes:

> Since they tend towards sensationalism, and to invoking strong emotional responses, movies lean naturally more towards madness than sanity (just as they are predisposed towards depiction of chaos and violence rather than with peace and order).[1]

The second observation is that cinema has for an extremely long time harbored a fascination for inner states of minds and *mindscapes*. This certainly is a matter for surprise, verging on the paradox. If one thinks about it, in its essential technological nature, cinema is most of all fitted to record external "reality"—let us not omit the Nabokovian quotation marks—to capture images of the physical, sensitive world that surrounds us. And yet the attraction for invisible worlds has always exerted its magnetic pull on filmmakers, as Marcel Oms once observed:

> As soon as cinema became aware of its own technical capabilities through special effects and other tricks, it started to appear, in the collective imagination, as a mechanical means not only to reproduce but also to *reveal* the invisible sides of our lives, while at the same time other figurative arts seemed to have exhausted such expressive capacities and turned towards abstraction.[2]

Cinema has always been driven by a strange pull for this paradox, verging on aporia, which may even be said to challenge its very nature. Besides, the issue of the representation of madness certainly is a privileged locus for the study of such attraction. As Patrick Fuery notes:

> The representational processes of the cinema construct a certain type of sign in order that narratives can develop and the spectator can make sense of the structures . . . . The issue here is when that which is being represented in cinema—images of madness—challenges the processes of cinematic representation, and consequently cinema itself.[3]

The complexity of the undertaking is thus twofold. Besides the issue of the representation of tormented subjectivities, how to represent what is categorized by our discursive environments as wholly other, or even, as a mere lack or *absence* of to use Foucault's terminology?

Such questions can hardly be answered within the scope of a few pages. That is the reason why this contribution will restrict itself to a short discussion on hallucinations in contemporary American films that have madness as their thematic core, and have opted for narrative strategies that promote the representation of delusional visions and hallucinations. In the first part, I will make some brief theoretical remarks concerning the status of hallucinations in the fiction film. This will be followed by a rapid analysis of four sequences. In conclusion, I will raise the question of viewer response to such films.

Filming Hallucinations

Broadly speaking, a hallucination is the perception of an object that has no reality or sensations which have no corresponding external causes. Hallucinations can be visual, aural, or related to taste, smell, and touch. In psychiatric terms, and per the often-quoted 1973 study by French psychiatrist Henry Ey (1900–1977),[4] hallucinations are the very essence of psychopathology insofar as they constitute a radical rupture with the reality principle.

They also are a crux; even though hallucinations are always real for the patient, they never are for the mental health practitioner. Their imperceptibility in "reality" makes it even more difficult to provide a fully satisfactory definition, as it rests on an impossible observation, an asymmetrical relationship between presence and absence.

This is the reason why one has to be very cautious when talking about "hallucinations" in films as though one were talking of the same phenomenon as in a psychiatric context. I would like to dismiss as unethical and unscientific claims made by some critics verging on the antipsychiatric and even sometimes downright New Age ideologies that the psychotic's hallucinations could be—or even should be—compared with the spectator's own position. Most schizophrenic patients who commit suicide do so because of the unbearable pressure imposed on them by hallucinations, from which they desperately try to escape—a far cry from most spectators' comfortable viewing experiences.

This is not to say, however, that hallucinations and the film experience have nothing in common. Some critics and film theorists have argued in favor of such proximity, starting with André Bazin and Christian Metz, who introduced the idea of cinema as a paradoxical hallucination. In his 2011 book *La subjectivité au cinéma*, Dominique Chateau argues that cinema is a space where consciousness fluctuates and reality is put to the test. He writes:

> While cinema may struggle to flesh out hallucinations, it nonetheless has something to do, as a projection of fantasies and images over reality, with

the transformation or distortion of percepts—be they true or false—into a position of in-between-ness where consciousness wavers.[5]

Another interesting lead may be offered by Raymond Bellour, who proposes in his essential study *Le Corps du Cinéma* (2010) a theoretical model of the film experience as primarily hypnagogic. This is even more convincing since Henry Ey, in his treatise on hallucinations, had distinguished between three major types of hallucinations:

- Hallucinations experienced during sleep such as dreams and nightmares
- Hypnagogic and hypnopompic hallucinations, close to those one may experience on the threshold between sleep and wakefulness (either when waking up or falling asleep) or in a state of hypnosis
- Delirious and alienating hallucinations

In the latter category, which mainly corresponds to the films to be considered, the subject alienates what is most intimate and personal and ends up perceiving it as words and acts that belong to the other, an other so radically other that it threatens to destroy him or her.

The terminological coincidence linking Bellour's film theories to Ey's psychiatric classification is rather telling. Cinema, as a fantastic—even "phantasmagorical"[6]—journey in a world of moving visual and aural perceptions that have no tangible reality yet still exist in front of our eyes—and the rest of the audience—has a hallucinatory quality, though one that is more akin to the hypnagogic experience than the alienating one experienced by psychotic individuals.

Filmmakers, on the other hand, seem to be more attracted by delirious hallucinations, the most radical, spectacular, and thrilling. This is where the art of narrative steps in. If cinema is essentially an adequate vehicle to place us in a state of hypnagogic reverie, then the crafting of mad narratives may result in achieving an *analogon* of psychotic hallucinations, or at least in the telling and *showing* of demented hallucinatory tales.

Generally speaking, conventional film narrativity is neutral and impersonal.[7] In movies dealing with psychopathology and hallucination, the issue is thus to deneutralize the narrative through strategies of enunciation so that the normal landscape can be turned into a "mental" mindscape, preferably a paranoid schizoid one, where madness can enter the representational field, and delirious hallucinations burst onto the big screen.

A Beautiful Mind (2001) and *Black Swan* (2010)

Ron Howard's Academy Award winner *A Beautiful Mind* is the film version of the already-romanticized version of John Nash's turbulent biography. The Princeton mathematician and 1994 Nobel Prize winner interpreted by Russell Crowe was a notorious paranoid schizophrenic, suffering from hallucinations. Howard's often melodramatic film endeavors to portray the genius, the family man, and the lunatic in one sweeping cinematographic movement. Despite a tremendous popular success and some critical recognition, the movie drew a lot of criticism from mathematicians and psychiatrists alike. In the latter's case, it is the representation of Nash's hallucinations that seems to have been the main cause of discontent.

Howard's decision was to transform all of Nash's hallucinations into elements pertaining to the *visual* narrative. The director went so far as to incarnate Nash's psychotic visions and turn them into characters of the film. Three actors thus fill in the parts of the hallucinations: Paul Bettany as Charles, the prodigal roommate, who accompanies Nash through his studies and later turns up in the company of his young niece Marcee (Vivien Cardone). The third hallucination is Ed Harris, who acts as secret agent Parcher. What mostly characterizes these delusional apparitions is their diegetic status. They seem to belong to the diegetic universe in which Nash and all the other characters evolve. During the first half of the film, this inclusion is the main directorial choice regarding the way hallucinations operate. They are invisible as hallucinations because of their excessive visibility. Besides, the filmic narrative is intent on deceiving the viewer as most of the shots are not subjectivized. On the contrary, the camera is positioned to deny access to Nash's subjectivity as long as possible, shunning subjective camera and semisubjective shots. The shot-reverse shot sequences, on the other hand, appear perfectly normal. Consequently, the hallucinations cannot be ascribed to the central character's consciousness and are not perceived as hallucinations by the viewer. This, of course, is not a new film trick. It had already been successfully used in David Fincher's *Fight Club* (1999), with the presence of Tyler Durden (Brad Pitt) to be retroactively decoded as a figment of the main character's imagination.

However, what makes *A Beautiful Mind* quite specific is the use of a highly conventional cinematography in entire sequences[8] that are supposedly moments of acute psychotic delirium. Because of this very conventionality, Ron Howard's film can be said to be an extremely manipulative narrative. By choosing not to distinguish between "landscape" and "mindscape," the film certainly cheats viewers above all. Because hallucinations can be normally perceived, they become the ultimate fakery. Hence the film's difficulties, once the delusional nature of the apparitions has been made clear—thanks to the sequence in the psychiatrist's office exactly halfway through the film—to remain intriguing during its second half. Eventually, the hallucinations become rather tedious ghostlike figures as the movie gallops to its happy ending. As the film's way of dealing with hallucinations boils down to a narrative trick, the central question—namely, what is going on *inside* this supposedly beautiful mind?—is left entirely *out of the picture*.

It may be worth mentioning that Darren Aronofsky's first film, *Pi*, released in 1998, also dealt with portrayal of a paranoid mathematician, though in a far less conventional way. *Pi*, however, was not a huge commercial success, unlike Aronofsky's fifth feature film, *Black Swan* (2010), a movie that offers an intense journey into psychotic territories.

Black Swan is a powerful film blending ballet, the quest for one's limits, and delusional psychosis. As we follow Nina (Natalie Portman) through her ascension to the very top of her art while she interprets the swan queen for a ballet company, we also follow her sinking into the throes of paranoid schizophrenia, which mostly takes the form of a cleaving of personality, in a clear parallel with the black and the white swans she must interpret. Drawing from influences such as Michael Powell's *The Red Shoes* and Robert Siodmak's *The Dark Mirror*, the film provides a spectacular variation on the motif of the doppelganger, moving in a carefully orchestrated crescendo from the first fleeting uncanny encounter of her own image to a climactic moment of self-destruction that recalls the end of Poe's 1839 short story "William Wilson."

As far as delusions and hallucinations are concerned, *Black Swan* greatly differs from *A Beautiful Mind*. The construction of a mindscape seems to be an absolute priority for the director. The film relentlessly follows Nina, and there is not one single sequence in which she is not present, possibly not even one shot if one accepts that every time we do not see her in the frame, we are sharing her point of view. In *Black Swan*, we seem to be nearing the apex of what an alienated narrative in the conventional feature film can be. Close-ups, medium close-ups and tracking-in shots recalling Polanski's *Repulsion* (1965) insistently follow the protagonist in her descent into madness, or perhaps her ascent, given the overall soaring composition of the film.

Besides, *Black Swan* relies heavily on "occularization," the spectator's adoption of a narrative vantage point through a direct or indirect levelling with a character's visual perception inside the film's narrative. In *Black Swan*, the gaze of the character and that of the camera coincide to such an extent that everything becomes possible. Psychotic delirium, particularly in the last breathless minutes of the film, is thus shown through an intense distortion of reality via maximal subjectification and internalization of the narrative instance. Aronofsky even takes the viewer so close to Natalie Portman's character that things ultimately become physical. The most striking hallucinatory sequences in the film are arguably those in which Nina sees herself metamorphosing into a black swan. These shots, such as the feathers suddenly growing in her back or her foot becoming a palm, captured in very close shots, are among the most penetrating of the film. They provide a striking experience for the viewer, illustrating or even fleshing out Michael Fuery's comments on the issue of looking directly at madness:

> We do not penetrate madness to see its impossibilities; we experience them as the rub against it. It is this initial site of resistance that shows us we are witnessing madness. It is a site that has become so invested with fear that the systems for representing it often carry a sense of the medusa—to gaze directly at madness will bring about a transformation of the self.[9]

Spider (2002)

David Cronenberg's *Spider* came out in 2002. The film is an adaptation of Patrick McGrath's eponymous novel, published in 1991. Resting its textual artifice on the literary tradition of the "madman's diary" as well as more paradigmatic unreliable narratives in the tradition of Edgar Allan Poe, McGrath's novel is a journey into the depths of schizophrenia in which Spider, the erratic narrator of his own life story, gradually traces his way back to his own past and the murder of his mother which he perpetrated in a totally delusional state, convinced that she had been replaced by another woman, a prostitute named Hilda with whom Spider's father was having an affair. While the novel, relying heavily on inner ghosts and hallucinations, might have provided Cronenberg with several spectacular sequences of visual delirium, the director chose not to include such scenes, opting instead for a starker mode of representation, making *Spider* "as bleak and reality-based as a movie about mental illness can be,"[10] in the same vein as Lodge Kerrigan's *Clean, Shaven* (1994). This is not to say, however, that hallucinations do not feature at all in *Spider*. On the contrary, they insidiously enter the film's narrative and give the spectator access to the truth behind Spider's delusional universe. The status of hallucinations in the film is rather complex. With one exception, they occur during moments of remembrance, either through reverie—long moments of analepsis that cannot be described as flashbacks but rather as recollections—or, more often, through moments of inner introspection via the writing of his own journal. On several occasions, we see Spider (Ralph Fiennes), alone in his garret room, scribbling incomprehensible hieroglyphs on a torn diary, before we understand we have been propelled back into his past. In these sequences, simply introduced by cuts instead of dissolves which have become the convention for such retrospective returns, we see Spider as an adult back physically to the territories of his childhood. Spider features on screen twice, as an adult and as a child (Bradley Hall), both as the witness and protagonist of his past. Such dual incarnation to signify a return to the past is not so unconventional, having already been used quite successfully by Ingmar Bergman and Woody Allen, among others. Besides, these scenes are not exactly instances of hallucinations but moments of retrospection. However, in *Spider*, the character's past is a delusional one, and his narrative quite unreliable. This is where hallucinations find their peculiar function. Instead of providing, as in *Black Swan*, moments of intense visual spectacle or, as in *A Beautiful Mind*, overly evident apparitions, hallucinations in *Spider* work their way discreetly through the character's visual memories shared by the spectator who, for a long while, will not be able to identify them as such. This is of course particularly true for the (non) metamorphosis of Spider's mother into Hilda, the prostitute who, Spider believes, has usurped her in the family home.

While Spider's delusion is total and will ultimately lead him to commit matricide, the spectator is trapped in a visual jigsaw puzzle, confused and unable to identify precisely who Hilda is, as both she and Spider's mother are interpreted by the same actress (Miranda Richardson) yet so differently that one can never be certain of their identity. While we, spectators, know we are following a madman's memories, we remain in a state of ambiguity, unable to know much more than the madman, until, that is, he also projects Hilda's face onto Mrs. Wilkinson's (Lynn Redgrave), the warden of the home he has found refuge in after having been left out of the asylum.

Hallucinations in *Spider* are thus used against traditional conventions in the context of a film staging a schizophrenic character struggling with his psychotic condition. Their eminently ambiguous status allows for the creation of an unreliable film text that avoids the pitfalls of excessive spectacularization.

Take Shelter (2011)

While still dealing with psychotic hallucinations, Jeff Nichols' *Take Shelter*, released in 2011, also provides an interesting variation on the theme of delusional visions. First, it shifts away from huge Oscar-winning productions to a more low-key, almost independent cinema. Second, it links hallucinations to other forms of fear, such as that of global destruction, stirring some deep-rooted American collective nightmares and bridging the gap between the personal and the apocalyptic.

Unlike what happens in the three films previously studied and in most films dealing with hallucinations, Curtis, the protagonist (Michael Shannon) does not entirely fall prey to his hallucinations. As the film unfolds, Curtis struggles against the onset of his psychotic disorder, trying to resist his gradual collapse, taking medication and consulting therapists. Repeatedly in the first part of the movie, he is plagued by nightmares from which he awakens in a state of terror. We mentioned earlier that images seen in dreams or nightmares are a form of hallucinations, distinct from psychotic delirious ones, and in most cases, closer to the viewers' experience than the latter. Hence this strange, even uncanny feeling of connecting back to reality when the nightmare comes to its abrupt end shared by both character and spectator.

Take Shelter does not propel the viewer into a deluded world of nightmarish hallucinations. Unlike *A Beautiful Mind*, its narrative is not based on withdrawal of crucial information—which allows for unexpected twists and spectacular revelations. It is the narrative of a crumbling psyche, on the threshold of catastrophe. As in *Black Swan*, the camera remains focused on the protagonist, yet apart from the nightmare sequences we do not share Curtis's visions. On the contrary, Michael Shannon's stony and tormented face remains the locus of a profound enigma.

Those who have seen the film do know, however, that an unexpected final twist—or twister, rather—will occur in the final sequence. Beyond its fantastic quality, reconnecting madness somewhat boldly with the genre of the supernatural, this final, apocalyptic moment combines a sense of doom with the triumph of what Derrida called "the truth of delirium."[11] In this instant of absolute revelation where the Book of Job meets that of John, the viewer experiences the catastrophic Word;[12] the madman's "hyper-acuteness of the senses," to echo Poe in "The Fall of the House of Usher," has indeed become a Revelation.

Conclusion

One could ultimately raise the issue of the ethics of such films. Beyond their mere spectacular effects and the thrill of experiencing delusion and psychotic alterity in a primarily entertaining way, is there a place in such movies for a viewer's ethical response to a disease that is often agonizing for those who suffer from it?

When confronted with patients suffering from hallucinations, mental health practitioners are generally advised to bring the patient to a state of "double-consciousness," infusing doubt into his or her certainty.[13] By twisting this statement ever so slightly, one may raise the following question: does the double consciousness of the film-spectator inform him about the single psychotic reality of the hallucination?

This may be doubted. To trigger viewers' empathy in the face of psychotic disorders, films should not remain within the boundaries of the classic Hollywood paradigm. The comfortable stability of the product is too big an obstacle to allow a truly meaningful insight into the thralls of such disturbed psyches. One must turn to more "borderline" movies to do so. Films like Polanski's *Repulsion*, Kerrigan's *Clean, Shaven* or *Keane*, or even, more recently, Bronstein's *Frownland*, do not necessarily shatter the cinematic conventions of the feature films, yet they disrupt them to such an extent that the viewing experience becomes an experience of alterity. Only through such heterological processes can filmmakers produce something ethically meaningful in front of the catastrophe of psychosis.

Notes

1. Jason Horsley, *The Secret Life of Movies: Schizophrenic and Shamanic Journeys in American Cinema* (Jefferson, NC: McFarland, 2003), 33–34.

2. Marcel Oms, "La vie quotidienne au cinéma: image de la folie, folie des images," *CinémAction n° 50* (1989): 88. [My translation]

3. Patrick Fuery, *Madness and Cinema: Psychoanalysis, Spectatorship and Culture* (London: Palgrave MacMillan, 2004), 15.

4. Henry Ey, *Traité des hallucinations*, 2 vols. (Paris: Masson, 1973).

5. "Si le cinéma représente tant bien que mal l'hallucination, il a quelque chose de fondamental à voir lui-même, en tant que projection, avec cette manière de projeter des fantasmes sur la réalité, de les métamorphoser en vrais-faux percepts, dans cet entre-deux où la conscience claudique. " [My translation]; Dominique Chateau, *La subjectivité au cinema* (Rennes, France: Presses Universitaires de Rennes, 2011), 82.

6. It should be remembered here that the Greek etymology of the word *fantasma* means "the sudden apparition of images," which somehow could stand as the most embryonic definition of the cinematographic experience.

7. "In classical Hollywood narration the conventions of continuity editing, unobstrusive cinematography, and realist sound design frequently elide the narrator's perspective and present it as an objective and ideologically neutral viewpoint on a story that unfolds naturally in space and time." James Stadler, *Pulling*

Focus. Intersubjective Experience, Narrative Films and Ethics (New York: Continuum Press, 2008), 68.

8. Hallucinatory sequences can also be very long (over 10 minutes) and include several diegetic developments.

9. Fuery, *Madness and Cinema*, 16.

10. Sharon Packer, *Movies and the Modern Psyche* (Westport, CT: Praeger Books, 2007), 167.

11. Jacques Derrida, *Mal d'archives* (Paris: Galilée, 1995), 136.

12. Julia Kristeva, *Folle Vérité: Vérité et vraisemblance du texte psychotique* (Paris: Seuil, 1979), 9.

13. I would here like to thank Pr. Vignoles of Le Vinatier Psychiatric Hospital (Bron, France) for his expertise and the richness of conversations we have had on the matter.

CHAPTER FOUR

Dissociative Identity Disorder in Horror Cinema (You D.I.D.n't See That Coming)

Michael Markus

Holland Perry: "Who are you?"
Niles Perry: "I'm me. Niles. Niles Perry."
Holland Perry: "Are you sure?"

—*The Other* (1972)

Dissociative identity disorder (DID, formerly known as multiple personality disorder) is a condition which has routinely been depicted in cinema since the silent era and, if the success of the recent television series *The United States of Tara* (2009–2011) is any indication, it continues to be a source of audience fascination today. Cinematic representations of DID can be found across the spectrum of major genres, from drama (*The Three Faces of Eve*, *Sybil*), to comedy (*Loose Cannons*; *Me, Myself & Irene*), to horror (*Dr. Jekyll and Mr. Hyde*, *Psycho*).

This chapter explores typical portrayals of DID in the latter genre. As several scholars have noted, mental illness is almost never depicted with sympathy or accuracy in horror films, and this is unquestionably the case when it comes to the representation of DID in such films.[1] However, I will focus on the rationale behind the horror genre's widespread adoption of this DID plot variation, which I refer to here as the "surprise DID plot structure" (SDID). I will argue that this plot structure appears frequently in horror films because it is so effective in producing a particular fear-response in audiences—one which other horror films generally do not produce. Finally, I will suggest that recent changes in the depiction of DID in films employing the SDID plot structure are largely a consequence of the exigencies of that plot structure itself.

The Emergence of the SDID Plot Structure

DID remains a highly controversial diagnosis within the psychiatric community.[2] Much of the controversy stems from the dramatic increase in diagnosed cases which occurred in the 1980s and early 1990s. However, its inclusion as a specific diagnosis in the fifth edition of the American Psychiatric Association's *Diagnostic and Statistical Manual* (*DSM-5*, 2013) indicates that many still view it as a genuine, and distinct, mental illness. At present, the key diagnostic criteria for DID are 1) the alternating presentation of two or more distinct personality states within a single person; and 2) amnesia experienced by the "host" personality for periods during which an alternate personality is in control.[3]

Leaving aside cases in which such symptoms were attributed by observers to demonic or spiritual "possession," documented instances of this symptomology have been located as early as the late 18th century.[4] Beginning in the last quarter of the 19th century, there was a significant proliferation of case studies, and this trend continued into the first decades of the 20th century. It is no coincidence that it was also during this period that the notion of the "split personality" began to percolate through American popular culture. Robert Louis Stevenson's novella *The Strange Case of Dr. Jekyll and Mr. Hyde* (1886) familiarized readers with the notion that a single human body might host two separate and distinct personalities.[5] Over the course of the next few decades several popular stage plays (some of which were explicitly based upon *Jekyll and Hyde*) focused on characters with split personalities, and between 1915 and 1923, no fewer than six American-made films did so as well. These early cinematic treatments of "split personality," such as *The Curious Conduct of Judge Legarde* (1915), *The Case of Becky* (1915), and *The Brand of Satan* (1917), established a basic framework of representation which is still often utilized today. In such films it is the main protagonist who is a sufferer of split personality—a fact which is typically established for the audience quite early in the film, although the protagonist herself or himself may initially be unaware of it due to the amnestic qualities of the condition. In each case the unfolding narrative focuses upon the struggles and challenges experienced by the afflicted protagonist, which are utilized to achieve various dramatic, suspenseful, and/or comedic effects.

Up to the late 1950s, the only films in the horror genre which dealt with the subject of split personality were the various iterations of *Dr. Jekyll and Mr. Hyde* (of which at least ten had appeared between 1920 and 1957), and these utilized the basic narrative structure noted above. Although in Stevenson's novella the fact that the brutish Mr. Hyde is actually the kindly Dr. Jekyll's alter ego is kept hidden from the reader until the final pages—thereby constituting a frightening and horrific "surprise ending"—this was never the case with the various stage and screen adaptations of it which followed. Both on stage and on screen, the true nature of Jekyll's relationship with Hyde is usually revealed to the audience early on.

In the late 1950s, a revival of interest in the clinical diagnosis of what was by that time commonly called "multiple personality" was accompanied by an increase in cinematic representations of it. The drama *The Three Faces of Eve* (1957), based upon an actual case study,[6] followed the representational pattern established in earlier film treatments of the subject. At the same time, it served to crystalize for audiences the "scientific" reality of the "multiple personality" diagnosis, and in so doing helped to lay the groundwork for an alternative pattern of cinematic representation which would soon emerge.

The groundbreaking horror films in which this alternative representational pattern was first established were Robert Day's *The Haunted Strangler* (1958) and Alfred Hitchcock's *Psycho* (1960), both of which utilized the Surprise Dissociative Identity Disorder plot structure (SDID). This plot structure, which continues to be utilized by horror filmmakers today, represented an entirely novel approach to the onscreen depiction of DID. Rather than focusing upon the travails of a protagonist whose DID is overtly acknowledged, films which employ this plot structure hide from audiences the fact that a major character, or even the main protagonist, suffers from DID. Indeed, knowledge of this fact is carefully concealed from the audience until it is suddenly revealed—usually towards the end of the film—in the form of a shocking "plot twist" or "surprise ending."

In *The Haunted Strangler* (1958), Boris Karloff plays James Rankin, a benevolent Victorian-era novelist and social reformer who becomes obsessed with proving that an innocent man had been executed 20 years before for a string of murders. Roughly halfway through the film, Rankin manages to locate the never-discovered murder weapon. The audience is then presented with a wholly unanticipated plot twist as Rankin's handling of the knife causes him to undergo a Jekyll-and-Hyde-style transformation into his long-dormant alter ego—a twisted, murderous fiend. The remainder of the film follows a fairly straightforward Jekyll and Hyde trajectory, with Rankin himself eventually coming to understand that *he* is the very murderer for whom he has been searching. The film, despite its title, eschews a supernatural explanation: as one character puts it, Rankin is "possessed" by "a side of himself he can't control. A dual personality that, without the knife, is incomplete."

Alfred Hitchcock's *Psycho* (1960) is, of course, a film which has been far more widely seen, and is considered far more influential than *The Haunted Strangler*. Nevertheless, the two films approach the representation of DID in strikingly similar fashions. In both films, the revelation that a major character has a second, murderous personality comes as a terrifying surprise to the audience. And in the 50 or so years since the release of these two films, the SDID plot structure which they pioneered has been employed by filmmakers time and again. Indeed, the potency of this particular plot structure is strongly attested to by the very fact that it has been reiterated so frequently. The SDID plot structure, it must be noted, is one which has been employed almost exclusively in horror films—and for good reason. Its effectiveness *as* a plot structure rests in its ability to generate a particular *type* of fear—one which horror films typically do *not* evoke.

Why SDID?

There is a substantial body of literature devoted to the exploration of issues surrounding the question of what, exactly, audiences find appealing about horror films. Given the wide range of approaches, both psychoanalytic[7] and cognitivist,[8] that film scholars have adopted, it should hardly come as a surprise that a multitude of answers to the riddle of horror's appeal have been proffered. Not all scholars agree, for example, that people who like horror films like them primarily because they enjoy the sensation of artificially-induced fear. Indeed, even among those who adopt a psychoanalytic approach there are differing perspectives on this question, with some suggesting that certain horror films, at least, provide the viewer with pleasure via the vicarious gratification of repressed, unconscious desires, as opposed to the arousal of repressed, unconscious fears.[9] One of the leading advocates of the cognitivist approach, Noël Carroll, has suggested that the fear engendered by horror is largely an unavoidable (and perhaps unsought) by-product of horror's *real* payoff—which, he claims, is the satisfaction of the audience's curiosity regarding unusual or impossible things.[10] Moreover, it is unquestionably the case that the success of *some* horror films must be attributed less to their ability to frighten than to their successful incorporation of other genre elements—such as comedy, drama, or action—into the narrative. Nevertheless, most scholars would agree that people who like horror films like them in large part because they enjoy, in some manner, the sensation of fear which these films elicit.

In general, successful horror films work by instilling in audiences both a fear of what the villain *is*, and a fear of what the villain *does* and *might do*. That is to say, horror films typically "other" the villain—be it demon, monster, or "psycho-killer"—in such a manner that the mere contemplation of her/him/it inspires fear and disgust. At the same time, audiences are also prompted to experience fear *for* the victims, and potential victims, of the villain.

Films which employ the SDID plot structure work, in part, by eliciting fear in these familiar ways. In *Psycho*, for example, "Mother Bates" is a horrifying and menacing figure who elicits fear and dread long before her true connection with Norman is revealed. However, what makes SDID films so memorable and effective is the fact that, in addition to evoking fear in these ways, they also elicit from audiences a separate and distinct sort of fear which most horror films do not evoke. Simply put, these films undermine the commonly held notion of the "unitary self" and they inspire in viewers the fear that *our own* experience of selfhood might well rest upon far more fragile, or even illusory, grounds than we are typically comfortable with acknowledging.

The "traditional" notion of the self as a unitary, stable, and continuous entity rooted in the cognitive process—an idea embodied in Descartes's dictum "I think, therefore I am"—has been unraveling for decades in the face of scrutiny from various quarters including philosophy, psychiatry, postmodernism and, most recently, evolutionary psychology and cognitive neuroscience. However, despite this fact, most people—including those who are fully aware of these developments—prefer to regard themselves, for all practical purposes, as "selves" in the traditional sense of the term. It is most likely the case that one of the main reasons for this is the simple fact that the alternative to the unitary self is, for most people, a profoundly disquieting one. David Spiegel, in attempting to explain why the *DSM's* diagnostic category of "Dissociative Disorders" (which includes under its rubric DID) continues to be so controversial within the psychiatric community, has suggested that even many psychiatrists are simply uncomfortable with the implications for the concept of selfhood which these diagnoses entail. Dissociative disorders, Spiegel contends, "force us to reexamine our assumptions about the solidity of identity and the consistency of our control over our minds and bodies."[11] And indeed, there is no question that challenges to these traditional assumptions can be deeply disturbing. One philosopher has gone so far as to contend that such challenges to our sense of selfhood constitute the very definition of "horror": "'Horror' is the title I am giving to the perception of the precariousness of human identity, to the perception that it may be lost or invaded, that we may be, or may become, something other than we are, or take ourselves for [.]"[12] The reason that films employing the SDID plot structure are so effective is that they elicit just such fears—and do so far more directly, and viscerally, than other horror films generally do.

Most horror films involving mentally ill villains portray the "mad slasher" or "psycho killer" as being, in most respects, akin to any other screen monster—grotesque, violent, and utterly alien. Audience members are no more encouraged to regard Hannibal Lecter or Leatherface as being "a person like myself" than they are to find commonality with Dracula or the Blob. This may seem a shockingly unfair and irresponsible way to depict mental illness (and indeed it is), but in many respects, it differs only in degree from the way the mentally ill have traditionally been portrayed in Western art. Sander Gilman argues that Western representations of illness, including mental illness, have always been largely instrumental. By depicting those with disease as radically unlike ourselves, we mentally quarantine ourselves from the possibility of dissolution which disease represents to us: "Then it is not we who totter on the brink of collapse," he contends, "but rather the Other."[13] If this is so, then the typical horror-film depiction of the "mad slasher" actually evokes one type of horror—namely, the potential existence of a monstrous, deranged killer—while simultaneously *insulating* audiences from another, perhaps more unsettling, horror: the possibility that our own mental state might *not* differ substantially from that of the madman. Gilman even ponders a question which gets to the heart of what animates the SDID plot structure: "What happens when it is not the identifiable "mad person" who turns out to be aggressive, but the "normal," nice kid next door? . . . Our shock is always that they are just like us. This moment, when we say, "they are just like us," is most upsetting."[14]

And of course, the SDID plot structure works precisely because the "mad slasher" is *not* "othered" in these films—or, at least, the "othering" does not take place until after the "surprise" has been revealed. Indeed, SDID films present viewers with a "psycho killer" who does not know, and has no way of knowing, that he or she *is* a "psycho-killer." In that moment of surprise in which it is revealed that the seemingly normal, even likeable, character with whom the audience had been encouraged to identify actually suffers from a mental illness characterized by alternating personality states and amnesia, audiences are forced to confront the frightening possibility that *anybody*—including themselves—might also be a person who is radically different from the person whom they imagine themselves to be. (In this context, Norman Bates's most famous observation—"we all go a little mad sometimes"—takes on an even more unsettling meaning.)

The degree to which SDID films succeed in prompting this disquieting revelation depends, in large part, on the degree to which they succeed in convincing the viewer to identify with the character who will ultimately be shown to suffer from DID. Although some film scholars criticize the term "identification" as ill-defined, we need not adopt a very stringent or elaborate definition of "identification" to find the concept of use. For our purposes, an audience can be said to "identify" with a character if they anticipate that the character is meant to represent the film's "main protagonist"; or, more generally, if they simply "like," or feel some sympathy for, a character. In his famous examination of the structure and elements of tragedy, Aristotle argued that "pity is aroused by unmerited misfortune, fear by the misfortune of a man like ourselves."[15] The fear to which Aristotle referred is not the audience's fear *for the character*, but fear *for themselves* which the plight of the character has inspired. Films which utilize the SDID plot structure work, ultimately, because they manage to convince the audience that the character who suffers from DID is "a man (or woman) like ourselves."

Recent Developments

Between 1970 and 1980, horror-film audiences would see the SDID plot structure recycled time and again in films such as *The Other* (1972), *Sisters* (1973), the "Millicent and Therese" segment of *Trilogy of Terror* (1975), *Schizo* (1976), and *Dressed to Kill* (1980). However, use of the SDID plot structure fell into abeyance during the 1980s and 1990s—a fact which might seem surprising given the huge proliferation of diagnosed cases of DID which occurred during this period. It is most likely the case that filmmakers abandoned the SDID plot structure during this period because they believed that it was losing its effectiveness: overuse had familiarized filmgoers with the possibility that a major character might suddenly be revealed to have an alternate personality. And, as we have seen, if the SDID plot fails to surprise, it fails to frighten.

It is therefore noteworthy that, beginning in the early 2000s, horror films utilizing the SDID plot structure once again began to appear: *Secret Window* (2004), *Hide and Seek* (2005), *High Tension* (2005), *My Bloody*

Valentine (2009), *The Uninvited* (2009), and *Silent House* (2011) have all employed it. This revival of the SDID plot structure has been largely facilitated by the willingness of filmmakers to employ certain representational techniques which, for the most part, had not been utilized in previous SDID films. Significantly, the use of these techniques—which are designed to make it more difficult for audiences to guess the surprise that the film has in store for them—directly impacts the way DID itself is depicted in these films.

As has been noted, it is almost never the case that mental illness is accurately (or sympathetically) depicted in horror films, and horror films depicting DID have never been an exception to this rule. The most obvious example of this is the fact that SDID horror films invariably depict the afflicted character's alternate personality as being a psychotic murderer, whereas this is simply not true in real-life instances of DID. However, other, more subtle inaccuracies have always been present in SDID films. DID has always been characterized as a "reality-oriented" disorder, as opposed to a species of psychosis. It is important to note, in this regard, that DID, as it has been defined across the various editions of the *DSM, can* entail certain symptoms which might otherwise be indicative of psychosis—namely auditory and (more rarely) visual hallucinations. However, the presence of delusional beliefs—another key aspect of psychosis—is *not* a recognized symptom of DID.

In general, early SDID films did not suggest that afflicted characters experience hallucinations. On the other hand, they did portray DID as a mental illness which involves elaborate delusions. For example, afflicted characters in these films commonly hold the delusional belief that their alternate personality is a living, breathing, externally existing person with whom they share some sort of relationship. Examples of this can be found in *Psycho, Sisters*, and *Dressed to Kill*. Needless to say, real-life sufferers of DID do not hold such delusional beliefs.

What differentiates the recent crop of SDID films from those of the previous generation is the fact that these newer films present to the audience the interwoven hallucinations and delusions of the afflicted protagonist without signaling to the audience that they *are* hallucinations and delusions. Protagonists are shown having conversations—and even engaging in physical altercations—with characters who are ultimately revealed to be their alternate personalities. Invariably, these alternate personalities are played by a different actor than the one who portrays the protagonist, and they are presented to the audience without the slightest indication that they exist only as a projection of the protagonist's psyche. Indeed, entire scenes are eventually revealed to have taken place completely within the mind of the protagonist. The enormously popular *Fight Club* (1999)—perhaps the sole example of a nonhorror film which utilizes the SDID plot structure—paved the way for this style of representation, and it has been adopted, at least to some degree, by every SDID horror film produced since then.

In its utter reliance upon the notion that DID entails all manner of hallucinations and delusions, this recent mode of representing DID is even less "realistic" than earlier depictions had been. Realism, of course, is not the point of a horror film; and filmmakers have adopted this mode of representation for the simple reason that it makes it more difficult for the audience to guess that a now-familiar plot twist is going to be sprung on them. The obvious hazard involved in utilizing this style of representation is that it may lead audience members to feel "tricked" or "cheated" by the film. On the other hand, the fact that filmmakers continue to risk this hazard might be taken as testimony to the uniquely disquieting potential of the SDID plot structure.

Notes

1. For sharp criticism of the portrayal of mental illness in horror films, see Otto F. Wahl, *Media Madness: Public Images of Mental Illness* (New Brunswick, NJ: Rutgers University Press, 1995). Scholars who employ cinematic representations of mental illness as a pedagogical tool almost never utilize horror films for that purpose: See Jacqueline Noll Zimmerman, *People Like Ourselves: Portrayals of Mental Illness in the Movies* (Lantham, MD: Scarecrow Press, 2003); David J. Robinson, *Reel Psychiatry: Movie Portrayals of Psychiatric Conditions* (Port Huron, MI: Rapid Psychler Press, 2003); Lisa D. Butler and Oxana Palesh, "Spellbound: Dissociation in the Movies," *Journal of Trauma and Dissociation* 5, no. 2 (2004): 61–87; and Danny Wedding, Mary Ann Boyd, and Ryan M. Niemiec, *Movies and Mental Illness: Using Films to Understand Psychopathology,* 3rd rev. ed. (Cambridge, MA: Hogrefe Publishing, 2010).

2. August Piper and Harold Merskey, "The Persistence of Folly: A Critical Examination of Dissociative Identity Disorder, "Part I: The Excess of an Improbable Concept," *Canadian Journal of Psychiatry* 49, no. 9 (2004): 592–600, and "Part II: The Defense and Decline of Multiple Personality or Dissociative Identity Disorder," *Canadian Journal of Psychiatry* 49, no. 10 (2004): 678–683; David Spiegel, "Dissociation in the *DSM-5*," *Journal of Trauma and Dissociation* 11, no. 3 (2010): 261–265; Joel Paris, "The Rise and Fall of Dissociative Identity Disorder," *Journal of Nervous and Mental Disease* 200, no. 12 (2012): 1076–1079.

3. American Psychiatric Association, *Diagnostic and Statistical Manual of Mental Disorders*, 5th ed. (*DSM-5*) (Washington DC: American Psychiatric Publishing, 2013), 291.

4. For the history of the DID diagnosis see Michael Fleming and Roger Manvell, *Images of Madness: The Portrayal of Insanity in the Feature Film* (London: Associated University Presses, 1985), 57–60, and Piper and Mersky, "Persistence of Folly, Part I," 596–597.

5. Henri Ellenberger's *The Discovery of the Unconscious: The History and Evolution of Dynamic Psychiatry* (New York: Basic Books, 1970) identifies parallels between Stevenson's popular novelistic treatment of split personality and emerging psychoanalytic concepts. A psychiatrist and a medical historian, Ellenberger convinces readers that literary developments paved the path to acceptance of Freud's and Jung's controversial (and difficult-to-prove) theories about dualism.

6. The real-life clinical outcome experienced by Chris Costner Sizemore, who was dramatized in the film as "Eve White," was far less tidy than that which was depicted in the film. Although she would eventually claim to have been cured of her condition, this resolution would not come until the mid-1970s, at which point over 20 personalities had presented themselves.

7. Steven Jay Schneider, ed., *Horror Film and Psychoanalysis: Freud's Worst Nightmare* (New York: Cambridge University Press, 2004).

8. David Bordwell and Noël Carroll, eds., *Post-Theory: Reconstructing Film Studies* (Madison: University of Wisconsin Press, 1996); and James B. Weaver III and Ron Tamborini, eds., *Horror Films: Current Research on Audience Preferences and Reactions* (Mahwah, NJ: Lawrence Erlbaum Associates, 1996).

9. Malcom Turvey, "Philosophical Problems Concerning the Concept of Pleasure in Psychoanalytical Theories of (the Horror) Film," in Schneider, ed., *Horror Film and Psychoanalysis.*

10. Noël Carroll, *The Philosophy of Horror: or, Paradoxes of the Heart* (London: Routledge, 1990), 184–193.

11. David Spiegel, "Dissociation in the *DSM-5*," 262.

12. Stanley Cavell, *The Claim of Reason: Wittgenstein, Skepticism, Morality, and Tragedy* (New York: Oxford University Press, 1979), 418–419.

13. Sander L. Gilman, *Disease and Representation: Images of Illness from Madness to AIDS* (Ithaca, NY: Cornell University Press, 1988), 1.

14. Gilman, *Disease and Representation*, 13.

15. Aristotle, *Poetics*, XIII, H. S. Butcher, trans., http://classics.mit.edu/Aristotle /poetics.2.2.html.

CHAPTER FIVE

Spirit Possession, Mental Illness, and the Movies, or What's Gotten into You?

Sean Moreland

The subjective experience of possession, characterized primarily by the feeling of being influenced by an overpowering, alien force beyond one's conscious control, shares much in common with the experiential aspects of many mental disorders. Cinematic attempts to capture the intensity of both experiences, often in an unsettling or disturbing way, have a long history. This chapter provides a brief, broad survey of how possession has been cinematically represented (especially in Anglo-American films) over the last century in ways that both explore and exploit these phenomenological intersections.

Throughout this chapter, the word *possession* will be used as shorthand for the concept anthropologist Felicitas Goodman calls "negative spirit possession," but adulterated by what Carol J. Clover calls "occult possession." According to Goodman, negative spirit possession includes a broad array of culturally specific phenomena that share the fundamental "experience of some uninvited evil entities assuming complete control over one's body."[1] I employ Goodman's more inclusive term rather than "demonic possession" because many of the films I discuss at least ostensibly posit something other than a specifically Christian supernaturalist conception to explain the troubling phenomena they screen. Clover's term "occult possession," on the other hand, is also more capacious than "demonic possession" but is specifically reserved for literary and filmic representations. It therefore usefully demarcates what I am discussing from the anthropological term "negative spirit possession," emphasizing the fictive dimensions of these cinematic narratives, however much they purport to be grounded in "real" phenomena.

Whether or not the demonic is diegetically framed as the cause of the possession in these films, Judeo-Christian conceptions of the demonic color each of these representations to some degree. The cinematic and narrative devices used by filmmakers to represent possession have been powerfully shaped by notions and earlier representations of demonic possession. As Brian Levack points out, the intersections between cinema and possession date to well before the technological advent of film, going back to the connections between theatre and exorcistic rituals in early modern Europe, "when Shakespeare and Ben Jonson exploited the theatrical potential of the subject." Since then

> there has been a close reciprocal relationship between demonic possession and the theater. Possession and exorcism are intrinsically theatrical: the demoniac, the exorcists, and those who observe the afflictions of the possessed are all involved in a performance in which they follow scripts that are encoded in their religious cultures. They learn these scripts from reading reports of other possessions, listening to sermons of ministers, or following the rituals in exorcist manuals. Even if the parties are not aware that they are performers, they nevertheless act the way their religion expects them to act. This reciprocal relationship between possession and exorcism on the one hand and the theater on the other buttresses the argument that both possession and the films based on them, including *The Devils* (1971) and *The Rite* (2011) as well as *The Exorcist*, are also horror shows—productions that excite fear, shock, and revulsion in the audience.[2]

Indeed, filmic explorations of the devil, demons, and of the idea of possession were among some of the earliest subjects portrayed with the dawn of film, and later filmmakers, consciously or otherwise, have drawn upon and reimagined these treatments. While they are widely different in style and in their diegetic explanations for the possession (or possession-like phenomena) they screen, the films discussed here are united by shared narrative and cinematic conventions. Whether they treat possession as a metaphorization of mental illness, or use the phenomenological characteristics of certain mental illnesses as poetic devices for conveying the horror and anxiety of possession, each of these films draws (or at least attempts to draw) affective power from common anxieties about the loss of self-control and self-identity, and thus should be considered as part of a continuum of filmic possession narratives.

It is also important to note that negative spirit possession, certain types of mental illness, and related altered states of consciousness overlap phenomenologically, a fact that makes possession films potentially disturbing even to audiences who lack a shared cultural and religious framework in which demonic possession is accepted as a "real" phenomenon. This means that ultimately, whether the film's diegesis presents the possession syndrome as explainable by naturalistic psychological principles (for example, in many films, some form of disassociative identity disorder, senile dementia, or depersonalization related to an epileptic condition function very much like an "uninvited evil entity") or as caused by occult, supernatural forces, whether it uses mental illness as a red herring for what is eventually supernaturally explained (1973's *The Exorcist*, 2014's *The Taking of Deborah Logan*) or vice versa (2001's *Session 9*, and more polemically 2006's *Requiem*), the most effectively unsettling possession films are those that explore the subjective overlap between these conditions. However, those films that are most effectively terrifying or disturbing in their exploration are also arguably the most exploitative, since they run the greatest risk of demonizing mental illness, both figuratively and literally. This is true even when the possession in the filmic narrative is explicitly attributed to an alternative (that is, nondemonic) supernatural entity (for example, as in the 2012 film *Possession*, a dybbuk, or in the intriguingly execrable 1978 film *Manitou*, a vengeful Native American shaman) or a stated psychiatric cause (for example, the psychiatrist's explanation of Norman Bates's introjection of his mother's persona in Hitchcock's 1960 *Psycho*).

It must also be noted that many modern clinical conceptions, including especially DID and epilepsy, are themselves importantly shaped by earlier conceptions of possession, and more broadly, the history of modern therapeutic psychology is deeply rooted in early modern European cultural conceptions of, and cultural practices linked to, witchcraft and demonic possession. Since the earliest advent of cinematic technologies in the last decade of the 19th century, however, film has both altered and interrogated the shifting interstices between the medicalization of mental illness, and still-widespread beliefs in the reality of possession.

From the earliest cinematic productions, some audience members have experienced watching film as a kind of compulsive and uncontrollable event; images flash by on the screen, and the senses are bombarded with visual, and later auditory, impressions that can produce powerful cognitive and affective responses. In this light, it is clear why film as a medium has had such a forceful correlation with narratives of spirit possession. Early cinema, arising contemporaneously with both psychoanalysis and modern clinical psychiatry near the close of the 19th century, was quick to explore the mingling of wonder and horror occasioned by the demonic. One of the earliest short films, Georges Méliès's *Le manoir du diable* (1896), exploited the visual capabilities of this new technology to represent the powers of the devil in a way that had never before been seen. While Méliès's film does not present the possessive powers long thought to be part of the devil's supernatural arsenal, possession and exorcism would play a role in early American biblical epics. Sidney Olcott's *From the Manger to the Cross* (1912) briefly portrays Jesus's curing of a demoniac as part of his early ministry. More dramatically, Cecil B. DeMille's *King of Kings* (1927) features a lengthy scene of Jesus casting seven spectral demons (each based on one of the seven deadly sins; see Luke 8:2 and Mark 16:9) from Mary of Magdala. While the brief biblical accounts themselves offer no phenomenological description of the experiences of the possessed, DeMille's film supplies something of this sort, and its phantasmagoric visuals and gender dynamics typologically anticipate those of *The Exorcist* and the many demonic possession films that follow it.

While they did not directly explore demonic possession, German expressionist classics including *The Cabinet of Dr. Caligari* (1920, dir. Robert Wiene) and *Dr. Mabuse, the Gambler* (1922, dir. Fritz Lang) portray variations of hypnotic trance as inculcating a kind of possession, as does the American horror film *White Zombie* (1932), which features a racially and sexually ambiguous voodoo master possessing the bodies of his "zombies." The Polish film adaption of S. Ansky's play *The Dybbuk* (1937, dir. Michal Waszynski) screens the phenomenon more directly, making it arguably the first feature film whose primary focus is occult possession.[3] The dybbuk in this case is portrayed as the jealous spirit of the possessed Leah's beloved suitor, Khonnon, whom her father had rejected. The film's penultimate scene, in which Rabbi Azriel performs an elaborate exorcism to cast Khonnon's spirit from Leah's body, is both beautiful and harrowing, as is its conclusion, in which Leah chooses to join Khonnon in death rather than live without him. Ultimately, *The Dybbuk* is an entirely different breed of possession film from *The Exorcist* and its horrific spawn; it is a film, in Ira Konigsberg's words, "about loss, about failed possibilities, about forlorn hopes," and "about the scarce boundary between the living and the dead, about the interpenetration of the dead into the world of the living."[4] Yet it is also a film that speaks powerfully to the connection between loss and mourning, depression and self-destruction; in short, it aesthetically captures the psychological themes of Freud's essay "Mourning and Melancholia" (1917) like no other film.

Overt spirit possession is, for the most part, absent from the films of the late 1930s through the late 1960s. The psychological experiences that possession films speak to, however, are not. Many post–World War II horror films explore the terrifying effects of alien influences, the loss of self-control, and self-identity and related anxieties. They tend to do so through more science-fictional, and less religious or mythic, conceits. Many films, most famously *Invasion of the Body Snatchers* (1956, dir. Don Siegel) portray extraterrestrial forces occupying human bodies in ways that clearly parallel spirit possession. Others, including *The Manchurian Candidate* (1962, dir. John Frankenheimer) displace malevolent spirits with malevolent Communist ideologies and brainwashing techniques to achieve related effects.

It isn't until the early 1970s that the modern occult possession film takes to, and takes over, the screen. While it is *The Exorcist* (1973, written by William Peter Blatty, dir. William Friedkin) that primarily initiates this craze, it is important to note that Blatty and Friedkin's film followed in the wake of a very different film about demonic possession, Ken Russell's *The Devils* (1971). Russell's film is a sexual extravaganza that combines horror with eroticism and social satire, and is based on Aldous Huxley's lightly fictionalized historical novel *The Devils of Loudun* (1952). Possession in Huxley's novel, and in Russell's film, has no supernatural trappings, but is instead explicitly attributed to a combination of religiously inspired mass hysteria and the consequences of repressed sexuality. Despite Huxley's critical attitude toward Freud, Freud's ideas on hysteria, repression, and female sexuality are in clear evidence in the novel, and Russell's film exploits them visually to sensational effect. Nevertheless, it was not until the theatrical release of *The Exorcist* that the modern possession film's popular formulae were truly established, and few films frame the interpretive tension between modern psychiatry and neuroscience and occult possession as forcefully as Friedkin's.

A large portion of *The Exorcist*'s screen time is spent foregrounding the lengthy and disturbing course of examinations Regan is subjected to by medical professionals. These invasive tests build tension that the film's subsequent scenes of exorcism serve as a catharsis for. In direct opposition to the cosmopolitan skepticism and liberal irony of *The Devils*, *The Exorcist* treats demonic possession as a serious, irreducibly supernatural and viscerally horrifying phenomenon. As Sharon Packer points out, "Director

William Friedkin fretted about adding too much medical detail—yet he delighted in tapping into" contemporary medical controversies.[5]

As the authors of "Horror Films and Psychiatry" explain,

> Initially Regan experiences non-specific behaviour changes which alarm her mother. Her doctor diagnoses ADHD and prescribes Ritalin which does not help. Medical tests (including neuroimaging) fail to demonstrate the aetiology. Regan develops seizures and agitation from being possessed, with her eyes rolling back, convulsions, foaming mouth, and purposeless violence. Seizures or pseudo-seizures have long been used to describe demonic possession. The differential diagnosis is wide, including psychotic disorders, mania, Tourette's syndrome, conversion disorder, histrionic personality and dissociative identity disorder.[6]

While it draws on contemporary medicine and psychology, a large part of *The Exorcist's* affective power derives from its gradual exhaustion of these as explanations. As terrified mother Chris MacNeil desperately seeks a cure for her daughter Regan's nightmarish condition, she is failed time and again by medical and psychiatric authorities, until she and Father Damien Karras are driven to enlist the aid of Father Lankester Merrin in attempting to exorcise Regan. *The Exorcist's* effect on many audience members was so powerful it convinced a number of them they, too, were suffering from demonic possession, eventually giving rise to the clinical concept of "cinematic possession neurosis."

Ballon and Leszcz describe this condition, "often associated with horror films," as one in which "psychotic disorders were associated with extreme cases of behavior resulting from film viewing," in which the symptoms consisted "of dissociative phenomena, anxiety states, and paranoid ideation, involved the narrative or imagery of the film."[7] They explain that it is

> a culturally shaped syndrome, whereby a film shapes the symptom presentation of pre-existing mental health conditions in vulnerable people. Vulnerable individuals include those who have issues with their identity, e.g. possessing varying degrees of borderline personality structures, and those coping with stress, such as a loss of a close relationship about which they feel ambivalent. A film's content can result in the introjection of a powerful cultural symbol for evil to compensate for this loss, resulting in paranoid ideation, dissociative states, and anxiety, all of which are highly influenced and shaped by the film narrative.[8]

Beyond such cases in which *The Exorcist* synchronized powerfully with the pathological tendencies of individual audience members, it also tapped into increasing social anxieties about the power and influence of cinema itself. *The Exorcist* appeared at a moment when film studies emerged as a discipline heavily invested in Freudian psychoanalytic and structuralist Marxist theories that emphasized the power of cinema to influence audiences on a preconscious level. Film theorists including Laura Mulvey, Christian Metz, and Robin Wood viewed film as a method of ideological interpellation, one that functioned primarily on an unconscious register. In the work of these thinkers at this time, film was seen as a vector for the ideological inhabitation of largely passive spectators, suggesting that possession could function as a metaphorization of spectatorship itself.

While *The Exorcist*'s critical and commercial success would spawn a legion of cinematic imitators, the link between film and possession would be differently sensationalized by many of the headlines and commentaries that appeared during the "Video Nasties" moral panic that surrounded straight-to-video horror films throughout the 1980s. Such accounts described impressionable youths and children as "obsessed" and "possessed" by horror films, driven to commit violent acts as a result of their influence. Horror films, many of them featuring demonic possession, became framed as possessive entities themselves. Such anxieties were simultaneously amplified and satirized by films including Sam Raimi's *The Evil Dead* (1981) and its increasingly comedic sequels (1987, 1992), David Cronenberg's *Videodrome* (1984) and Lamberto Bava's *Demons* (1985). Raimi's film offered a Grand Guignol variation on the theme of demonic possession as an epidemic that was, however differently envisioned, also the focus of *The Devils*. Cronenberg displaced the idea of a spiritual or demonic possessing entity altogether, replacing it with paranoiac, techno-organic version of Marshall McLuhan's theory of media as a sensorial prosthesis. Bava's film embodied the same anxieties that gave rise to cinematic possession neurosis by portraying an epidemic of demonic possession, visualized with gruesome physical transformations, occurring among the audience of an avant-garde grindhouse theatre, an idea that would be imitated by later films including *The Video Dead* (1987).

Other horror films from this period veered more toward naturalist psychological explanations, while still carrying over some of the uncanny horror of *The Exorcist*. The indie horror/thriller film *Pin* (1988, dir. Sandor Stern), for example, portrays a young man whose dissociative, and eventually psychotic, behaviors are portrayed in ways that parallel demonic possession. Similarly, the unsettling and atmospheric film *Session 9* (2001, dir. Brad Anderson), shot primarily in the abandoned Danvers State Hospital in Massachusetts before its demolishment, probes the parallels between abuse-triggered dissociative identity disorder and possession.

The first decades of the 21st century have seen a greater focus on exploiting the resemblance between demonic possession and unusual epileptic conditions on the one hand, and on the idea of demonic possession as a kind of epidemic contagion on the other. The perceived connection between epilepsy and possession is an ancient one. Owsei Temkin explains that the "morbid conditions with which epilepsy in the Western world becomes increasingly associated from about the beginning of the Christian era" are subsumed under possession, "ascribed to the intrusion of a god, demon, or ghost into the body of a hitherto normal individual who now behaves like a willing or reluctant instrument of the intruder."[9]

Sallie Baxendale adds, "The association of epilepsy with supernatural possession, represented in art forms throughout the ages [. . .] remains a popular theme in 21st-century cinema," with many films reinforcing "the idea that seizures open up a portal to a demonic (or less frequently, divine) realm."[10] While *The Exorcist* had previously emphasized the failed attempts of Regan's doctors to explain her condition as related to epilepsy, three more recent films, each of them loosely based on the tragic case of Anneliese Michel (1952–1976), reinforce this association. Michel had been diagnosed with epilepsy, depression, and depressive psychosis before undergoing, at her own insistence and that of her pious Catholic parents, a harrowing series of exorcisms that eventually culminated in her death. This case became the subject of Felicitas Goodman's influential study *The Exorcism of Anneliese Michel*, which in turn was the major inspiration for Scott Derrickson's *The Exorcism of Emily Rose* (2005).

While it finally pushes the viewer toward a supernatural interpretation of events, this legal procedural/supernatural horror hybrid emphasizes the resemblance between Emily's possessed state and her epileptic-like seizures. In Baxendale's words,

> Although there is a superficial battle of science vs. the church in the courtroom, viewers are left in little doubt as to the supernatural nature of Emily's afflictions in the flashback sequences. No least, because supernatural happenings gradually creep into the main narrative, as the story unfolds in the courtroom. While it is not for clinicians to dictate the shape or form of any artistic endeavor, "The Exorcism of Emily Rose" is troubling, not only because this 21st-century treatment reinforces the ancient links between demonic possession and epilepsy but also because the strapline for the film is "Based on a True Story."[11]

Hans-Michael Schmidt's more somber and less exploitative treatment of Anneliese Michel's story, *Requiem* (2006) pushes the interpretive envelope in the other direction, clearly underlining mental illness stemming from epilepsy as the root of its young victim-protagonist's suffering. *Requiem* is a powerfully understated and sympathetic film, but it reached a much smaller audience than Derrickson's genre hit, which inspired a slew of low-budget imitators, most egregiously the wretchedly exploitative and tediously formulaic *Anneliese: The Exorcism Tapes* (2011) and the slightly more imaginative *The Devil Inside* (2012).

The demonic-possession-as-contagious-epidemic, on the other hand, was popularized by the inventive Spanish mockumentary horror film *Rec* (2007, dir. Jaume Balaguero), its Spanish-language sequels, and its American remake *Quarantine* (2008, dir. John Pogue and John Erick Dowdle). While the Spanish films overtly attribute their horrific epidemic to a weaponization of the demonic, *Quarantine* downplays the demonic dimensions of its epidemic, following earlier epidemic horror films including *28 Days Later* (2002) in emphasizing instead a bioweaponized variation of rabies.

More interesting in their exploration and exploitation of the subjective overlap between possession and mental illness are two recent possession films, the American indie mockumentary *The Taking of Deborah Logan* (2014, dir. Adam Robitel) and the stylish Australian horror film *The Babadook* (2014, dir. Jennifer Kent). *The Taking of Deborah Logan* links demonic possession not to a trauma-induced dissociative state or to an epileptic condition, but to senile dementia. Presenting itself as part of a documentary film about the effects of Alzheimer's, the film begins by harrowingly documenting the disintegration of Deborah's memory, personal identity, and relationship with her friends and family, ostensibly due to the progression of her illness. As the film continues, overtly supernatural elements emerge and intensify, and by its midpoint the film has abandoned any semblance of psychological subtlety, gleefully embracing its occult possession theme and horror-genre conventions.

With its striking visual echoes of German expressionist films including *Nosferatu* and *Caligari*, and classic American horror films including *The Shining* (1980) and *The Exorcist*, *The Babadook* pays homage to the many cinematic treatments of possession that influenced its creation. It deals with possession as a way of allegorizing grief and trauma, the interpenetration of the living by the dead, and is in this respect much closer to Waszynski's film *The Dybbuk* than it is to *The Exorcist*. *The Babadook* attains a memorable balance between exploiting mental illness as a source of fear and horror and exploring possession as a way of sympathetically and imaginatively portraying the crushing power of isolation, anxiety, and grief. At the same time, its extensive use of visual reference and homage enables it to uniquely explore the long-shared history between occult possession and mental illness in film, making it an ideal note on which to conclude this chapter.

Notes

1. Felicitas Goodman, *How About Demons? Possession and Exorcism in the Modern World* (Bloomington: Indiana University Press, 1988), 88.

2. Brian Levack, "The Horrors of Witchcraft and Demonic Possession," *Social Research* 81, no. 4 (2014): 921–939.

3. A term I take from Carol Clover's essay "Opening Up," as it is more capacious than "demonic possession" but also somewhat divorced from the anthropological term "negative spirit possession" used by writers including Patrick McNamara and Felicitas Goodman, which I hope will emphasize the fictive dimensions of these cinematic narratives, however much they are, or purport to be, grounded in "real" phenomena. Carol J. Clover, *Men, Women and Chainsaws: Gender in the Modern Horror Film* (Princeton: Princeton University Press, 1992), 65–113.

4. Ira Konigsberg, "The Only 'I' in the World: Religion, Psychoanalysis, and 'The Dybbuk,'" *Cinema Journal* 36, no. 4 (1997): 22.

5. Sharon Packer, "Demon Drugs or Demon Children," *Monstrous Children and Childish Monsters: Essays on Cinema's Holy Terrors*, Markus P.J. Bohlmann and Sean Moreland, eds. (Jefferson, NC: McFarland, 2015), 175.

6. Susan Hatters Friedman, Fernando Espi Forcen, and John Preston Shand, "Horror Films and Psychiatry," *Australasian Psychiatry* 22, no. 5 (2014): 447–449.

7. B. Ballon and M. Leszcz, "Horror Films: Tales to Master Terror or Shapers of Trauma?" *American Journal of Psychotherapy* 61, no. 2 (2007): 211–230.

8. Ballon and Leszcz, 224.

9. Temkin, Owsei, *The Falling Sickness: A History of Epilepsy from the Greeks to the Beginnings of Modern Neurology* (Baltimore: Johns Hopkins University Press, 1994), 86.

10. Baxendale, Sallie, "Epilepsy on the Silver Screen in the 21st Century," *Epilepsy & Behavior* 57 (2016): 270–274.

11. Baxendale, 271.

CHAPTER SIX

Hitchcock: Master of Suspense and Mental Illness

Mark O'Hara

Perhaps best known for his spoofs such as *Blazing Saddles* (1974), Mel Brooks in *High Anxiety* (1977) devotes his entire send-up of suspense films to Alfred Hitchcock.[1] Brooks includes shots of the legs of busy airport travelers, reverse zooms from high perches, a tense soundtrack—all of the conventions and off-balance plotting of the master, along with plentiful winks toward the viewer. In a re-creation of the shower scene from *Psycho* (1960),[2] Brooks's character Dr. Richard Thorndyke is pummeled not with a knife but with a newspaper wielded by a belligerent bellboy played by Barry Levinson; the camera pans from Thorndyke's stunned face on the floor up to the tub drain, where the black ink flows like blood.

An amalgamation of vaudevillian goofiness and self-reflexive shtick (the camera twice crashes through the "fourth wall" and disturbs the actors), *High Anxiety* is a farce that offers merely cartoonish depictions of characters with diagnoses of mental illness. Although the film elicits laughter, it is useful to recall Wahl's explanation: "Americans identify media as their main source of knowledge about mental illness, and because mental illness appears so frequently in American visual discourse."[3] Alfred Hitchcock's 1960 film *Psycho* is often blamed for reinforcing negative attitudes toward mental illness and people who are diagnosed with mental illness. Leading character Norman Bates is a relentless predator and murderer. But many of Hitchcock's other films feature characters who face psychological issues in more realistic ways.

In the 1958 movie *Vertigo*,[4] for example, John "Scottie" Ferguson, a police detective forced to retire because he has developed an intense fear of heights, accompanied by acute dizziness, falls in love with a mysterious woman that he has been hired to follow. Small details in the film, such as events that trigger Scottie's anxieties—and the coping mechanisms he develops to deal with them—portray the protagonist as a flawed but likable character.

Acrophobia—and the vertigo/dizziness induced by it—acute melancholia, guilt complex: these are the terms assigned in the film to the disorders affecting Scottie, played by Jimmy Stewart. In today's clinical lingo, diagnosticians might add a few more, certainly including obsessive compulsive disorder and perhaps voyeurism and scopophilia. Scottie's career as a police detective has made him well aware of criminal law, but his neglect of ethical principles causes him barely to skirt the line of criminality. Long an effective law enforcement officer and respected citizen, Scottie exhibits behaviors that conflict with his reputation. Because of his recent trauma—witnessing a patrol officer trying to help him but falling to his death, in the scene that opens the film—Scottie has a visceral reaction to heights and has retired from the force. Nevertheless, he is able to blend into society; he even feels well enough to allow himself to be convinced by a friend to take on a sort of private detective job: following Gavin Elster's wife Madeleine, whom Gavin believes is somehow possessed by the spirit of her great-grandmother, Carlotta Valdes.

The subplots of *Vertigo* seem to pivot on Scottie's relations with women. Well into middle age, he appears comfortable with Midge Wood (Barbara Bel Geddes), who had actually broken their engagement years before. Their conversation in her apartment is tinged more with familiarity than flirtation. When Scottie first spots Madeleine Elster (Kim Novak), however, he is taken with her classic beauty, and accepts the task of shadowing her. What may have begun as curiosity becomes obsession. Madeleine's movements among unusual locations—Carlotta's portrait in a gallery, her house, and her grave—fascinate Scottie; he is attracted more when he apparently saves her life after she jumps into San Francisco Bay.

Scottie's years as a detective do not serve him well in romance. The gaze that he directs at Madeleine becomes slanted with desire: as he falls in love, he does not appear to realize his betrayal of his college friend Gavin as well as of his own professionalism. Ravetto-Biagioli comments that the shift "between being captivated by the image of Madeleine and being captive of Scottie's obsessive gaze forces us to see the relation of seduction to obsession, blurring the lines between possessing and being possessed by the gaze."[5] Scottie goes from policing the social order to experiencing chaotic emotions. What Scottie fails to detect are the layers of deception that this woman, whose real name is Judy Barton, and Gavin Elster have piled upon him.

Unaware that Elster has killed the real Madeleine, throwing her out of the bell tower of San Juan Bautista just before Scottie can reach the top of the tower, Scottie believes that he is responsible for Madeleine's death. In his portrayal of the guilt-addled Scottie Ferguson, James Stewart shows a shocked passivity, as though he is incapable of responding to the unfair characterizations at the hearing over Madeleine's death. In his study of mental illness in the media, Wahl states that consumers constantly watch depictions of people with mental health issues as comical, different, or dangerous, and these images carry on the negative stereotypes that lead to the stigmatization of real persons with psychosocial disorders.[6] Even after Scottie forces Judy Barton to remake herself into Madeleine, the role she had played previously, Scottie is not viewed unfavorably.

Even though Gavin Elster is guilty of planning the murderous ruse, it is Judy who appears the recipient of the harshest punishment. She loves Scottie enough to allow him to dress her as Madeleine. However, she overlooks the gold necklace that she had worn during the charade, and when Scottie spots it, his anger seems justified. Perhaps his returning to the mission is his attempt to force Judy's confession, but the trip results in her death. Regardless of the variables that make up the equation of Scottie Ferguson's likability, losing the woman he loves for the second time can only continue to affect his mental health.

Tippi Hedren plays the title character in Hitchcock's 1964 film *Marnie*.[7] Opening shots show Marnie carrying a suitcase along a train platform. Bernard Herrmann's suspenseful string music draws in viewers as the camera stops on a marquee poster: "Alfred Hitchcock's Suspenseful Sex Mystery." We don't see Marnie's face until, washing out dark hair dye, she tosses back her head to reveal her face framed by her true blonde hair. Swiftly-paced sequences tell us about Marnie: she has stolen nearly $10,000 from her employer, Mr. Sidney Strutt, who is describing her to two detectives. Among Strutt's denigrating comments is the odd (and foreshadowing) phrase, "Always pulling her skirt down over her knees as though they were a national treasure." The narrative reveals that Marnie has developed paralyzing fears of storms, of intimacy with men, and of the color red; she is also an unrepentant liar and thief. A publisher named Mark Rutland, played by Sean Connery, falls in love with Marnie, and after a series of suspenseful complications, coaxes her into marriage.

Marnie is surely one of Hitchcock's more troubled female leads. The director is to be admired for not naming Marnie's disorders beyond her being "sick" or having kleptomania. In one scene we hear girls who are jumping rope and chanting, "Call for the Doctor, Call for the Nurse, Call for the Lady with the Alligator Purse. . . ." This rhyme echoes the school children singing in *The Birds*; it seems appropriate here because no one in the rhyme is able to give a correct diagnosis for the afflicted child. One of Marnie's problems is her unusual relationship with her mother, Bernice Edgar. With stolen money Marnie buys her mother a mink scarf. Her mother reacts indifferently, even when Marnie sits on the floor and rests her head on her mother's lap. Resentful of her mother's attentions toward a girl whom Bernice is babysitting, Marnie soon asks bluntly, "Why don't you love me?" The scene ends with Marnie receiving a slap from her mother, and going to lie down before dinner. The following scene reenacts the start of a traumatic night from Marnie's childhood. A window shade tapping, red light flooding the screen, Marnie seems beset by a dream. She awakens when her mother, standing in the doorway, calls her for dinner. Marnie comments that she was having the "same dream," and the feeling of cold started when her mother entered the room.

One method that Hitchcock frequently uses to build both suspense and characterization is dichotomous in nature. In Marnie's case, we viewers notice her revulsion by the color red, as when she spills ink on her sleeve—like a sudden blooming of blood—and alarms her coworkers when she rushes out of the office to the bathroom. Obsessively scrubbing at the stain, Marnie utilizes the defense mechanism of denying the near-hysteria of her reaction. Accompanying her shocked behavior is the Hitchcockian artifice of the red filter filling the shot whenever Marnie spots the provocative color. Although the filter may be heavy-handed, it serves to highlight how sudden and unwelcome are the emotions evoked by redness—and ultimately by the repressed trauma that generates these emotions.

This two-sided technique—Marnie's panic attacks triggered by physical factors, and heightened through the red filtering—is often accompanied by noises like knocking or rapping, and especially by the flashing and din of thunderstorms. Called in for Saturday overtime work, Marnie meets Mark Rutland in the empty office complex. Rutland appears to have been grooming her for a relationship, but as Marnie sits down to a fresh piece of paper in the typewriter, a storm suddenly crashes upon them, tossing a tree limb through a window and shattering display cases containing pre-Columbian art—the last of Rutland's mementos of his deceased wife. Her face frozen in terror, Marnie retreats to the far end of the room. He embraces Marnie against the paneling; she accepts passively, crying, "Stop the colors"; the racket and strobing lightning have transfixed her. After a few seconds Rutland gives her a kiss that is not returned, and it seems that he has exploited Marnie's vulnerable state. However, Marnie recovers and does not seem to remember or react to the stolen kiss.

As in *Vertigo*, the romantic subplot of *Marnie* serves to show the more "normal" sides of Hitchcock's characters. By film's end, Marnie is apparently "cured," and Mark Rutland has attained his goal of seeing her "fixed." Viewers witness portrayals of the lived experience of Marnie Edgar's character, and perhaps come away with sharper understanding of her complex behaviors, and more importantly, of what caused them. In fact their cause is what's most intriguing about the film: the seemingly minor character of the mother, Bernice, appears only a few times, but when in flashback we see her working in her own apartment as a prostitute, waking the six year-old Marnie so that Bernice can use the only bedroom with a sailor, we are introduced to the depravity whose result is the anguish that has stayed with Marnie into adulthood. From a 21st-century perspective, the mental illness of the male lead of Alfred Hitchcock's 1945 mystery *Spellbound*,[8] John Ballantyne (Gregory Peck), is not a fault within himself but a disability imposed upon him by society. He is treated differently as a result of his nonnormative behaviors. Whether they are physiological or psychological, impairments are socially conditioned and framed.[9] Other phrases suggest the easy marginalization of postwar lingo: "emotional problems of the sane," "the locked doors of his mind," "the illness and confusion disappear," imply that talking with a psychoanalyst results in a "disappearance"—or sure cure.

No movie of Hitchcock's uses more clinical language than *Spellbound*— not modern clinical terminology, but phrases like "guilt complex" and simplified theories of Freudian psychology. Even the setting is the clinic, the place in history where citizens were removed in order for their disorders to be examined. This clinical gaze comes from medical doctors with the power to make decisions and order interventional treatment.[10] The institution is called Green Manors, and the retiring head psychiatrist, Dr. Murchison (Leo G. Carroll), presides over the entrance of his replacement, Dr. Anthony Edwardes (Gregory Peck). The protagonist is the only woman on staff, Dr. Constance Petersen (Ingrid Bergman), and she falls in mutual infatuation with Edwardes at first contact. The doctors have apartments in this institution, and Petersen leaves her rooms to visit the library, ostensibly to borrow Edwardes' latest book but really to visit his apartment to pursue a romance. Soon they kiss. Their embrace is interrupted, however, when Edwardes seems frozen in revulsion: he's staring at the lines in the fabric of Petersen's robe. At their first meeting a few hours earlier, Edwardes acted unduly alarmed at a pattern that Petersen had drawn on the tablecloth with a fork, rectilinear lines shaped like a pool. She soon discovers the man she's in love with is only posing as Dr. Edwardes. As he has amnesia, he cannot say his real name (we discover later that it's John Ballantyne, and his knowledge of medicine hints that he is some sort of doctor).

Gregory Peck's masterful acting, enhanced by the minute details of Hitchcock's direction, sketches Edwardes's/Ballantyne's character as extremely complex yet likable. Growing agitated whenever he spots patterns of parallel lines—especially against a white background—he enters a state resembling fainting before he recovers. The dedication depicted by Bergman seems so real that viewers' disbelief remains suspended when Petersen leaves her place of work, Green Manors, for Manhattan to follow Ballantyne after he is suspected in the murder of the real Dr. Edwardes.

It is safe to say that the director's agenda is to make *Spellbound* suspenseful, and that the police chasing a "madman" (as a radio report calls Ballantyne) and his psychiatrist/girlfriend does not supply enough "white-knuckled" moments. Perhaps that's why Ballantyne is at times portrayed as menacing. Hiding out in the house of her mentor, Dr. Alexander Brulov, Petersen lies about her relationship with Ballantyne, claiming they're married. Acting as a gentleman, Ballantyne takes the couch and leaves the bed to Petersen, but in the middle of the night, sleepless, he enters the bathroom and stirs up some shaving soap. Caught in a spell of anxiety by the black brush bristles against the white soap, Ballantyne retreats to the bedroom, where he stands beside the sleeping Petersen. Holding a straight razor, he's transfixed by the lines in the bedspread. Tense moments pass. Ballantyne silently leaves the room to descend the stairs, where a wakeful Dr. Brulov sits at the far end of the parlor. Hitchcock's famous camera work cuts in here, showing a long shot of Brulov chattering away, with occasional close-ups of the razor in Ballantyne's hand.

That the murderer of the eminent Dr. Edwardes turns out to be his predecessor at Green Manors, Dr. Murchison, is an indicator of the unjust blame directed toward John Ballantyne. (Further irony surfaces when we ponder Murchison's comment that his own reason for retiring from Green Manors was his "crumbling," or some unspecified psychological disorder.) A character's perceived mental illness is a variable that cannot be ignored in the viewing of a film, as suggested by Dr. Petersen when she refuses to let Ballantyne surrender before the murder is solved: "If you turn yourself in in your condition, there is no afterward." In fact, John Ballantyne has been objectified by the part of society intent on disciplinary action.

Foucault comments that it is "the fact of being constantly seen, of being able always to be seen, that maintains the disciplined individual in his subjection."[11] Dr. Petersen may be breaking the law, but she is also protecting a loved one from the power collected through observing and controlling the populace.

In 1963's *The Birds*,[12] the supporting character Lydia Brenner, played by Jessica Tandy, has an inordinate fear of abandonment. She's the mother of Mitch Brenner (Rod Taylor), the lawyer who meets Melanie Daniels (Tippi Hedren) in the bird shop. After Melanie drives 60 miles out of San Francisco to deliver love birds to the Brenner house, using the cover story of visiting the teacher Annie Hayworth, she meets Mrs. Brenner and finds her distant. Mrs. Brenner watches Melanie move throughout the house, and questions Mitch about her presence and her reputation as a scandalous socialite. In a conversation with Annie Hayworth, Melanie learns that Mrs. Brenner can be difficult to deal with—as Annie had discovered while in a relationship with Mitch. Having lost her husband, Mrs. Brenner now cannot stand the thought of being alone.

In a famous scene, Mrs. Brenner drives her pickup truck to the farm of a friend, only to find the inside of the house in disarray and the owner dead in his bedroom, apparently killed by birds. Running in panic, dropping her purse as she heads to the truck, Mrs. Brenner cannot even summon words to speak to a farmhand, or to Mitch and Melanie as she arrives home. Of course this is one bit of characterization and one tense moment of many to come. It is followed, however, by a break in which Melanie brings tea to Mrs. Brenner, and they converse, Mrs. Brenner confiding her wish to be stronger than she is, and Melanie offering to go to the schoolhouse to pick up Cathy, Mitch Brenner's younger sister. In the cinematic condensing of time, Melanie grows closer to the entire Brenner family, helping Cathy through several bird attacks and falling in love with Mitch.

Strangers on a Train (1951)[13] opens with shots of the legs of two men as they leave their taxis and board a train, the waist-down perspectives highlighting the similarities of the soon-to-be compartment-mates. Guy Haines, played by Farley Granger, is a social-climbing tennis player whose girlfriend's father is a U.S. senator, while Bruno Antony, played by Robert Walker, reveals himself early as a rich and risk-taking sociopath. After Antony talks his way into an easy acquaintance with the younger man, discovering Haines's hatred for the wife who will not divorce him, Antony proposes the two should "swap" murders, with Haines killing Antony's meddlesome father and Antony killing Miriam Haines.

That Antony is Haines's secret self, or doppelganger, is suggested through several images and conversations. First, the two often dress alike, in well-tailored suits and fedoras; Antony also continually appears as Haines's shadow, stalking him from the steps of the Jefferson Memorial or from the stands of a tennis court. The main plot hinges on Antony's interpretation of the exchange on the train, which Haines took as a joke. Viewers are struck by Antony's aberrant behavior when he catches Miriam Haines on an island at an amusement park and strangles her. Hitchcock enhances this scene by showing the murder: not directly but in the reflection of Miriam's large eyeglasses that have fallen in the grass. Further, the shot lingers in the lens to feature Antony's hands before he picks up the glasses as a keepsake, and then the lighter that he'd dropped, the lighter that Haines had left behind in the train car.

Antony's psychopathology is unique. His conversational style is familiar, his manner insouciant. Able to endear himself swiftly to strangers, he introduces himself to Haines' circle and insinuates himself into conversations with Senator Morton (Leo. G. Carroll) and Mrs. Cunningham (Norma Varden), the wife of a judge. A small but definite turning point in the perception of Bruno Antony comes when he places his hands around Mrs. Cunningham's neck, in a demonstration of a technique of murder that is intended to be humorous and witty. As Antony commences his mock choking, Barbara Morton (Patricia Hitchcock), the sister of Haines' girlfriend Anne Morton (Ruth Roman), steps behind Mrs. Cunningham. Barbara is appalled at the spectacle of this man, whom she suspects of murdering Miriam Haines and framing Guy Haines, reenacting the crime. And the scene indeed becomes a reenactment as Antony is for a second time transfixed by Barbara Morton—by her resemblance to Miriam Haines. Staring at her eyes framed by large glasses, Antony tightens his grip on the now-whimpering Mrs. Cunningham. Antony's occasional bouts of paralysis remind viewers that he is operating with an array of disorders, not the least of which is an outsized ego.

The mix of Bruno Antony's social ease and edginess fits Merskin's concept of the compensated psychopath, a figure that "defies convention, breaks rules, and fearlessly flaunts convention. He is predatory and to be feared, and yet he is alluring, manipulative, powerful, and successful."[14] Despite the knowledge possessed by viewers—about Antony's premeditated murder of Miriam Haines, about his obsessive stalking of Guy Haines, about the past transgressions that have made Antony's father seek to "commit" him—Bruno Antony's gentlemanly charade is beguiling, making his character almost likable. His determination to frame Haines for Miriam's murder is simply an extension of his neglect of truth and decency: "For Bruno, the act of killing Miriam was as ethically and mechanically pure as one of the death sentences handed down by the judge he harangues at

Senator Morton's party."[15] Bruno Antony falls short, however, of Norman Bates's status as serial killer: both men follow no code of morals, but Bates' sinister manners attract more stigmatization.

Lead characters in Hitchcock's *Vertigo, Marnie, Spellbound, The Birds*, and *Strangers on a Train* behave in ways that cause their titles to be listed more as suspense films, as opposed to *Psycho*, which has been dubbed by some critics as the "granddaddy of modern horror films." Although Alfred Hitchcock keeps shock value high on his shelf of cinematic devices—think of the demise of Detective Arbogast in *Psycho*, or our glimpse of Norman's mother—the director gives away measurements of his understanding of the dimensions of human behavior most clearly in his studies of suspense. Hitchcockian characters defy normative behavior; viewers are alarmed when they see a person who seems agreeable suddenly turn murderous. Finally, Hitchcock's use of tropes continually activates viewers' cultural catalogs. That's why Mel Brooks has so much material to lampoon.

Notes

1. Mel Brooks and Madeline Kahn, *High Anxiety*, DVD, dir. Mel Brooks (1977; Los Angeles: 20th Century Fox, 2006).

2. Anthony Perkins and Janet Leigh, *Psycho*, DVD, dir. Alfred Hitchcock (1960; Los Angeles: Universal Pictures, 1998).

3. Otto Wahl, *Media Madness: Public Images of Mental Illness* (New Brunswick, NJ: Rutgers University Press, 2006).

4. James Stewart and Kim Novak, *Vertigo*, DVD, dir. Alfred Hitchcock (1958; Los Angeles: Universal Pictures, 1999).

5. Kriss Ravetto-Biagioli, "Vertigo and the Vertiginous History of Film Theory," *Camera Obscura* 25, no. 75: 100–114 (2010). *Academic Search Complete*, EBSCOhost (accessed August 6, 2015).

6. Wahl, *Media Madness*, 164–165.

7. Tippi Hedren and Sean Connery, *Marnie*, DVD, dir. Alfred Hitchcock (1964; Los Angeles: Universal Pictures, 2001).

8. Ingrid Bergman and Gregory Peck, *Spellbound*, DVD, dir. Alfred Hitchcock (1945; Los Angeles: Anchor Bay Entertainment, 1998).

9. Abram Anders, "Foucault and 'the Right to Life': From Technologies of Normalization to Societies of Control," *Disability Studies Quarterly*, 33, no. 3 (2013), http://dsq-sds.org/article/view/3340 (accessed August 9, 2015).

10. Jonathan Joseph, *Social Theory: An Introduction* (Washington Square: New York University Press, 2003), 165.

11. Michel Foucault, *Discipline and Punish* (New York: Vintage, 1977), 187.

12. Tippi Hedren and Rod Taylor, *The Birds*, DVD, directed by Alfred Hitchcock (1963; Los Angeles: Universal Pictures, 2000).

13. Farley Granger and Robert Walker, *Strangers on a Train*, DVD, directed by Alfred Hitchcock (1951; Los Angeles: Warner Home Video, 1997).

14. Debra Merskin, "Smooth Operator: The Compensated Psychopath in Cinema," in *Mental Illness in Popular Media: Essays on the Representation of Disorders*, ed. L. C. Rubin (Jefferson, NC: McFarland & Company, 2012), 54.

15. Peter J. Dellolio, "Hitchcock and Kafka: Expressionist Themes in 'Strangers on a Train,'" *Midwest Quarterly* 45, no. 3 (Spring 2004), 249. Academic Search Complete, EBSCOhost (accessed August 14, 2015), 99.

CHAPTER SEVEN

McMurphy the Trickster, Foucault, and *One Flew Over the Cuckoo's Nest*

Mark O'Hara

A trickster in a cinematic work often starts out in a position of imprisonment or other restraint.[1] The protagonist of *One Flew Over the Cuckoo's Nest*, Randle Patrick McMurphy, struggles and arguably prevails against the institution that wishes to discipline him. His resistance to people in power reflects the nature of the trickster as a character type that can change audience members' attitudes toward characters who are portrayed as mentally ill.

One Flew Over the Cuckoo's Nest was one of the most renowned cultural artifacts of the 1970s. The movie assumes a stance that is against psychiatry and institutionalization. It also paints a positive picture of the rebellious antics and tactics of Randle Patrick McMurphy who, in his role as trickster, is determined not only to challenge authority but to cause the "patients" around him to take stands for their own dignity and liberation. Of course, in the film, McMurphy tweaks his role as patient/prisoner with a modern mix of bawdy humor, reckless violence, and relentless defiance of control. Randle Patrick McMurphy is a crusader for his fellow patients, one who never stops in his attempts to "stick it to the Man."

Michel Foucault was a 20th-century French educator, philosopher, and historian; his genealogical ideas about the human sciences are very useful in an analysis of Milos Forman's *One Flew Over the Cuckoo's Nest*,[2] based on Ken Kesey's novel. Randle Patrick McMurphy, played by Jack Nicholson, achieves archetypal status through his rendition of a likable rascal out to overthrow medical and legal tyrants wherever he meets them. Having "played" the prison system and convinced his warders that he (and they) might be better off if "R. P." were transferred into the clinical system, McMurphy meets Nurse Ratched (Louise Fletcher in the film) and the supposedly deviant collection of patients over whom she holds sway. Here are visible a series of Foucauldian themes, mainly covering the development and commingling of the sciences of sociology, psychology, and psychiatry with the older institution of penalty. Foucault posits that

> psychiatric or psychological experts, magistrates concerned with the implementation of sentences, educationalists, members of the prison service, all fragment the legal power to punish;. . .one is handing over to them mechanisms of legal punishment to be used at their discretion: subsidiary judges they may be, but they are judges all the same.[3]

How does McMurphy fit the profile of an ideal "offender"? First, he is subjected to procedures that are intended more as supervision than punishment—but end up as both. For instance, he is prohibited from certain areas; he is watched closely and monitored to a degree corresponding to his increasing rebellion; he is obliged to take medication. In short, McMurphy faces a clinical "gaze" whose purpose is to record and transform his state of mind and change his criminal behaviors—and to continue the surveillance and modification after he has been changed.[4]

The Foucauldian concept of the soul, propounded in *Discipline and Punish*, assists in describing the effects of the apparatuses of power upon the bodies of the characters in this study. The concept of a soul related to materiality and not spirituality serves as a support beam in Foucault's structural analysis of technologies of control. Insubstantial in itself, this soul nevertheless reflects the ways in which the body is invested by power relations, as well as how it is surrounded by a juridico-medical enterprise that continues to collect knowledge for the purpose of distributing and utilizing power.[5] "The soul is the effect and instrument of a political anatomy; the soul is the prison of the body"[6]:

> [I]t is produced permanently around, on, within the body by the functioning of a power that is exercised on those punished—and, in a more general

way, on those one supervises, trains and corrects, over madmen, children at home and at school, the colonized. . .[7]

All of the makers of meaning within the collaborative genre of film provide multiple relationships and plot points that exemplify power relations.

With R. P. McMurphy it is relevant to reference Foucault's idea of the soul: his character incurs the most forceful apparatuses of discipline of any characters in the film. It could be argued, however, that McMurphy's role as advocate and activist grants a certain agency for resistance. Hughes writes that activism against ableist policies and procedures should not be reduced to the intentions of individual persons with disabilities, but it should also not be reduced to the bodiless technologies of discourse.[8] Despite his perseverance in subversive behaviors—such as arranging an actual fishing trip for his fellow "inmates," or bribing attendants in order to set up a sexual tryst for young Billy Bibbit, McMurphy is eventually caught in the network of power running through this state hospital. In Kesey's novel the motif of surveillance is more noticeable: Chief Bromden's paranoid tone is apparent in the first line, "They're out there,"[9] as he pushes his broom slowly about the antiseptic halls. Kesey's invention of Bromden as the first-person narrator enables the reader to overhear the workings of power at its source, as the Chief, who feigns an inability to speak, hear, and react "normally," is allowed to sweep even during the meetings of the board of directors. The metaphor of fog suggests that events or agendas around the facility are hidden, perhaps unethical or even illegal; the fog also characterizes the deadened states of consciousness that drugs impose upon the patients. In the film, not many doctors appear; "Big Nurse" Ratched is their surrogate. She represents the medical establishment in her decisions about the patients: whether or not they are dangerous; whether they should be treated or forced into submission; even the psychiatric judgment of what part of free will was involved with their "offenses."[10] So much of Randle Patrick McMurphy's "treatment" exemplifies Foucault's propositions about how criminology, sociology, and the other "human sciences" combine to legitimize the sentences and procedures in operation in modern clinical and justice systems. A crucial effect arises from this combination: the penal system has assumed so many extrajudicial elements and such a large body of knowledge that the judge is no longer seen purely as the person who punishes; criminal justice perpetually invokes systems other than itself.[11] McMurphy is out to "play" whichever system that purports to control him, however.

Foucault's theory of the binary materializes clearly in *One Flew Over the Cuckoo's Nest*. Running throughout the film are several oppositional relationships, from color symbolism—in which McMurphy initially appears in dark clothing and wool cap while Nurse Ratched is dressed in white—to the general milieu of the institution—in which power-laden actions like unwarranted lobotomization are cast in striking relief against the small bodies of the patients, who are virtually powerless. In *Power/Knowledge* Foucault speaks against the tendency toward reductionism, asking why it is that humans tend so quickly to resort to the weak logic of contradiction.[12] In viewing a situation, Foucault believes, "one must try to think struggle and its forms, objectives, means and processes in terms of a logic free of the sterilizing constraints of the dialectic."[13] Foucault traces the marginalization that occurs with binary thinking:

> Generally speaking, all the authorities exercising individual control function according to a double mode; that of binary division and branding (mad/sane; dangerous/harmless; normal/abnormal); and that of coercive assignment, of differential distribution. . .how a constant surveillance is to be exercised over him in an individual way).[14]

R. P. McMurphy is identified early as a troublemaker, an offender, a person who does not obey sovereign power or disciplinary tactics. Nurse Ratched certainly notes his noncompliance and punishes him with various procedures, including electroshock; McMurphy defies his branding and survives all attempts to break his will, however, until Ratched stumbles upon a gap in McMurphy's armor: he defends those weaker than himself.

Three-quarters into the 20th century—1975—is an imperative date in a genealogical review of films featuring characters diagnosed with mental illness. The years of the 1960s and 1970s saw the contestation of psychiatric authority, and a reduction in the number of mental institutions, along with the democratization of procedures in many institutions that remained open.[15] The popularity of *One Flew Over the Cuckoo's Nest* suggests strong cultural biases in favor of depictions of distrust of those in power.[16] In fact, the years between the release of Ken Kesey's novel (1962) and the release of the film span roughly the rise and decline of American involvement in the war in Vietnam/Southeast Asia, a time of growing disillusionment and protest in American culture. Paralleling the intergenerational anger of the Vietnam era, the film blames parents for the psychoses of their children, and shows authority figures imposing arbitrary and oppressive rules upon the patients/inmates. Furthermore, the Oregon mental institution of *Cuckoo's Nest* functions as a stand-in for a repressive state.[17] The power structures wielded by the hospital—with the stern, neatly-coiffed Big Nurse as their agent—represent a coldly calculating agenda that ignores civil rights and annihilates individuality.[18] This film clearly does not assume the conservative establishment view that institutionalizing persons with psychological disabilities is the best course: *One Flew Over the Cuckoo's Nest* could be positioned at the top of the list of films supporting ideas promoted by the antipsychiatry movement. The film brims with binary oppositions between humans and the practices of control exemplified by state institutions.[19] Rutten et al. clarify the protagonist's reaction to power: "McMurphy's resistance becomes significant when he disturbs the public order and the dominant discourse, which prescribes that people with 'mental health problems' need to be isolated from society in psychiatric state hospitals."[20] Both the novel and the film present positive depictions of antiauthoritarian ideology, sentiments that were popular in the 1960s and 1970s, and that also fit the thinking of the antipsychiatry movement.[21] Both texts reinforce the discourse of the imposition of disability status upon humans who are impaired—the major discourse informed by the social models of disability. In fact, *One Flew Over the Cuckoo's Nest* suggests that the institution of psychiatry and the protocols it has engendered are responsible for creating "mental health problems."[22]

Randle Patrick McMurphy can be characterized as a liberator because he treats his fellow patients as mature humans who deserve to make their own decisions—an idea that reinforces a theme in *One Flew Over the Cuckoo's Nest* that individuals should exercise their free will instead of obeying the dictates of hierarchical powers.[23] Whether he is leading a protest over television rights in the ward by cheering for a fantasized baseball game, or organizing a fishing trip during which he introduces his fellow patients as doctors (repeating the old trope about "who's running the asylum?"), McMurphy strives continually to liberate and empower the men surrounding him. Further, McMurphy can be seen as a Christ figure, working for the good of common people until he is betrayed—by Billy Bibbit, who soon kills himself, Judas Iscariot-like; "Mac" is then symbolically crucified through lobotomization, and "rises" briefly before Bromden smothers him, whispering "You're coming with me."[24] Bassil-Morozow categorizes McMurphy as a "human type" of trickster, who tends to lack abilities to transcend the human frame and sustains bodily harm: his body suffers because he "has crossed the line into the dangerous territory and disrupted the established order of things" within the oppressive psychiatric hospital.[25] The physical restraints on McMurphy's body—including the facility itself, assaults from orderlies, and through ECT and lobotomization—exemplify the Foucauldian idea of biopower. However, I would argue that McMurphy's influence continues after death: Bromden uses his friend's idea of tearing up the heavy control panel in the tub room and, with water spraying everywhere, Bromden throws the appliance through the mesh window and runs away, the camera staying on him as he recedes. It is significant that Bromden does not leave McMurphy alive, as McMurphy would have served as a continuous warning of oppressive institutional control. Instead, Chief carries Mac's message of self-liberation with him, and the other patients back in the hospital shout happily as the big man escapes.

McMurphy can also be romanticized as a rebel who challenges "Big Nurse" Ratched's authority; when McMurphy states that the patients are no more troubled than the average person "on the street," he is pointing out the tendency to otherize and stigmatize, or to draw a line between "us and them."[26] All aspects of the patients' lives are regimented, and their treatments can hardly be called rehabilitative; patients are in fact punished if they step out of their "sick roles" to exhibit more normative behaviors.[27] The character Billy Bibbit, for instance, played by Brad Dourif as an insecure and stuttering quasi-adolescent, regains poise and confidence after R. P. McMurphy sets Billy up for his first sexual experience. Appalled by Billy's rebellion, her authoritarian rule threatened, Nurse Ratched shames Billy into guilt-ridden compliance and suicide. Through invoking Billy's mother and her incipient dissatisfaction with his behaviors, Ratched locates Billy's deviance within the domain of the family and uses the mother's influence to control the son. Billy fails to reject dependence on his mother, a condition for claiming his manhood. Foucault describes the shift away from the public status of family affairs that was a hallmark of the classical age—when societies locked away citizens for debauchery or prodigality but did not categorize these "offenses" as marks of insanity: "In the nineteenth century, conflicts between individuals and their families became a private affair, and took on the allure of a psychological problem. . . .To attack the family was to flirt with the world of unreason."[28]

By mentioning Billy Bibbit's mother, Nurse Ratched nullifies the traditionally supportive role of the family in the care of a troubled member, and manipulates Billy into such mortifying guilt that he names his friend McMurphy as the culprit behind the promiscuity on the ward. This head nurse's behavior suggests an element of hypocrisy in the representation of those who care for the mentally ill characters in film: dominant American ideologies view nursing as a respectable profession, yet films tend to portray mental health nurses as uncaring and even aberrant.[29] After destroying Billy's self-worth, Ratched continues to devalue her own authority when she retaliates against the other patients on the ward, and particularly when she orders the lobotomy that is meant to neutralize McMurphy's disruptive influence. Foucault describes the home as the natural location where the family helps to fight illness, the place that existed *before* the hospital (which before the 18th century was really no more than a poorhouse, or even a warehouse to imprison any type of person society found offensive), the family and home as the place to receive loving care and let the illness dissipate through its natural course.[30] Having fallen asleep and missed his planned escape, McMurphy witnesses Billy's fate, and attempts to murder Ratched. Now that the disciplinary regime has trapped McMurphy, his demise is imminent. Although the "Big Nurse" can seem caring, even liberal, in her promotion of group therapy, her patronizing manner cannot hide her steely belief in the psychiatric hospital as a place of surveillance and control.[31] Ratched's group therapy sessions are more of "a Gestapo-like questioning" than helpful dialogues.[32] In short, she is skilled at casting aspersions and airs of unreason upon the less powerful humans surrounding her.

It is fitting that R. P. McMurphy has tricked the prison officials who had him in custody but transferred him to the psychiatric hospital, as these actions further support his role as a trickster. At once social critic and clown, McMurphy breaks countless hospital rules in order to subvert management styles that he deems oppressive, to promote independence and self-esteem in his fellow patients, and finally, simply to amuse himself. Similarly, the conventional trickster is a primal figure, both creator and destroyer, who breaks social taboos, often entertains both others and him/herself, and undergoes punishments that remind onlookers/listeners of the consequences of breaking societal rules.[33] Hyde characterizes the confidence man as a typically American hero/trickster, a wanderer in a land of opportunity, an opportunist who can say anything he wants at any time[34]—an apt description for "R. P." Because of his antics and oppositional attitude toward the Establishment, McMurphy can also be compared to comical cartoon characters such as Bugs Bunny, whose mischief keeps viewers enthralled;[35] McMurphy might also strike viewers of the film as a compilation of characteristics of Kesey's circle of friends from The Merry Pranksters. Jack Nicholson preserves much of McMurphy's bravado in the film, showing the scintillating self-confidence of a scar-marked gambler, roguish Korean War vet, hard-fighting (and fornicating) logger, and, in one of Kesey's monologues, quasi-cowboy slang-speaker, cocky and eager to establish himself on the ward:

> Then you tell Bull Goose Loony Harding that R. P. McMurphy is waiting to see him and that this hospital ain't big enough for the two of us. I'm

accustomed to being top man. . . .Tell this Harding that he either meets me man to man or he's a yaller skunk and better be outta town by sunset.[36]

R. P. McMurphy's demeanor is complicated: good natured but volatile, loyal yet rebellious—all hallmarks of the trickster. Cinematic tricksters also sometimes serve as therapists, bringing patients to the point of crisis and finally reflection: McMurphy carelessly exposes repressed psychic material, an action that ultimately allows those with whom he shares the ward to connect with each other.[37] The irony lies in an ages-old character type being marked by the modern, medicalized construction of mental illness. In earlier times McMurphy might have been accepted as an eccentric and diverse presence, but in the United States of the 20th century, he and his behaviors are marked as defective and categorized for separation from mainstream life.

Several aspects of Milos Forman's film diverge from the novel's representations of mental illness. Gone is Ken Kesey's famous invention of the Native American, "Chief" Bromden, as the first person narrator, along with Bromden's storytelling devices that suggest symptoms of schizophrenia. Slapstick comedy, violence, and distorted depictions of reality are altered or missing from the movie.[38] For instance, Nurse Ratched's face does not contort surrealistically, and there is no mention of fog machines or the "Combine," Bromden's metaphors for hidden hegemonic controls, disciplinary technologies, and destructive agendas. Camera shots, angles, and editing perspectives are also divorced from Bromden, showing third-person omniscience and a traditional, straightforward storyline.[39] Kesey's early postmodern prose style—present tense, first person psychedelic, as it were—is also elided. Milos Forman's statement, "I like to reveal the inside through the surface,"[40] suggests the director's penchant for indirect characterization and subtle social satire; the viewer/ spectator, however, must remember that the film and book are largely different texts. R. D. Laing posits that the mind is located within a person and therefore is not accessible to the other (a psychoanalyst, for example);[41] perhaps the decision not to use unusual effects to simulate psychoses is the director's way of endeavoring to copy his version of reality as closely as possible—without exploiting the medium of film to infer what a character is experiencing. A vastly condensed dramatization that locates institutional inequities mostly within one spiteful nurse, the film fails to expose the injustices leading to the categorization and internment of "the mentally ill"—unless the themes of injustice can be developed solely through the symbols of sterile hospital corridors, locked doors, and electroshock therapy. Foucault cites major institutions such as psychiatric and penal facilities as having limited importance when they are viewed for their economic significance; however, these institutions are crucial to the continued functioning of the "wheels of power."[42] Forman's film was both a popular and critical "hit," but regardless of its artistry and literalness, Kesey's opus also installs images of increasing dominance of disciplinary regimes and unseen wielders of power.

One must wonder what changes would be made if *One Flew Over the Cuckoo's Nest* were to be rewritten and reshot. If a filmmaker attempted to follow Ken Kesey's vision more closely, the product would surely display more surrealistic effects in attempting to suggest states of aberrant perception; it might retain the narrative wanderings of Chief Bromden, and it would probably feature countless permutations of hallucinations experienced by the characters—brought about both through psychoses and through mind-expanding drugs. Kesey speculated on being both the screenwriter and director of his own work: "I could do it weird. I could do it so that people, when they left there, they couldn't find the exit."[43] Still, the much-lauded 1975 film retains its iconic status more than 40 years after its making, one of the most famous movies to attack psychiatry and its gazes and glances, as well as to promote patient rights and dignity.

Notes

1. Helena Bassil-Morozow, *The Trickster in Contemporary Film* (New York: Routledge, 2012), 24.

2. Jack Nicholson, *One Flew Over the Cuckoo's Nest*, DVD, dir. Milos Forman (1975; Los Angeles: United Artists, 2010).

3. Michel Foucault, *Discipline and Punish* (New York: Vintage Books, 1977), 21.

4. Ibid., 18.

5. Ibid., 24.

6. Ibid., 30.

7. Ibid., 29.

8. Bill Hughes (2012), "What can a Foucauldian Analysis Contribute to Disability Theory?" in *Foucault and the Government of Disability*, Shelly Tremain, ed. (Ann Arbor: University of Michigan Press, 2012), 80–81.

9. Ken Kesey, *One Flew Over the Cuckoo's Nest* (New York: Viking Press, 1962), 3.

10. Foucault, *Discipline*, 22.

11. Ibid.

12. Michel Foucault, *Power / Knowledge: Selected Interviews and Other Writings 1972–1977* (New York: Vintage Books, 1980), 143.

13. Ibid., 143–144.

14. Michel Foucault, *The Birth of the Clinic* (New York: Vintage Books, 1994), 199.

15. Helen Spandler, "Spaces of Psychiatric Contention: A Case Study of a Therapeutic Community," *Health & Place* 15 (2009): 672.

16. Michael Ryan and Douglas Kellner, *Camera Politica: The Politics and Ideology of Contemporary Hollywood Film* (Bloomington: Indiana University Press, 1988), 10.

17. Claude J. Smith, "Finding a Warm Place for Someone We Know: The Cultural Appeal of Recent Mental Patient and Asylum Films," *Journal of Popular Film & Television* 27, no. 1 (1999): 43.

18. Elaine B. Safer, "'It's the Truth Even If It Didn't Happen': Ken Kesey's *One Flew Over the Cuckoo's Nest*," *Literature Film Quarterly* 5, no. 2 (1977): 132.

19. Kris Rutten, Griet Roets, Ronald Soetaert, and Rudi Roose, "The Rhetoric of Disability: A Dramatistic-Narrative Analysis of *One Flew Over the Cuckoo's Nest*," *Critical Arts: A Southwest Journal of Cultural & Media Studies* 26, no. 5 (2012): 638.

20. Ibid., 639.

21. Ibid., 641.

22. Ibid.

23. William L. Blizek, "Religion and Spirituality in the Movies," *International Journal of Religion & Spirituality in Society* 2, no. 3 (2013): 110.

24. Ibid.

25. Bassil-Morozow, *The Trickster*, 33–34.

26. Rutten et al., "The Rhetoric of Disability," 639.

27. D. Quinn, "One Flew Over the Cuckoo's Nest," *Teaching Sociology* 171, (1989): 122.

28. Michel Foucault, *History of Madness* (New York: Routledge, 2006), 91.

29. Keri de Carlo, "Ogres and Angels in the Madhouse: Mental Health Nursing Identities in Film," *International Journal of Mental Health Nursing* 16, no. 5 (2007): 346.

30. Foucault, *Clinic*, 17.

31. deCarlo, "Ogres," 344.

32. Bassil-Morozow, *The Trickster*, 132.

33. Esther Clinton, Jane Garry, and Hasan El-Shamy, "The Trickster, Various Motifs," *Archetypes & Motifs in Folklore and Literature: A Handbook* (2005): 472–480. EBSCOhost (accessed June 4, 2014).

34. Lewis Hyde, *Trickster Makes This World: Mischief, Myth, and Art* (New York: Macmillan, 1997), 11.

35. Paul Nastu, "Kesey's *One Flew Over the Cuckoo's Nest*," *Explicator* 56, (1997): 48–50.

36. Kesey, *Cuckoo's Nest*, 19.

37. Bassil-Morozow, *The Trickster*, 56.

38. Nastu, "Kesey's *One Flew Over the Cuckoo's Nest*," 48.

39. Marsha McCreadie, "*One Flew Over the Cuckoo's Nest*: Some Reasons for One Happy Adaptation," *Literature Film Quarterly* 5, no. 2 (1977): 28.

40. Milos Forman, quoted in McCreadie, "Some Reasons," 128.

41. Ronald David Laing, *Self and Others*, vol. 2 (New York: Routledge, 2013), 3.

42. Foucault, *Power / Knowledge*, 116.

43. Kesey, quoted in Safer, "It's the Truth," 132.

CHAPTER EIGHT

"Nature Played Me a Dirty Trick": Illness vs. Tolerance in Gay-Themed Film

Eric J. Sterling

Homosexuality was designated by the American Psychiatric Association (APA) as a mental illness until December 15, 1973, when it was removed from the list of mental disorders.[1] Peter Zachar and Kenneth S. Kendler claim that "sexual practices such as masturbation and homosexuality were considered to be signs of a progressive psychic decline,"[2] but in 1970, the APA began to be pressured into removing same-sex preference from its classifications of mental illnesses. One reason for the APA's decision to remove homosexuality as a category in their *Diagnostic and Statistical Manual (DSM)* was that organizations in America were openly discriminating against gays and then justifying their prejudice by pointing to the APA's classification in the manual. Another reason is that psychiatrists discerned that gays resembled heterosexuals in their desire for committed and caring long-term relationships, undermining the stereotype that gays solely desired sexual acts with various and indiscriminate partners. Furthermore, the removal occurred because "positive personal encounters reduce negative attitudes about outgroups,"[3] reversing negative opinions deriving from a lack of contact with members of outgroups.

For instance, during the Holocaust, the Nazis criminalized intermarriage with Jews, prevented them from working jobs or going to school with "Aryans," prevented "Aryans" from shopping at Jewish businesses, and subsequently removed Jews from cities and their neighbors while placing them in ghettos. The purpose in separating them from the rest of the population was in part to prevent Jews from becoming a sympathetic outgroup, for "Aryans" could gullibly believe Nazi anti-Semitic propaganda and consequently be indifferent to their plight (and even want to persecute Jews themselves) if they never interacted with Jews. It is easier to hate, or feel prejudice toward, those members of an outgroup when one does not have any knowledge about, or encounters with, them. Watching movies about an outgroup, such as homosexuals, serves as a visual interaction (and identification) with them and can lead to understanding, sympathy, respect, and acceptance. When examining the gay films *Victim* (1961), *The Children's Hour* (1961), *Bent* (1997), and *Brokeback Mountain* (2005)—all set before 1973—viewers can discern sympathetic portrayals of homosexuals in an era in which they suffered widespread oppression; the persecution and prejudice they endure lead gay characters who are not initially mentally ill to experience mental disorders they would not have suffered had they been treated with kindness and respect rather than with cruelty and homophobic oppression. This chapter will focus on the mental illnesses that gays experience due to external prejudices and oppression as well as the film's significant impact upon creating understanding of homosexuals and sympathy toward their plight regarding the prejudice they encounter. Audience sympathy for these oppressed characters helped influence public opinion about gays in a positive way over the decades, resulting in a more tolerant society.

Self-Loathing

Although the APA correctly removed homosexuality from its *DSM*, oppression and hatred often lead gay victims to self-loathing, which occurs when the characters start to accept the homophobic prejudice that is prevalent in their society. Self-loathing is dangerous because the characters start to believe that they deserve the oppression they encounter because their sexual orientation is considered abnormal, unnatural, or deviant. For instance, in *Victim*, the first movie ever to use the word "homosexual," Henry (Charles Lloyd-Pack), who is forced to sell his successful barbershop to pay off blackmailers, laments to barrister Melville Farr (Dirk Bogarde): "Nature played me a dirty trick."[4] Henry's comment indicates that he believes that his sexual orientation is unnatural and abnormal because it conflicts with what people in his society consider natural and normal. Adding to his shame is his belief that his homosexuality derives from "nature," so he realizes that he cannot change, that his "abnormality" extends beyond his control and derives from a higher source. His low self-esteem, verging on borderline personality disorder (BPD), comes from him experiencing (undeserved) shame from his homosexual sexual desires that the majority of his fellow citizens (and British law) consider to be abhorrent and from being unable to change and conform. His inability to conform to societal sexual norms has led to his imprisonment four times because homosexual acts violate Section 11 of the British Criminal Law Amendment Act of 1885; these arrests have rendered him anxious and neurotic, and thus vulnerable to blackmailers, who use photographs of him to coerce him to sell his beloved barber shop and flee to Canada; his anxiety and neurosis lead to his fatal heart attack when Sandy the blackmailer appears at his shop and starts to destroy it.

Similarly, in *Victim*, stage actor Calloway (Dennis Price) pays a significant part of his income to the blackmailers yet defends his homosexuality by saying, "I've never corrupted a *normal*. Why should I be forced to live outside the law because I find love in the only way I can?"[5] Calloway's defense suggests that he considers homosexuality to be a mental illness and abnormal behavior, for he suggests that it is the opposite of "normal" (heterosexual) comportment. In addition, his employment of the word "corrupted" suggests that he considers homosexual intercourse to be a "corruption," a negative deviation from heterosexual sex. Thus, in *Victim*, the idea that homosexuality is unnatural and immoral has been instilled into the minds of gay characters such as Henry and Calloway, destroying their self-esteem and causing self-loathing and depression.

In *The Children's Hour*, Martha (Shirley MacLaine) starts to hate herself after she is accused of being a lesbian. When the grocery boy stares at her and giggles, she yells, "I've got eight fingers, see? And two heads. I'm a freak." Upon her discovery that she is indeed a lesbian, she laments to Karen (Audrey Hepburn) that they can never leave the house again because of the rumor that they are lesbian lovers, "We've been famous . . . . We're bad people. There's always been something wrong [with me] . . . . I can't keep it any longer."[6] Martha, like many women who feel persecuted, suffers from depression because of low self-esteem, feelings of helplessness, and pessimism.[7] Martha loathes herself because she unconsciously accepts the societal prejudice that being gay signifies that there is something wrong with her, that she is sinful. She feels ashamed of herself although she has done nothing wrong and has never touched Karen in a sexual way.

Likewise, in *Bent*, Max (Clive Owen), while on the transport train to Dachau, feels ashamed for being gay. Max hates himself for punching his gay lover Rudy (Brian Webber II) to death (on orders from Nazi guards) and for denying his sexual orientation, saving his life by assuring the guards that he is not gay. When gay prisoner Horst (Lothaire Bluteau) tries to comfort him by touching him, Max pulls away, saying, "You mustn't do that. For your own sake. You mustn't touch me. I'm a rotten person."[8] Max's self-loathing derives from his denial of his sexual orientation and his realization that his family has disowned him because he is gay. When Max tells Uncle Freddie (Ian McKellen) that he wants to reconcile with his family, his uncle replies that because he is gay, "Maybe they don't want you back."[9] Max's self-loathing leads to his incessant escape of reality through his abuse of alcohol and drugs, his self-destructive behavior, and his depression.

Trauma

In *Bent*, Max's desire to hide his sexual identity leads to a traumatic event on the train to Dachau. To please the Nazi guards and to save his life, shortly after Max is forced to punch his lover Rudy until the man dies, he must then have sexual intercourse with the corpse of a teenage Jewish girl whom the Nazis have recently murdered. If he does not have sex with her, if he cannot get an erection (if he is "bent"—an actual term the Nazis used in German), he will also be killed. He relates the humiliating experience to Horst flatly and tonelessly, as if he is almost in a catatonic state:

> Just dead, minutes . . . bullet . . . in her . . . they said . . . prove that you're . . . and I did . . . prove that you're . . . lots of them, watching . . . laughing . . . drinking . . . he's a bit bent, they said, he can't . . . but I did. . . I hit him, you know. I kissed her. I killed him. Sweet lips. Angel. . . I proved that I wasn't. . . [Silence] And they enjoyed it. . . And I said, I'm not queer.[10]

Traumatized by having to help kill his lover, he must then publicly humiliate himself in front of the guards; as a gay man, it would be hard enough for him to have an erection with a woman, but to do so with a female corpse as guards mock him is utterly debasing. The frequent ellipses in the aforementioned quotation demonstrates his shock, as if he is too humiliated to speak coherently. In fact, after the incident, he can no longer remember Rudy, even though they have been longtime lovers who live together until the Nazis raid their apartment. It seems clear that this shocking episode causes Max to suffer from post-traumatic stress disorder (PTSD).

Similarly, Ennis Del Mar (Heath Ledger) experiences a life-changing traumatic event in *Brokeback Mountain.* Del Mar tells his lover Jack Twist (Jake Gyllenhaal) that when he was nine, his father forced him to witness a murder scene involving two gay men. Ennis says, "They found Earl dead in a irrigation ditch. They'd took a tire iron to him, spurred him up, drug him around by his dick till it pulled off."[11] Del Mar is traumatized because he was so young when he saw the aftermath of the horrific murders and because of the implied threat from his father, who Ennis admits might even have been responsible for the crimes. The father forced his son to see the dead gay cowboys, even the one with the penis ripped off, to threaten his son: if Ennis ever engages in homosexual sex, this could (and should) be what happens to him. The sight renders Del Mar paranoid and fearful for the rest of his life of being identified as a gay man, making him neurotic and anxious. This traumatic event clearly hinders Del Mar from ever maintaining a sustained romantic relationship, and he continually finds excuses to refrain from spending his life with Twist.

While camping, Ennis expresses his fear that he and Jack will be murdered for being gay: "we're around each other and this thing grabs on to us again in the wrong place, wrong time, we'll be dead."[12] He constantly fears that people suspect that he is gay and even stops attending church because he considers the congregation a "fire-and-brimstone crowd"[13] that attacks him personally when they condemn homosexuality. Ennis asks Jack, "You ever get the feelin'. . . when you're in town, and someone looks at you, suspicious. . . like he knows. And then you get out on the pavement, and everyone, lookin' at you, and maybe they all know too?"[14] Jack Straw similarly becomes anxious when a suspicious rodeo clown refuses to let him buy him a drink and starts talking about him to others. Ennis asks Jack if his wife Lureen (Anne Hathaway) suspects that he is actually gay or normal (as if gay is the opposite of normal) because the men constantly doubt their own true identity and fear the consequences of being outed. The two men's paranoia and neuroses are symbolized by the two shirts, one inside the other.

Although many viewers are touched by the image of Del Mar's shirt hanging inside of Twist's, showing the inextricable emotional bond between them, Ennis finds the shirts hiding within the deep recess of Jack's closet, which is itself a "shallow cavity."[15] So Ennis' shirt hangs within Jack's inside a niche within an obscured closet in a tiny town in Wyoming. Jack even hides the shirts from his own parents. The shirts, like the men, are hiding inside a closet, and although a touching symbol, the shirts' image is disturbing, representing the terror the men feel of being identified as gay men in a homophobic culture. The shirts bond together in a way the two men can never do because of their paranoia. Are the shirts a symbol of their relationship or a substitution for it? Living one's daily life in constant fear inevitably leads to paranoia and anxiety because they cannot be themselves or live life in a manner that is normal for them, and they (Del Mar, in particular) constantly fear that they are being watched and suspected of "inappropriate behavior." Part of the depression the two men feel derives from their inability to be themselves and participate in the long-term relationship they desire.

Del Mar's paranoia is apparent at the end of the film when he learns of Twist's untimely death. Twist's wife, clearly not concerned about her husband's demise, nonchalantly explains that a tire blew out and broke Jack's nose and jaw, killing him. Del Mar thinks back to the traumatic sight he witnessed as a child and suspects, without proof, that Twist must have been cruelly murdered in a homophobic attack. He envisions "a MAN being beaten unmercifully by THREE ASSAILANTS, one of whom uses a tire iron."[16] Paranoia becomes commonplace for Ennis, inhibiting his ability to sustain a romantic relationship or live happily.

Anxiety, Depression, and Suicide

The oppression that the gay characters experience causes anxiety and depression that, in turn, sometimes leads to suicide. In *Victim*, John "Boy" Barrett (Peter McEnery) embezzles money in order to pay off blackmailers who threaten to reveal his sexual orientation to the public, which would cost him his job and friends while subjecting him to public humiliation. Because homosexuality was illegal in England in 1961, when *Victim* was filmed, and not decriminalized until 1967,[17] Barrett faces a prison sentence for being gay; rather than go to jail, he commits suicide, one of two gay characters in *Victim* who takes his own life. To the police, Barrett's major crime, the film suggests, is not that he steals money but rather that he is gay. When Barrett readily confesses that he has stolen the money, the policemen ignore his embezzlement and focus on the motive; they want to know why he stole the money (blackmailed for being gay), leading him to commit suicide in his prison cell. Barrett and Henry become anxious and depressed because they are despised simply for being themselves; if people do not want to be hated for embezzlement, they can simply refrain from stealing, but people cannot stop being who they are or experiencing normal urges.

In *Victim*, the gay characters are frequently reminded that their lives are considered worthless. For example, despite knowing that Barrett desperately seeks a place to stay, Sylvie (Dawn Beret) refuses to allow her husband Frank to let him spend the night, asking, "Why can't he stick with his own sort?"[18] She implies that gays are inherently different beings than heterosexuals, so the latter should refrain from interacting with or helping homosexuals, as if they are a different species. She speaks her insulting question loudly so that Barrett will hear—as if gays lack feelings or that their feelings do not matter. Frank lamely consoles Barrett about not letting him stay in his house, saying that gays are persecuted less now than witches were in Salem: "It used to be witches. At least they don't burn you."[19] The camera zooms in on Barrett's face several times, including after Frank's insincere comment, to manifest the terror that the oppression he encounters causes him. Deputy Inspector Harris (John Barrie) observes that approximately 90 percent of blackmail cases involved homosexuality.[20] Hugh David notes that gays were targeted so often by blackmailers that the term "blackmailer's charter" became a common term, and that between 1921 and 1963, the number of homosexuals targeted rose greatly, as high as 24 percent in some years, leading to many emotionally scarred lives.[21] Unsurprisingly, Barrett's anxiety becomes so great that he fears blackmailers over an innocuous photo: he is simply crying while barrister Melville Farr puts his arm around his shoulder—not proof of homosexuality, but the photo still terrorizes a man suffering from great anxiety. It is not surprising, then, that Barrett commits suicide. When talking to Farr about blackmail, Henry laments that "Barrett is well out of it,"[22] suggesting that as a persecuted homosexual man, Barrett is better off dead than incessantly hounded and despised. The persecution has rendered Barrett so depressed that he chooses to end his life.

An effect of incessant persecution (such as institutionalized homophobia) is anxiety and depression, which, unfortunately, sometimes lead to self-destructive behavior, even suicide. This is apparent in *The Children's Hour* when Martha commits suicide after her depression, brought upon when people accuse her of being a lesbian, seizes control of her. For eight days, she refuses to leave her house and sits despondently on her chair. She has been banned from the ladies clubs and even from stores, so in order to eat, she must have food delivered to her house. Her best friend Karen has also been accused of being gay, ruining her marriage plans, and Martha feels responsible. It is unclear from the film whether Martha is a lesbian or if the accusations render her so depressed and confused that she incorrectly accepts them as factual. She confesses to Karen, "I've got to tell you how guilty I am. . . . It's all my fault. I ruined your life, and I ruined my own . . . . I feel so sick and dirty. I can't stand it anymore."[23] For years she has lived with Karen, yet her sexual desires have gone unfulfilled. Peggy Thoits notes that "members of groups that are weakly integrated suffer from disappointment and misery because their escalating passions, unregulated by norms or relations with others, inevitably go unfulfilled. [Emile] Durkheim called this kind of suicide 'egoistic suicide,' because individuals in poorly integrated groups are more likely to succumb to despair caused by unchecked and unfulfilled personal desires."[24] Martha then hangs herself because the accusation and its ramifications render her depressed and hopeless.

Conclusion

Rather than portraying gays as abnormal beings, effeminate caricatures, or sexually-obsessed perverts, *Victim* characterizes the protagonists as sympathetic, three-dimensional, normal human beings. Producer Michael Relph called *Victim* "the first wholly adult and serious approach to homosexuality that the British cinema had made, with gays portrayed as 'human being[s] subject to all the emotions of other human beings, and as deserving of our understanding.'"[25] Such an honest and sympathetic portrayal offered hope and benefitted the mental health of gay viewers. Bogarde notes, "The countless letters of gratitude which flooded in were proof enough of that [inner peace given to homosexuals], and I had achieved what I had longed to do for so long, to be in a film which disturbed, educated, and illuminated as well as merely giving entertainment."[26] Renowned gay British filmmaker Terence Davis was moved by *Victim*: "The fact that it features a sympathetic homosexual protagonist— the first in British cinema—was no small matter, and the effect it would have had on a boy of 16 struggling with his own homosexual feelings is incalculable."[27] Gay films such as *Victim*, *Brokeback Mountain*, *Bent*, and *The Children's Hour* helped successfully to diminish the mental illness suffered by homosexuals through their humanizing and sympathetic protagonists. The aforementioned films actively undermine the social stigma and inaccurate stereotypes about homosexuals that many people inevitably encountered and naively accepted as truth. Male gay characters such as Farr, Del Mar, Twist, and Max are manly, not effeminate. Homosexual characters such as Farr, Del Mar, Twist, and Martha are virtuous and kind people, not abnormal beings or sexual predators. Most of the characters in these gay films desire long-term and emotionally satisfying relationships, not merely indiscriminate sex acts with any available partners, as the stereotypes suggested. Part of the reason why psychologists considered homosexuality to be a mental illness was the mistaken belief that, unlike heterosexuals, gays were incapable of having long-term romantic relationships and that their relationships were based primarily on the physical, not the emotional, with many partners. The realization that gays were no different than heterosexuals in desiring permanent and monogamous romantic bonds proved instrumental in the acceptance of gays.

One essential factor in the portrayal of gays in the films is perspective. Each of the films addressed in this chapter is presented almost exclusively from the perspective of homosexuals, which allows them to tell their stories and dreams, demonstrate that they are human beings with feelings like any other people, and show the audience the tremendous hurt caused by homophobia. The sympathetic, first-person portrayals in these films generated significant empathy, understanding, and respect for gays, which, in turn, created a more tolerant attitude toward them. A rare instance of a homophobic perspective actually creates more empathy for gays. In *Victim*, heartless Miss Benham (Margaret Diamond), an ugly spinster and blackmailer, speaks of gays with great prejudice and paranoia: "They disgust me. . . . They're everywhere—everywhere you turn. . . . Somebody has to pay for their filthy blasphemy." Alan Burton and Tim O'Sullivan note that Benham is "bitter and vicious, with an almost psychotic hatred of homosexuals."[28] Thus, heterosexual viewers feel more tolerance for gays when they witness the mean-spirited, homophobic diatribe by the unsympathetic Benham, whose hysteria suggests that some homophobic people are actually latent homosexuals and suffer from their own mental disorders. Undoubtedly, Relph undermines Benham's bigotry, employing her homophobia to present gays as victims who should be treated empathetically. Toleration and understanding led to kinder treatment of gays, which, in turn, led to diminished mental illness in gays because they felt more accepted and thus less anxious and depressed.

Notes

1. Paula Caplan complicates this statement by noting that "ego syntonic homosexuality" (self-acceptance) was removed from the manual but that "ego dystonic homosexuality" (anxiety over one's homosexuality) remained for years, which is problematic when gays live "in a culture that scorns and demeans lesbian and gay men." Paula Caplan, *They Say You're Crazy: How the World's Most Powerful Psychiatrists Decide Who's Normal* (Reading, MA: Addison-Wesley, 1995), 180–181.

2. Peter Zachar and Kenneth S. Kendler, "The Removal of Pluto from the Class of Planets and Homosexuality from the Class of Psychiatric Disorders: A Comparison," *Philosophy, Ethics, and Humanities in Medicine* 7, no. 4 (2012).

3. Ibid., 7:3.

4. Janet Green and John McCormick, *Victim*, film, dir. Basil Dearden, 1961, Allied Film Makers, United Kingdom.

5. Ibid., my italics.

6. John Michael Hayes, *The Children's Hour*, film, dir. William Wyler (United Artists, 1961).

7. Robert G. Meyer, *The Clinician's Handbook: The Psychopathology of Adulthood and Adolescence*, 2nd ed. (Boston: Allyn and Bacon, 1989), 118.

8. Martin Sherman, *Bent*, film, dir. Sean Mathias (1997, MGM), DVD.

9. Ibid.

10. Ibid.

11. Larry McMurtry and Diana Ossana, "*Brokeback Mountain*, the Screenplay," in *Brokeback Mountain: Story to Screenplay* (New York: Scribner, 2005), 53.

12. Ibid., 52.

13. Ibid., 60.

14. Ibid., 71, first ellipsis mine.

15. Ibid., 91.

16. Ibid., 87.

17. *Victim* was made primarily to overturn the antigay law.

18. *Victim*.

19. Ibid.

20. Ibid.

21. Hugh David, *On Queer Street: A Social History of British Homosexuality, 1895–1995* (London: HarperCollins, 1997), 17, 153–154.

22. *Victim*.

23. *The Children's Hour*.

24. Peggy Thoits, "Sociological Approaches to Mental Illness," in *A Handbook for the Study of Mental Health: Social Contexts, Theories, and Systems*, eds. Allan V. Horwitz and Teresa L. Scheid (Cambridge: Cambridge University Press, 1999), 131.

25. John Coldstream, *Dirk Bogarde: The Authorised Biography* (London: Weidenfeld & Nicolson, 2004).

26. Christopher Pullen, *Gay Identity, New Storytelling and the New Media* (Basingstoke: Palgrave Macmillan, 2008), 87.

27. Michael Koresky, "Queerness and Melancholia: An Excerpt from Terence Davies," September 4, 2014, http://www.brooklynrail.org/2014/09/film/queerness-and-melancholia-an-excerpt-from-terence-davies, accessed April 23, 2016.

28. Alan Burton and Tim O'Sullivan, *The Cinema of Basil Dearden and Michael Relph* (Edinburgh: Edinburgh University Press, 2009), 237.

PART II

Television: The Small Screen

CHAPTER NINE

Women's Agency as Madness: "The Yellow Wallpaper" to Penny Dreadful

Laura E. Colmenero-Chilberg

Madness . . . the word brings a cascade of popular cultural images to mind. Some may think of Norse berserkers running headlong into battle; others of Shakespeare's Ophelia broken by "love madness" from the cruelty of her beloved Hamlet,

> When down her weedy trophies and herself
> Fell in the weeping brook. Her clothes spread wide;
> And, mermaid-like, awhile they bore her up:
> Which time she chanted snatches of old tunes;
> As one incapable of her own distress,
> Or like a creature native and indued
> Unto that element: but long it could not be
> Till that her garments, heavy with their drink,
> Pull'd the poor wretch from her melodious lay
> To muddy death.

Perhaps the image that comes to mind is of the abandoned forever-bride Miss Havisham from Charles Dickens's *Great Expectations*. Or maybe if you're a traditionalist, it is the ancient Greek maenads madly worshipping Dionysus, the "raving ones" dancing in a frenzy intoxicated by wine and their revels. Or if the images that pop into mind are more recent, maybe you think of *The Hobbit*'s Gollum, driven mad by his obsession with "his precious" or the insane fan in Stephen King's *Misery*. The possibilities seem endless. While we see images of both male and female madness throughout history, one thing is very clear—much of the discourse about madness has revolved around the condemnation of and an attempt to control women.

What do we mean when we say "madness"? Andrew Scull's definition in *Madness in Civilization* is "massive and lasting disturbances of reason, intellect and emotions" resulting in "sadness, isolation, alienation, misery and the death of reason and of consciousness."[1] When in the company of madness, the "sane" feel a frisson of horror seeing the images, hearing the sounds, witnessing the irrationality, all calling up a primal fear and with it the stigmatizing label of madness. What then is the difference between madness and mental illness? The medicalization of madness began during the 19th century when it became the purview of males in the medical profession and soon became mental illness. Today, mental illness is a social construct largely defined by the *DSM-5*, a quite controversial diagnostic tool. This essay, however, will focus on the original definition of madness.

The history of women and madness, in particular what became known as hysteria, will be our focus. Throughout western history we have seen this deviance "named" in a variety of ways when applied to women stigmatizing those who are uppity, who are sinful, and who are mad. The focus of this study is two historical works of literature that defined female agency as madness, Charlotte Bronte's *Jane Eyre* and Charlotte Perkins Gilman's "The Yellow Wallpaper" compared to several examples of modern and contemporary popular culture including Tennessee Williams's *A Streetcar Named Desire*, Quentin Tarantino's movie *Kill Bill*, and the television series *Penny Dreadful*. While we might expect that in the past women might have been controlled by the threat of the label "insane," we'll see that today this same kind of women's agency is also often seen as "crazy," continuing a long-standing tradition of controlling women by defining them as insane.

History of Madness and Women[2]

The earliest image of madness in women can be found from around 1900 BCE in Ancient Egypt. The condition is thought to have been hysteria, a term based on the Latin word for uterus, a mental disorder that is automatically identified as a "female malady." The explanation for why women suffer from this mental disorder remains constant throughout much of history: the spontaneous movement of the uterus in women's bodies. Symptoms included seizures, a sense of suffocation, and fear of impending death. Treatment was logical within the context of the time period; the uterus had to be driven back to its proper location. Foul-smelling and pungent odors were placed near a woman's mouth and nose and sweet-smelling ones next to the vagina thus driving and drawing the uterus back to where it belonged. It is also interesting to note that another term for madness, "lunacy," also has ties to women. *Luna* is Latin for the moon, and lunacy is madness often thought to have been brought on by the moon. Clear links can be drawn between women's "lunacy" and their menstrual cycles, motherhood, and sexuality.

The ancient Greeks also saw the uterus as the offending part of the body and its irregular movement as the cause of women's madness. The reason for the movement, however, differed somewhat from the Egyptian explanation. The organ suffered from melancholy brought on by a lack of carnal satisfaction. Unmarried, sterile, and widowed women were encouraged to engage in sexual activity to stop movement of the uterus, but if it did occur, the cure was the same odor treatment as used by the ancient Egyptians. When we look at another ancient culture, Rome, we find that the physician Galen suggested similar remedies including purges, herbs with strong odors, getting married, and limiting those activities that could excite women.

Greek and Roman explanations and treatments retained authority even after the fall of Rome. Like Hippocrates, Trotula de Ruggiero, the first woman physician in Christian Europe, identified abstinence as the root cause of hysteria and melancholy in women. Abbess Hildegard von Bingen, another woman physician, used a religious explanation; these mental disorders were incurable and the result of original sin, for which she held men and women equally responsible. St. Thomas Aquinas, however, took the more popular path of misogyny identifying women as defective and inferior and totally responsible for original sin, and also, therefore, their madness. It is at this time in history that women with these disorders began to be the target of supernatural explanations for their mental ailments with exorcism identified as the appropriate cure. In the early Middle Ages, exorcism was not considered a punishment for women's sin but instead was a cure for the illness caused by the sin. By the late Middle Ages, with the publication of Heinrich Kramer and Jacob Sprenger's *Malleus Maleficarum*, a witch hunter's manual, attitudes change;

it's all about punishment for women's demonic possession, not treatment of the mental disorders.

Throughout the Renaissance and into the modern age, the focus of explaining mental disorders in women was still on the uterus. For example, Victorian women carried smelling salts in case of fainting, which probably had more to do with tight corsets than wandering uteruses. The strong and malodorous smell of the salts was believed to return the womb to the proper location in the body, after which the woman would awaken. It was not the salts that brought a woman back to her senses; they returned the uterus to its proper location and the woman's body to equilibrium. In late 19th-century America, beliefs about what caused madness in women included grief, use of abusive language, suppressed menstruation, sexual promiscuity, epilepsy, overexertion, disagreement with the dominant religious beliefs, and failure to accept male authority, all of which could result in imprisonment in an asylum.[3] These ideas about women and the causes of their insanity would not change until the 20th century.

Today, we still focus primarily on women. According to "Behavioral Health Trends in the United States: Results from the 2014 National Survey on Drug Use and Health" sponsored by the U.S. Department of Health and Human Services,[4] women are more likely to suffer from a serious mental illness than men except in the case of schizophrenia, autism spectrum disorder, and ADHD. Madness remains woman-identified.

Women's Madness, Traditional Gendered Roles, and the Mass Media

Beliefs about correct gender behavior are threads running through every part of society, and training in doing gender right begins at birth and runs throughout the life course.

Traditionally, women are identified as dependent, men as independent; women as caregivers, men as breadwinners; women as passive, men as aggressors; women as incompetent, men as powerful, often over women. Women are required to provide self-denying generosity, to limit their physical location primarily to their homes, and not to engage in adventurous or sexual behaviors. Women are required to look pleasing as well as to be chaste, emotional, nice, and flexible. On the other hand, men are encouraged to compete, to be adventurous, courageous, and sexually active. They are to limit all emotions except for aggression and anger, and be rational, logical, and independent. Madness, which can be seen as rampant emotionality, is the very antithesis of logic and rationality and, therefore, seen as a feminine characteristic.

Images in the media, both past and present, still often represent traditional gender roles, but what about images related specifically to women and madness? Do these, too, identify a narrow role for women, a role that is both confining and limiting?

Jane Eyre and "The Yellow Wallpaper"

Let's look at two historical works of fiction that deal with women and madness—*Jane Eyre* and "The Yellow Wallpaper."

Charlotte Bronte's *Jane Eyre* provides us with the character of Bertha Mason, Rochester's mad wife. Confined and hidden in the attic (the original madwoman in the attic[5]), Bronte describes Bertha as both hideous and violent.

> In the deep shade, at the further end of the room, a figure ran backwards and forwards. What it was, whether beast or human being, one could not, at first sight, tell: it groveled, seemingly on all fours; it snatched and growled like some strange wild animal; but it was covered with clothing; and a quantity of dark, grizzled hair, wild as a mane, hid its head and face.[6]

Bertha's madness is inherited from her mother ("a madwoman and a drunkard"), and like her mother, after marriage Bertha becomes "intemperate and unchaste." She fails to meet many of the traditionally required characteristics of a woman of the Victorian time period; most particularly, she breaks the sexual behavior rule. Described as a "monster of sexual appetite," Bronte ties Bertha's madness to her female sexuality, reporting that during blood-red moons she becomes most vicious and destructive, hallucinating a familiar who tells her "to burn people in their beds at night, to stab them, to bite their flesh from their bones."[7]

At first glance Bertha appears to be the insane foil to Jane's sane grounded pragmatism. But is she, or is Bertha really the cautionary example to rein in Janes' passionate and independent nature? Worried about the possibility of descending into love madness, Jane says,

> [I]t is madness in all women to let a secret love kindle within them, which, if unreturned and unknown, must devour the life that feeds it; and if discovered and responded to, must lead, [will-o'-the-wisp]-like into miry wilds whence there is no extrication.[8]

And when pressured by Rochester to become his mistress, Jane attempts to stave off her own madness.

I will keep the law given by God; sanctioned by man. I will hold to the principles received by men when I was sane, and not mad—as I am now, it is because I am insane—quite insane: with my veins running fire, and my heart beating faster than I can count its throbs.[9]

It is not only a fear of madness that concerns Jane, but also a fear of the loss of her sense of self.[10] She comes to realize that her relationship with Rochester will never be one of equal partners, an idea clearly but subtly communicated by his gently couched threat:

[I]t is your time now, little tyrant, but it will be mine presently: and once I have fairly seized you, to have and to hold, I'll just—figuratively speaking—attach you to a chain, like this (touching his watch guard).[11]

While Bronte never discusses wandering uteruses, the failure of Bertha to conform to society's expectations resulted in her incarceration in her own private asylum. The message is clear: if Jane does not control her own passions and toe the gender line, Rochester may have to lock her up too.

Charlotte Perkins Gilman's "The Yellow Wallpaper"[12] continues the same themes seen in *Jane Eyre*. A woman's perceived madness is seen as both a symptom of and a cause of a woman's descent into madness. The story centers on another Jane, a woman who has been confined by her husband John, usually in their upstairs bedroom (another madwoman in the attic). The room has been papered in a horrible shade of yellow. "The color is repellant, almost revolting; a smouldering unclean yellow." The confinement is a Victorian "neurasthenic rest-cure" and is prescribed by John, a doctor, because he believes she is suffering from "but temporary nervous depression—a slight hysterical tendency." The neurasthenic rest cure was developed by a well-respected physician, S. Weir Mitchell, during the 19th century. Treatment included enforced bed rest, isolation, force-feeding, and massage. Perkins Gilman's description of this cure in "The Yellow Wallpaper" rings particularly true because she had actually been a patient of Weir's after suffering what today would be called acute postpartum depression after the birth of her daughter. In her autobiography, *The Living of Charlotte Perkins Gilman*, she reports Weir's prescription: "Live as domestic a life as possible. Have your child with you all the time. . . . Lie down an hour after each meal. Have but two hours' intellectual life a day. And never touch pen, brush, or pencil as long as you live."[13]

It is clear that John places the blame for the condition directly on Jane, whom he sees behaving in a way that perpetuates "a false and foolish fancy."[14] Whatever the reason, she is expected to spend most of her time resting in the ugly yellow bedroom, overseen/spied on by her husband and servant, and ordered to rest and spend her life passively, isolated, and with no mental activity. With nothing to occupy her, her focus and then her obsession becomes the horrible yellow wallpaper.

Jane's first hallucination is eyes—bulbous and unblinking—all over the yellow walls, constantly watching her. This may be an indirect reference to a new form of prison developed during the Victorian period, the panopticon, a prison where inmates are always within the sight of guards, paralleling Jane's feeling that she is being watched. Although originally a nursery, the room has other prison-like characteristics including bars on the windows and rings mounted on the wall, bringing to mind shackled prisoners.

Jane's delusion soon changes. In addition to the eyes, she begins to see a figure moving beneath the wallpaper. "[I]t is like a woman stooping down and creeping about behind that pattern."[15] Eventually Jane begins to tear the wallpaper off the walls, trying to get to the figure imprisoned behind it, but by the time it is all removed, Jane herself has begun creeping about the walls telling John, "I've got out at last . . . in spite of you and Jane. And I've pulled off most of the paper, so you can't put me back!"[16] Jane is no longer Jane but has become the woman trapped behind the wallpaper.

Perkins Gilman's short story gives us both a view of how women were controlled by the male application of the label "mad" and how the imposition of that stigmatizing label may intensify the harmful effects of the mental disorder.

A Streetcar Named Desire, *Kill Bill*, and *Penny Dreadful*

Switch time periods to the mid-20th century through present day and we find a very different collection of popular culture choices.

A mid-20th century investigation of the madness of women can be seen in Tennessee Williams's *A Streetcar Named Desire*. Williams identified the main theme in all his fiction as "the destructive impact of society on the sensitive, non-conformist individual."[17] Blanche DuBois aptly illustrates this kind of person. Beautiful, delicate, sexually promiscuous, dependent "on the kindness of strangers," and somewhat eccentric in attitude, speech, and dress, Blanche loses her job and her family home and turns to her sister and brother-in-law, Stella and Stanley Kowalski, for support. Raised with her sister in shabby refinement, Blanche is unable to accept the lifestyle of the Kowalskis, seeing it as vulgar and brutal. Initially merely unwelcomed by her brother-in-law, tensions continue to rise, culminating in Blanche's rape by Stanley. Stella chooses to believe Stanley over her sister about the rape and tells her friend, "I couldn't believe her story and go on living with Stanley."[18] It is Stella that calls the asylum to institutionalize her sister.

Blanche's emotional and eccentric nature coupled with her sexual promiscuity breaks the gender rules, and her punishment is to be publicly indicted, imprisoned, and labeled crazy. Just as in *Jane Eyre* and "The Yellow Wallpaper," it is the male that controls a woman's life and dispenses punishment for what he deems unwomanly and deviant behavior through rape and the label "crazy."

Kill Bill 1 and 2, on the other hand, provide us with the character of The Bride, an atypical woman who on the surface fails to fit the traditional characteristics of a woman. A martial-arts-trained assassin and part of the Deadly Viper Assassination Squad (DiVAS), The Bride becomes tired of that life, falls in love, becomes pregnant, and is at the church about to be married when the DiVAS arrives, led by Bill—her past boss, lover, and father of her unborn child. The squad kills everyone and Bill shoots The Bride in the head. She falls into a coma and awakens four years later with a steel plate in her head and no child, catapulting her on a campaign of revenge against the DiVAS. She plans to kill them all, saving Bill for last so he can suffer the anticipation of his impending death. She is successful in her revenge but discovers that her daughter lived and was raised by Bill. The Bride kills Bill, and she and her daughter go off together, mother and child reunited.[19]

The character of The Bride at first does not seem to conform to the traditional woman's role script—she is aggressive, courageous, and adventurous and uses logic to guide her actions—all traditionally male characteristics. But it is clearly emotion and the denial of motherhood that guides her path of revenge. Her grief at the assumed death of her child pushes her over the line from sanity to insanity. Where her past assassinations were business, the death of the DiVAS is personal, maternal, and ruthlessly violent. There are no accusations of insanity directed at The Bride, but the impetus for her actions is clearly outside of the norm and as a result of behaviors that have typically resulted in a label of insanity.

The last example of contemporary mass media is Showtime's series *Penny Dreadful*,[20] a unique mash-up of Victorian horror characters which include Dorian Gray from Oscar Wilde's *The Picture of Dorian Gray*; Victor Frankenstein, the Monster, and an updated Bride of Frankenstein from Mary Shelley's *Frankenstein*; Van Helsing, Renfield, and Count Dracula from Bram Stoker's *Dracula*; and Dr. Henry Jekyll from Robert Louis Stevenson's *Strange*

Case of Dr. Jekyll and Mr. Hyde. Add to this set of literary characters Sir Malcolm Murray, an African explorer; Ethan Chandler, an American werewolf gunslinger; and Vanessa Ives, a sometimes demon-possessed witch.

The character of Vanessa Ives certainly falls into the category of mad hysteric. She is over-the-top emotional, sexually promiscuous, a practitioner of witchcraft, and a target of the devil. The season 3 opener finds her dirty, unkempt, and eating like an animal, somewhat reminiscent of Bertha in *Jane Eyre*. Her bouts of deep depression and catatonia fit well within the criteria of madness established for the time period. But it is not only Vanessa who suffers from deep pits of depression from which it is a struggle to escape. In fact, most of the male characters, too, have these same troubles, and almost all have their origins in family issues, usually seen as the concern of female characters.

Victor Frankenstein, an opium addict, allows his fascination with science to lead him to take on the role of God and create life—the original male Monster, a second male creature, and a female Bride. Victor is horrified by the first creature, both because of his shocking physical deformity and the anger he directs at his maker. In turn the original Monster despises Victor. In revenge the Monster kills the second male, with whom Victor had bonded. Trying to placate the creature, Victor creates a Bride for him, but she rejects both Victor, the father figure who incestuously lusts after her, and the Monster. Suffering from grief and betrayal by the "family" he has created, Victor enters a lingering drug-fueled depression.

Sir Malcolm lets his obsession with Africa stand in the way of being a "good father." He loses his son because the young man is unable to achieve his father's high standards, dying in the attempt; he loses his daughter to vampirism, and his wife is killed by his mistress. His disastrous family relationships send him over the edge into alcohol abuse and depression.

It is family, too, that haunts Ethan Chandler, as well as his uncontrollable and violent werewolf alter ego. At the end of season 2, Chandler's father kidnaps his son and has him transported in chains back to the American Southwest. Guilt at the murders he unknowingly commits when in his werewolf form and his clearly coming from a severely dysfunctional family contribute to Chandler's own isolation and depression and the denial of his love and abandonment of Vanessa.

Hysterical behavior in *Penny Dreadful* does not limit itself to a single gender but paints both sexes with its brush. Throughout history, we have seen women controlled by men who determine when their behavior is "rational" and when it is "mad."

Popular culture throughout history has reflected this image of women, and we still see elements of that today. However, we are also seeing the redefinition of gender roles in some of these fictional works to include male characters who clearly have adopted some characteristics of women's madness.

Notes

1. Andrew Scull, *Madness in Civilization* (Princeton, NJ: Princeton University Press, 2015), 11.

2. Cecilia Tasca et al., "Women and Hysteria in the History of Mental Illness," *Clinical Practice & Epidemiology in Mental Health*, 8 (2012): 110–119.

3. Katherine Pouba and Ashley Tianen, "Lunacy in the 19th Century: Women's Admission to Asylums in United States of America," *Oshkosh Scholar*, 1 (2006): 95.

4. Sarra L. Hedden et al., "Behavioral Trends in the U.S.: Results from the 2014 National Survey on Drug Use and Health," *National Survey on Drug Use and Health* (Washington, DC: Department of Health and Human Services, 2014), 28.

5. Sandra M. Gilbert and Susan Gubar, *The Madwoman in the Attic: The Woman Writer and the 19th Century Literary Imagination*, 2nd ed. (New Haven, CT: Yale Nota Bene, 2000).

6. Charlotte Bronte, *Jane Eyre* (London: Oxford University Press, 1969), 370.

7. Elaine Showalter, *The Female Malady: Women, Madness, and English Culture, 1830–1980* (New York: Penguin Books, 1985), 67.

8. Bronte, 201.

9. Bronte, 404–405.

10. Barbara Hill Rigney, *Madness and Sexual Politics in the Feminist Novel* (Madison, WI: University of Wisconsin Press, 1978), 33–34.

11. Bronte, 341.

12. Bronte, 201.

13. Anne Stiles, "The Rest Cure, 1875–1924," BRANCH: Britain, Representation and 19th-Century History, ed. Dino Franco Felluga, Extension of Romanticism and Victorianism on the Net, accessed May 4, 2016, http://www.branchcollective .org/?ps_articles=anne-stiles-the-rest-cure-1873–1925.

14. Charlotte Perkins Gilman, "The Yellow Wallpaper." *The Norton Anthology of Literature by Women*, eds. Sandra M. Gilbert and Susan Gubar (New York: W.W. Norton and Company, 1985), 1156.

15. Perkins Gilman, 1155.

16. Perkins Gilman, 1161.

17. Jacqueline O'Connor, *Dramatizing Dementia: Madness in the Plays of Tennessee Williams* (Bowling Green, OH: Bowling Green State University Popular Press, 1997), 5.

18. Tennessee Williams, *A Streetcar Named Desire* (New York: Signet, 1951), 133.

19. Quentin Tarantino, *Kill Bill*, 2003.

20. John Logan, *Penny Dreadful*, Showtime.

CHAPTER TEN

Orange Is the New Color for Mental Illness

Mary L. Colavita, Kate Lieb, Alexis Briggie, Sonal Harneja, and Howard L. Forman

Sometimes the feelings inside me get messy like dirt. . . and I like to clean things, pretend the dirt is the feelings. This floor is my mind. That is coping. And the COs don't care because they like things clean. And that is called symbiosis.

—Suzanne Warren, *Orange Is the New Black*

It could be said that two of America's favorite activities are incarcerating people and making television shows about incarcerating people. Whether documentary (*Making a Murderer* on Netflix), reality TV (*60 Days In* on A&E), or drama (*The Night Of* on HBO), America can simply not get enough entertainment based around this topic. It should be no wonder that a population that incarcerates approximately one out of every 100 adult citizens would have an interest in this topic.[1]

Incarceration rates in the United States have more than sextupled in the last 40 years, from just below 200,000 in 1970 to just over 1.5 million in 2014.[2] For growth of such magnitude, it is unlikely that a single explanation will be sufficient. Certainly the rising crime rate from the 1960s through the 1970s, including a doubling of the homicide rate, did much to stir the sense that stemming the tide demanded greater deterrence through punishment.[3] Some theorists pin the rise in incarceration on the political leaders elected during this era, with the Nixon administration focusing on increasing sentencing lengths, the Reagan administration starting the "War on Drugs," and the "Three Strikes" policy of the Clinton administration leading to life imprisonment of many repeat offenders.[4]

Unrelated to increases in crime and political responses to it, those in the public health sector have a different explanation of increased incarceration rates, one that gained its momentum from the civil rights movement and was spurred on by humanitarian impulses. This movement, called deinstitutionalization, was the sum of all actions taken to remove people from state hospitals and integrate them into the greater community. In 1954, there was the first report of chlorpromazine successfully treating psychosis in the United States.[5] Within a few years, psychiatrists working with the most severely mentally ill patients—patients who would have been confined to state hospitals for the remainder of their lives and exposed to treatments of certain discomfort without clear benefit—came to regard this drug as a "miracle drug."[6]

The advent of the antipsychotic era (the class of which chlorpromazine would be known once additional similar drugs were developed) allowed for the possibility that masses of people could rejoin society at large. The civil rights movement encouraged people to question state-imposed limitations of personal autonomy, as occurred in the Jim Crow South. State psychiatric hospitals filled with involuntarily committed patients were similarly viewed as "cruel and inhumane."[7] Such institutions deprived citizens of their rights to freedom. Under the guise of promoting integration of state psychiatric patients into the communities they came from, the federal government took many financial steps to ensure the closure of state hospitals. Federal benefits programs including Supplemental Security Income (SSI), Social Security Disability Insurance (SSDI), Medicaid (insurance funded through state and federal funding) and Medicare (federally funded health insurance) were all created during the 1960s. When created, patients hospitalized in state mental hospitals were specifically excluded from receiving these benefits, leaving states to shoulder the financial burden for housing and treating these patients.[8] Since many patients would become immediately eligible for these programs following discharge, there was not a tremendous financial carrot for states to discharge patients from their wards regardless of whether infrastructure was in place yet to treat them effectively.

Deinstitutionalization did not lead to the dreamed-of vision of severely and persistently mentally ill patients living in the community and receiving outpatient psychiatric treatment suitable to their needs. In fact, today there are only 35,000 state hospital beds for the mentally ill, yet there are 10 times more severely mentally ill persons housed in prisons and jails.[9] This is almost the exact inverse of the state of affairs in 1969, when there were over 350,000 state hospital beds and fewer than 30,000 severely mentally ill inmates.[10] This has led many to term "deinstitutionalization" as "transinstitutionalization."[11]

Jenji Kohan's Netflix series *Orange Is the New Black* is one of many television series that has familiarized mainstream audiences with the trajectory of mental illness within the legal system. Based on the 2010 memoir of Piper Kerman, the series revolves around Kerman's actual experiences at the minimum-security Federal Correctional Institution in Danbury, Connecticut (more widely known as the facility that has housed various television, music, and business personalities). The TV show follows the main character, renamed "Piper Chapman," who is sentenced to 15 months in the fictional federal prison of Litchfield Penitentiary for her involvement in a drug smuggling operation ten years prior. The show focuses on Piper's experiences with the other inmates in real time, while interweaving flashbacks to build the backstories of these supporting characters.

Following its premier on July 11, 2013, the series began to receive critical acclaim for humanizing and illuminating the diversity of the prisoners and their experiences. In addition to addressing issues of sexuality, gender, race, ethnicity, age, and family, the series also reflects on the above legal and social trends that impact some of our more psychiatrically complicated criminal offenders. The effects of transinstitutionalization are displayed quite vividly. We see the plight of the mentally ill inmates of Litchfield and witness possible missed opportunities for care both prior to and during incarceration. *Orange* portrays issues that often arise from incarcerating severely mentally ill patients, who tend to be more vulnerable to victimization by other inmates within the prison system.

The show appropriately speaks to the prevalence of mental illness among female offenders and the social relevance of this trend. Although men are incarcerated at much higher rates than women, mental illness is present in a higher percentage of female inmates. As a reflection of these trends, the absolute number of female mentally ill inmates is higher than prison population statistics alone would predict. Many would be surprised to learn that 14.5 percent of male jail inmates have severe mental illness, yet that percentage pales in comparison to the 31 percent of female inmates who suffer from severe mental illness[12] Moreover, incarceration of women, regardless of race, is rising at a more rapid rate than men's incarceration, according to former New York state commissioner of corrections, Phyllis Harrison-Ross, MD. Before her death in January 2017,

Ross was a psychiatrist, pediatrician, and medical school professor emeritus.[13] Perhaps the general public intuits this trend without necessarily accessing specific statistics, and this recognition partially explains the popularity of this production at this given time.

Suzanne Warren, most commonly referred to as "Crazy Eyes" in *Orange Is the New Black*, is a 32-year-old black female incarcerated at Litchfield Penitentiary. She is the prototype of the mentally ill incarcerated woman with a violent past who will urinate on your floor if you reject her. She smacks her head feverishly when in distress, has been "removed from the puppy program," breaks into Shakespearian soliloquies when the opportunity arises, and she "will cut you, bitch." Suzanne herself comments that she has had repeated visits to the psychiatric ward for her diagnosis of intermittent explosive disorder: "When I get angry, sometimes I can't control myself. . . . They give me medication to make me calm, but that just makes me sleepy. Sometimes they tie me down like a balloon, so I don't fly away. Once you go to psych, you're lost to psych." It is for this role that actress Uzoamaka Aduba received Primetime Emmy wins for Outstanding Guest Actress in a Comedy Series in 2014 and Outstanding Supporting Actress in a Drama Series in 2015, and the Screen Actors Guild Award for Outstanding Performance by a Female Actor in a Comedy Series for two years in a row.

Making a psychiatric diagnosis in a real human being can be quite difficult; formulating a diagnosis in a fictional character, although possible, is increasingly complicated due to the obvious limitations of not being able to explore various aspects of the character's history in adequate detail and not being afforded the opportunity to experience in vivo transference, which has significant diagnostic and therapeutic utility. Through the juxtaposition of Suzanne's flashbacks with her present journey, it becomes quite obvious that her fragile sense of self has been compounded by repeated experiences of loss, familial shifts, and complex racial/social identifications. As a young black child adopted by white parents who eventually have their own biological daughter, Suzanne repeatedly experiences alienation from the community of which she desperately struggles to be a part.

Suzanne displays many features of mental illness, and although she is widely known as "Crazy Eyes," we prefer to call her by her name so as not to perpetuate the stigma that has been imposed upon her throughout much of her life. To parallel Suzanne's emphatic response to one of her fellow inmates, "No! I am not crazy. I am unique!" In the following chapter, Suzanne's rich history will be explored to identify the various cognitive, personality, and affective components that she displays and the coping skills that she has developed as a means through which she strives to reconcile and protect her complicated sense of self.

Although it is difficult to confirm Suzanne's cognitive functioning due to limited information regarding her developmental milestones and academic accomplishments, it may be assumed that Suzanne exhibits traits of neurodevelopmental disability based on her repeated deficits in communication and interaction with her fellow inmates. In other words, were she not incarcerated, she would likely have qualified for special services through commissions for the developmentally disabled and the cognitively impaired (previously known as "mental retardation") as well as from her local office of mental health or its equivalent, which specifically serves persons with general mental illness.

She either comes on too strong and scares others away, or she leaves herself so vulnerable that she becomes an easy target for manipulation. This is displayed quite vividly in the first season, when Suzanne develops a rapid and unreciprocated attachment for Piper, the newest inmate at Litchfield. She nicknames her "Dandelion," writes poetry for her, threatens other inmates in Piper's defense, and places a request, unbeknownst to Piper, that they share a room. She is unable to perceive Piper's lack of interest, as she continues to refer to her as her wife and as she sings about their partnership as a "chocolate and vanilla swirl." These deficits in communication further resonate throughout the course of the second season, as Suzanne falls under the influence of a new inmate, Vee, who acts as a motherly figure in order to manipulate and exploit Suzanne's vulnerabilities. She uses Suzanne as a pawn in her drug operation, has her commit dangerous acts with little reward, and then has her assume responsibility for a very violent crime against another inmate that she did not commit. As explained in *DSM-5*, "gullibility" and poor awareness of risk are often features of intellectual disability, as these patients can be easily led, victimized, and exploited by others resulting in unintentional criminal involvement and false confessions.

Also consistent with neurodevelopmental disorder, Suzanne displays repetitive behaviors in response to difficult self-management of emotions, as illustrated by frequent episodes of hitting herself repeatedly on the head while saying "no no no no no." She seems to be hyperreactive to sensory input, often demonstrating irritability and self-harming behavior when overstimulated. Her insistence on sameness and her struggle to achieve personal independence is quite literally displayed by her maintenance of the same hairstyle for approximately a quarter of a century. In real life and in psychiatric circles, we witness similar repetitive behaviors in persons diagnosed with autism spectrum disorder, which falls under the rubric of "developmental disability."

We are given insight into the pervasiveness of Suzanne's developmental difficulties, via flashback, when 10-year-old Suzanne is pushed by her mother to socialize with her sister, Grace, and Grace's friends, who are four to five years younger: "We just feel it's important for Suzanne to have the same social development as Grace. . . . You know which kids suffer in this world, Melanie? The ones who are told they're different." As spectators, we wonder about the inadvertent stress imposed on Suzanne by denying Suzanne's differences from her sibs (who are white while she is black). Even viewers who have no professional background in either psychology or sociology ask themselves if this homogenization further deprived Suzanne of an individual identity, and further strained this intellectually challenged child's ability to understand herself.

When at the party, Suzanne struggles to read the room, and takes her turn to complete a princess-themed story telling game with a very macabre ending: "But then, a dragon came, swooping in, breathing fire out of its dragon nostrils—some of the family runs outside, but the little girl gets trapped inside, screams for help, sits and cries by herself and gets burned up by the fire and dies alone." This scene illuminates both the vast age difference between Suzanne and her six-year-old peers and her difficulty adapting to their social needs. Further, the character in the story parallels Suzanne and the loneliness that she herself experiences as a little girl who is constantly reminded that she is different, as she desperately struggles to be like those around her. Suzanne echoes, "I'm not weird, I'm just like everyone else."

Suzanne's desperation for love and validation comes with such vulnerability to repeated victimization that her suspected neurocognitive diagnosis is likely complicated by the oftentimes comorbid pathology of disinhibited social engagement disorder. This diagnosis is characterized by indiscriminate social behaviors that result in complicated peer relationships in response to a pattern of insufficient care. Like many mentally ill women who are incarcerated, it seems that Suzanne has a history of suspected trauma and poor attachments. We never learn about Suzanne's biological parents, but it is possible that they were abusive or neglectful of Suzanne. Perhaps she was malnourished or exposed to harmful drugs.

Although her adoptive parents appear quite loving and supportive, it seems that they don't understand Suzanne's needs and limitations. In the flashback wherein a 4–5-year-old fairy-winged Suzanne comes to visit her newborn sister Grace for the first time, she notes that Grace looks much more like her mother and father, as she is their biological child. She rapidly attaches to Grace, commenting, "Hello Grace, I'm your best friend and your big sister, Suzanne. Just me and you, you and me, you and I."

She then has a tantrum when her parents try to lift the baby up from her arms, but is quickly appeased by a maternal black nurse who seems to be more attuned to Suzanne's physical and emotional needs. The baby nurse relates to Suzanne calmly and provides her with a hairstyle that is maintained for decades. This hairstyle remains unchanged until restyled by Vee, one of Suzanne's more sinister maternal figures in prison. It isn't until the third season, when Suzanne develops an attachment to a more supportive maternal figure with Tasha "Taystee" Jefferson, that we eventually see our character able to gain some autonomy, style her own hair, and engage in her first reciprocal romantic relationship in a carefully paced manner.

Suzanne's resoundingly fragmented and unstable sense of self in the context of repeated trauma contributes to her behavioral pattern most consistent with borderline personality disorder (BPD). As mentioned earlier, Suzanne has a history of unstable interpersonal relationships that result in frantic and potentially psychotic attempts to avoid abandonment, even if this means taking the blame for a crime she didn't commit. When Vee critically assaults one of the other inmates, she encourages Suzanne to assume responsibility by convincing her that she committed the violent act. Vee then disappears, which reactivates Suzanne's struggle with abandonment. This sense of abandonment is then exacerbated by the stress of being interrogated for a violent crime that Suzanne is not sure that she committed. In response to the simultaneous loss of her love object and stress of being interrogated, Suzanne becomes briefly psychotic, strips naked in the hallway, becomes internally preoccupied, and displays thought disorganization: "I thought I was mopping in the warehouse, turns out I was slocking in the greenhouse. I must have mixed up ware and green or mop and slock. That can happen, right?" During these scenes, she frantically attempts to attach to others to reconcile her fragmented sense of self, insofar as attaching to the detectives: "Those men who were here said I did—shouldn't I believe them?" The psychosis resolves once Suzanne develops the aforementioned healthy and supportive attachment to Taystee, who encourages her autonomy.

Also in line with BPD, Suzanne demonstrates affective instability, impulsivity, and transient stress-related dissociation, most evident when she blacks out during rageful violent acts. This is illustrated in season 2, when Suzanne freezes up onstage at the Christmas play. She flashes back to an episode from youth wherein her mother forces her to sing at her high school graduation, and she similarly freezes, shouts, and repeatedly strikes herself in the head. After the Christmas play, Suzanne is mocked by her peers, and in a panic, she runs outside and ragefully punches Piper while shouting: "No Mommy, I don't want you! You're always pushing me to do these things. Pushing me. No more, Mommy! No more!" This scene illustrates both the complicated relational and trauma pattern that contributes to BPD, in addition to the affective instability and dissociative episodes that can result.

Though it is hard to pigeonhole a fictionalized character into diagnostic groups, we can use Suzanne to look more broadly at the experiences of mentally ill persons who are incarcerated. In a June 2016 interview with *Variety*, Uzo Aduba reflected on the social conversation that is brought about by her character: "She is not in full possession always of herself. It asks a lot of questions: How is it that someone who isn't in full possession of herself winds up in this form of rehabilitation? Is it rehabilitating? Is this the form of treatment she should be receiving?"[14]

Notes

1. Bruce Western and Becky Pettit, "*Collateral Costs: Incarceration's Effect on Economic Mobility*," The Pew Charitable Trusts, 2010, http://www.pewtrusts .org/~/media/legacy/uploadedfiles/pcs_assets/2010/collateralcosts1pdf.pdf.

2. The Sentencing Project, "Fact Sheet: Trends in U.S. Corrections," December 2015, http://sentencingproject.org/wp-content/uploads/2016/01/Trends-in -US-Corrections.pdf.

3. Bruce Western and Steve Redburn, "The Underlying Causes of Rising Incarceration: Crime, Politics, and Social Change," in *The Growth of Incarceration in the United States: Exploring Causes and Consequences*, National Research Council of the National Academies, National Academies Press, 2014, http://www.nap .edu/read/18613/chapter/6#112.

4. Todd R. Clear and Natasha A. Frost, *The Punishment Imperative: The Rise and Failure of Mass Incarceration in America* (New York: New York University Press, 2014).

5. N. William Winkelman Jr., "Chlorpromazine in the Treatment of Neuropsychiatric Disorders," *JAMA* no. 155 (1954): 18–21.

6. Thomas A. Ban, "Fifty Years Chlorpromazine: A Historical Perspective," *Neuropsychiatric Disease and Treatment* 3, no. 4 (August 2007): 495–500.

7. Daniel Yohanna, "Deinstitutionalization of People with Mental Illness: Causes and Consequences," *AMA Journal of Ethics* no. 10 (October 2013): 886–891.

8. E. Fuller Torrey, et al., *The Shortage of Public Hospital Beds for Mentally Ill Persons: A Report of the Treatment Advocacy Center*, 2015, http://www.treatmentad-vocacycenter.org/storage/documents/the_shortage_of_publichospital_beds.pdf, accessed February 22, 2017.

9. E. Fuller Torrey, et al., "Treatment of Persons with Mental Illness in Prisons and Jails," TACReports.org, Research from the Treatment Advocacy Center,

April 8, 2014, accessed February 22, 2017, http://www.TACReports.org/storage /documents/treatment-behind-bars/treatment-behind-bars.pdf.

10. Gregory Sokolov and Talmadge Jones, "Mental Health Courts and the Criminalization of People with Mental Illness" (Slideshow/Lecture presented at general meeting of NAMI Sacramento, Sacramento, CA, March 9, 2007), accessed February 22, 2017, http://www.namisacramento.org/advocacy/docs/Mental%20 Health%20Court-Board%20of%20Sup-3-9-07.pdf.

11. SJ Prins, "Does Transinstitutionalization Explain the Overrepresentation of People with Serious Mental Illnesses in the Criminal Justice System?" *Community Mental Health Journal* 47, no. 6 (2011): 716–722.

12. David Cloud, *On Life Support: Public Health in the Age of Mass Incarceration* (New York, NY: Vera Institute of Justice, 2014).

13. Phyllis Harrison-Ross and James E. Lawrence, "Women in Jail: Mental Health Care Needs and Service Deficiencies" in *Women's Mental Health Issues across the Criminal Justice System*, eds. Rosemary L. Gido and Lanette Dalley (New York: Pearson, 2009).

14. Geoff Berkshire, "Uzo Aduba on 'Orange is the New Black' Season 4, the Big Death and Mental Health," *Variety*, July 21, 2016, http://variety.com/2016/tv /news/uzo-aduba-orange-is-the-new-black-season-4-interview-suzanne-crazy -eyes-warren-poussey-washington-samira-wiley-1201799903/.

CHAPTER ELEVEN

Suffering Soldiers and PTSD: From Saigon to Walton's Mountain

Haley Gienow-McConnell

A discussion was begun in earnest in 1980 by George Gerbner about the stigmatizing effects wrought by media portrayals of mental illness in his landmark essay "Stigma: Social Functions of the Portrayal of Mental Illness in the Mass Media." Through his appraisal of mental illness in popular media, Gerbner concluded that the mentally ill represent "a stigmatized group that serves as a lightning rod for [viewers'] pent-up insecurities and, at the same time, demonstrates the moral and physical price to be paid for deviance."[1] He recommended that further and ongoing research be conducted into the nature and influence of popular portrayals of mental illness in order to mitigate its stigmatizing effects.

In the years since, a significant literature has emerged to attest to the powerful presence and influence of mental illness as it appears in myriad forms in our culture.[2] In their essay "Mental Illness Depictions in Prime-Time Drama: Identifying the Discursive Resources," Claire Wilson et al. conclude that "The media has been shown to be the public's single most important source of information about mental illness, and that these sources are generally very negative." Furthermore, they found that certain patterns and themes were persistent in these sources and, as a result, "In these circumstances, the frequent exposure to the same understandings of mental illness can create self-validating impressions of the correctness of those understandings."[3] In sum, mental illness in popular media is a highly informative and high-stakes issue.

Much has been written about film and its portrayals of mental illness.[4] Increasing attention is being devoted to the topic of mental illness on television, as well as to the presence of disability in general on the small screen.[5] Since, as Gerbner and others have argued, media images of mental illness are powerful influences on public consciousness, the history of these images cannot be overlooked.

The following is a discussion of how CBS television's *The Waltons*, one of the most popular and enduring prime-time dramas of the 1970s and early 1980s, handled the topic of mental illness, and specifically how it contributed to popular perceptions of post-traumatic stress disorder (PTSD).[6] It is also a discussion of how *The Waltons* was distinct among other on-screen examples of the Vietnam experience in the 1970s and early 1980s. Given that *The Waltons* was a long-running television serial which aired from 1972 to 1981 but depicted events set in rural Virginia from 1933 to 1946, *The Waltons* makes for an interesting case study of mental illness in popular culture, since it simultaneously depicted story lines about mental illness in the United States during World War II, the milieu in which the show was set, while reflecting attitudes towards mental illness during the post-Vietnam era of the late 1970s and early 1980s, the milieu in which the show was produced and viewed.

During its final few seasons on the air, *The Waltons* broached mental health disabilities via several story lines that explored the psychological and emotional ramifications of war.[7] The most noteworthy example was an episode entitled "The Tempest" (2/05/81), which depicted the challenges faced by Curtis Willard, husband of eldest Walton daughter Mary-Ellen, upon his return from service in World War II and reunification with his wife. The story went that Mary-Ellen married local country doctor Curtis Willard around the time that war was breaking out in Europe. A couple of years hence, Curtis was drafted into the medical corps and stationed to serve at Pearl Harbor. Following the Japanese attacks on Pearl Harbor, Curtis was presumed dead in the fray, forcing Mary-Ellen and their son John-Curtis to resume a life without him. In actuality, Curt survived, though was severely injured and in a coma for some time. Audiences learned that, after convalescing in a veterans' hospital, Curt decided to remain estranged from his family. His decision was informed by his belief that they would be better off without him. The trauma endured through witnessing the attacks on Pearl Harbor, and through coping with the injuries that resulted, negatively impacted Curt's mental health and his sense of identity. In addition to the psychological trauma wrought by the events of Pearl Harbor, Curt's mental health was further impacted by a physical trauma he endured in the fray. He explained to Mary-Ellen "I can never be a real husband, Mary-Ellen. I can never father another child. I'm not a whole man, and I'm never gonna be one."[8] In Curt's own words, the combination of these traumas left him feeling "empty and lifeless."[9]

As eldest son John-Boy explained in the episode's opening narration: "A chill settled on Walton's Mountain that first autumn after the conclusion of the Second World War. Mary-Ellen had been caught up in a whirlwind love affair that seemed certain to add a new member to the family. But a storm was brewing to the south, a storm that ended her romance and called her to a distant part of the country in search of a man she believed to be dead."[10] The language used from the episode's outset was telling. Rather than referring to Curt's psychological and physical challenges in clinical terms, his struggles were referred to in descriptive, metaphorical terms. The experience of service-induced post-traumatic stress, it was suggested, was a disruptive albeit temporary phenomenon. It was a problem to be weathered, with the expectation that with time and the right attitude, the "storm" would pass. The ensuing episode revolved around Mary-Ellen's struggle to understand Curt's behaviors and choices as he adjusted to civilian life a changed man. Whereas before his service Mary-Ellen knew Curt to be "a good husband and father and a fine doctor," in other words, an upstanding member of his Walton's Mountain community, post-service the townsfolk of Curt's new haunt in Larksburg, Florida, described him as "nothing but trouble."[11] Upon reuniting with Curt and learning of his challenges post-service, Mary-Ellen echoed the townsfolk's disapproval and exclaimed to Curt "The Great Warrior. Killed at Pearl Harbor. Decorated for heroism. Reported in all the newspapers. Just look at you now!"[12]

The townsfolk and Mary-Ellen's sentiments generally reflected the overall perspective on PTSD espoused in the episode, a perspective that was more critical of the individual living with the psychiatric illness than of the circumstances and politics which led to said individual being traumatized in war. This perspective distinguished *The Waltons* among many of its celluloid contemporaries, whose messages tended toward anti-Vietnam rather than anti-veteran rhetoric. While the perspective adopted on *The Waltons* towards war and PTSD was in keeping with the sentiments of the World War II world in which the show was set, its echoes in the contemporary world of the 1970s and 1980s—in which it was viewed—were problematic. Because of the unique temporality of *The Waltons*, determining its position in mental health historiography is complex.

Some has been written about the history of Vietnam and the post-traumatic stress experience in film.[13] By contrast, almost nothing has been written about Vietnam and post-traumatic stress in television. Considering the preeminence of television in the 1970s' cultural landscape, and television's power to shape public consciousness about mental illness, such an examination is important. By the 1970s television had morphed from the "toy with a flickering image" of its inception to a "powerful and influential communications medium" that commanded "an important place in the lives of most Americans."[14] And with only three major networks competing for an audience share throughout the 1970s and early 1980s, what shows like *The Waltons* said about mental illness mattered because their reach was vast.

While the literal war in Southeast Asia concluded in 1975, for many Vietnam veterans another war, battled on a psychological front, was just beginning. Yet the mental health and overall well-being of returned Vietnam veterans were given short shrift on the national agenda.[15] The war in Vietnam was a war that most Americans wanted to forget. As Stephanie A. Slocum-Schaffer explained, "Quite simply, the nation did not want to be reminded of its disastrous defeat in Vietnam. Thus, bitter and frustrated soldiers, many with drug dependencies, came home to a bitter America that was at best indifferent and at worse . . . overtly hostile."[16]

If the plight of the mentally anguished Vietnam veteran was fading from social justice marches, nightly newscasts, and presidential debates as the 1970s wore on, it was becoming increasingly visible on screen in fictionalized accounts. Throughout the 1970s and 1980s, myriad depictions of the far-ranging consequences of the Vietnam War appeared in film. Film historian Robert Niemi observed "During the war and in the decades since, fiction and non-fiction films about Vietnam have engaged in an elaborate and always emotionally charged dialogue about the war's meaning and consequences." As compared to the typically patriotic and battle-charged films which emerged following World War II, Niemi explained "From rancorously partisan defenses and denouncements of American involvement, Vietnam War cinema has generally evolved into something more ideologically nuanced and elegiac."[17] For example, films such as *Coming Home* (1978), *The Deer Hunter* (1978), *First Blood* (1982), *Combat Shock* (1986), and *Jacknife* (1989) all broached the topic of the psychological distress endured by returning Vietnam veterans. Though these films had distinct plots and employed unique narrative devices, the commonalities that they shared were that they were produced during the post-Vietnam era, they spoke directly of the Vietnam experience and were generally critical of the war, and they used the more epic and provocative medium of film to tell their stories.

This brings us back to the curious example of *The Waltons*. The heavy pall cast by the Vietnam War, some have argued, contributed to the popularity of the Great Depression and World War II setting of *The Waltons* during the 1970s. James Person Jr. explained that "*The Waltons*, despite its setting and themes, was fresh and appealed to the nation's sense of nostalgia and soul-searching during the twilight years of the Vietnam-War era."[18] *Waltons* historian Mike Chopra-Gant echoed Person and declared, "by the time *The Waltons* first appeared on American television screens in 1972, Americans . . . had been discomfited by the implicit inhumanity of the USA inscribed in appalling images of the terrified, agonised faces of helpless Vietnamese children bathed in American napalm while American troops stood by, seemingly immune to their suffering." By contrast *The Waltons* was seemingly an anodyne.[19] And in some respects, this was true. Episodes like "The Graduation" (February 21, 1974), where the central crisis revolves around the decision to allocate the family's meager financial resources toward a new suit for eldest son John-Boy, or for a new cow for the family, represented a salve of sorts for audiences, as they were firmly rooted in the specifics of a rural family struggling through the Great Depression.

However, although *The Waltons* was an historically-situated television drama, upon closer analysis of other specific story lines on *The Waltons*, such as that of "The Tempest," it was evident that American audiences did not always escape the turbulent world in which they lived while viewing *The Waltons*. Many story lines covertly referred to issues contemporary to the 1970s and early 1980s, while using the medium of television, and the historical backdrops of the Great Depression and World War II, as inert spaces in which to hash out such issues. When eldest son John-Boy referred to Curt and Mary-Ellen's life just prior to his service in World War II as "the waning hours of a simpler era," his remarks were pointed. Story lines like the "The Tempest" could be interpreted literally as the story of one man's emotional hardships in the aftermath of service in World War II, but they could also be interpreted allegorically as relating to the post-Vietnam world. The tendency to produce historical fiction with contemporary resonance was not exclusive to *The Waltons*. In fact, it was a significant aspect of American television in the 1970s, according to Malgorzata Rymsza-Pawlowska. She explained that among the most popular television series were "programs that emphasized characterization to introduce relatable protagonists and that involved current political and social issues." These programs were "characterized as 'relevance' programming because of the way that they deliberately foregrounded the realities of life in the 1970s."[20]

By contrast, shows like *The Waltons*, and its contemporary *Little House on the Prairie*, consciously foregrounded the past in their storytelling, while referring to contemporary issues in coded and implicit ways. Due to their historical settings, *Little House* and *The Waltons* offered a unique breed of realistic and relevance programming. Rymsza-Pawlowska elaborated: "In this programming context, *Little House* made similar avowals of realism. . . . As one critic observed, the show 'dishe[d] up today's hardships as 1870s hardships.' If relevance programming aimed to advance television's position by emphasizing its ability to represent and attend to social issues, shows such as *Little House* took the additional step of placing these issues within a historical milieu."[21]

Thus, it behooves us to consider *The Waltons* as a legitimate and illuminating contribution to the discussion of mental health and the military on-screen in the 1970s and 1980s. Though set during the 1930s and 1940s, its relationship to the time in which it was produced was significant. *The Waltons* represented a counterpoint to the Vietnam films of the era, which tended to be contemporaneous to the period they were made, and overt in their commentary on the consequences of the Vietnam War. Of historically based television dramas like *The Waltons*, television historians S. Robert Lichter, Linda S. Lichter, and Stanley Rothman argued, "Sometimes the disguise is elaborate enough to produce a genuinely covert political statement, with scripts that tackle controversial political issues symbolically or even allegorically."[22] For example, when Mary-Ellen sets out to reconnect with her estranged husband, she asks a local resident of Curt's new hometown for directions to his home and is told to "Just look for the first junk heap you come to."[23] The literal interpretation of this exchange was that Curt failed to adjust and thrive upon his return from service. The subtext was that some returning service-persons living with mental illness, including Vietnam veterans by extension, not only struggled emotionally, they struggled socially and financially as well. And while these problems may have appeared insurmountable in the real world in which viewers lived, when filtered from Walton's Mountain through the cathode-ray tube, they appeared more manageable, requiring little more than a good attitude and perseverance to overcome.

Television historian Ella Taylor described the Waltons as "an imaginary idealized family set in an imaginary, idealized past, equipped with the insights of applied psychology. They offer us a world in which traditional values of faith and kindness, persistence and initiative, respond to modern dilemmas of identity and development, and in which the apho-ristic, material language of common sense mingles happily with contem-porary psychological wisdom."[24] As a result, *The Waltons* offered an illuminating perspective on representations of PTSD on-screen in that it addressed the modern dilemma in the nostalgic framework of the 1940s, and couched its discussion of PTSD in 1940s sensibilities—and therefore in detached and reassuring tones. This basic formula through which *The Waltons* handled topics such as mental illness was common in television depictions of disability in this era. According to Paul Longmore, "in the 'social problem' dramas seen during the 1970s and 1980s, the subjects of our worries were addressed, but without deep examination. In such cases, television and film provide quick and simple solutions. They tell us that the problem is not as overwhelming as we fear, that it is manageable, or that it is not really our problem at all, but someone else's."[25]

Indeed, in episodes of *The Waltons* where characters were affected by disabilities, if the character affected by disability was a nonrecurring character, the disability could not be reversed. Its effects were permanent. In episodes where a member of the Walton family or a recurring character of the series was affected by disability, typically the disability was not permanent, and medical intervention, combined with perseverance, faith, and family, mitigated the effects of the disability. In this way, the Waltons, by overcoming their own disabilities and relegating permanent disabili-ties to nonrecurring characters, suggested this message to the viewing audience: Disability is not for us. Disability is for someone else. The writ-ers of the series thereby created a safety net between the audience and disability. In the case of Curtis Willard, he resided in a kind of no-man's-land of disability and mental illness. He was a Walton by extension, hav-ing married a Walton daughter, and so was expected to confront and overcome his PTSD. Indeed, Mary-Ellen was prescriptive in her appraisal of how best to manage Curt's PTSD, as was typical of scenarios wherein the Waltons confront disability. After her initial reunion with Curt, Mary-Ellen telephoned her younger sister Erin to give her an update. "There's something very wrong with him," she reported of Curt. "I have to stay here. I have to get to the bottom of this."[26] And yet the episode made clear that though Mary-Ellen had strong opinions about how Curt should confront his PTSD, she would not be present for Curt's recovery, nor would they resume their marriage. There was hope for Curt if he adhered to the Walton way and readjusted to civilian life, but his recovery was not meant for audience consumption. The onus of recovery was his individ-ual burden to bear, and total redemption in the form of reconciliation with Mary-Ellen was not possible.

Although disability was embraced as a relevant social problem in series such as *The Waltons*, its deployment was not without its risks. It had to be handled in a certain way because "Disability happens around us more than we generally recognize or care to notice, and we harbor unspoken anxieties about the possibility of disablement, to us or to someone close to us. What we fear, we often stigmatize and shun and sometimes seek to destroy. Popular entertainment depicting disabled characters allude to these fears and prejudices, or address them obliquely or fragmentarily, seeking to reassure us about ourselves."[27] In addressing the topic of disability frequently, *The Waltons* conceded that disability was a relevant social issue, but in relegating permanent disabilities to non-recurring characters, *The Waltons* reassured its audience that this social problem was, as Paul Longmore put it, "not really our problem at all, but someone else's."[28]

In reality, mental health is everyone's concern. The way mental illness is perceived and treated is informed by myriad social, political, and cultural factors, not the least of which includes popular culture. Even the seemingly most innocuous examples of mental illness in popular culture, examples such as *The Waltons*, are influential and have consequences. It is important to be media savvy and critical of these images, and it is important to understand that these images have a history, a history that has been overlooked. Mental illness means different things at different times. What we consider to be mental illness and best practice in a given period is different from our definitions and approaches in another period. Therefore, images of mental illness on-screen such as *The Waltons*, despite their shortcomings, should not be discounted as outdated treatments of the subject, but rather as important historical artifacts of the place and meaning of mental illness in our culture at a given time. Understanding the history and evolution of these images puts us in better stead to have productive, timely, and context-specific discussions about mental illness and its place in our current culture.

Notes

1. George Gerbner, "Stigma: Social Functions of the Portrayal of Mental Illness in the Mass Media," in *Attitudes Toward the Mentally Ill: Research Perspectives*, ed. J. Rabkin, L. Gelb, and J.B. Lazar (Washington, DC: U.S. Government Printing Office, 1980), 45–47.

2. See Otto F. Wahl, *Media Madness: Public Images of Mental Illness* (New Brunswick, NJ: Rutgers University Press, 1995); D.I. Diefenbach, "The Portrayal of Mental Illness on Prime-time Television," *Journal of Community Psychology* 25, no. 3 (1997): 289–302; Diana Rose, "Television, Madness, and Community

Care," *Journal of Community and Applied Social Psychology* 8, no. 3 (1998): 213–228; J.R. Cutcliffe and B. Hannigan, "Mass Media, 'Monsters' and Mental Health Clients: The Need for Increased Lobbying," *Journal of Psychiatric and Mental Health Nursing* 8, no. 4 (2001): 315–321; John Coverdale, Raymond Nairn, and D. Claasen, "Depictions of Mental Illness in Print Media: A Prospective National Sample," *The Australian and New Zealand Journal of Psychiatry* 36, no. 5 (2002): 697–700; Otto F. Wahl, "Depictions of Mental Illnesses in Children's Media," *Journal of Mental Health* 12 (2003): 249–258; Otto F. Wahl, "News Media Portrayal of Mental Illness," *American Behavioral Scientist* 46, (2003): 1594–600.

3. Claire Wilson, Raymond Nairn, John Coverdale, and Aroha Panapa, "Mental Illness Depictions in Prime-Time Drama: Identifying the Discursive Resources," *Australian and New Zealand Journal of Psychiatry* 33 (1999): 232.

4. See, for example, David Robinson, *Reel Psychiatry: Movie Portrayals of Psychiatric Conditions* (Port Huron, MI: Rapid Psychler Press, 2003); Krin Gabbard and Glen O. Gabbard, *Psychiatry and Cinema* (Chicago: University of Chicago Press, 1987); Danny Wedding and Mary Ann Boyd, *Movies and Mental Illness: Using Films to Understand Psychopathology* (Columbus: McGraw-Hill College, 1998); *Mental Illness in Popular Media: Essays on the Representation of Disorders*, ed. Lawrence C. Rubin (Jefferson, NC: McFarland, 2012).

5. See Paul Longmore's landmark essay, originally published in 1985, "Screening Stereotypes: Images of Disabled People in Television and Motion Pictures," in *Why I Burned My Book and Other Essays on Disability*, ed. Paul K. Longmore (Philadelphia: Temple University Press, 2003); Beth Haller, *Representing Disability in An Ableist World: Essays on Mass Media* (Louisville: Advocado Press, 2010); *Different Bodies: Essays on Disability in Film and Television*, ed. Marja Evelyn Mogk (Jefferson, NC: McFarland, 2013).

6. Earl Hamner and Ralph Giffin, *Goodnight John-Boy: A Celebration of an American Family and the Values That Have Sustained Us Through Good Times and Bad* (Nashville: Cumberland House Publishing, 2002), 64.

7. Including *The Waltons*, "The Children's Carol," dir. Lawrence Dobkin (December 5, 1977; Warner Home Video, 2008), DVD; *The Waltons*, "The Conscience," dir. Gwen Arner (January 4, 1979; Warner Home Video, 2012), DVD; *The Waltons*, "The Obstacle," dir. William H. Bushnell (January 11, 1979; Warner Home Video, 2012), DVD; *The Waltons*, "The Lost Sheep," dir. Walter Alzmann (November 1, 1979; Warner Home Video, 2009), DVD; *The Waltons*, "The Furlough," dir. Harry Harris (February 21, 1980; Warner Home Video, 2009), DVD; and *The Waltons*, "The Whirlwind," dir. Nell Cox (January 22, 1981; Warner Home Video, 2002), DVD.

8. *The Waltons*, "The Tempest," dir. Gabrielle Beaumont (February 5, 1981; Warner Home Video, 2002), DVD.

9. Ibid.

10. Ibid.

11. Ibid.

12. Ibid.

13. See Lauri E. Klobs, *Disability Drama in Television and Film* (Jefferson, NC: McFarland, 1988); Christian Keathley, "Trapped in the Affection-Image: Hollywood's Post-Traumatic Cycle (1970–1976)," in *Screening Disability: Essays on Cinema and Disability*, eds. Christopher R. Smith and Anthony Enns (Lanham, MD: University Press of America, 2001); Sharon Packer, "Cold War Paranoia and Postwar PTSD," in *Movies and the Modern Psyche*, ed. Sharon Packer (Westport, CT: Praeger, 2007).

14. Stephanie A. Slocum-Schaffer, *America in the Seventies* (Syracuse: Syracuse University Press, 2003), 179.

15. Ibid., 129.

16. Ibid., 209.

17. Robert Niemi, *History in the Media: Film and Television* (Santa Barbara, CA: ABC-CLIO, 2006), 152.

18. James E. Person Jr., *Earl Hamner: From Walton's Mountain to Tomorrow* (Nashville: Cumberland House, 2005), 75.

19. Mike Chopra-Gant, *The Waltons: Nostalgia and Myth in Seventies America* (London: I.B. Tauris & Co. Ltd, 2013), 2.

20. Malgorzata J. Rymsza-Pawlowska, "Broadcasting the Past: History Television, 'Nostalgia Culture,' and the Emergence of the Miniseries in the 1970s United States," *Journal of Popular Film and Television* 42, no. 2 (2014): 83–84.

21. Ibid., 83–84.

22. S. Robert Lichter, Linda S. Lichter, and Stanley Rothman, *Prime Time: How TV Portrays American Culture* (Washington, DC: Regnery Publishing, 1994), 9–10.

23. *The Waltons*, "The Tempest," 1981.

24. Ella Taylor, *Prime-Time Families: Television Culture in Postwar America* (Berkeley: University of California Press, 1989), 103.

25. Paul Longmore, "Screening Stereotypes: Images of Disabled People in Television and Motion Pictures," in *Why I Burned My Book and Other Essays on Disability*, ed. Paul K. Longmore (Philadelphia: Temple University Press, 2003), 132.

26. *The Waltons*, "The Tempest," 1981.

27. Paul Longmore, "Screening Stereotypes," 132.

28. Ibid.

CHAPTER TWELVE

Mirth and Mental Illness: Television Comedy and the Human Condition

Kristi Rowan Humphreys

According to Susan Brink of the *Los Angeles Times*, "Mental illness, long taboo or distorted by the media, is making its way into the fictional lives of television characters. Once, mentally ill people were commonly portrayed as homicidal maniacs, evil seductresses and assorted buffoons. Sometimes, they are still. But they are also lawyers, doctors, mobsters and detectives—not always lovable folks, but increasingly understandable human beings."[1] Recently, this shift has made a successful foray into television comedy. With shows like *Monk* (2002–2009), *Raising Hope* (2010–2014), and *Anger Management* (2012–2014), we find mentally ill characters who are lovable and funny.[2] These shows center on characters struggling with everything from nervous breakdowns to Alzheimer's disease and obsessive compulsive disorders; yet just as individuals in reality who deal with similar illnesses are capable of any range of emotions from laughter to anger in addition to life's successes and failures, these shows underscore the human qualities of these fictional characters—connecting the imperfections of the mentally ill to the imperfections of the human race. The comedy does not function to ridicule mentally ill characters, but rather to expose their humanity—their human abilities to laugh, solve mysteries, care for others, and diagnose illnesses. I argue that these shows apply comedy to mental illness successfully because they focus on respect for the characters, depicting them not as abnormal or marginalized, but rather as imperfect—a quality binding the entire human race. As *Monk*'s Executive Producer David Hoberman claims, "The more we can portray damaged people as heroes, the better off we'll all be."[3]

In 2014, when Leonardo DiCaprio was nominated a fourth time in acting categories for an Oscar award, and lost a fourth time, James S. Murphy wrote an article in *Vanity Fair* about this phenomenon and what he calls the "Pitt-Hanks Continuum." He states that the "Pitt-Hanks Continuum can be used to predict how likely an actor is to win an Academy Award. The more like [Brad] Pitt an actor's style and roles are, the less likely he is to win. The continuum also explains why the Academy favors actors playing characters who are disabled, mentally ill, gay, or ugly."[4] He finds that DiCaprio has not been embraced by the Academy because he plays characters who do not invite us to share their positions. Like Pitt, he is "cool," and "cool guys don't win Oscars."[5] Whereas this chapter is not about DiCaprio, awards, or even films, it is about mentally ill characters who invite us, the audience, to share their positions, and I believe this quality especially has much to do with their success in the comedy genre.

Monk and Obsessive-Compulsive Disorders

In the crime comedy *Monk*, we find an obsessive-compulsive character, Adrian Monk (Tony Shalhoub), who solves crimes as an expert private detective. Unlike other prime-time examples addressing mental issues, such as *The West Wing* or *The Sopranos*, *Monk*'s mental illness is not a side story or extraneous character information, but rather, it is integral to the plot of the series. In the first episode, "Mr. Monk and the Candidate," Monk's disorders, and their concomitant stigmas, are spelled out explicitly, when the San Francisco mayor's wife, Miranda St. Clair (Gail O'Grady), asks Monk how he can possibly investigate anything successfully because she has been told he is "germaphobic, afraid of the dark, heights, crowds, and milk." Monk's personal assistant, Sharona Fleming (Bitty Schram), responds by claiming, "We're working on the milk. He's making good progress on milk." This scene is noteworthy for multiple reasons. First, Monk and Sharona not only admit openly to his mental illness, but also, embrace his need for and progress in therapy. Second, and perhaps more important, the scene demonstrates Miranda's desire to define Monk by his disabilities. She supposes mental illness precludes him from "investigating anything," and this statement embodies a stigma that operates to marginalize and devalue the mentally ill, regarding mental disabilities in particular as barriers to leading normal, happy, and successful lives. Monk and Sharona assimilate his condition, claiming they are "working on it," and subsequently, solve the crime successfully.

This stigma is again both underscored and dispelled later in the episode. Despite his best efforts, Monk lets a criminal escape when his fear of heights prevents him from pursuing the man, who climbs down a tall building. The police captain responds to this mistake by saying to Monk, "Don't expect a medic to help you because after this, you're a leper." In other words, when Monk's mental illness hinders him, the captain is quick to regard his disorder as cause for rejection, as basis to label him an outcast—a common trope in popular culture. However, when Monk succeeds, despite his defects, we are reminded of the danger of assumptions and stereotypes. This scene exemplifies how the show respects the mentally ill character, depicting the flaws of humanity in general, and encouraging us to share this imperfect position. Despite the rejection, Monk alone is capable of solving the case, which negates the captain's unfair assessment of his condition. Monk is able to thrive despite, and even because of, his disorders, and this compels others, including viewers, to regard mental illness differently—not as leprosy, but as common human imperfection. Consequently, *Monk* invites us all, as uniquely flawed human beings, to share in Monk's position, as part of the human condition involves managing the judgments of others.

Whereas these treatments of mental illness are important, they are not entirely unique to the comedy genre. However, the ways in which Monk's disorders feed the comic dialogue of the series are unique. Monk, Sharona, and other characters regularly poke fun, in playful manners, at his disabilities, thus highlighting the show's management of these issues as imperfections, rather than aberrant human qualities. For example, in part two of the episode "Mr. Monk and the Candidate," Sharona quits as his assistant, claiming, "I think I have to find a normal job before I go completely crazy." Monk playfully responds, "Like me." Then, when Sharona returns to her role as Monk's assistant, he thanks her by saying, "I'll never forget you." She replies, "You never forget anything." Later, Monk won't eat a canned good because the can is dented, and he asks if Sharona wants it. She replies, "Of course, I want it; I'm not the mental case." Finally, Miranda St. Clair attempts to explain something to Monk, comically saying, "You seem like an intelligent person . . . *on occasion*." While these examples are from one episode alone, they represent the spirit of the entire series. By programming mental illness for comedy, while maintaining

Monk's ability to thrive, despite his condition, the show normalizes Monk—it aligns the faulty qualities of his mental disorders with the imperfections of the human race.

In fact, Monk's disorders, in many ways, function not to weaken his abilities, but to strengthen them. In discussing *Monk* and phenomenology, Talia Welsh reveals, "Monk is distracted by things that we would likely ignore, but it is *because* he is distracted by so many seemingly inconsequential things that he notices incongruous elements that solve the cases."[6] Monk's crime-solving abilities are so closely intertwined with his mental disorders that he exemplifies the ways in which our combined qualities, ones we may consider "proper" or "flawed," function together to compose inimitable personalities in every individual. Monk himself acknowledges the binary nature of his gifts, regarding them as both blessings and curses. When Sharona asks, "How does it feel always being right?" He replies, "Terrible." Welsh reveals that like most of us, "Monk's curious talents have a dark side."[7] *Monk* welcomes us to share this position, as we recognize our own dark sides—the imperfections and insecurities we manage every day—and the show's comedy functions to bring these identifications to light.

Monk regularly doubts himself and his abilities, and his condition compels him to state these insecurities explicitly. He often admits, "I'm not sure if I'm going to be able to pull this off." Recalling, again, the "Pitt-Hanks Continuum," uninhibited insecurity and statements of self-doubt, such as this, are not regarded by popular culture as "cool" statements—a quality of Monk's character that strengthens our connection to him. His mental illness obliges him to state the insecurities most individuals attempt to conceal. We find Monk's honesty, even though motivated by disability and revealed through comedy, refreshing, because it reflects our own struggles with the flawed human condition.

Raising Hope and Dementia

Raising Hope is a show about a 20-something-year-old male, Jimmy Chance (Lucas Neff), who has a romantic fling with a convicted female murderer. When she ends up having their baby in prison, just before her execution, Jimmy decides to raise the baby with the help of his family— his mother, Virginia (Martha Plimpton), his father, Burt (Garret Dillahunt), and his grandmother, Maw Maw (Cloris Leachman). Maw Maw suffers from dementia, and her oscillation between sanity and insanity constitutes much of the humor of the show, as she rarely wears a shirt, frequently refers to her grandson as her late husband, occasionally attempts to breastfeed Jimmy's baby, and can often be found curled up under Burt's desk attempting to give birth to puppies. Whereas this disease is no laughing matter in real life, by programming it for comedy, the show underscores our own humanity, which is complicated regardless of illness or disability. Consequently, Maw Maw also incites us to share her position, as the binaries of her condition—much like Monk's illness comprises abilities functioning both for and against him—expose the imperfect humanity of her character.

This is made especially clear in the brief moments she is lucid—scenes that function as some of the most humorous segments of the show. In the first episode, "Pilot," Virginia runs out of the house chasing Maw Maw. When Burt asks her what's wrong, Virginia replies, "She's lucid . . . it's been almost 5 minutes." Burt says, "Whoa, that is a long one." Maw Maw reveals the reality of their situation during this sane moment, yelling, "So you're telling me that I just let all of you live in my house for free? Unbelievable! Pack up your circus and go find another teat to suck on." While Virginia and Burt are concerned, within seconds, Maw Maw returns to insanity—a state that is more convenient for Virginia and Burt. We know Maw Maw is no longer lucid because she asks Virginia to tell Jimmy to pick up something from the butcher on the way home, as the Greensteins are coming over for dinner and she has only pork chops in the icebox. Relieved, Virginia responds, "We're good now." Likewise, in the episode "Dead Tooth," Virginia recognizes Maw Maw has shifted back into lucidity, so she concernedly responds, "Uh, oh, somebody found her marbles." Seizing the opportunity, Burt states, "I've been waiting for this. Maw Maw, I'm your son-in-law Burt. You've lost your mind, and you're never lucid for very long, so listen up." Comprehending him, Maw Maw replies, "I understand. Go. Let's do this." In these moments, the show venerates Maw Maw's character, giving her a lucid, independent voice, even briefly, and providing a glimpse of both her straightforward personality and her life before dementia. These scenes lay bare the awareness that the characters are more than their illnesses, that mental illness does not diminish a person's value. The family often dismisses Maw Maw's comments and actions because they regard them as illogical, but because the show gives her moments of clarity and transparency, we, the viewers, are pressed to defend her humanity—seeing her as flawed rather than "crazy."

The series further respects Maw Maw's character by portraying her not only as the most intelligent member of the family, but often as the most logical and sensible, even while battling dementia. In the episode "Mrs. Smarty Pants," Jimmy decides to go back to school to earn his GED, but he is struggling to understand what is being taught. He admits to his parents that he is considering asking his educated girlfriend, Sabrina (Shannon Woodward), to tutor him. The parents caution him, claiming, "We have worked way too hard to keep Sabrina from finding out how stupid you are." To prove his need for a tutor, Jimmy tells his parents to ask him a basic math question. When they can't, astonished, Virginia says, "We're too stupid to even think of a question!" She calls for Maw Maw, yelling, "Come here and ask Jimmy a math question." Maw Maw enters the room and asks, "If the radius of a circle is six, what is the area?" Virginia condescends, saying, "A *math* question, Maw Maw." Maw Maw replies, "This *is* math. The formula is πr^2." Dubious, Burt whispers, "Is she even lucid right now? Square pies?" Maw Maw is revealed to be the most intelligent and educated member of the family. Similarly, in the episode "Cheaters," Maw Maw and Jimmy are sitting on the couch eating ice cream. Maw Maw has not been lucid for days and believes she has just had her heart broken by a soldier preparing to leave for the Korean War. Jimmy, too, was recently rejected by Sabrina. In her demented state, Maw Maw says, "War. It's not just hard on the soldiers." Jimmy plays along with Maw Maw's delusion, stating, "Yeah, well maybe Korea will be the last one, Maw Maw." She replies, "Well, they wouldn't call it falling in love, if you didn't get hurt sometimes. But you just pick yourself up and move on. There are other fish in the sea." Jimmy looks at her, astonished that her advice, even through the veil of insanity, is so sensible and helpful. The comedy succeeds because the show respects Maw Maw's character in scenes such as these, illuminating her as intelligent, wise, and nurturing, even while battling mental illness.

The family has grown comfortable with Maw Maw's insanity, to the extent that her lucid moments are burdensome because they are abnormal. In other words, the abnormal (Maw Maw's insanity) has become normal, and the normal (Maw Maw's sanity) has become abnormal. The family members have adapted to this reality, and they reflect the ways in which we, as humans, adjust to our own conditions. Furthermore, the process of discovery that is involved in these adaptations also composes much of the comedy of *Raising Hope*. The family often unearths new ways of both improving life for Maw Maw and accommodating her idiosyncrasies. For example, in the episode "Dream Hoarders," Burt discovers Maw Maw possesses virtuoso Jenga skills, but these talents reveal themselves only when he plays the recording "Istanbul (not Constantinople)" by The Four Lads. He mentions this breakthrough to Virginia, who replies, "I know! It's weird how music kicks in certain things in her brain. Like the other day, I found out 'America the Beautiful' makes her poop faster!" The process of discovery that accompanies any unpredictable illness is a foundational aspect of the series, and the comedy allows us to work through these challenging issues. We recognize the imperfections of the human condition in Maw Maw's character, and through humor we can identify with those defects in ways that inspire mirth and connection.

Anger Management and Anger Issues

Anger Management features former baseball player turned anger management therapist, Charlie Goodson (Charlie Sheen), who successfully and comically treats patients with mental illnesses, and who has a daughter with obsessive-compulsive disorder. This show differs from previous examples, in that the main character is both therapist *and* patient. But the show embodies a similar spirit because Charlie is also both competent and flawed, as the show makes explicit his efforts to work through his own anger issues, even while helping his patients do the same. Charlie treats many patients with anger issues, but Charlie's character is ironically the most compelling example of imperfection. He often attempts to connect with his patients by admitting his own weaknesses and shortcomings. For example, in the episode "Charlie and the Slumpbuster," he claims to have had a bout of night terrors after sleeping with an unattractive woman, whom he used as his "slumpbuster," which means that his baseball slump ended when he slept with the most unattractive girl in town—the "slumpbuster." He admits, "Like all of you, I've made mistakes, and yesterday, one of those mistakes reared its ugly head. Look, the lesson here is whatever you do, never use a slumpbuster." Whereas Charlie is attempting to use his experiences to normalize the issues of his patients, through comedy, we recognize Charlie's own disabilities. Obviously, the lesson he should have learned is not solely, or even largely, "never to use a slumpbuster." The real issues with Charlie lie much deeper—something with which the show allows us, the viewers, to identify and connect.

Charlie perpetually attempts to treat his patients by assimilating their issues and revealing his own similar faults, which, alone, is reflective of our imperfect human conditions. We each embody a desire to connect, to find commonalities with one another, and Charlie personifies this need. In multiple episodes, Charlie treats prison inmates dealing with anger issues. Attempting to connect, he exposes his own troubles, and in an interesting turn, the inmates often diagnose and advise him, sharing their own related experiences. However, their stories are illogical and humorous. When they claim not to like someone or something, they respond through murder or arson. One inmate talks about losing his girlfriend, in an effort to identify with Charlie's loss of a client, but the inmate claims to have killed a man upon discovering his involvement with the girlfriend. The comedy lies in the inmate's claims that this is also the best solution for Charlie's anger.

We connect further with Charlie because he makes mistakes. Even as a therapist, he is characterized as flawed—as requiring therapy and connection himself. This is revealed through comedy, and we identify with Charlie's human need to relate. In the episode "Charlie's Patient Gets Out of Jail," one of Charlie's inmate patients, Cleo (James Black), is released, and with nowhere to go, Cleo asks to stay with Charlie. He allows this, but soon discovers Cleo sleeping with Charlie's ex-wife. Charlie permits him to stay, and the next morning over breakfast, Cleo says to Charlie, "You know, I'm proud of you. In group [therapy], you tell us to let go of our anger, and you do it. *You really walk the walk.* Thank you. Because under normal circumstances, a guy comes into your house, eats your food, sleeps in your bed, oils up your ex-wife—a guy could get pretty upset about that." Charlie responds, "Well, I always say to *lead by example.* Could you pass the butter please?" Cleo replies, "Oh, yeah," and he takes a slice of butter for himself before passing it to Charlie. Charlie explodes, yelling, "That's my butter! You didn't ask! You just took it! And now you're just going to smear it all over your toast right in front of me!" Cleo interjects, "If you don't want me using your butter, all you have to do is say so," to which Charlie responds, "We're not talking about butter," as he appropriates a dispute over butter to help him deal with his anger over the ex-wife. By aligning Charlie's imperfections with those of his patients, in addition to his efforts to manage those defects, the show respects the characters, the therapeutic process, and allows us to do the same—encouraging us to share their positions in the human struggle.

Television comedy has a unique function regarding mental illness and popular culture. It allows us to laugh at our own human condition, giving us permission to address even the most difficult or taboo aspects of humanity in ways that inspire mirth and identification. Moreover, television comedy reminds us that we are all human, and despite individual illnesses, disabilities, or conditions, we can relate to being imperfect—and these imperfections are often amusing. Our flawed condition equalizes us, and once we concede this, we are more able and willing to laugh at ourselves. Television comedy unifies us on this level, allowing us to unveil our insecurities, share the positions of others, and laugh at our own complications, and humor succeeds in this capacity because the shows respect the mentally ill characters, depicting them as capable, successful, and ultimately, human. Instead of marginalizing or devaluing the mentally ill, comedy allows us to see beyond the disability and recognize characters as fellow human beings working through their own individual struggles, discovering independence and fulfillment, despite setbacks. Ultimately, these shows bring to the fore issues commonly concealed, and this gives us permission to address, and even laugh at, our own wonderfully imperfect human condition.

Notes

1. Susan Brink, "Mental illness sans clichés," *Los Angeles Times*, November 13, 2006, http://articles.latimes.com/2006/nov/13/health/he-mediaside13.

2. For this study, I viewed the following: *Monk: Season One.* Universal Studios Home Entertainment, 2010. DVD; *Raising Hope: Season One.* 20th Century Fox Home Entertainment, 2010. DVD; *Raising Hope: Season Two.* 20th Century Fox Home Entertainment, 2010. DVD; *Anger Management: Season One.* Lionsgate, 2012. DVD.

3. Quoted in Brink.

4. James S. Murphy, "The Pitt-Hanks Continuum: Why Leonardo DiCaprio Didn't Win the Oscar," *Vanity Fair*, March 3, 2014, http://www.vanityfair.com /hollywood/2014/03/leonardo-dicaprio-oscar.

5. In 2015, DiCaprio finally won an Oscar for his portrayal of a grief-stricken and abandoned frontiersman in the wilderness in *The Revenant*. Consistent with Murphy's assessment, DiCaprio wins for a role that loses the "cool" aspect, as he takes on the challenge of becoming a type of character rarely represented on the big screen.

6. Talia Welsh, "Mr. Monk and the Phenomenological Attitude," in *Mr. Monk and Philosophy: The Curious Case of the Defective Detective*, ed. D. E. Wittkower (Chicago: Open Court, 2010), 6.

7. Welsh, "Mr. Monk," 12.

CHAPTER THIRTEEN

Mentally Ill Mobsters: From Cagney's *White Heat* to *Scarface* to *Bugsy* and *Crazy Joe*

Vincent LoBrutto

Mob activity in organized crime, especially in the higher echelons where the capos reign, under most circumstances would be considered at least socially unstable. Many mobsters exhibit mental illness, aberrant behavior and murderous tendencies upon which they often act. Mental illness can strike anyone, but the combination of being mobbed-up and having untreated mental illness can often be a lethal prescription.

Tony Soprano, the television mob boss played brilliantly by James Gandolfini, experiences panic attacks and begins therapy with a psychiatrist who learns her client's profession and swears to keep his secret. A morning event with ducks at his outdoor pool starts his psychological journey beginning in a traditional manner and progressing to Soprano's deep venting about "family" members and the pressures of his work. What is unique here is that while he is in therapy he continues to be just as vile, violent, and vicious. *The Sopranos* investigates the dichotomy between mental illness and violence in mob culture. Tony can see a psychiatrist for help, but the mob life teaches there is only one way out—at the end of the barrel of a gun.[1]

In the world of cinema there are numerous examples of mob mental imbalance—some are fictional characters and some are based on true-life crime figures. Three of these real figures have nicknames that identify their mental state. "Crazy Joe" was Italian-American Joseph Gallo, who was part of the Colombo crime family. In the low-budget movie *Crazy Joe* (1974), Peter Boyle plays "Crazy" Joe Colombo as a man willing to do anything illegal: hits, all kinds of murder, and involvement in all the rackets, as well as the heroin trade. Eventually, because of his erratic and ultraviolent out-of-control behavior, Joe Gallo was banished by the mob, which became his mortal enemy. Oddly enough, he was accepted by the counterculture of the era, probably because of his antiestablishment rants and his ability to move one way and then the opposite way. Ultimately, the mob got to Joe Gallo. In the film he was shot repeatedly sitting at a restaurant table against the wall as he drew his pistol and fired back. He managed to get outside in the dark where the gang was waiting and fired rapidly and incessantly until he was dead in the street. The true story happened on April 7, 1972, at 4:30 in the morning, between seafood courses at Umberto's Clam House in Little Italy. Gallo was celebrating his 43rd birthday with his sister and bodyguard. Four gunmen burst in. Twenty shots were fired, hitting Gallo in the back, elbow, and buttock. Mortally wounded, Gallo stumbled into the street and collapsed. He was taken to a hospital where he died in the emergency department.

Benjamin "Bugsy" Siegel was a Jewish-American mobster who was a "dapper dan" of his day. He is considered the father of Las Vegas, developing the desert retreat in 1946. Before that Siegel was gambling in and out of flourishing joints on the outskirts of Vegas. He also kept company with prostitutes of all stripes. At times Siegel made Hollywood his beat. Benjamin, or "Ben," got the nickname "Bugsy" because his behavior would seem normal, at least for a mobster without mental illness, but Ben suffered from a brain ailment and would display aberrant and violent behavior, usually unprovoked. He complained of crippling headaches. His girlfriend Virginia Hill was a mob gal who passed information for a gang and was involved romantically with other mob figures before she fell for Siegel. It was a tumultuous relationship filled with heated arguments and infidelity. It was at her home where Siegel was murdered while reading the Los Angeles Times. The deadly shots came through a window and one hit him on the side of the head, ironically ending the headaches forever. No one was ever apprehended or even identified in the murder.

In the 1991 motion picture *Bugsy*, directed by Barry Levinson and starring Warren Beatty as the title character and Annette Benning as the glamourous Virginia Hill, Benjamin Siegel goes crazy when everyone keeps calling him Bugsy. His reaction is to stare them down until they squirm. Throughout the picture, literally at the drop of a hat, Siegel exhibits a lava-hot temper and acts of unspeakable violence.[2]

Alphonse Gabriel "Al" "Scarface" Capone is connected to mob activity like white on rice. He was an Italian-American who died in prison of syphilis at age 48. In between, he was responsible for the infamous St. Valentine's Day Massacre where mob members of a rival gang were brutally slaughtered by Capone gunmen. His territory was Chicago, and his reign of terror included bombings, shootings, robberies, and general mayhem.

Al Capone was a man capable of both planned and spontaneous violence delivered to his foes by his henchmen. Capone was nicknamed "Scarface" because of a physical slash mark on his face. He received the ugly mark back in 1917 when he was a bouncer at a dance hall. He encountered New York hood Frank Galluccio with his sister Lena and a date, Maria Tanzio. Capone began smiling at Galluccio's sister. Lena was annoyed and asked her brother to do something about it. As Frank was in the process of reacting, Capone leaned over to Lena and made a rude comment about her posterior. Frank exploded in rage. One thing led to another, with Capone charging at Gallucio and Gallucio pulling out a pocket knife. One of his moves caught Capone on the left cheek. The result was a gash requiring 30 stitches.

Alphonse Capone's mental stability functioned well when applied to his mob leadership skills, but his overall psychological fitness suffered from an unhealthy obsession for his sister and he had a murderous temper just barely under control.

There are three films based on Al Capone:

Scarface (1932), directed by Howard Hawks, starring Paul Muni as the Scarface character, Antonio "Tony" Camonte, and Ann Dvorak as his kid sister Francesca, is an early talkie based on the life of Al Capone. This film is from the pre-Code era, prior to a form of censorship that took over the movie industry. It is an excellent example of why the Code was established; this film has overt sex, a lot of female anatomy revealed, and a pointed suggestion of incest between Camonte (the Capone character) and his sister. The violence is relentless, sudden, prolonged, and murderous. Machine gun fire permeates the entire picture. The movie exhibits an undeniable truth that this Scarface is out of control and murderously angry when least expected.

Scarface (1983) is a reimagined version of Capone's story directed by Brian DePalma and starring Al Pacino as a Cuban Tony Montana (an updated Scarface). His incestuous emotions for his kid sister Gina (played by Mary Elizabeth Mastrantonio) return front and center in this version. This reboot has Scarface coming over on the Mariel boatlift, meant as a humane gesture to Cuba by President Jimmy Carter. The result of this gesture is Castro's release of unwanted criminals and other lowlifes into Miami. Pacino's performance is masterful. When the camera zooms in tight on him and then tight on Gina—whether dancing with a man or otherwise—a high pitched musical/electronic tone builds as Tony Montana gets so angry he could burst, because he desires his sister in a sexual way and can't stand other men with her. Ultimately, he even murders his best friend and partner Manny (Steven Bauer) then finds out Gina and Manny were married. Tony is unstable mentally in his own right and the mountains of cocaine he ingests fuel his instability. He is violent in every way from the beginning to end of this almost three-hour epic picture. Montana kills enemies by pistol and with automatic weapons in the machine gun category, with a gang war updated since the 1932 version. Both the 1932 and 1983 versions have a motif which is an ironic mantra: both men see the words "The World is Yours." Muni sees it on an electric sign outside his window and Pacino sees it on an air blimp and a statue in his home. Of course, the Capone characters are around only for a short time, as in the end both characters meet their demise. In the 1932 picture there is in an alternate ending where, after being arrested, Camonte is hanged by the state.

The 1983 version is a particularly popular film, especially among a young demographic. The fascination of the viewer experiencing pathological behavior on the screen is partly a case of cheering for the bad guy, partly an antiestablishment attitude, partly for the excitement generated by witnessing screen violence, and partly because the audience fantasizes what it would be like to be in a mindset where violence is in the forefront and control has broken apart.[3]

The Untouchables (1987) is directed by Brian DePalma and features Robert DeNiro as Capone and Kevin Costner as his relentless law enforcement tracker, Elliot Ness. The film is loosely based on the hit television series from the 1960s. This Capone does not have a sizeable scar on his cheek (as do Paul Muni and Al Pacino in the other two films), nor does it address the incestuous feelings he had toward his kid sister, as in the original and rebooted version. In *The Untouchables* Capone has far less screen time. As far as temperament, DeNiro's Capone is a man who seems to be in control but inside is teeming with florid rage. The classic set piece in this film is a room with a very oversized table. Men in formal wear are seated at a dinner party. Menacingly, Capone stands over the group holding a wooden baseball bat. He doesn't say so, but one of these men has betrayed him. Capone walks around the table giving a speech, repeating words and getting more frightening in his tone, becoming steadily more agitated, suggesting his pathological temper is about to blow. He stops and stands over one particular man. To the horror of all, Al Capone lifts the bat high over his head then comes down with brutal force, beating the man to death with repeated hits while blood flies in multiple directions. Intended anger and real violence trample through the picture.[4]

Dutch Schultz, known as "Dutch," "The Dutchman," or "Dutch Uncle," was a vicious mob man who liked tuxedos, as well as a fine suit, fine drink, fine food, fine beverages, women, and a cigar or cigarette; he was insatiably jealous of anyone—friend or foe—who would get near his girlfriends. *The Cotton Club* (1984) directed by Francis Coppola, sports an all-star cast of talented actors, singers, and dancers of African-American backgrounds. This legendary club was in Harlem, New York, and was visited by the elite, famous, the very rich, and the very mobbed-up. The painful irony is that during the 1920s the performers were all black and many of the women were light-skinned African Americans, but no blacks could sit at a Cotton Club table and enjoy the food, wine and liquor, and the spectacular shows featuring one great African-American act after another. This was strictly for the amusement of the privileged white race.

In *The Cotton Club*, Dutch Schultz, played by James Remar in full tilt, loves black music and holds black men in high esteem. The Dutchman is considered crazy because at the drop of a hat he can spray a whole room with machine gun bullets or take out an individual for practically no reason at all with the spitfire of his pistol. He is greedy and wants all the numbers rackets in Harlem; he's not willing to share. Ultimately Schultz is left dead in a pool of blood.[5]

Mad mobsters were created by screenwriters' typewriters borrowing attributes from the real thing; their behavior is often amplified in the violence they commit and their state of mental health.

One of the most infamous movie mob men is portrayed by James Cagney in *White Heat*, in a full-out performance as Cody Jarrett, a criminal without a heart, dictatorial and as vicious as they come. Jarrett's illness is often expressed out of nowhere when Cody gets buzz-saw headaches/seizures which toss him around the room with pain and torment that can only be relieved by the touch and cradling of his mother. Cagney holds his head, grimaces, and makes sounds of pain that start quietly and then explode out of his mouth. This representation of mental illness worked in 1949 when audiences shared the perception that fits were part of mental illness. Today's perception of Cody's mental condition might have been more interior, a little less physical, quieter, and without the body choreography demonstrated by the extraordinary manic movements of James Cagney.

The main character of *Kiss of Death* (1947) is Nick Bianco, portrayed by Victor Mature. He is a low-level hood with a wife (who later commits suicide) and two young daughters who are put up for adoption. Deep down inside he is a decent man who was raised in an environment where there were hardly any choices to live an honest and decent life.

The psychopath of this piece is Tommy Udo, played to the hilt by Richard Widmark. In one of the more memorable scenes in the film, a legendary example of uncontrolled violence, Tommy Udo pushes an elderly woman in a wheelchair down a flight of stairs to her death just to get back at her informer son. Udo has a signature laugh that is more like a cackle and starts evenly and then escalates in rhythm and volume. He has no regard for anyone and has a razor-sharp temper perpetually ready to go off in ways no one can predict.[6]

Sergio Leone's almost four-hour masterpiece *Once Upon a Time in America* (1984) is a time-tripping film. The character of "Noodles" (Robert DeNiro) and his friends grow up from childhood to adulthood, but the scenes are not presented in chronological order. Leone takes his characters back and forth in time, not always landing in what would seem to be a logical timeframe. DeNiro's point-of-view dominates the film. His tormented mind is obsessed by the police murder of the youngest member in his gang. He is haunted by the ghosts of his life. The epic shows Noodles and the other characters grow from kids to old men. Noodles's obsessions are beyond normal, but it is another character Max, played by James Woods with alternating control and then fire, who is severely mentally ill. Max is called crazy by Noodles and others. At the sound of the word he goes ballistic because his dad was "crazy" and died in a mental institution. Maximillian's actions are irrational, sudden, and often without thought. He has so many enemies his life is endangered. At the end it is unclear whether his body is being ground up and shredded in a garbage truck as the vehicle moves towards the camera.

True Romance (1993) is directed by Tony Scott with an original screenplay by Quentin Tarantino. It is basically a story of two unlikely lovers—a call girl, Alabama Whitman (Patricia Arquette), and a once-lonely movie, pop culture, and Elvis freak, Clarence Worley. A key character with mental illness leads to spontaneous and murderous violence partway into the picture. It occurs after Clarence has acquired (stolen, actually) an ultra-large amount of cocaine he found in a briefcase owned by crazed mob boss Vincenzo Coccotti, played with both reserve and rage by Christopher Walken. The scene takes place in a room where Coccotti and his gang interrogate and grill Clarence's father Clifford (portrayed by Dennis Hopper), a former cop who is trying to help his son. Hopper delivers one of the most racist and self-destructive monologue/speeches in motion pictures. He begins by establishing that Vincenzo is Sicilian, then employs a torrent of "N" words and a story woven with hate and disgust as he taunts the mob boss. Vincent seemingly takes it and turns as if to leave, then turns around again and fires a pistol into Clifford until he is as dead as a door nail. Yes, it was motivated, but to kill a man for basically calling him a racist name is far from normal behavior. And why does Coccotti wait until it's over? He doesn't shoot him at the sound of the first, second, or third 'N' word or ugly slur against the Italians, instead he smiles and turns to associates and then back to the tied-up Clifford. He is just beginning to burn with rage, but does not show it to anyone. He gives his victim the respect of finishing with the bile that has been coming out of his mouth. When Clifford stops, Coccotti turns and the result, after repeated pistol shots, is a dead man sitting.

Fight Club (1999) is based on a novel by Chuck Palahniuk that was published in 1996. The film stars Edward Norton and Brad Pitt and was directed by David Fincher. The film was initially a success and over the years has become a cult classic, especially for young men in their very late teens and early twenties. *Fight Club* is not about the Mafia, but because of the nature of the story, it could be. Edward Norton is an unnamed narrator suffering from insomnia. Through his treatment he becomes addicted to support groups. Later his apartment is destroyed by an explosion and he calls Tyler Durden, a soap salesman he befriended on an airplane flight. They switch homes, with the narrator getting the skinny end of the stick. They engage in a fist fight outside a bar which eventually leads to the two men forming a fight club. Many more clubs materialize. Project Mayhem is born and there is much violence and police involvement. The truth behind this unique mob or gang is revealed when it becomes clear that the narrator and Tyler Durden are the same person. Someone has a mental illness; it is most likely the narrator, but perhaps not.

The world of mob gang violence, mental illness, and instability has great range and will always be with us. The names change, the methods change, and some of the crimes have changed. One could say you have to be crazy to be in this life and as demonstrated here—many are.

Notes

1. Brett Martin, *The Sopranos: The Complete Book* (New York: Liberty Street, 2000).

2. Peter Briskin, *Star: How Warren Beatty Seduced America* (New York: Simon & Schuster), 431–51.

3. Douglas Keesey, *Brian De Palma's Split-Screen: A Life in Film* (Jackson: University of Mississippi), 156–65.

4. Vincent LoBrutto, *By Design: Interviews with Film Production Designers* (Westport, CT: Praeger), 188.

5. Gene D. Phillips, *Godfather: The Intimate Francis Ford Coppola* (Lexington: University of Kentucky Press) 226–43.

6. Aljean Harmetz, "Richard Widmark, Film's Hoodlum and Flawed Hero, Dies at 90," *New York Times*, March 27, 2008.

CHAPTER FOURTEEN

How Traditional Holiday TV Movies Depict Mental Illness

Martin J. Manning

Pop culture often addresses serious issues, such as mental illness, in informal ways, sometimes striving to understand the rationale behind irrational acts. Literature, TV serials, and comics offer more opportunities for character development than movies and so can show more nuanced and multilayered renditions of mentally ill characters. In contrast, movies must make major statements in a short time, and thus tend to polarize mentally ill characters as villains or victims. A special genre of winter holiday films—often promoted as "holiday specials"—addresses depression and suicide and even psychosis during the holiday season.

Films about Halloween follow the spirit of the scary neo-pagan celebration and offer some of the most dramatic examples of these themes. Occasionally, films about Christmas can be easily confused with Halloween-themed entertainment, as shown by the film *Black Christmas*.[1]

Winter Blues and Seasonal Affective Disorder (SAD)

People in every culture celebrate holidays. Although the word "holiday" literally means "holy day," most American holidays are not overtly religious but are more commemorative in nature and origin. Because the nation is blessed with a rich ethnic heritage, it is possible to trace some of the American holidays to diverse cultural sources and traditions, even when holidays take on a distinctively American flavor. Americans share three national holidays with many countries, including New Year's Day, Easter Sunday (the major religious celebration in the Christian world), and Christmas Day.

The holiday season begins right before Thanksgiving and stretches into January. It theoretically ends with New Year's Day—but may extend longer for those who celebrate Orthodox Christmas and other variations. Store displays and home Christmas decorations stay up to the end of the month, if not longer.

During this preholiday period, frenetic shopping starts on the day after Thanksgiving and peaks on Christmas Eve. The day after Thanksgiving brings the all-important Black Friday shopping day, which has developed into a holiday tradition of its own, of sorts. On that day, merchant associations voice predictions that the current year, unlike the previous year, will be successful for holiday sales. Catalogs swamp the mail while the newspapers and TV and radio shows advertise "must-have" products. After-Christmas sales, store returns, and cashing in on gift cards stretch out the official holiday season a little longer. Then there are the holiday parties, Santas at the mall, holiday music, and other material trappings we associate with this period.

The rites that surround holidays have been adopted, or even invented by, this pervasive marketing, to the point that the celebration of holidays and the business of holidays have become inseparable. Both December and January bring several seasonal celebrations: New Year's Day and Martin Luther King Jr. Day (in January); Christmas, Jewish Hanukkah, and Afrocentric Kwanzaa celebrations (in December). All holidays conjure up iconic images, such as Baby New Year and Santa Claus. Just before Christmas, Hindus and Jains celebrate the birthday of Ganesha, India's popular elephant-headed deity, which is also an iconic image. There is not just one Christmas but many Christmases: New England Christmas, Southern Christmas, and many different Latin American traditions. Then there is Orthodox Christmas in all its varieties.

Such commercialization is not an artifact of the mid-to-late 20th century. Its origins go back much earlier. In February 1900, one of the nation's leading trade papers, the *Dry Goods Chronicle*, set out the modern vision of the commercial possibilities of holidays.[2] "Easter, in common with the other great festivals of the year," the trade journal related, "has already been recognized as a basis of trade attraction, and, while it commemorates an event which is sacred to many, yet there is no legitimate reason why it should not also be made an occasion for legitimate merchandizing." Two months later the *Dry Goods Chronicle* further generalized the commercial interest in such festivals:[3] "Never let a holiday . . . escape your attention, provided it is capable of making your store better known or increasing the value of its merchandise."[4] The modern, up-to-date businessperson realized the economic potential in holidays, exploited them through sales and advertising, and took the lead in promoting them. Whether the occasion was Easter or the Fourth of July, Thanksgiving or Memorial Day, "wide-awake" retailers were to conjure up "the spirit of hearty celebration" for the purposes of merchandising and consumption.

One of the most important sources of holiday promotion has been the media. Ads for holiday sales appear in the newspapers, films, and television. Films themselves have done their part as well. Films with holiday themes are especially popular at Christmas. In fact, it is almost obligatory that a new crop of Christmas-themed movies comes out around Thanksgiving. Halloween has its own genre of films, with horror films and slashers (with their mentally-ill/cognitively-impaired murderers) as a specific (and now outdated) subgenre of horror. Recall Charlie, Freddy, Michael, and Jason. *Halloween* (1978) and its various sequels (1981, 1988, 1989) are perhaps the best known of these films.

White Christmas, Holiday Blues

Seasonal affective disorder (SAD), which is often conflated with "holiday blues," interferes with some people's enjoyment of the holiday season. SAD is a medical term and is attributed to specific biological responses to environmental changes (such as the shortened days and dimming of sunlight), yet those blues and anxieties are often attributed to other factors: loss of a loved one during that period or feelings of being overwhelmed by the holiday demands (buying presents; obligations to attend or to give holiday parties; gift-giving, buying and receiving; writing greetings to family, friends, and business associates; and other activities associated with these celebrations). This may be a time of sadness for persons who feel alone and alienated by the commercialization of the season and the media's promotion of holidays as feel-good events.

Other holidays can catalyze untoward feelings, but it is the overly promoted and hyped end of the year that seems to affect people the most. Interestingly, SAD usually starts in the autumn, when most stores and commercial enterprises start to promote their holiday wares. When it persists, SAD can obstruct enjoyment of the holiday season. Certain holiday films tap into that sense of sadness, and the need for assurance that such sadness will pass.

Holiday films about Thanksgiving and Christmas show wide variations in mood and content. Some are upbeat and stress family togetherness, but some films show the negative side of the holiday season. There are some old favorites that replay on TV each year, and are more reliable than the weather. Still, Hollywood releases new Christmas-themed films annually, with plots about dysfunctional families and relationships, where a mentally ill family member or associate disrupts the family dynamics. A specific film from 1995, *Home for the Holidays*, presents a paradigm of such plots. In that film, a dysfunctional family gathers together for Thanksgiving. After losing her job and discovering her daughter's plans to spend Thanksgiving with her boyfriend, Claudia Larson decides to spend her holiday with her neurotic mother and her aunt. Needless to say, she does not have a good time.

Some films, such as *It's a Wonderful Life* (1946) and *Miracle on 34th Street* (1947), touch on mental illness, but their searing messages became diluted after the films became holiday classics. These two films are often shown together during the holiday season (from Thanksgiving through Christmas), although their themes are distinctive and each evokes a very different emotional response. For example, the central plot of Frank Capra's *It's a Wonderful Life* revolves around a man, George Bailey (James Stewart), who attempts suicide, but the film sends an endearing message instead as it ends: "no man is a failure who has friends."

This movie (and the character that James Stewart portrays) fosters the "myth of the holiday blues." That movie, more than any available scientific data, has led the public to believe that the December holiday season inevitably brings sadness and even suicide, when, in fact, suicides drop to their lowest levels in December.[5] Unfortunately, news articles have perpetuated that myth, as noted by the Center for Disease Control (CDC).[6]

Capra's wonderful movie shows a hapless man, drunk and depressed, teetering on the brink, ready to end his life on Christmas Eve. Then an angel appears and shows him how the world is a different, better place because of the lives he has touched.

The details deserve attention. George Bailey has spent his entire life giving of himself to the people of Bedford Falls. He has always longed to travel but never had the opportunity to leave town because he felt obliged to prevent rich skinflint Mr. Potter from taking over the entire town. George and his family own a modest loan company, which was founded by his generous father. On Christmas Eve, George's Uncle Billy loses the business's $8,000 as he attempts to deposit the funds in the bank. George expects the bank examiner to discover the shortfall later that night, and then realizes that he will be held responsible and sent to jail. According to this catastrophic thinking, the company will collapse, which will allow Potter to take over the town.

Thinking that his wife, their young children, and others whom he loves will be better off with him dead, he contemplates suicide. In response to the prayers of his loved ones, a gentle angel named Clarence comes to earth to help George, with the promise of helping him earn his wings. Clarence shows George what would have happened had he never been born. In a nightmarish vision in which the Potter-controlled town is sunk in sex and sin, those George loves are either dead, ruined, or miserable. George realizes that he has touched many people in a positive way and that his life has truly been a wonderful one.[7]

In *A Miracle on 34th Street*, Kris Kringle (Santa Claus) is put on trial after an unkindly "psychiatrist" at Macy's deems Kris to be delusional. The evaluation has been engineered by an embittered woman who works for Macy's. At Kris's sanity hearing, a young lawyer not only proves Kris Kringle sane but even gets the U.S. Post Office to admit that Santa does exist!

Although it is considered to be a classic Christmas film, *Miracle on 34th Street* actually begins with the Macy's Thanksgiving Day Parade. Opening scenes show customers shopping in Macy's. The sight of children visiting Santa Claus at Macy's signals that the Christmas shopping season is underway. The film spans these two holidays: Thanksgiving Day to Christmas Day.

Miracle on 34th Street has two main themes. The first concerns Susan Walker and her mother, Doris, and their eventual belief in Santa Claus. The second concerns the socially (and legally) defined concepts of sanity and insanity.[8] Doris is a realist, her attitude toward life colored by her own failed marriage, which was not the fairy tale she envisioned it would be. She has imparted the same sour and cynical attitude to her impressionable six-year-old daughter, Susan. Susan does not believe in make-believe. She spurns "fantasies" associated with Christmas, such as Santa Claus. When Santa Claus becomes an invaluable addition to Macy's, and impresses Mr. Macy himself, Doris learns that the man who calls himself Kris Kringle believes he is the real Santa Claus.[9]

Doris suspects that Kris is insane after he gives his name as Kris Kringle on his Macy's employment card. She brings in Sawyer, who confirms that Kris is "crazy" and that he should be fired, as Doris contends. After Kris calls Sawyer a quack and hits him with his umbrella, Sawyer has Kris committed to an insane asylum. A formal hearing will determine if Kris should be permanently committed, as recommended by the examining psychiatrist. The hearing will allow Fred Gailey to defend Kris and ultimately prove that Santa Claus does exist!

The subplot stresses that Santa really exists and that the self-identified Santa (Kris) is not necessarily "crazy," as claimed. This aspect of the film challenges formal psychiatric diagnoses and asks how sanity (or insanity) is determined and by whom. To counter allegations that Kris is psychotic, Kris Kringle's young defense lawyer, Fred Gailey, arrives with three letters, all addressed to Santa Claus, North Pole. He submits those letters to the court as proof that Kris is the same Santa. The judge tells him he needs more support for his claims about Santa Claus.

Bailey then beckons to the guards to open the doors, at which point the post office employees (who work for the "U.S. Post Office, an entity of the United States government") enter with bags of letters, all addressed to Santa. They dump the letters on the judge's desk. The attorney chides the judge, "Your Honor, every one of these letters is addressed to Santa Claus. The Post Office has delivered them. Therefore, the Post Office Department, a branch of the federal government, recognizes this man Kris Kringle to be the one and only Santa Claus."

Judge Henry X. Harper responds, "Since the United States Government declares this man to be Santa Claus, this court will not dispute it. Case dismissed." The judge has sufficient proof. If an official government agency acknowledges the existence of Santa Claus, so does he. Kris is free. The film comes to an end having preserved the spirit of Christmas and uplifting spirits.

Although *It's a Wonderful Life* and *Miracle on 34th Street* are the best-known films in the holiday and mental illness genre (as it were!), there are others that are of interest. In *Christmas Eve* (1947), also called *Sinner's Holiday*, a greedy nephew of eccentric Matilda Reid seeks her judged incompetent so he can administer her wealth, but she will be saved if her three long-lost adopted sons appear for a Christmas Eve reunion. This film evokes memes about mental illness that are even more relevant today, as an epidemic of Alzheimer's threatens our aging society.

I'll Be Seeing You (1945) was released in the last year of World War II. Shell-shock or combat fatigue (now called "post-traumatic stress order" or PTSD) would soon become a serious postwar issue for returning vets.[10] A shell-shocked soldier (Joseph Cotten) on Christmas furlough leaves the battleground and meets a prison parolee (Ginger Rogers). The story begins.

Hallmark and Lifetime Films

Holiday specials have been a continuous part of television since 1947. Major programming revolves around Christmas, Easter, New Year's, and Thanksgiving. The first such film, *The Story of Easter*, aired on NBC in

1945 as an Easter Sunday evening program. It told the religious story of the celebration through narration over religious paintings, scripture readings, and songs. Annual traditions include the Charlie Brown specials, beginning with *A Charlie Brown Christmas*, on CBS in 1965. Other Charlie Brown holiday specials appeared on Thanksgiving, Easter, Halloween, and Valentine's Day.

One Hallmark film that directly addresses the theme of mental illness during the holiday season is *A Season for Miracles* (1999). When a young woman's niece and nephew are threatened with foster care after her drug-addled sister is hospitalized following yet another overdose, she goes on the lam with the children and lands in the low-key town of Bethlehem, Pennsylvania, just before Christmas. One unlikely coincidence after another offers this unlucky trio opportunities for happiness.

Silent Night, Lonely Night (1969) is a made-for-TV movie that features mental illness. Over the Christmas holidays in a small New England college town, a man and a woman share a brief interlude. He is there to visit his wife, who is a mental patient at the university, and she is there visiting her son, who is a student, after discovering her husband's infidelity. Alternatively, how do we make sense of the character of Scrooge in Dickens's *A Christmas Carol*, with its varied screen and television interpretations, both live and cartoons? Was his miserliness a form of mental illness? Depression increases frugality, to be sure, but the jury is still out on this one.

Disney and *Hans Brinker*

Mental illness as part of the holiday celebration appears frequently in one of the best-known purveyors of family entertainment, Walt Disney. One important story that portrayed this theme quite convincingly was presented as a 1962 Disney two-part television special, *Hans Brinker; or, The Silver Skates*, on Walt Disney's *Wonderful World of Color* television show. The TV show is based on the book by Mary Mapes Dodge but the book and the television version diverge.

Set in 1860s Holland along the famed Zeider Zee, young Hans Brinker finds himself responsible for supporting his family after his father, Raff Brinker, is accidentally injured. A log hits the father in the head as father, son, and other men try to keep the dike from crashing. The father needs an operation. Hans and his sister Gretel travel to Amsterdam in search of funds to pay for their father's surgery. Their only hope lies in the city's annual ice skating race, where Hans must face off against his archrival, Ludwig Schimmel, in hopes of winning the prize money.[11]

In her book entitled *Hans Brinker, or the Silver Skates: A Story of Life in Holland* (1865), Dodge exposes the hardships of poverty and elaborates on the daily grind needed to eke out a subsistence living. Compared to the more explicit Disney version, Dodge shies away from the mental illness issues and deflects attention away from Raff Brinker's amnesia and the reactions of family members and neighbors to his violent outbursts that follow his traumatic brain injury (TBI).[12] Instead of highlighting speculation that Raff is either mentally ill or even an imbecile, Dodge emphasizes the poverty-stricken straits that befalls the Brinkers after the accident.

In *Hans Brinker*, the title character is forced to look for work, doing even odd jobs, while his father is injured. The Disney film juxtaposes opposites to make a major visual impact. There are beautiful scenes of snowy vistas. The St. Nicholas festival (December 6) is celebrated in the town mayor's lavishly decorated house, where well-dressed children enjoy plentiful food and drink. This imagery stands in sharp contrast to Hans's experience. Hans looks through the window at the festivities that he knows his family will not experience. His father, seen as the strong head of the family in the beginning of the film, has become a helpless, uncommunicative parent and remains that way until he undergoes successful surgery at the end of the film. In the film, we witness the accident after we have already gotten to know Raff as his usual self. So, film spectators regard the accident as a temporary setback rather than all-encompassing. In the book, Dodge offers no clues about Raff's character before his accident. Our only glimpse of his real self is fleeting, when Dodge propels the story forward at the very end, to show us what the characters have become.

Halloween and Horror

Horror fans cherish Christmas, too, but seemingly derive their holiday cheer from watching out-of-control persons with psychosis dressed as Santa while wielding an ax. Certain films, advertised as holiday films by their titles, are often more horror films than holiday feel-good family film. Christmas films as horror have all the features of their Halloween counterparts, with the mentally ill slasher and the not-exactly-innocent victims. An example would be the cult classic *Black Christmas*, first produced in 1984 then again in 2006. The plot in both original and remake centers around Billy Lenz, whose mother hates him. One night he watches as his mother and her boyfriend kill his father. Billy retaliates by killing them and poking one eye out of his sister Agnes, who is also his daughter, the result of a forced incestuous relationship with his mother. Billy is confined to a sanitarium for the criminally insane, much like Michael Myers in the *Halloween* movies.

Later he escapes, only to kill the sorority girls now living in the house that he once called home. The sorority girls are confined there over the Christmas holiday, and that may be the film's only link to holiday specials.[13] Otherwise, the film intertwines Oedipal themes and slasher memes, to prove that the worst of the worst can occur on days that should be reserved for the best of the best. Christmas is no different from Halloween in *Black Christmas*.

Notes

1. For plots of the *Halloween* films (original and sequels, with commentary), see Leslie Y. Rabkin, *The Celluloid Couch: An Annotated International Filmography of the Mental Health Professional in the Movies and Television, From the Beginning to 1990* (Lanham, MD: Scarecrow Press, 1998) 312, 459–460.

2. Norman Rosenthal, *Winter Blues: Everything You Need to Know to Beat Seasonal Affective Disorder*, 4th ed. (New York: Guilford Press, 2013). See especially chapter 12, "How Can I Help?: Advice for Family and Friends"; Part 3: Celebrating the Seasons: chapter 13, "A Brief History of Seasonal Time"; chapter 16, "Creating with the Seasons"; and chapter 17, "Words for All Seasons." Three other books of interest include Lawrence C. Rubin, ed., *Mental Illness in Popular Media: Essays on the Representation of Disorders* (Jefferson, NC: McFarland, 2012), which is a collection of essays from domestic and international scholars on a wide range of fields that explore representations of mental illness across various media of popular culture. The second is Andrew Scull, *Madness in Civilization: A Cultural History of Insanity from the Bible to Freud, From the Madhouse to Modern Medicine* (Princeton, NJ: Princeton University Press, 2015); chapter 10: "Desperate Remedies" (pp. 290–322) and chapter 11: "A Meaningful Interlude" (pp. 322–357) discuss the various depictions of mental illness in various media, e.g., film, theater, and opera. See especially "Madness and the Movies" (pp. 351–357) in chapter 11, which begins with a discussion of the first classic silent film that revolved around mental illness, *The Cabinet of Dr. Caligari* (1920). Other films discussed in this section are not holiday films about mental illness but they are specific to the mental illness genre. Some, like *The Snake Pit* (1948), were a breakthrough in their time. Finally, see: Michael Fleming and Roger Manvell, *Images of Madness: The Portrayal of Insanity in the Feature Film* (Rutherford, NJ: Fairleigh Dickinson University Press, 1985).

3. Leigh E. Schmidt, *Consumer Rites: The Buying and Selling of American Holidays* (Princeton, NJ: Princeton University Press, 1995); Sharon Packer, "Beating Those Holiday Blues," *SoHo Life*, December 2012, 20.

4. Schmidt, 18.

5. Greg Eghigian, "The Holiday Syndrome: Who Exactly Came Up with the Idea of Those Christmas Blues?" *Psychiatric Times*, December 6, 2016: 1.

6. Sharon Packer, "Beating the Holiday Blues," *SoHo News*, December 2012, 20; Centers for Disease Control website, http://www.cdc.gov/. See also "Holiday Suicides: Fact or Myth?" http://www.cdc.gov/ViolencePrevention/suicide/holiday .html, which denounces the myth that suicides occur more frequently during the holiday season. For a good overview of the film's theme and allure, see Michael Willian, *The Essential It's a Wonderful Life: A Scene-By-Scene Guide to the Classic Film*, 2nd ed. (Chicago: Chicago Review Press, 2006): ix–x.

7. See Willian for a comprehensive scene-by-scene guide and timeline to the film's action. There are also charts labeling the different stores and buildings in the film's downtown scenes.

8. Rabkin considers this film the casebook on the foolishness and narrow-minded literalism of shrinkdom, centered in the character of the Macy's store psychologist who Rabkin describes as the "embodiment of a contemptible, hen-pecked ass," p. 107.

9. See Sarah P. Danielson, *Miracle on 34th Street* (North Digton, MA: World Publications Group, 2006), which recounts the story line and the history of this Oscar-winning holiday classic in words and pictures. See especially p. 94.

10. See the Internet Movie Database (IMDb), www.imdb.com, for a plot and analysis of this overlooked film.

11. *Walt Disney's Wonderful World of Color*, Season 8, Episode 14, "Hans Brinker; or the Silver Skates: Part 2" (January 14, 1962). Originally shown in two one-hour segments. This was the best version of the story, with magnificent location filming, especially during the skating competition!

12. Marilyn H. Karrenbrock, "Mary Mapes Dodge," p. 150, in "American Writers for Children Before 1900," *Dictionary of Literary Biography*, vol. 42, ed. E. Estes (Detroit: Gale Research, 1986), 146–160.

13. For an interesting discussion on this, see Erik Piepenburg, "Scary Holiday Movies: See You When You're Sleeping," *New York Times*, December 23, 2015, http://www.nytimes.com/2015/12/27/movies/scary-holiday-movies-see-you -when-youre-sleeping.html?hpw&rref=arts&action=click&pgtype=Homepage &module=well-region&region=bottom-well&WT.nav=bottom-well&_r=1.

CHAPTER FIFTEEN

Cotard's Syndrome in *True Detective*, Alien Invaders, Zombies, and Pod People

W. Scott Poole

"I'm the person least in need of counseling in this entire fucking state."

So claims Rustin Cohle in the enormously popular, deeply chilling, first season of HBO's hit series *True Detective*.

Not everyone would agree.

Cohle's precise, systemic nihilism makes him an unlikely television hero. He spends much of the series arguing a deeply unsettling worldview. He succeeds so admirably that many viewers found the optimistic rejoinder to Cohle's ideas in the last episode soporific in relation to the rest of the series intensity.

"I'd consider myself a realist" he tells his dubious partner Marty Hart (Woody Harrelson), "but in philosophical terms I'd call myself a pessimist." Marty somewhat reluctantly prods Cohle to explain what that means and Cohle responds that, "it means I'm bad at parties." Guffawing, Marty says, "let me tell you, you ain't great outside of parties either."

Rust Cohle's philosophy goes further than the tradition of modern pessimism. In episode 3 of the series, entitled "The Locked Room," he suggests that the eyes of the dead contain a revelation, the sudden discovery that they are waking up from "the dream of being a person." Cohle under-stands human experiences, even the most intensely felt emotional experi-ences, as a series of chemical, electrical, and molecular processes. In fact, for Cohle, our subjective experience of ourselves as persons, and certainly as individuals, represents nothing more than the elaborate neurological mapping necessary for our brains to process experience. We are not per-sons. We are our own metaphors.[1]

Most critics and culture watchers agree that Matthew McConaughey's delivery of these ideas from the far reaches of speculative philosophy gave tremendous depth to a show that already offered a many-layered blend of neo-Gothic weird fiction with the police procedural. The series, not sur-prisingly given its conflation of classic horror fiction with true crime nar-ratives, deals explicitly with the blurred boundaries of madness, sanity, and moral evil. In fact, we are left pondering several times throughout the season whether or not Cohle himself bears responsibility for some or all of the murders; whether his "nihilism" has taken on its popularly under-stood dimensions in his character and exploded into a murderous war against life itself.[2]

The *DSM* would diagnose Rust Cohle with major depressive disorder. Indeed, Cohle's case falls into the category of "severe with psychotic fea-tures" given that a focus on "death" and "nihilism" is integral to his philoso-phy. In this medicalized reading of Cohle, his worldview masks a worship of the death impulse, a desire to negate the premises and possibility of life itself. He does not have a philosophy. He displays a set of symptoms.[3]

The horror tradition, especially the "new horror" that began to appear in the late 1960s, has been described from a psychoanalytic perspective as both "nihilistic" and "paranoiac." Horror fandom recognizes this and sometimes celebrates the appellation. It's easy to find online fan lists of "the worst [best] nihilistic films available."[4]

Nihilism has a peculiar history in relation to concepts of sanity. It is perhaps the only philosophical position, not excluding solipsism, that has invited diagnosis. One of its first uses in English, according to the Oxford English Dictionary, appeared in John Charles Bucknill's 1854 *Criminal Lunacy*. In an odd juxtaposition, the author claimed that a devotion to "rationalism" in Continental philosophy has led to "an absolute nihilism."[5]

The most interesting early effort to ponder nihilism in relation to men-tal health appears in Cotard's syndrome. Named for the French alienist who classified it in 1880, the malady includes a range of symptoms from believing oneself dead, to the idea that one's internal organs have disinte-grated or, most important in philosophical terms, the belief that one does not exist as a person.

Called *Le délire des négation* or "the delirium of negation," Cotard's syndrome does not appear in the current *DSM* and its symptoms are placed under the rubric of delusional disorders in *DSM-5* 297.1. The World Health Organization identifies it as symptomatic of a larger disorder. Psychiatry currently regards it as a set of "nihilistic delusions" that accompany schizophrenia. A brief discussion of Cotard's in the summer 2012 issue of the *Journal of Neuropsychiatry* called it "an infrequent condition with monothematic, nihilistic delusions" that can "lower the threshold for violence against others." Hello, Rust . . . or so it might seem.[6]

Subjective rejection of the subjective experience of personhood has several implications for the examination of mental health and horror tropes in popular culture. First, horror's tendency to suggest nihilism as a deeper wisdom about the world jostles with the "positive psychology" trend that began in the 1990s. This movement discouraged a theoretical and contextual construction of mental illness and focused instead on behavioral modification leading to ill-defined notions of happiness. This, William Davies has argued, represented a larger philosophical change in the goal of psychiatric care. Efforts at normalization gave way to therapies to promote happiness.[7]

Second, the medicalization of nihilism ignores an outré, if well-regarded, tradition in speculative philosophy that regards nihilism as something other than a manifestation of a Freudian death drive or as Lacan's notion of attraction and repulsion to the unknown. Several important texts, all of them with explicit links to the horror genre, introduce nihilism as a basic premise for understanding the world rather than a symptom.[8]

Finally, we find a contradiction within popular horror texts themselves over the nature, or ephemerality, of a human person. Some horror tales purposefully avoid the logic of their own self-representation amid flumes of gore and frightening suggestions about the nature of human experience. The demands of commodity production and enthusiastic audience reception frequently prevent films in this allegedly "nihilistic" genre from asking deeper questions about the reality and stability of the self in relation to the larger world of time and things.

The first point requires relatively little argument. The popularity of horror as a genre has actually waxed and waned in relation to American optimism and social crisis. The golden age of the new horror opened in the cataclysmic year of 1968 with *Night of the Living Dead* and closed in 1984 with *Nightmare on Elm Street*. The 1990s proved a slough for both cinematic and literary horror in an era of economic boom and an atmosphere in which neoconservative intellectuals referred to "the end of history" with a sense of elation, insisting that the end of the Cold War meant that democratic reform and free market liberalism would prosper together. Only after 9/11 did a reinvigorated horror genre appear, not only in film but also television, video games, literature, and graphic novels.

In recent years, the horror genre has become more intricately hard-wired into nihilism as a set of ideas rather than simply creating a series of representations that produce a nihilistic affect. A philosophical litera-ture, doubtful of the stability of personhood and the necessity of normal-ization in human behavior, has used the horrific fantastic as a vehicle and reflective tradition. These efforts self-consciously follow the small collec-tion of tales and short novels of H. P. Lovecraft (1890–1937), who asserted that horror must have a "cosmic" dimension that creates "a profound sense of dread."[9]

Lovecraft doubted the substantiality of personhood and believed that representations of emotional affect and even personal belief systems are epiphenomena that human beings engage in to avoid the universe's pro-found lack of interest in their affairs. "Sensations," no larger framework of meaning or even systems shaped by human intellect, are primarily responsible for human values, he told James Morton in 1930.[10]

The horror tales that flowed from this worldview mythologized Love-craft's philosophical premises by creating monstrous alien gods, "Great Old Ones," with no particular interest in human beings. He made his pro-tagonists purposefully uninteresting, in part because their fate is either a welcomed ignorance or, more often, a voyage across what Lovecraft called "the black seas of infinity" that ends in questions about the possibility of human consciousness and meaning.[11]

A large number of recent works have followed Lovecraft in using the horror genre itself as a premise for nihilism. These works have included Eugene Thacker's three-volume *Horror of Philosophy* series, Dylan Trigg's *The Thing: A Phenomenology of Horror*, Benn Woodard's *Slime Dynamics*, and Michel Houellebecq's older work *H.P. Lovecraft: Against the World, Against Life.*

Thomas Ligotti's 2010 *The Conspiracy Against the Human Race* perhaps represents the most sustained and straightforward case for nihilism as a mood and even an aesthetic in line with what the best of the horror genre has proposed about humanity's predicament. Ligotti's short stories are deeply philosophical, aesthetically sophisticated and are perhaps the tru-est heir of Lovecraft's work. In his nonfiction that argues a pessimistic antinatalism, he also offers a powerful target for those in the psychiatric profession who would seek to medicalize nihilism as a system of a larger disorder.

Understanding Ligotti requires some definition of the personhood he denies. He's not a simple determinist (as Lovecraft sometimes seemed to be). He does assert that we have a consciousness but sees that fact as the primary tragedy, evolution's "single calamitous event" and "the parent of horrors." Consciousness acts as "a parent of horrors" in terms of giving us a self-awareness of suffering that makes many experiences utterly unendurable while pushing us toward a creation of a notion of "self" that anchors us against the inescapability of death but also makes us aware of our impending demise.[12]

Consciousness also acts as a parent to the genre of horror narrative. Ligotti, building off some of Lovecraft's comments in his *Supernatural Horror in Literature*, suggests that an awareness of the supernatural comes from the human act of stepping outside of nature, the paradox of having a consciousness wholly determined by nature that imagines it has an integrated self-exercising free will. The very experience of the uncanny comes from a sudden realization of death, that we'll all at least find a personal resolution someday to the philosophical problem of "why is there something rather than nothing."

Horror tales depend on the paradox of belief in a fully intact self. Inanimate puppets that move, the undead that come to life, indescribable Lovecraftian horrors with a profound indifference to the human, manage something more dreadful than suspending the laws of nature. They suggest to us, Ligotti writes, "that we are not what we think we are" and derail our efforts at repressing, denying, and sometimes asserting with all the force that comes with lack of conviction that we are Persons with a Destiny living a Life that, the revealing and paradoxical joke explains, "is better than the alternative." Horror suggests that we are perhaps a broken, self-aware mechanism, an accident, a sarcasm. This can elicit an uncanny response in which our disposition begins to display symptoms reminiscent of Cotard's and, if we express the ideas too loudly and to a concerned medical professional, may give lead to our diagnosis.[13]

The notion of Cotard's syndrome as a delusion, or the more recent conception of its particularities as symptomatic of schizophrenia, assumes that sanity requires us to subscribe to an optimistic philosophical view about not only the nature of life and of death but the nature of the self. Psychoanalyst David Livingstone Smith has described this premise by noting that his field "works on the assumption that the healthy and the viable are at one with the highest in personal terms." Nihilism thus becomes "viewed as signs of a pathological state and treated thereafter."[14]

Popular culture, particularly in the realm of horror, enables us to play with such ideas without risking the terror of the disappearing self, the lurking fear of being a puppet unaware of its truest fate. Human beings, even when they expose themselves to horror, work terribly hard to avoid drawing any ultimate conclusions about personhood. We are, Ligotti claims, exceedingly careful that we "do not catch on to any monkey business that would leave us stripped of our defense mechanisms."[15]

Ligotti's work, per *True Detective* writer and showrunner Nic Pizzolato, proved especially pertinent for the series. He has said that in Ligotti's "nightmare lyricism" he found a new definition of "the hardboiled detective" and a way to think about horror in which the monster and the self are interchangeable. However, the series did end on that off-key optimistic note, something of a conversion on the part of Cohle from his allegedly unhealthy state of mind even though this change in worldview made even less narrative than philosophical sense.[16]

True Detective has not been alone in using themes from the gothic and horror traditions to secure a kind of ultimate victory for the triumphant human personality that sees survival of the person, and the species, as the primary, ineluctable value. Horror, especially in its cinematic form, has safeguarded the sublime (quotes implied) nature of the human person. In fact, those subgenres that tend to steer clear from the "Hollywood ending," that are supposedly the most daring in their willingness to kill the characters we empathize with, are actually the least nihilistic. They pretend to test the borders of our optimism and then either save the hero or turn their horrific death into Nietzschian tragedy (precisely what the philosopher believed gave meaning to human suffering). We often partake communally in cinematic terror agreeing that our most deeply held values about human life and personhood are at risk; how else do we explain the nervous thrill in a packed audience waiting to see a particularly harrowing horror film? However, we risk a peek at the void only to have these commodities powerfully reaffirm what for most human beings provides their core of absolute meaning, that they are a person and that it's better that they are than that they are not.

Zombie tales offer an intriguing example. The zombie film, particularly in the hands of George Romero, has frequently offered piquant social commentary, challenging various aspects of American experience. Kim Paffenroth makes a convincing argument that Romero's oeuvre has challenged classism, militarism, consumerism, racism, and misogyny with ever greater perspicuity.[17]

The zombie seemingly offers an ultimate image of nihilism, a monster that sacrileges the very notion of a stable human person. Vampires transcend human limitations while other traditional creatures of film and folklore represent humans transformed as various were-creatures and witches.

Monsters of cosmic dread shore up the boundaries of the human by presenting us with a threatening Other that displays no human characteristics, reaffirming the meaningfulness and exceptional nature of human experience.

Zombies are animated rotting corpses. Worse, their decaying flesh suggests they have sloughed off personhood and yet continue to mill about, blasphemies of our need to be, and act, as persons. They sometimes follow the impersonal routine they pursued before death, most famously in Romero's *Dawn of the Dead* when we are told that zombies are stumbling to the mall because "they just remember that they want to be there."[18]

However, social critique in the zombie genre, even the most radical, does not question the basic premise of human existence. Romero's films in particular have moved close to an identification of humans and zombies, the suggestion that "we are them and they are us" to such a degree that, in at least two of his major films, audience sympathies are directed toward the zombie itself. However, it's notable that even in these cases we are not encouraged to face the possibility that we are chemical epiphenomena or even to see the zombie as a kind of postmodern "Danse Macabre." Romero's sympathetic zombies are on their way to becoming human, wakening up to the wonders of personhood, usually evidenced as communicative skills and autonomy.[19]

Our most popular current zombie fictions don't even bother with wondering about zombie personhood and depend heavily on what Kyle William Bishop calls the "invasion sub-genre." These apocalyptic and postapocalyptic scenarios center on a small group of diverse survivors with varied personalities, backgrounds, and skills that allow viewers to identify with at least one of these characters. The personhood of such characters, both valorized and sentimentalized, radically contrasts with the undifferentiated hordes that threaten efforts to rebuild the world before the coming of the zombie menace.

A wonderfully entertaining example appears in the gun-toting partisans of humanity's survival in the television (and comic) series *The Walking Dead*. Our heroes are driven not only by the desire to survive and the assumption that this is an unmitigated good; they want to recreate "normal" human experience, which, in the television series, recently materialized as a first-world, indeed, suburban experience (a sort of gated community in fact!) under threat. The spin-off series, *Fear the Walking Dead*, has raised our expectations further. Not only does the zombie not call into question personhood, the human spirit will struggle to maintain rather traditional notions of family, even as it plays with the soap opera and talk show conventions of the "dysfunctional family" trying to "make it work."

We fans, and I am a fan of all these fictions, are tricked; an ideological prank is played. We are shown corrupted flesh that has lost all semblance of humanity, indeed to such a degree that we are asked to question the boundaries of the human and nonhuman (thus the much discussed, though entirely obvious, irony of the title "The Walking Dead"). However, filmmakers and showrunners explore the terror of such a narrative to, at least in the final frame, remind us of some notion of collective humanity. Even the bleakest of such visions—here we think immediately of Danny Boyle's important *28 Days Later*—avoids what Lovecraft calls "the sheer artistic nightmare" and "take(s) a definite stand in sympathy with mankind and its welfare."[20]

Ironically, the supposedly staid, conservative 1950s produced one of the most startling conceptions of the human self to appear in horror film. Generally regarded as a critique of 1950s conformity or a comment on Cold War paranoia, *Invasion of the Body Snatchers* (1956) borrows such tropes but also burrows deeply into our ideas about personhood and the value of human experience. Most distressing for some viewers even today, the film can be read as taking the side of the invading body snatchers, whose creation of empty pod puppets triumphs over the conventionalities of sentiment. As Ligotti points out in his reading of the film, becoming a pod person really does not seem so bad in comparison to the emotional dilemmas and the malignant narcissism of the male lead and some of his fellow townsfolk.[21]

So why does the film end with Dr. Bennell (Kevin McCarthy) screaming in traffic a warning that no one at first attends? What's McCarthy's interesting example of 1950s male hysteria about?

The "body snatchers" are not coming to torture us, kill us, or rule over us. They are simply creating homunculi, organic mannequins and fleshy puppets. The possibility of this in the narrative, and its seductive appeal, calls into question the possibility of an individuated human self. How different, really, are the pod folk from the daily round of human experience in which, the film constantly reminds us, feels both tortured and attenuated by "all that's going on in the world?" The difference is that the parent of horrors, personal consciousness, has ceased to haunt their minds. The "body snatchers" are the trust exorcists. Rather than giving the victims of Ligotti's "conspiracy against the human race" a dubious sense of inviolable self, they free them from the haunted consciousness.

In the last moment of *Invasion of the Body Snatchers*, evidence of this conspiracy prompts the authorities to act. However, credit goes to filmmaker Don Siegel for an ending so unlike most 1950s sci-fi horror, in which the army and the scientific community unite successfully against the threat. We're left wondering if Dr. Bennell and the rest of the human race will continue with their masquerade of essentialist selfhood or not.

Nihilism of the self lives at the roots of the horror tradition, both in the work of H. P. Lovecraft and in filmmakers' increasing desire to turn terror into despair in post-1968 horror films and literature. However, even in the far reaches of experimental horror culture, the self has remained an invincible citadel while the notion of a universe firmly on our side has been bloodied and gored into unrecognizability. In this commitment to an essential value, the horror genre has sided with prevailing psychiatric opinion that to suffer the loss of self signifies the truly unbearable monstrousness, a delusion that must be cured or, in your average zombie, serial murderer, or possession drama, destroyed or exorcized.

So much in the horror tradition acts then as a surprising bromide, appealing to us because it offers danger to the self in order to rescue it. The human self, or at least the idea of it, can survive even as human bodies are gored, possessed, tortured, and turned into rotting versions of their former owners. When you consume such material you are a person reaffirming your unbreachable self. You're not a pod person; your true self can escape the demon that possesses you; you can save the last bullet to preserve that precious personhood. A true detective can decide that stars show evidence that all is not void (rather than the actual astronomical corpse lights they are). Thinking otherwise might require a diagnosis and a program of treatment. Don't you, after all, want to feel better?

Notes

1. The neurological mapping notion of consciousness has been most fully developed by Michael S. A. Graziano in *Consciousness and the Social Brain* (New York: Oxford University Press, 2013).

2. Philosopher Paul J. Ennis described both the influences on Cohle's ideas and his own understanding of how they influenced the character's representation in a February 2014 interview. See Matt Patches, "Ask a Philosopher: What's Up with True Detectives Rust Kohle?" in *Vulture: Devouring Culture*, Feb. 28, 2014, accessed December 14, 2015, http://www.vulture.com/2014/02/philoso pher-assesses-true-detective-characters-rust-cohle-marty-hart.html#.

3. This essay bypasses the controversy over the growing collapse of symptom into syndrome (and vice versa) in the APA and in various revisions of the *DSM*. Philosophical nihilism has, at different times, been read as both symptom and syndrome, though most recent tendencies are to view it as a sign of a deeper malady. Hannah Decker examines the controversy in *The Making of the DSM-III: A Diagnostic Manual's Conquest of American Psychiatry* (Oxford: Oxford University Press, 2013).

4. Han-Yu Huang, *Horror and Evil in the Name of Enjoyment: A Psychoanalytic Critique of Ideology* (Bern: Peter Lang Press, 2007), 38.

5. "Depersonalization disorder" might be considered the fruit of a solipsistic worldview, though it's not an exact match, bearing some relation to so-called "out of body" experiences. See Depersonalization Disorder, *DSM-IV* 300.6, Diagnostic and Statistical Manual of Mental Disorders, 4th ed. Nihilism features a generally peculiar taxonomic history. Its most widespread use in the 19th century occurred in relation to the political situation in czarist Russia after the publication of Mikhail Bakunin's "Reaction in Germany" (1842) and its more widespread usage after the publication of Turgenev's "Fathers and Sons" (1862). Freud did once make an interesting connection between the symptoms of paranoia and the attitude of modern philosophy, but this stray comment has never been fully developed in medical literature. See Sianne Ngai, Ugly Feelings (Cambridge, MA: Harvard University Press, 2005), 399n. 7.

6. Cotard's syndrome is described in detail in a report following an August of 1892 "congress of French alienists" that took place at Blois. The modern discussion of the term that uses "nihilism" as a general description of symptoms appears in Hans Debruyne et al., "Cotard's Syndrome," *Journal of Psychiatry* 2, no. 1 (July 2011): 67. See also "We Are All Zombies Anyway" in the "Letters" section of *Journal of Neuropsychiatry* 4, no. 3 (Summer 2012): 21.

7. See William Davies, *The Happiness Industry: How the Government and Big Business Sold Us Well-Being* (London: Verso Books, 2015), 174–179, 260–261.

8. See Jacque Lacan, chapter IVX, "Love of One's Neighbor, in *The Ethics of Psychoanalysis*.

9. H. P. Lovecraft, "Supernatural Horror in Literature," in *Eldritch Tales: A Miscellany of the Macabre* (London: Gollancz Press, 2011), 425, 6.

10. See David E. Schultz and S. T. Joshi, eds., *H.P. Lovecraft: Letters to James P, Morton* (New York: Hippocampus Press, 2011), 220–221.

11. Lovecraft referred to human consciousness as "a momentary incident . . . the life, images and thoughts of mankind are of the utmost triviality and ridiculousness." See *H.P. Lovecraft Selected Letters III* (Sauk City, WI: Arkham House), 261.

12. Thomas Ligotti, *The Conspiracy Against the Human Race* (New York: Hippocampus Press, 2010), 31, 51, 60.

13. Ligotti notes that psychiatry has tended to see speculative pessimism as "a maladaptation"; see *Conspiracy*, 44.

14. David Livingstone Smith, *Why We Lie: The Evolution of Deception and the Unconscious Mind* (New York: St. Martin's Griffin, 2007).

15. Ligotti, *Conspiracy*, 29.

16. I see no reason to engage with the absurd discussion, picked up by several major new outlets, that Pizolatto "plagiarized Ligotti" in *True Detective*. This accusation appeared five months after he talked at length to the *Wall Street Journal* about the influence of *The Conspiracy Against the Human Race* on his ideas. The claim rests on a notion of plagiarism that works for college exams and

research papers but not the nature of writing fiction and shows no awareness of influence, pastiche, and homage.

17. Kim Paffenroth, *The Gospel of the Living Dead: George Romero's Visions of Hell on Earth* (Waco, TX: Baylor University Press, 2006).

18. *Dawn of the Dead*, dir. George Romero (1978).

19. The increasingly self-aware "Bub" in *Day of the Dead* (1985) began this trend. Romero continued to explore the idea in *Land of the Dead* (2005).

20. Lovecraft, "Supernatural Horror," 446.

21. Ligotti, *Conspiracy*, 91.

CHAPTER SIXTEEN

House, Monk, Dexter, and Hannibal: "Super-Powered" Mentally Ill TV Characters

Lisa Spieker

In contemporary television, mental illness has taken center stage. Writers use it as a basis for character development (e.g., by allowing characters to overcome limitations associated with their illness) as well as motivation for dramatic plot elements (such as a worsening condition or romantic rejections of the afflicted characters due to their illness). However, in some cases mental illness is written in such a way that it professionally enables the characters who suffer from it to such a degree that it is turned into a veritable superpower: protagonists no longer seem to succeed professionally *despite* their various mood-, obsessive-compulsive-, or personality disorders but *because of them*.

Western culture's fascination with mental illness is not a recent development and neither is the association of mental illness with heightened creativity or genius. Socrates was quoted by Plato to have said that "madness, provided it comes as the gift of heaven, is the channel by which we receive the greatest blessings, madness is a nobler thing than sober sense . . . madness comes from God, whereas sober sense is merely human."[1] Touched with divine fire, artists were liberated from the limitations of custom and convention and were capable of great feats of creativity.[2] Over time this understanding of mental illness was discarded in favor of other discourses that saw mental illness alternately as a form of divine punishment, demonic possession, or the result of one's own moral transgressions. The conflation of mental illnesses and creativity or genius was picked up again during the Renaissance and the romantic era when being called "mad" became a point of pride for artists and melancholia in particular was said to heighten the poet's creativity.[3]

These days the stance towards the mentally ill seems to oscillate between fear, stigmatization, or ridicule on the one hand and fascination or even romanticization on the other.[4] I suggest that these vacillations between stigmatization and romanticization are mirrored in cultural products such as television shows. Popular contemporary television shows can express deep-seated cultural beliefs about the nature of disorders of the mind and allow us to gauge which aspects or interpretations the general audience wants to engage with. Even though there are several other shows that feature mentally ill characters, this paper will only focus on Adrian Monk (played by Tony Shalhoub) in *Monk*, Gregory House (Hugh Laurie) in *House, M.D.*, Dexter Morgan (Michael C. Hall) in *Dexter* and Will Graham (Hugh Dancy) in *Hannibal*. I hope to show how these shows present mental illness as the basis of their protagonists' success and discuss what the popularity of the trope may signify about the contemporary stance towards mental illness in Western culture.

Adrian Monk, the "defective detective"[5] and star of the police procedural / sitcom that bears his name, suffers from a severe case of obsessive-compulsive disorder (OCD). Most of his OCD-related behavior presents itself in the categories of cleaning, ordering, checking, and counting compulsions, as well as obsessive worries about having left on the oven or about losing personal items like keys. He also admits to having more than 300 phobias. Some of his phobias are very common, such as fear of heights, needles, snakes, germs, or crowds, whereas others are rather unusual, such as his fear of milk. While many of these symptoms are highly debilitating—in many instances Monk cannot arrest fleeing suspects or criminals because he finds himself paralyzed by his fear of heights[6] or germs[7]—others constitute the basis of his prowess as a detective. Adrian Monk's obsession with cleanliness and symmetry enables him to notice minute clues that escape his colleagues' attention, which ultimately leads him to solving the case. In a scene reminiscent of Sherlock Holmes's meticulous analyses of crime scenes, Monk infers—to the incredulity of other police investigators—that they are looking at a premeditated murder rather than a burglary gone sour as the perpetrator had waited for his victim at least an hour. Like Holmes, who could famously distinguish brands of cigars based on the ashes[8] or notice small idiosyncrasies of typewriters,[9] Adrian Monk possesses extraordinarily acute senses and can sniff out the brand of cigarettes which the perpetrator smoked while he waited. Monk also has an eidetic memory[10] that enables him to reconstruct crime scenes to the last detail. Both the acuteness of his senses and observations as well as his flawless memory are depicted as traits connected to his OCD: throughout the entire series, Monk's brilliant observations and reasoning are interrupted by compulsive gestures (e.g., touching lamps) and anxious questions concerning topics of his obsessive worrying or similar behavior. This direct juxtaposition of socially sanctioned and pathological behavior is not only exploited as a basis for the series' jokes but also suggests a connection. The link is further emphasized by scenes in which Monk's constant scanning of the environment for things that could cause him distress leads to his discovery of vital cues as well as his repeated assertion that his ability to notice and remember so much is "a gift . . . and a curse."[11] While one could argue that Monk's catchphrase is merely a reference to the hardships of an excessive ability to remember minutiae rather than his obsessive-compulsive disorder, a therapist he sees briefly further stresses the connection between his OCD and his detective skills: he suggests that Monk uses his analytical powers as a prop to avoid dealing with his "real problems."[12] In other words, his unique focus on the irregularities of the crime scene or case at hand are born out of Monk's need to cope with his generalized anxiety and his wife's violent death, just as his obsessions and compulsions are. The ninth episode in the third season drives the connection home: frustrated by his recurrent inability to fill out the role of police officer completely, Monk gives in to his psychiatrist's urging and starts to take an experimental drug to reduce the symptoms of his OCD. While Monk does feel more at ease and no longer suffers from his obsessions, compulsions, or phobias, he also loses his crime-fighting superpowers along with his ability to read social cues or even care about the case he is working on.[13] Convinced that he cannot have the gift without the curse, he finally stops taking the pills and becomes his obsessive-compulsive and brilliant self again.

Another figure in contemporary television with exceptional analytical powers and a severe mental illness is Doctor Gregory House. He suffers from recurrent depressive episodes, is addicted to Vicodin, and has alternately been diagnosed with narcissistic personality disorder or "sociopathy."[14] The latter two are ascribed to him because of his disregard for the feelings of others, egocentrism, difficulty in maintaining mutually intimate relationships, the fact that his self-esteem is based on his intellectual and diagnostic success, his narcissistic need for admiration, self-aggrandizement, manipulativeness, and failure to follow hospital rules and laws.[15] Despite these conditions, House mostly remains a high-functioning medical doctor and brilliant diagnostician who can solve the most baffling cases. While these disorders severely disable House personally and socially—over the course of the show he was fired,[16] incarcerated,[17] committed to a mental hospital,[18] on the brink of death,[19] and repeatedly alienated even his most indulgent friends and fellow doctors—they also constitute the basis for his diagnostic success: When House says that he became a doctor to treat illnesses, not patients,[20] he means it. To him, patients are diagnostic puzzles to be solved rather than human beings in need of help. As puzzles, they provide interesting intellectual challenges and opportunities to prove his diagnostic superiority over other doctors. Thus, finding a treatment or cure for the patient is not the goal but rather a test of his diagnostic endeavors: "if the treatment works, he can know *for sure* that his diagnosis was correct."[21] House's focus on an impersonal challenge rather than the patient at hand makes for his abysmal bedside manner but it also explains his extraordinary tenacity and drive. Exactly *because* he uses cases to satisfy his narcissistic need for admiration and to support his instable sense of self-worth,[22] finding the correct diagnosis is of intense personal importance to House and motivates him, time and again, to do whatever it takes. "Whatever it takes" includes manipulating his team and superiors, threatening, mocking, and deceiving patients and their families in order to get them to agree to risky or experimental treatment, and coercing his team into breaking into their patients' houses to gather clues, all of which match the diagnostic criteria of narcissistic and antisocial personality disorder, respectively.[23] House's willingness to overstep legal, ethical, and social rules usually ends up saving his patients, so his more benevolent fellow doctors see his actions as House's idiosyncratic and overbearing way to act in the patient's best interests. Patients generally come to House and his team when other doctors are stumped for answers, making House both a last resort and his actions a necessary evil. It needs to be pointed out, though, that House does not restrict this antisocial behavior to getting ahead in his cases. He constantly manipulates, cheats, lies, and breaks rules in order to get what he wants—regardless of whether this means winning a bet with a friend, antagonizing his superiors, or acquiring drugs.

Even though House also seems to delight in breaking the rules for the fun of it, he also suffers from his inability to foster and maintain the mutually intimate personal relationships he craves.[24] Yet, like Adrian Monk, House essentially must remain his disordered self. Like Monk, House believes that a more ordinary way of relating to the world may lead to more happiness but is ultimately incompatible with his unique analytical gift. Unlike Monk, who seems to choose a life with obsessions, compulsions, and phobias out of a sense of duty as a police officer, House has less altruistic reasons; for him it is better to possess unique talents and be unhappy than to be normal and content.[25]

Dexter Morgan, blood splatter analyst by day, serial killer by night, would trade his deviations for normalcy in an instant; having been traumatized at a very young age, he is, by his own account, incapable of relating to others and even of experiencing the full range of human emotions. In frequent monologues, he agonizes over his alienation from society, the performative quality of all his interactions, wonders what it would be like to *truly* feel happiness or sadness, and considers his secret lust for violence.[26] Because of these traits, Dexter Morgan has been diagnosed with sociopathy—or rather, antisocial personality disorder (ASPD).[27]

Dexter Morgan is no ordinary serial killer: He kills only those who "truly deserve to die." Because his adoptive father, Harry, noticed Dexter's violent and anti-social tendencies early, he developed a plan to both stop his son from spending his life in jail and to "harness [Dexter's] violence toward some form of justice."[28] Harry insisted that Dexter needs to follow a "code" whenever he gives in to "his dark passenger": he can only kill those who are guilty of violent crimes and either escaped punishment or remained unredeemed and thus still constitute a danger to society. As a result, Dexter carefully vets all his victims to ensure they fit the code, and kills in a ritualistic and antiseptic fashion that "echo[es] the US' 'medicalized' death penalty practices."[29] Both Dexter and Harry consider Dexter's actions a corrective to a legal system that cannot always protect citizens from violence as well as it should due to bureaucratic loopholes or human fallibility. Dexter and his killing therefore become necessary evils in that they break the law to better serve the law's purpose, which is protecting the innocent.[30] Dexter's ASPD and his disconnection from others in combination with Harry's code as moral compass make Dexter the ultimate vigilante: he is unencumbered by emotions that could blur his judgement, untouched by the violence he commits yet in control of his bloodlust, isolated enough to freely give in to his violent urges, and a masterful manipulator and liar who (for the most part) manages to hide his double life from his coworkers at the Miami PD and his family. Problems only arise when Dexter becomes increasingly attached to others, such as his girlfriend Rita and their children, because it makes him vulnerable to threats by other killers and causes him to make mistakes due to a lack of sleep and focus.[31]

FBI special agent Will Graham in *Hannibal*, a crime drama/psychological thriller, suffers from an "empathy disorder." No such condition exists in real life, but the audience quickly understands that Will Graham can empathize with anyone, cognitively and emotionally. His character represents pure empathy, i.e., the logical opposite to the concept of "sociopathy." As a profiler, Will Graham needs to empathize with serial killers in order to reconstruct their thinking and methods. While his disorder enables him to provide insights so keen that they seem to be based on mind reading rather than the human faculty to take other perspectives, it becomes clear that it also takes its toll: over the course of the first season Will Graham becomes increasingly unstable because he cannot shield himself from the thoughts, associations, and emotions of the serial killers he investigates. Without "forts in the bone area of his skull"[32] that keep the grotesque yet aestheticized acts of violence at bay, he is forced to share serial killers' emotions and thoughts as if they were his own. His sense of self becomes increasingly elusive and unstable until he (almost) cannot tell anymore whether he has turned into a serial killer himself. Unlike the characters discussed previously, Will Graham has a condition that is entirely fictional, yet it illustrates the mythologization of mental illness and the diffuse way in which it is used to explain superhuman abilities.

Considering the reasons for the rise of sociopathic yet hypersuccessful characters, Adam Kotsko argues that television has created its own version of sociopathy that departs from the clinical definition in several ways and only retains the most enabling and mythical attributes: according to Kotsko "the fantasy sociopath is somehow outside social norms—largely bereft of human sympathy . . . and generally amoral—and yet is simultaneously a master manipulator, who can instrumentalize social norms to get what he or she wants."[33] Unlike real life sociopaths, Gregory House and Dexter Morgan are at times able to empathize, forge and maintain personal relationships, or even care deeply for others. House has a close friend in his fellow doctor James Wilson and an admittedly unstable romantic relationship with his supervisor. Dexter cares for his sister Debra, his son, and his girlfriends. Despite their severe problems to relate, show their true selves or trust others, they gradually overcome some of the interpersonal limitations associated with their condition over the course of the show—without much therapy to speak of. Endowed with a lack of moral intuition and empathy, yet free from extreme impulsivity, or the incapacity to experience mutually intimate relationships, the fantasy sociopath is enabled to function professionally on superhuman levels, whereas real people with ASPD face severe impairments in personality and interpersonal functioning.[34]

Building on Kotsko, I suggest that contemporary television has not only constructed a fantasy sociopath but is in the process of creating an entire fantasy psychopathology. There are several possible explanations for this phenomenon. Kotsko suggests that the immense popularity of fantasy sociopaths is related to a profound cultural unease. According to him, "the average person" is painfully aware of the problems that arise from an attachment to social norms as well as the way those norms are successfully exploited or ignored by "the people who run our world."[35] The average person then projects the opposite of their limitations onto their "conquerors"—which gave rise to the figure of the fantasy sociopath and its intense popularity in contemporary television.[36]

While I agree with Kotsko that there seems to be a demand for larger than life characters that possess incredible skills—a fascination also expressed in Western culture's current interest in superheroes and super-villains—his explanation cannot account for the general rise of characters with mental illnesses other than ASPD. I therefore propose that the conflation of (analytic) genius and mental illness as well as the creation of a fantasy psychopathology can be explained by the two opposing reactions to mental illness in Western culture: fascination and stigmatization. I further suggest that these positions are not as contradictory as they might seem. In his seminal work on stigma, Erving Goffman states that in order to facilitate interactions with strangers and to reduce the cognitive effort required by these encounters, we as a society have developed means of categorizing people and established assumptions according to which attributes are "ordinary and normal for members of each of these categories."[37] Furthermore, we have expectations concerning the types of people we are likely to meet in specific settings. Based on a person's appearance, the setting of the encounter, and the resulting normative expectations on how the individual in question ought to be, we form a working hypothesis on a stranger's social identity, which Goffman called "virtual social identity."[38] A person's virtual social identity includes not only personal attributes such as creativity but also structural ones such as occupation. If an individual differs in one or several attributes from other members of the category available to him/her and if the aspects in which he/she deviates are found to be less desirable, these attributes constitute a stigma. Regardless of other positive traits, an individual is then "reduced in our minds from a whole and usual person to a tainted, discounted one"[39] and in the most extreme cases considered to be "not quite human."[40] Mental illness, despite the efforts and successes of various advocacy groups, still constitutes a stigma. Goffman further claims that "[w]e tend to impute a wide range of imperfections on the basis of the original one."[41]

For example, in the case of anorexia nervosa, one of the additional imperfections commonly ascribed is narcissism; in the case of depression it is weak will based on the assumption that depressed persons could pull themselves together if they really wanted to. However, in some cases we tend to simultaneously "impute some desirable but undesired attributes, often of a supernatural cast, such as 'sixth sense,' or 'understanding.'"[42] Goffman cites the example of blind people, who are sometimes assumed to be great judges of character, as if their impairment allowed them to draw on "special channels of information un-available to others."[43] Likewise, the superhuman abilities of perception, memory, analytical genius, empathy, or manipulation are ascribed on the basis of the characters' original stigma, their mental illness. However, it should be kept in mind that all characters discussed here are enabled professionally by their conditions, yet ultimately miserable. The only way they can achieve happiness is by learning to overcome their disorder, which frequently involves relating emotionally to "normals,"[44] i.e., nonstigmatized or healthy individuals, and often results in a decline of their special powers. The making of mental illness that can currently be found in television therefore simultaneously allows for an increased visibility of disorders of the mind in public discourse and puts forth a romanticized and even positively mythological view on them but also stresses the characters' isolation, unhappiness, or even his/her failure to be a "full human being,"[45] that is capable to experience the entire range of emotions.

Notes

1. Plato, *Phaedrus and the Seventh and Eighth Letters*, trans. Walter Hamilton (Middlesex: Penguin, 1974), 46–47.

2. Plato, *Phaedrus*, 68.

3. Roy Porter, *Madness: A Brief History* (New York: Oxford University Press, 2002), 65–83.

4. See also Porter, *Madness*, 65–83; M. C. Angermeyer and H. Matschinger, "The Stigma of Mental Illness: Effects of Labeling on Public Attitudes towards People with Mental Disorder," *Acta Psychiatrica Scandinavia* 108 (2003): 304–309.

5. *Monk*, "Mr. Monk and the Candidate," dir. Dean Parisot, written by Andy Breckman, USA Cable Entertainment, July 12, 2002.

6. Ibid.

7. *Monk*, "Mr. Monk Takes His Medicine" dir. Randall Zisk, written by Tom Scharpling and Chuck Sklar, NBC, August 20, 2004.

8. See Arthur Conan Doyle, *A Study in Scarlet* (London: Ward Lock & Co., 1888); Arthur Conan Doyle, *The Hound of the Baskervilles* (London: George Newnes Ltd., 1902).

9. Arthur Conan Doyle, "A Case of Identity," in *The Adventures of Sherlock Holmes* (New York: Harper & Brothers, 1892), 56–75.

10. Interestingly, Sheldon Cooper (played by Jim Parsons) on CBS's *The Big Bang Theory* is another highly intelligent fictional who has OCD and an eidetic memory. With him, however, the connection between these two conditions is never made explicit.

11. *Monk*, "Mr. Monk Goes to the Carnival," dir. Randall Zisk, written by Siobhan Byrne, ABC, August 2, 2002.

12. *Monk*, "Mr. Monk Goes to the Asylum," dir. Nick Marck, written by Tom Scharpling and David Breckman, USA Cable Entertainment, August 9, 2002.

13. *Monk*, "Mr. Monk Takes His Medicine."

14. While both the depressive episodes and the addiction to Vicodin are thematized in the show itself, the diagnosis of either a narcissistic personality disorder or sociopathy can only be found in secondary literature.

15. See Mark Alicke, "House and Narcissism: Why Are Flawed Heroes Simply Irresistible?" in *House and Psychology: Humanity is Overrated*, ed. Ted Cascio and Leonard L. Martin (Hoboken: John Wiley and Sons, 2011), 143; Adam Kotsko, *Why We Love Sociopaths: A Guide to Late Capitalist Television* (Winchester, UK: Zero Books, 2012), 2. Henceforth, the clinically more accurate term "antisocial personality disorder" will be used to refer to what Kotsko calls sociopathy.

16. *House*, "Both Sides Now," dir. Greg Yaitanes, written by Doris Egan, Fox, May 11, 2009.

17. *House*, "Que Sera Sera," dir. Deran Sarafian, written by Thomas L. Moran, Fox, November 7, 2006.

18. *House*, "Broken (Part One and Two)," dir. Katie Jacobs, written by Russel Friend, Garrett Lerner, David Foster, and David Shore, Fox, September 21, 2009.

19. *House*, "The Softer Side," dir. Deran Sarafian, written by Liz Friedman, Fox, February 23, 2009.

20. *House*, "Pilot: Everybody Lies," dir. Bryan Singer, written by David Shore, Fox, November 16, 2004.

21. Kotsko, *Sociopaths*, 90.

22. For a more detailed discussion of House's sense of self-worth see Kotsko, *Sociopaths*, 84–93, and Alicke, "Narcissism," 143–151.

23. American Psychiatric Association, *Diagnostic and Statistical Manual of Mental Disorders*, 5th ed. (Washington, DC and London: American Psychiatric Publishing, 2013).

24. His neediness is frequently commented upon both by other characters—his supervisor and sometime romantic partner Lisa Cuddy calls him the "long-distance runner of neediness"—and by House himself. See *House*, "Don't Ever Change," dir. Deran Sarafian, written by Doris Egan and Leonard Dick, Fox, February 5, 2008, and *House*, "Birthmarks," dir. David Platt, written by Doris Egan and David Foster, Fox, October 14, 2008.

25. See Kotsko, *Sociopaths*, 92.

26. For a more detailed analysis of Dexter Morgan's ruminations about his feelings, appropriate emotional reactions, and the way he fakes them, see Bella Depaulo, ed., *The Psychology of Dexter* (Dallas: Benbella Books, 2010).

27. To cite just one example: Adi Jaffe, "The Killer Within," in *The Psychology of Dexter*, ed. Bella Depaulo (Dallas: Benbella Books, 2010), 147–154.

28. Kotsko, *Sociopaths*, 83.

29. Kotsko, *Sociopaths*, 84.

30. Cf. Kotsko, *Sociopaths*, 85.

31. *Dexter*, "Living the Dream," dir. Marcos Siega, written by Clyde Phillips, Showtime, September 27, 2009.

32. *Hannibal*, "Apéritif," dir. David Slade, written by Bryan Fuller, NBC, April 4, 2013.

33. Kotsko, *Sociopaths*, 2.

34. Ibid.

35. Kotsko, *Sociopaths*, 7–8.

36. Kotsko, *Sociopaths*, 7.

37. Erving Goffman, *Stigma: Notes on the Management of Spoiled Identity* (New York: Touchstone, 1986), 2.

38. Ibid.

39. Goffman, *Stigma*, 3.

40. Goffman, *Stigma*, 5.

41. Goffman, *Stigma*, 14.

42. Goffman, *Stigma*, 14–15.

43. Goffman, *Stigma*, 15.

44. Goffman, Stigma, 16.

45. Kotsko, *Sociopaths*, 10.

PART III

Novels, Poetry, Memoirs, and Short Stories

CHAPTER SEVENTEEN

Sanity and Perception in Philip K. Dick's *Clans of the Alphane Moon*

Aaron Barlow

In his 1964 novel *Clans of the Alphane Moon*, Philip K. Dick presents a third way of looking at people whose lives and attitudes move from the norm. For the most part, throughout the history of Europe and America, such people have either been removed from society or society has attempted to bring them into the fold. In both cases, these people, or their differences, become unmentionable in society. Dick presents the possibility of chosen separation—not exclusion—accompanied by acceptance (even celebration) of difference. This embrasure of alterity is at the heart of much of Dick's work, of course, but it is of even greater significance here.

Since the publication of *Clans*, cultural possibilities for alterity manifestation have expanded in ways that could not have been predicted—through the internet and the social media that have grown particularly strong over the past decade. One of the peculiar aspects of the novel (and even of the short story that sparked it), however, is that it can be seen as a metaphor for aspects of contemporary social media—especially for the groups that separate themselves from the mainstream centering around belief in specified conspiracy theories, end-of-time convictions, and other fragmented 'truths' built from personal needs of all sorts. The communities of otherness that result have striking similarities to the clans of the novel though it was never Dick's intent to outline any 'real' future. Instead, he was looking at the idea of the unknown or unseen other through the lens of definition of mental illness. This chapter is an attempt to make sense of that in a much-changed world.

In Philippe de Broca's 1966 film *Le Roi de cœur*, the struggles of World War I allow the overlooked inmates of an insane asylum to spend a day as the residents of the nearby town—the only outsider being a British soldier (Alan Bates) trying to save the town by disarming a German explosive on a timer. At the end of the movie, the former inmates return to their asylum—trailed by Bates.

The movie follows Ken Kesey's novel *One Flew Over the Cuckoo's Nest* by four years. Experience working in a mental hospital tied to his own use of drugs, particularly LSD, had led Kesey to question just who is insane—those society decides to lock away or those with the keys. He makes it even more complicated: many of the inmates in the institution where most of the book takes place have committed themselves voluntarily—they locked themselves up. They prefer the regularized "inside" to what they experience as the chaos without. Is that insane?

That question, raised in both works, is classic and it used to be commonplace: who's crazy, those inside or their minders? Or, by extension into politics, the people or their leaders? This was a prime focus of American discussion during the 1960s, when it seemed that leaders at all levels had spiraled away from any real connection to reality—or that reality wasn't really all that it was cracked up to be in the first place, certainly not in terms of sanity. But the discussions are much older: Hamlet or his uncle? Does either reflect sane leadership? Who commands reality in Chaucer's "The Miller's Tale"? Today, we continue the concern if not the talk. People's beliefs—even people seeming sane—in nonsense is often unshakeable . . . and "people" includes members of the ruling classes everywhere. It is also resurging today, when our leaders seem continually to be other than what they seem. And people, even those leaders, continue to believe in things that are demonstrably false.

The question of normative sanity is resurging in importance today, even though we don't talk about it as much as we used to—not seriously, at least, and in hushed tones. Ours is a time when our leaders seem continually to be other than what they are and whatever sanity they claim appears to be a function of individuality and, oddly, is often excused as political expediency. This is a time when, also, deviation from the norm is less acceptable than ever. It is a time when people, even American leaders, insist on believing in things that are demonstrably false. And that insistence spreads across political, class, ethnic, and religious spectra.

Maybe it has ever been so.

In his 1953 short story (the precursor to his 1964 novel *Clans of the Alphane Moon*) "Shell Game," Philip K. Dick has one of his characters comment, "A myth can be picked up by a whole society, believed and taught to the next generation. Gods, fairies, witches—believing a thing doesn't make it true. For centuries, Terrans believed the Earth was flat."[1] Donald Trump and millions of Americans insist that Barack Obama wasn't born in Hawaii. There are still people convinced that the moon landings were a hoax, that the twin towers were brought down by the CIA, that Lee Harvey Oswald didn't act alone, that Area 51 contains proof of alien visitation. "False flag" has become a commonplace explanation, no matter the incident. This Gilbert-and-Sullivan ("Things are seldom what they seem/Skim milk masquerades as cream"[2]) view of the world even set off a chain of events that led a sociology professor, James Tracy, to lose his job at Florida Atlantic University. In regard to the mass shooting at Sandy Hook Elementary School in Connecticut, he "repeatedly questioned whether the shooting— and other recent mass shootings reported by the media—actually happened."[3] Conspiracies are increasingly seen everywhere and in everything.

Thing is, recognizing that others are being crazy doesn't make you sane—or your beliefs rational or the conspiracies you see real (or false, for that matter). Nor does deciding you are the crazy one somehow give you a better perspective or the bragging rights of being different. This is the point Dick makes in *Clans* and in the body of his work as a whole.

Annie Ross wrote in her 1952 lyrics to Wardell Gray's tune "Twisted":

My analyst . . . said I was the type that was most inclined
When out of his sight to be out of my mind.[4]

These lines are packed with implications, including ones about control, assumptions, self-flattery and relative rationality—all topics Dick would also address. They show, certainly, a willingness to see oneself as the crazy one, reveling in difference in a way that has almost disappeared today, paradoxically in that we now take mental illness more seriously as treatable and mainstreamable than in the past. That is, we see it as a problem we can solve, believing that its "sufferers" are not irredeemable but able (with drugs and counselling) to eventually lead "normal" lives, ones worthy of a lack of notice. Because we don't any longer completely write off those with psychiatric troubles, however, we tend to lose them as metaphors and as vehicles for satire.

Crazily, this has led us to lose sight of our own fragile sanity and the weaknesses of our own subjective (and even variable) stances, grabbing hard onto our personal visions of our own sanities and truth *as truth* in a world increasingly—and documentably—crazy. We can't talk about it.

This has also led us to use diversity as a norming tool, as a means of accommodating difference so that we can then, conveniently, ignore it. It can also make reading a certain kind of book or seeing some movies uncomfortable for some readers and viewers—unless they are shown a path at the end for movement by the different into certain kinds of conformity, generally some sort of acceptance of the particular difference as acceptable as an anomaly—as unworthy of mention. While we claim to celebrate difference, our actions suppress it.

What de Broca, Kesey, and Ross are presenting is something subtly but significantly different from contemporary mainstreaming: their characters are not asking for acceptance from the broader society or a milieu where no one admits to noticing their difference but for the space to live as they see fit. This, for the greater part of society today, is unsettling. Their challenge to conformity, while popular for a time (along with more direct attacks) in the 1960s, is one few of us in the early 21st century are willing to face. More than at any time since World War II, we acquiesce, feeling we have to do things in certain ways.

When someone shows us, by their own actions, that it isn't really true that difference can be ignored, we either find excuses for their special circumstances (a means of ignoring) or turn away. Nonconformity, to have an impact or simply not to be suppressed, now must center on the trivial. Tattoos, septum rings, and odd hair colors replace the substance of alternatives to the mainstream—and make us forget that, for many, the alternative was not simply a choice of style but a necessity determined by inability to force the vagaries of a particular individuality into the confines of conformity. The people in the de Broca movie and the Kesey novel and the narrator of Ross's song aren't trying to be different. They just *are*.

Attitudes toward the different have changed. Take, for example, the greatest success of mainstreaming of our time, homosexuality. Once it was considered an illness on the level of those depicted in *Clans*. Today, especially since the legalization of gay marriage, homosexuality is on the verge of becoming part of the unnoticeable, so normal an aspect of being in society has it become. The exuberance of difference, of a distinct gay culture may well disappear as the unique identity—even when openly hidden—of being gay no longer has more significance than, say, having blue eyes. The same, of course, has been happening for centuries in

America as minorities and immigrants have assimilated into the broader culture. They change that culture for the better, yes, but something good is often also shed—or becomes mere decoration. It may be that acceptance of homosexuality is a triumph for recognition of the importance of alterity within society, but it might also be the same sort of embrasure by the norm that makes difference disappear or become simply decoration (as it does in Alice Walker's short story "Everyday Use"). Or an unmentionable.

Among the deaf, there are those who don't want operations allowing them to hear, not willing to lose the tight-knit community they now inhabit. Yet the pressure to be normalized into the larger culture is strong and, most of us would argue, ultimately necessary. "Mainstreaming" is the word of the day, and has become so in part because of the belittling nature of the old separations.

Unfortunately, one side effect of mainstreaming is a loss of respect for the substance of difference. Difference, in its manifestations, is to be ignored. Once accommodated, it must no longer exist. Another side effect is the loss of a method for discussing difference in art. Illness, among other things, can no longer be a metaphor for the value of distinction.

As a result of all of this, the sheer joy of being unique degrades. No longer can the Luisas of the world luxuriate in their own being, as Luisa does in *The Fantasticks*:

Please, God, please!
Don't—let—me—be—normal![5]

Today, it has become: Please go, please, don't let anyone treat me as anything but normal!

And that may be good—as far as it goes.

But it also can be stultifying. We have become so attuned to the idea of normal being the goal that we have reached the point where any recognition of variance runs the risk of being judged offensive. We hesitate to call anyone fat or old or bald (or any variety of other things) not because these things aren't clear to everyone but because calling attention to these traits highlights deviation from the norm—and that, we have come to believe, is a slap in the face.

Movies like *Le Roi de cœur* or Hal Ashby's 1971 *Harold and Maude* would be approached gingerly today (if made at all)—and *One Flew Over the Cuckoo's—Nest* would be criticized for its naïve take on the variances of mental illness (among other things). The song "Twisted," though still sometimes recorded, might be taken as callous disrespect if it were new.

Clans of the Alphane Moon would be dismissed, were a contemporary Philip Dick to manage to see it published today, as ignorant and insulting. Its basic premise, after all, is based on stereotyping of people suffering from mental illnesses, a doubly heinous crime, for stereotyping is as bad as singling out sufferers of any difference at all from the norm. The novel's plot, logic, and characters also step outside of the expected, further removing it from today's constrained acceptable.

Yet it is just these flaws that make it timely, for it becomes a novel that can awake us from the smugness of our narrow preconceptions and the limitations of our own visions.

Dick, through much of his writing, argues for seeking another way (or ways) of looking at the normal, the different and, in fact, anyone struggling to come to terms with their own existence within a milieu of normalization or even massive differentiation. His concern was right in line with the zeitgeist of the 1960s on the heels of the conformist 1950s that he had struggled against in both his personal life and his writing.

Today, in a society with its own conformity every bit as powerful as that of the "fabulous fifties," though different in compass, we also have need for someone who can present a little of the value of nonconformity while still respecting those needs of individual respect and generalized equality. Dick, if we allow ourselves to look beyond our own norms, can still provide that.

In the 1960s, Dick was relatively unknown outside of the small community surrounding the science fiction genre. His 1962 book, *The Man in the High Castle*, had won science fiction's most prestigious award, the Hugo for Best Novel, but that meant little to anyone not already a fan of the genre. He would not break out until after Ridley Scott's 1982 movie *Blade Runner* (adapted from Dick's novel *Do Androids Dream of Electric Sheep?*) had achieved cult status in the 1990s. Unfortunately, Dick died just before the movie's release.

Though Dick did see himself as a visionary, he never thought of himself as a predictor of the future. He simply tried to reflect his own concerns and those of his milieu. Though he can be seen as having predicted Ronald Reagan (in "The Mold of Yancy" and elsewhere) and had created a character who seems to foreshadow *both* Obama and Trump (Jim-Jam Brisken, an African-American "news clown" in a trademark red wig who becomes president), seeing into the future was never his purpose nor his goal. Though *Clans of the Alphane Moon* does present, we discover, 21st-century dilemmas over belief, Dick was concerned not with what *might* happen in some haphazard future but with what *was* happening around and within him. The fact remains that this very 1960s novel (in respects beyond even its considerations of mental illness) still manages to speak to very real concerns appearing today—though it does so in tones and voices we might not want to hear.

Dick has left us a body of work that may speak to America more than 30 years after his death as vividly as it did to the small science fiction community he addressed in his lifetime. He has become known far beyond the science fiction community for his visions of dystopia, personal salvation, and more. "Phildickian" has become something of a *thing* and cultlike adoration now accompanies his name.

Though not one of his better-known novels, *Clans of the Alphane Moon* fits squarely within the pattern of explorations that has kept his novels vibrant and popular even as times have changed. Yes, the 1960s were a time of questioning not only who was running the asylum but what the asylum was—which was inside, which out? Is there a difference? Yes, since then, Americans have become much more sanguine in their confidence that they know the truth, that they each are the sane one.

Americans also have come to believe, on the other hand, that their truth is common. But, at the same time, visions of "truth" have fragmented even in public perception, something Dick had always explored. The old Quaker joke hits closer today than ever before but Dick (who had Quaker connections anyhow) would have appreciated its truth even more than 50 years ago: Two people in the simple clothes of Quakers of the past are sitting on a bench watching the world go by. One turns to the other, "I think that the whole world is crazy, except for me and thee." A pause. "And sometimes I am concerned about thee."

The clans of the title of Dick's novel are named for contemporary 1960s images of mental disorders, stereotypes that many today would find offensive. They include the Pares (paranoiacs), the Manses (the manic-depressives), the Skitzes (schizophrenics), the Heebs (hebephrenics), the Polys (polymorphic schizophrenics), the Deps (depressives) and the Ob-Coms (obsessive-compulsives). They live in Adophville, Da Vinci Heights, Joan d'Arc, Gandhitown, Hamlet Hamlet, and Cotton Mather Estates—depending on the nature of their "affiliation." The Ob-Coms don't seem to have a town of their own and that of the Deps isn't named. As Charles Dee Mitchell describes the home world of these clans, "Alpha III M2 is a small moon in the Alpha Centauri system used by Earth as a global mental facility. The moon was one giant hospital treating all known forms of mental derangement. The fact that these break down to only a half dozen or so reflects the mid-sixties when the novel was written."[6] Mitchell, like others, goes on to connect the novel to Dick's own experience as a psychiatric patient, but I would hesitate to push that too far.

It doesn't really matter that Dick's categories are capricious and, even for his time, uninformed. His divisions are little more than sly parts of his somewhat comedic frame; never are they meant to be a reflection of professional psychiatric thinking. Behind the satire, Dick is certainly exploring the place of so-called mental illness in relation to healthy society, but he has little interest in exploring the putative diseases of the various groups. Anyway, as Lord Running Clam, a "Ganymedean slime mold" character in the novel, states categorically, "'Insane'. . . is, strictly speaking, a legal term."[7]

It's also a choice:

> "If you'll stay here," Chuck said, "on Alpha III M2 and not return to
>   Terra—"
> "I am staying here," Mary said. "I've already worked it out." She indicated
>   Ignatz Ledebur. "Not with him; this was only for a little while and he
>   knew it. I wouldn't live in Gandhitown—it's not the place for me, not
>   by any stretch of the imagination."
> "Where, then?"
> Mary said, "I think Da Vinci Heights."
> "Why?" Incredulous, he stared at her.
> "I'm not sure. I haven't even seen it. But I admire the Manses; I even
>   admire the one I killed. He never was afraid, even when he was
>   running for his tank and knowing he wouldn't make it. Never in my
>   life have I seen anything resembling that, not ever."
> The Manses," Chuck said, "will never let you in."
> "Oh yes." She nodded calmly. "They certainly will."[8]

This has nothing to do with the reality of mental illness (whatever that may be) but with the realities of structure, perception, and choice. It has to do with the ways a society defines itself, its insiders and its fringe. It has to do with norms and behavioral expectations. Finally, it has to do with the decisions one makes about how one lives one's life.

It is in this last that *Clans of the Alphane Moon* relates most significantly to both *One Flew Over the Cuckoo's Nest* and *Le Roi de cœur*. All three posit mental illness—at least for some people—as a choice. Or rather, recognition of personal difference from the norm as a choice: one can either admit what one is or pretend to toe the standard line.

Of course, as anyone who has struggled with psychiatric disorders knows, choice has very little to do with the work to stabilize oneself in the face of out-of-control aspects of . . . what? Personality? Chemistry? But that doesn't really matter, for that's not what any of these works explores. In all three of them, the conventions of mental illness become devices for exploring the idea of sanity itself. They become means for questioning our assumptions about normalcy—not for exploring the reasons some individuals find their roads veering away from the main drag.

If "insanity" is a legal term, "sanity" must be one, too. In terms, it would follow, of the natural world—that is, the one beyond human constructs—both are irrelevant as they are human fictions.

There are two plot strands in Dick's novel, one concerning the attempt by the residents of the moon to retain independence and the other tracking the deteriorating relationship of Mary and Chuck Rittersdorf back on Earth and, finally, on the moon. Unfortunately, according to Jason Koornick, one of the best and most knowledgeable commentators on Dick's fiction, "With its over-the-top weirdness and convoluted plot structure, *Clans of the Alphane Moon* can be best understood by those with an 'acquired taste' for PKD's style."[9] Koornick sees the book as a work of irony and humor—which it most certainly is—but the novel offers a great deal more than that, as Koornick would probably agree. Reviewing the book online, Bob Wright says it deals "with the human situation before (and yes, quite often to the detriment of) the science. *Clans of the Alphane Moon* is about marriage and divorce, sex and impotence, blackmail, guilt, and self-loathing."[10] Ultimately, though, it is about the meaning of sanity. The importance of the novel today—the reason for reading it—lies in its depiction of the struggle to adapt to a particular mindset while still operating effectively within the broader universe. What makes the novel distinct from the early story of Dick's is this: the adaptation fails in "Shell Game," leaving most of the characters dead and the remnants bent on a course that could prove disastrous to the rest of humanity. Dick, when he wrote the short story, had not yet reached the conclusions about beings and being that would color his career from the 1960s on, ones that posit that there is always the possibility of alternative to destruction. He writes of Mary toward the end of the novel, from the perspective of Chuck: "She, as well as he, as well as everyone on Alpha III M2 including the arrogant Mans rep Howard Straw, struggled for balance, for insight; it was a natural tendency for living creatures. Hope always existed, even perhaps—God forbid—for the Heebs."[11] This is also the conclusion shown by de Broca, when the soldier, Plumpick, shows up at the asylum, naked, and by Kesey, when inmate Bromden smashes the window and leaves the institution.

What makes Dick's novel work is what at first seems simply an amateurish (or rushed) grafting of the Rittersdorf story onto an expanded (from the short story) and much more sophisticated and subtle vision of the society of the moon. On the surface, this book seems simply a cobbling together, a cheap means of reaching the Ace Books word count that Dick had to meet in order to take advantage of that new celebrity (even if only in the science fiction community) resulting from the Hugo award. And that is certainly the case. The parts of the novel can seem uncoordinated and their combination gratuitous. If we don't know their genesis, they can even seem . . . crazy, following a logic unavailable to the rest of us.

Part of the genius of Dick is that he does not follow the rules of his art but ones from other sources completely—even imagined ones, making it possible for him to explore deviation in ways that more rule-bound writers cannot. Yet he still manages to make his work (most of the time) accessible and enjoyable. Even if those in the know about literature look down their noses at him for what they see as a lack of craft, Dick valued his unique explorations and the unique aspects of the characters he created—and even his process of creation. The characters may not fit the norm, but they survive despite being different, and there are plenty of readers who appreciate that more than adherence to standards of authorial craft.

The problem, as Dick might see it, in contemporary society is that we feel it necessary to normalize people *in order* for them to survive. We can't let anyone be different. Not even novelists.

This novel *is* different. Even its characters are. From that "Ganymedean slime mold" Lord Running Clam to the TV comic Bunny Hentman (a precursor to that Jim-Jam Brisken of "Top Stand-By Job" and *A Crack in Space*) to the various inhabitants of the moon, none makes much sense in our standardized terms of character development. Not even the Rittersdorfs do.

Nor should they. Each character exists in a subjective frame that each believes objective—except, of course, for a few of the people on the moon and Lord Running Clam who understand that subjectivity is the norm and objectivity a fiction. The slime mold with the oxymoronic name—the most bizarre of the characters—is the only one who approaches sanity—except for Chuck himself, even though Chuck has been suicidal early in the novel. In fact, when, at the end of the book, Lord Running Clam asks Chuck what his plans are, he says he is going to:

> "Go ahead and found my own settlement," Chuck said. "I'm calling it Thomas Jeffersonburg. Mather was a Dep, Da Vinci was a Mans, Adolf Hitler was a Pare, Gandhi was a Heeb. Jefferson was a—" He hunted for the correct word. "A Norm. That will be Thomas Jeffersonburg: the Norm settlement. So far containing only one person, but with great anticipations for the future."[12]

The point, the final one of the novel, is that even normalcy is only another deviation, simply one of a number of possibilities. The difference, for Chuck, is that his Norm community is tiny. It does not have the strength of numbers that allows it to dominate back on Earth or in our own time. The Norms, even if the community grows, will have to negotiate as equals with all of the other clans. The fact of deviation from the norm becomes a commonplace, not an aberration. The pressure to conform disappears.

The pressure to pretend that all one sees is conformity also disappears. That is, overt recognition of difference is not seen as an affront but as a natural part of interaction; alterity itself become part of the norm. Furthermore, even when, in the novel, traits associated with different of the groups are denigrated, the individuals are not put down because of them. If they are criticized (and they are), it is for their particular personalities. There are no games, no pretenses, no imagining that not mentioning something makes it invisible. Or, to follow one of our contemporary bits of mass insanity, that makes it disappear.

Notes

1. Philip K. Dick, "Shell Game," *The Collected Stories of Philip K. Dick*, vol. 3 (Los Angeles: Underwood/Miller, 1987), 196.

2. Arthur Sullivan and W. S. Gilbert, "Things Are Seldom What They Seem," in *The Complete Annotated Gilbert and Sullivan*, ed. Ian Bradley (Oxford: Oxford University Press, 1996), 227.

3. Susan Svrluga, "University Fires Professor Who Says Sandy Hook Was a Hoax," *The Washington Post*, January 6, 2016, https://www.washingtonpost.com /news/grade-point/wp/2016/01/06/university-fires-professor-who-says-sandy -hook-was-a-hoax/.

4. Annie Ross, "Twisted," *King Pleasure Sings/Annie Ross Sings* (New York: Original Jazz Classics, 1992).

5. Tom Jones and Harvey Schmidt, *The Fantasticks: 39th Anniversary Edition* (New York: Applause Theatre & Cinema Books, 1990), 38–39.

6. Charles Dee Mitchell, "Philip K. Dickathon: Clans of the Alphane Moone," Worlds Without End blog, http://blog.worldswithoutend.com/2011/12/philip-k -dickathon-clans-of-the-alphane-moon/#.Vzxv5pErJhE.

7. Philip K. Dick, *Clans of the Alphane Moon* (Boston: Houghton Mifflin, 2013), 207.

8. Ibid., 210–211.

9. Jason Koornick, "Review of Clans of the Alphane Moon," Philip K. Dick Fan Site, http://www.philipkdickfans.com/literary-criticism/reviews/review-by -jason-koornick-clans-of-the-alphane-moon-1964/.

10. Bob Wright, "*Clans of the Alphane Moon* by Philip K. Dick," PARSEC, http://www.cs.cmu.edu/afs/cs/usr/roboman/www/sigma/review/alphanemoon .html.

11. Dick, *Clans*, 221.

12. Ibid., 217.

CHAPTER EIGHTEEN

Medea, Mothers, and Madness: Classical Culture in Popular Culture

Daniel R. Fredrick

Nothing repulses or shocks a community more than when a mother kills her child(ren), turning from mother to murderer, from a Madonna to a Medea. In literature, that character—Medea, who gets revenge on her cheating husband by stabbing to death their two young boys—is the archetype for today's murderous mothers. In the news of the last few decades, there seems to be an endless supply of prolicidists who could be labeled as modern-day "Medeas." There is Andrea Yates, for example, who, in 2001, drowned her five children to save them from hellfire.[1] Or Lianne Smith, who, in 2010, suffocated both her girl and boy with a plastic bag to avoid surrendering them to government care, a legal requirement because her boyfriend Martin Smith (last names are coincidental) was charged with pedophilia, specifically raping Lianne Smith's eldest daughter for 11 years.[2] Diane Downs could also take this label because back in 1983 she shot her children to free up her dating schedule with Robert Knickerbocker.[3] Then there is Kenisha Berry, who duct-taped her newborn's mouth and nose (to suffocate both the air and the cries for help), leaving "Baby Hope," in 1998, to die in a dumpster.[4] Nor should we forget Susan

Eubanks who, in 1997, murdered her sons to inflict revenge on her ex-husband, a strikingly close parallel to the acts and motives of Euripides's Medea.[5] Unfortunately, the list could go on ad nauseam.

These Medea-type mothers appear frequently in current news reports. Do not these mothers share our biological instinct to rear, protect, and nurture offspring? Do they not share our biological drive to disseminate (and keep) one's DNA in the gene pool? Murdering one's offspring is bizarre for a range of reasons, culturally and biologically, and yet it is a reality. Thus, it should behoove us to explore a wide range of insights into this uncomfortable topic, including the literary and interpretive, to understand more about the features and motives of murderous mothers. This essay will examine Euripides's character Medea to see in what ways she, as a fictional archetype, corresponds to real-life prolicidists.

Homicide: One of The Leading Causes of Death in Children

Today's children are presumably far safer than they must have been in ancient Corinth, the city where Medea murdered her two sons. Rare is the child today without a bicycle helmet, knee and elbow pads, carbon monoxide detectors, allergy-free pillow covers, and daylight savings. Yet, a stupefying statistic from the research of Jaana Haapasalo and Sonja Petaja shows that prolicide (the murder of offspring by a parent) is a leading cause of childhood death.[6] The Centers for Disease Control and Prevention (CDC) list homicide as the third most common cause of death for children ages one through four.[7] The CDC registry, the National Violent Death Reporting System (NVDRS), distinguishes deaths involving legal intervention (e.g. police or prison custody), unintentional violent deaths, "undetermined intent," suicide, and homicide. Homicide is defined as "death resulting from the use of physical force or power, threatened or actual, against another person, group or community when a preponderance of evidence indicates that the use of force was intentional."[8] These specific statistics do not distinguish between parents, relatives, babysitters, or strangers, although that data is available elsewhere, and varies dramatically by region.

Prolicide shocks us today, but we should remember that it was a normal part of many ancient cultures. The Spartans, without flinching, tossed weak-looking newborns over cliffs while the Aztecs sacrificed children for the sake of bumper crops. Even today, we learn of mothers in some countries who are driven to murder female infants because of birth quotas (preferring to keep males) or to spare the girls from a life of abuse.[9]

Profile of the Prolicidist

If homicide is a leading cause of childhood deaths and quite often parents are to blame, it makes sense to identify some features of a prolicidist. The research of Haapasalo and Petaja states that mothers who kill their children were typically "single, young, and living in difficult circumstances."[10] Let's consider these features as they relate to the prolicidists listed earlier: Yates, to start, was not single, nor young. She was 37 at the time of the murders. As far as "living in difficult circumstances," the Yateses had their troubles. They were, for sure, not affluent, living for a long time in a trailer. But Yates seems to have only one of these prolicidist features, for she was neither young nor single. Lianne Smith was even older than Yates, committing her crime at 45. Although unmarried, Smith was dating Martin Smith for a very long time, so she was not alone, as so many single mothers are. Furthermore, Smith was financially secure, owning and running a business in Barcelona, Spain, with her partner Martin, who also earned money from his roles on TV as a hypnotist. In Smith's case, "difficult circumstances" cannot refer to financial difficulties. Instead, Smith's difficulty was figuring out how to protect her boyfriend from the police. Like Yates, Smith only has one of the features of a prolicidist. The other mothers listed earlier also show a mix of the features delineated by Haapasalo and Petaja: Downs was 28 and single but facing no unusually difficult financial circumstances. Perhaps Berry and Eubanks fit the full description. Berry was 20, single, and financially destitute. Eubanks was 33, single, and faced several difficult circumstances, being in massive debt and constantly avoiding her abusive, estranged husband. These infamous prolicidists have "enormous variation in the circumstances surrounding [their] crimes."[11] But to what extent does Medea, the archetype, fit the description as described by modern psychologists?

Single

Is Medea single? Recall that at the start of the drama, Jason is an honored guest in Creon's palace for reasons of which Medea is unaware: Jason marries the princess Glauce. Jason's new wife would force Medea into divorce because ancient Greece was a monogamous culture.[12] How Jason was able to secure a divorce goes unanswered, but presumably his marriage to Medea, a barbarian, was deemed invalid. Was it the fact that Medea was single that triggered her desire to commit prolicide, or was it the *suddenness* of being single? Jason and Medea had no ordinary marriage, no ordinary bond. Medea was in many ways Jason's mentor and superior, for, without her magic, Jason never would have mastered the "fire-breathing bulls" nor gotten past "the serpent that kept watch over the Golden Fleece."[13] Brian Lush explains that the marriage of Jason and Medea was more like a "contract between two aristocratic male warriors . . . than a typical Greek marriage."[14] Thus, one can imagine how the sudden rupturing of not only the marriage contract but the warrior's contract affected Medea. What we can be sure of is that Medea's relationship status is blurred due to the fact that there was no official divorce, and perhaps worse, no official marriage. Similarly, the status of real life Medeas are difficult to classify. For example, how would one define Downs's relationship status? She was involved in parallel relationships, for legally Downs was married, but she was living a single life. She was both betrayer and betrayed. Perhaps one's *feelings* about one's own relationship status override any legal definition of "single"? If so, this is a key similarity among the fictional Medea and modern Medeas who feel single though still legally married.

Age

Age is the most objective feature of the prolicidist. But Medea's age is unknown. She is likely over 30 because she is greatly accomplished in the most urbane and advanced types of sorcery, possessing the power to bring about what I call designer resurrections, wherein the recipient is renewed to life in the more virile years of the early 20s, a gift we hope she bestows on her boys once safe in Athens, and plausible given the fact that Medea protects their corpses, propping them up as if alive next to her in the chariot, a macabre moment of affection similar to Smith cuddling the corpses of her children through the night after asphyxiating them with a plastic bag. Hence, we can assume that because Medea possesses advanced abilities in sorcery and magic, she must be older; but whatever her age, Medea has incredible, youthful energy to survive as a fugitive, to murder anyone who gets in her way, and to plan and execute a royal assassination. It is possible that many modern Medeas are driven by the same youthful energy even if they are older. Yates, for example, was strong enough and possessed the stamina to hold down flailing children as they drowned. Without detailing the physicality one needs to commit murder, there is enough ambiguity in Haapasalo and Petaja's description of a prolicidist to say that just as a prolicidist can feel single even though married, she can also feel and act younger even though older.

Difficult Circumstances

If the terms "single" and "age" can cause some ambiguity, we will face even greater ambiguity with the phrase "living in [a] difficult circumstance." Shelton and Hoffer offer a working definition, noting that a difficult circumstance would include living in poverty, suffering from a lack of education, and domestic abuse.[15] Medea was for sure in a psychologically difficult circumstance, but she was not facing poverty like Yates or Berry. In fact, for her entire life, Medea knew nothing of poverty, brought up as a princess in Colchis, bestowed with a luxurious heirloom, gold and fine thread, which she strategically discarded, using it as a weapon to kill Glauce rather than pawning it for cash later in exile. In contrast to Medea, most prolicidists are struggling in financially difficult circumstances.

Whereas financial circumstances of prolicidists vary, they all experience severe mental or emotionally difficult circumstances. On this point, real life prolicidists are closely aligned with Medea. Yates, for example, suffered from postpartum psychosis and possible bipolar disorder. At the time of the murders, Yates had an irrational belief that Satan was influencing her children, while Downs was diagnosed with narcissistic and histrionic personality disorder.[16] Susan Eubanks was suffering from domestic abuse, and Berry was for sure suffering from mental issues, evidenced by her later conviction of killing her second child—six years after killing her first (ironically while working as a prison guard). For Medea, Jason's betrayal causes her insufferable mental torment which sets her on the path to murder her children. But what exactly are the motives?

Altruistic Filicide: The Murdered Life

According to the research of Susan Hatters-Friedman and Phillip Resnick, there are five main motives why mothers kill their children, a list compiled after studying over a hundred cases of child murders (that occurred within a span of two hundred years). The categories are as follows: (1) Altruistic Filicide, (2) Acutely Psychotic Filicide, (3) Unwanted Child Filicide, (4) Accidental Filicide, and (5) Spousal Revenge Filicide.[17] To some extent, Medea's motives fit neatly in three out of five categories, yet two of the categories (unwanted child filicide and accidental filicide) are not relevant to Medea's story nor the prolicidists discussed here.

The first category, altruistic filicide, is a key trope in *Medea* and is common among real-life prolicidists. In altruistic filicide, the mother kills the child(ren) to release him or her from any form of suffering. Medea's altruistic motive is based on her fear that Creon's soldiers, upon learning of the assassination of the king and princess, will hunt down and butcher the boys. Reid and Gillett confirm this idea but indeed play down Medea's situation, stating that Medea worries about a "suspect step-family who would perhaps not have their best interests at heart."[18] Medea states her position better: "I'll not leave sons of mine to be the victims of my enemies' rage."[19] Recall that Smith shared a similar sentiment, but far less dramatic in terms of life or death. Smith believed that her enemies, the UK authorities, were hunting down her children, but the goal was to protect rather than murder them. In short, prolicidists believe that murder is an act of kindness. This explains why, in the days before the crime, Smith enjoyed a final vacation at the beach with her children before squeezing a plastic bag around their heads. Altruism also explains Yates's motive. To drown the children would spare them from a life of demonic torture. Succinctly put, the altruistic prolicidist reasons that the act of mothering is reciprocal to the act of murder.

Acutely Psychotic Filicide

The second category is called acutely psychotic filicide. It may seem obvious that any mother who murders her own child must be suffering from serious psychiatric problems. However, a recent study challenges the Haaposolo and Petaja study, concluding that, surprisingly, few of the women who murdered their own children "suffered from real psychiatric problems" but did have "troubles."[20] No doubt, confirming psychosis is far more difficult than identifying troubles. Obviously, all the prolicidists highlighted in this section faced troubles. (They murdered their own children, after all.) Thus, we need to look for acutely psychotic traits which are peculiar to murdering mothers so that we can determine what constitutes a "trouble." Sarah LaChance Adams argues that a mother's ambivalent feelings toward her children arise from the mother's attempt to "achieve both intimacy and separation" from them.[21] This ambivalence is a psychological trouble indeed and one with which Medea deeply struggles. For example, Medea reveals that she cannot kill the children because she is moved by their "young, bright faces."[22] Thus, she decides to take the boys to Athens; that is, she will embrace the intimate connection. But, as if hearing voices, Medea screams out an opposing view. She flips her decision. The children will die by her hand, not the hand of her enemies. Medea continues to change her mind, at times choosing intimacy, then choosing separation. Finally, she chooses separation (by death) but not without a last moment of intimacy wherein she feels their hands, their lips, their noble faces and bodies, caressing the "soft skin" while listening to their "breath pure." For sure, Medea's ambivalence identifies a key trouble; must this trouble be acute psychosis? Even though Medea's psychosis is hard to diagnose, it is self-evident that her mental instability is a significant motive for killing her children.

Spousal Revenge Filicide: Battle or Childbirth

The final category, spousal revenge, is the most infrequent reason for why parents murder their children.[23] In the prolicidists noted throughout this essay, only Eubanks was motivated by spousal revenge, a feature which connects her the most to Medea. One piece of evidence that Medea is fueled by spousal revenge is Medea's own confession. At the end of *Medea*, Jason valiantly attempts to save his children, but by the time he reaches their bedroom, Medea has already seated their corpses beside her in her flying chariot. Chariot hovering, Medea shouts to Jason, revealing her motive for the crime, that it was Jason's new marriage which led her to kill the children.

But is sexual jealousy really what motivates Medea? Is the drive to reproduce children ultimately more powerful than the drive to care for them? Surely, reproductive drives will vary among individuals, and as for Medea, it seems that being "wronged in bed" is reason enough to seek vengeance.[24] Seeing Medea's plight from a different perspective, however, Maria Mackay urges us to consider the biopoetic aspects of the *Medea*, arguing that Medea's anger is not ultimately fueled by sexual jealousy but "founded in [Jason's] emotional and material disinvestment" in her and the children.[25] In a sense, then, destroying Jason's children is the logical move, for in doing so she removes *Jason's* DNA from the gene pool, a significant blow to a regal line. Medea suffers nothing biologically because she is still able to reproduce. Thus, Medea's choice to murder her sons is simultaneously fueled by passion while cooled by reason, a paradox noted by Stuart Lawrence, who suggests that at the end of the drama, Medea's reason and passion are not polarized, but fused, one in service to the other: "Medea herself is now two people: Medea the agent and Medea the victim of Medea the agent."[26] Lawrence's ideas are important to note, for they force us to consider gray areas regarding any final comments about, or condemnation of, Medea, now that we have covered her multiple motives.

Gray Areas?

The saving grace of Euripides's *Medea* is that it is, of course, fiction. Even so, it is hard to withhold moral condemnation of the title character. Yet, Reid and Gillett, for example, believe that the moral condemnation one may have for Medea can be clouded if he or she compares Medea to the pregnant women in the following scenarios. First, Reid and Gillett want us to consider "Melissa" who has decided to end her pregnancy at seven and a half months because her partner left her. Knowing that the baby is still in utero, would we feel that Melissa is as horrible as Medea? Or consider the case of "Nada." She is six months pregnant and has hypertension-of-pregnancy syndrome so severe that if her blood pressure rises excessively, she could die. The only way to ensure Nada's survival is to abort the child. Whereas the Melissa scenario may still make one uncomfortable, the Nada scenario is no doubt not as controversial, for parents are under no legal or religious obligation to die for their children. Finally, and less sympathetically perhaps, we have "Olga," who is five and a half months pregnant and, after some soul searching, decides her child will be "too great a burden" and thus will undergo an abortion. From these hypothetical scenarios, we realize that "The closer we get to conception, the more ambiguous are our intuitions about the moral judgments of the concerned [i.e. the child]."[27] These scenarios, I argue, however, although intriguing, do not relate to Medea nor the prolicidists highlighted in this piece, for they deal with unwanted, unborn children.

So, what possible conclusion could a literary interpretation offer on such a dark and heinous crime? What do we say when such a disturbing piece of Greek drama so closely and so often aligns with harsh human reality? After all, isn't a Medea far more likely to appear in the news than an Oedipus or an Orestes? The key difference, of course, is that Oedipus and Orestes murdered adults, not children. Because children are innocent, vulnerable, and defenseless, it would be remiss of me to recline, to recommend that readers merely take in my analysis for its modest insights into a classic Greek drama and how it relates to modern-day news. Rather, I shall urge the reader to continue his or her perusal of the subject in the hope that prevention and cure is found. But where would one start? Perhaps the first step is to consider the ideas of Barbara Barnett, who prescribes that we "present infanticide in the broader context of gender inequity and to examine disparities in punishments for women convicted of murdering their children."[28] How soon should we get started? If we read the news for the next three months, there is a strong chance we will learn of a new case of prolicide somewhere in the world.

Notes

1. Jim Yardley, "Mother Who Drowned 5 Children in Tub Avoids a Death Sentence," *New York Times*, March 16, 2002.

2. Sam Greenhill, "Lianne Smith Jailed for 30 Years for Murdering Her Baby Son and His Sister, 5, in Their Spanish Hotel Room," *Mail Online*, July 3, 2012.

3. Sean Dooley, "The Diane Downs Story: 1983 Murder Case Focuses on Mom," *ABC News*, May 12, 2010.

4. "Woman Accused of Abandoning Babies," *Lubbock Avalanche-Journal*, August 10, 2003.

5. Tony Perry, "4 Boys Killed; Wounded Mother Is Suspect," *Los Angeles Times*, October 28, 1997.

6. Jaana Haapasalo and Sonja Petaja, "Mothers Who Killed or Attempted to Kill Their Child: Life Circumstances, Childhood Abuse, and Types of Killing," *Violence and Victims* 14, no. 3 (1999): 219–239.

7. Sara G. West, "An Overview of Filicide," *Psychiatry (Edgmont)* 4, no. 2 (2007): 48–57.

8. Ibid.

9. Cheryl Meyer and Michelle Oberman, *Mothers Who Kill Their Children: Inside the Minds of Moms from Susan Smith to the Prom Mom* (New York: New York University Press, 2001), 2–8.

10. Jaana Haapasalo and Sonja Petaja, "Mothers Who Killed or Attempted to Kill Their Child: Life Circumstances, Childhood Abuse, and Types of Killing," *Violence and Victims* 14, no. 3 (1999): 219.

11. Meyer and Oberman, *Mothers Who Kill Their Children*, 2.

12. Walter Scheidel, "A Peculiar Institution? Greco-Roman Monogamy in Global Context," *The History of the Family* 14, no. 3 (2009): 280.

13. Euripides, *Medea and Other Plays*, trans. Philip Vellacott (New York: Penguin Books, 1963), 31.

14. Brian Lush, "Combat Trauma and Psychological Injury in Euripides' Medea," *Helios* 41, no. 1 (2014): 30.

15. Joy Shelton et al., *Behavioral Analysis of Maternal Filicide* (Cham, Switzerland: Springer International Publishing, 2015), 70.

16. Deborah Denno, "Who Is Andrea Yates? A Short Story about Insanity," *Duke Journal of Gender Law & Policy* 10, no. 1 (2003): 1–139.

17. Susan Hatters-Friedman and Phillip J. Resnick, "Parents Who Kill: Why They Do It," *Psychiatric Times* 26, no. 5 (2009): 10–12.

18. Matthew C. Reid and Grant Gillett, "The Case of Medea: A View of Fetal-Maternal Conflict," *Journal of Medical Ethics* 23, no. 1 (1997): 23.

19. Euripides, *Medea and Other Plays*, 30.

20. Clotilde Rouge-Maillart et al., "Women Who Kill Their Children," *American Journal of Forensic Medicine and Pathology* 26, no. 4 (2005): 323.

21. Sarah LaChance Adams, *Mad Mothers, Bad Mothers, and What a "Good" Mother Would Do: The Ethics of Ambivalence* (New York: Columbia University Press, 2014), 32.

22. Euripides, *Medea and Other Plays*, 49.

23. Phillip Resnick, "Child Murder by Parents: A Psychiatric Review of Filicide," *Psychiatry* 126, (1970): 325.

24. Helene Foley, "Medea's Divided Self," *Classical Antiquity* 8, no. 1 (1989): 80.

25. Maria Mackey and Arlene Allan, "Filicide in Euripides' Medea: A Biopoetic Approach," *Helios* 41, no. 1 (2014): 64.

26. Stuart Lawrence, "Audience Uncertainty and Euripides' Medea," *Hermes* 125, no. 1 (1997): 53.

27. Matthew C. Reid and Grant Gillett, "The Case of Medea: A View of Fetal-Maternal Conflict," *Journal of Medical Ethics* 23, no. 1 (1997): 20.

28. Barbara Barnett, "Medea in the Media: Narrative and Myth in Newspaper Coverage of Women Who Kill Their Children," *Journalism* 7, no. 4 (2014): 420.

CHAPTER NINETEEN

Narratives in *The Snake Pit,* *I Never Promised You a Rose Garden,* and *Girl, Interrupted*

Jessica N. Lee

In his 2012 "Teaching about Mental Health and Illness through the History of the *DSM,*" Joshua W. Clegg declares that "the ways that mental illnesses are defined have always been, and continue to be, principally by consensus rather than in terms of organic pathology."[1] The implications of Clegg's statement imbue representations of mental illness in popular culture with particular significance, highlighting the ways in which reflections of popular culture as seen in books and movies affect and are affected by the consensus that governs how mental illnesses are determined. In what follows, I trace the evolution of diagnosing psychiatric illness in the United States. In particular, I juxtapose the development of the American Psychiatric Association's (APA) *Diagnostic and Statistical Manual of Mental Disorders (DSM)* with narrative accounts, each based on the author's experience with inpatient psychiatric hospitalization. This comparison provides a unique perspective through which to view the ways in which an ever-evolving diagnostic system necessarily affects depictions of mental healthcare.

The function of diagnostic labels in the United States' mental health system holds significant rhetorical force and material consequences.

Diagnostic labels are dangerous in their potential to stigmatize those diagnosed. Yet categorizing and labeling a person's mental health distress, while criticized, also serve an important rhetorical function. Specifically, defenders of diagnostic labels point to the ways in which such a system allows medical professionals to learn from and utilize treatments that others have attempted for persons with similar, if not the same, diagnoses. Additionally, defenders of diagnostic labels cite the ways in which this categorization of illness can add to the body of medical knowledge and advance more effective treatments.

In the absence of a system that would allow for the effective treatment of individuals suffering from mental afflictions without the need for a diagnostic label, it becomes necessary to acknowledge the rhetorical force and material consequence of diagnostic labels by understanding the framework in which they are situated. In particular, recognizing the impossibility of a "theory-neutral" system of classification for mental illness, as well as acknowledging assumptions about mental illness reflected in different classification schemes employed in mental illness diagnostic systems such as the APA's *DSM* can do much to mitigate any harmful consequences of categorizations that would unnecessarily pathologize difference.

1918: *Statistical Manual for the Use of Institutions for the Insane,* National Committee for Mental Hygiene

Before the advent of the classification system the United States uses to determine types of mental issues today, as represented in the *Diagnostic and Statistical Manual of Mental Disorders,* the *Statistical Manual for the Use of Institutions for the Insane,* first published in 1918, served as a tool for health practitioners to record and keep track of mental health abnormalities. The *Statistical Manual* was primarily concerned with the biological manifestations of mental distress and, as such, contained instructions for its users on "how to prepare uniform 'statistical data cards for each patient, including mostly demographic information (age, ethnicity, occupations, etc.)' along with some basic information about the presenting 'psychosis.'"[2] Although revised in 10 subsequent editions, the overall biological method identifying and organizing mental health issues persisted into the 1940s.

1946: *Medical 203,* Office of the Surgeon General, U.S. Army Service Forces

The widespread practice of classifying mental illness primarily by its biological effects was disrupted in 1946 by *Medical 203,* a medical bulletin of military nosology for the United States Army directed by psychoanalyst William Menninger, a World War II brigadier general and the head of psychiatry in the Office of the Surgeon General.[3] *Medical 203* was revolutionary for the ways in which it reframed thinking about mental health issues. Rather than primarily focusing on biological and behavioral deviations, *Medical 203* attempted to identify and organize shared environmental and/or experiential precursors for various manifestations of mental distress. Some scholars speculate that this shift from focusing on the biological to the psychological causes of mental pathology was also, in part, motivated by World War II and the Holocaust and a subsequent desire to renounce anything German-related, including the "systematic study of psychopathology that had distinguished the German school."[4]

1946: *The Snake Pit* (novel)

This shift in U.S. psychiatry from psychopathology to psychoanalysis is the context in which Mary Jane Ward's *The Snake Pit* was received. Published in 1946 as a work of fiction, Ward nevertheless "admitted that *The Snake Pit* is based on personal experience" and as such was understood as an "important document in the education of the public [. . .] call[ing] attention to the inadequacies of even [the U.S.'s] better institutions for the mentally ailing."[5]

In *The Snake Pit*, the protagonist is Virginia Cunningham, a recently married woman who has unexpectedly found herself in an unfamiliar, frightening environment. Part of the fear Virginia experiences has to do with the gaps she has in her memory, specifically her inability to recall how or why she has come to be in such a place, or what the place itself even is. Gradually, Virginia is able to piece together where she is—a mental hospital—but returning to her "everyday" life with her husband (who himself seems, at times, unreal to Virginia) proves to be immensely difficult, as she deals with both the precipitating reasons for and the devastating effects of her hospitalization.

The Snake Pit provides a personal perspective of how shifting approaches to diagnosis—in particular, how diagnosis rooted in psychoanalytic understandings of mental health—impacted mental healthcare. The book's only direct statement of what Virginia "has" comes well into the advancement of the plot, and is even then only revealed by Robert, Virginia's husband, as opposed to her presumed "diagnoser," her psychiatrist, Dr. Kik. Robert informs Virginia of her diagnosis during one of his visits to the hospital. Robert and Virginia have a picnic outside, spreading a blanket out on the grass. However, when Virginia becomes weepy about being separated from Robert because of the hospitalization, Robert stands up and declares, "'I think we had better sit on a bench now. I'll put the rug around you. You mustn't catch a cold.'"[6] In response, Virginia laments, "'I wouldn't mind having a cold, double pneumonia or something I could understand. [. . .] What's the matter with me? Is it a brain tumor?'"[7] Robert and Virginia's subsequent exchange is as follows:

> "God, no," [Robert] said. "Whatever made you think that?"
> "I don't know," Virginia said. "I just now thought of it."
> "It's a nervous breakdown," he said.
> "That doesn't sound so bad, does it?"
> "It takes time, that's all."[8]

Why is Virginia only told of her diagnosis now, several months into her hospitalization and after nearly a dozen shock treatments?[9] And why is the announcement of her diagnosis made so casually, almost as an aside, by her husband, and not by her doctor? Whether this is even her "official" diagnosis is anyone's guess, as Virginia's conversations with her doctor make no mention of what she is being treated for. I argue that such a cavalier attitude towards Virginia's diagnosis is indicative of the general societal attitude toward diagnosis at the time, when the *Statistical Manual for the Use of Institutions for the Insane* and its biological explanations and categorizations of mental illness were being discarded for *Medical 203*, with its heavy emphasis on psychoanalysis. More important than Virginia's diagnosis seems to be determining the root cause of her mental distress. For those who would believe the diagnostic process is an example of a way to determine the root cause of a mental illness, the minimization of Virginia's diagnosis in her treatment can be understood as a devaluing of determining specific biological causes and subsequent medicinal responses in favor of identifying the "powerful emotional charges, usually attached to certain infantile and childhood developmental practices" that Virginia is repressing and thereby causing her mental distress.

1952: *DSM-I*

The next stage of the U.S. mental health diagnostic system is embodied in the first edition of the *Diagnostic and Statistical Manual of Mental Disorders* (*DSM-I*), which was published in 1952. For the most part, there was little difference between the *DSM-I* and *Medical 203*, as both shared the conceptualization of mental health issues as rooted primarily in environmental causes. It was the *DSM-I*'s reiteration of a focus on psychoanalysis that led, in part, to the need for a subsequent edition. Shorter explains that "the psychoanalytic period began to be rung out with the introduction of effective new pharmaceutical agents."[10] In particular, the tricyclic antidepressant imipramine was launched in the United States in 1959, shifting approaches to mental healthcare back to biology.

1964: *I Never Promised You a Rose Garden* (novel)

It was within this context that Joanne Greenberg's *I Never Promised You a Rose Garden* was published. First printed in 1964 under Greenberg's pen name, Hannah Green, *Rose Garden*, like *The Snake Pit*, was semiautobiographical: "In real life, [Greenberg] was 'Deborah' [the protagonist of *Rose Garden*] and Dr. Fromm-Reichmann was 'Dr. Fried' [Deborah's psychiatrist]."[11]

In *Rose Garden*, 16-year-old Deborah is institutionalized by her concerned parents following Deborah's increasingly antisocial behavior and recent episode of self-harm. Deborah divides her time between reality and a world which exists in her mind, named "Yr." What first began as a coping mechanism for the harshness she experiences in reality, however, is rapidly overwhelming Deborah and blocking her ability to interact in the "real world," separate from Yr. Upon being hospitalized, Deborah is treated by the famous Dr. Fried, who takes Deborah on as her sole clinical case in the midst of a life of research, teaching, and lectures. Together, Dr. Fried and Deborah determine the significance of Yr for Deborah, in particular, the corresponding traumatic events in Deborah's life that have caused her to create Yr's elaborate infrastructure. Though Deborah does eventually recover, choosing reality over Yr, Greenberg resists providing an immediate, tidy moment of transformation, instead depicting the shades of grey often present in one's quest towards mental health. Deborah's journey towards becoming a functioning member of society is gradual, as she goes from being restricted to the ward, to the hospital grounds, to having town privileges, to living outside the hospital in the neighboring town while continuing to participate in therapy at the hospital. Deborah also suffers several setbacks requiring repeated hospitalizations but, importantly, such hospitalizations do not send Deborah back to square one. Instead, Deborah continues to learn and grow from her relapses, the overall effect of which is a nuanced portrayal of living and ultimately functioning with mental illness.

Given the waning popularity of psychoanalysis, the aftermath, in part, of a renewed interest in biological understandings of the workings of the mind, it is perhaps not surprising that, unlike *The Snake Pit*, the reader learns Deborah's diagnosis fairly early on in the novel. Depicting Dr. Fried's deliberation of whether to take on Deborah's case, Greenberg introduces readers to Deborah's formal diagnosis through the eyes of Deborah's future psychiatrist, a point of view automatically imbued with authority by virtue of her credentials. That readers learn of Deborah's diagnosis through Dr. Fried's point of view also stands in stark contrast to how *The Snake Pit*'s protagonist's diagnosis is declared, almost an aside by her husband as a "nervous breakdown." In *Rose Garden*, readers learn of Deborah's diagnosis when Dr. Fried "[sat] down with the [Deborah's case] folder, opened it, and read it through."[12] Deborah's initial diagnosis is schizophrenia, a conclusion that is partially explained by subsequent notes on the results of testing: "Tests show high (140–150) intelligence, but patterns disturbed by illness. Many questions interpreted and overpersonalized. Entire subjective reaction to interview and testing. Personality tests show typically schizophrenic pattern with compulsive and masochistic component."[13] This greater emphasis on testing and diagnosis in comparison to *The Snake Pit* thus reflects the evolution of the U.S. diagnostic system, as diagnosis moves to take center stage.

1968: *DSM-II*

In the late 1960s, despite the waning popularity of using psychoanalysis to understand and treat mental distress, the framework of *DSM-II*, published in 1968, varied little from *DSM-I*. The impetus for the second edition of the *DSM*, managed by Ernest Gruenberg, was the forthcoming eighth edition of the World Health Organization's *International Classification of Diseases* (ICD), thus prompting a desire to coordinate the U.S. diagnostic system accordingly.[14] Clegg notes, however, that "the account of this process, as well as *DSM-II* itself, makes it clear [. . .] that the ICD was changed much more than was the *DSM*."[15]

1980: *DSM-III*

The advent of the *DSM-III* in 1980 marked a "profound break" from the previous classification systems of *DSM-I* and *DSM-II*. Shorter comments that "the success of the new psychopharmacology had demonstrated that the brain was involved in illness after all and that biological perspectives were the field's future."[16] In 1973, the APA commissioned a new edition of the *DSM* and asked Robert Spitzer, a biometrician at Columbia University, to direct the task force. The displacement of psychoanalysis with diagnoses entailed "explicit attempt[s] to remove all evidence of early psychodynamic explanations for disorders."[17] Of particular significance was the concept of diagnostic criteria, "the list of symptoms a patient would require in order to 'get into' the diagnosis."[18] With these diagnostic criteria came "the removal of explicitly theoretical descriptions,"[19] which Clegg argues "left *DSM-III* without any clear basis for the diagnostic categories provided, other than the consensus of clinical judgment."[20] This "consensus of clinical judgment" was considered valid when compared with empirical evidence, reflecting "the growing belief that the diagnosis and treatment of mental disorders would have to be based on 'data.'"[21] With the *DSM-III*'s "medicalization" of psychiatric diagnoses came a reframing of the understanding of the very concept of mental illness itself. No longer necessarily caused by traumatic events of the past, mental illness was now presumed primarily the product of biological, anatomical issues.

1987: *DSM-III-R*

With this renewed focus on the biological causes of mental illness, the accuracy of diagnostic criteria came under scrutiny. In response to data from new studies that were inconsistent with the *DSM-III*'s diagnostic criteria, revisions on the third edition began in 1983, a short three years after the first publication of the third edition. Clegg observes that revisions in the *DSM-III-R* "included renaming and reorganizing some categories (perhaps the most significant of these changes being the addition of the new category 'developmental disorders'), removing and adding a small number of categories, and changing some of the diagnostic criteria for various disorders."[22] The basic etiological perceptions of mental illness that saw such problems as stemming from biological matters, however, remained the same.

1993: *Girl, Interrupted* (novel)

Seven years after the publication of *DSM-III-R* and one year before the publication of *DSM-IV*, *Girl, Interrupted*, a memoir by Susanna Kaysen, was published in 1993. Although *Girl, Interrupted* recounts Kaysen's experiences as a psychiatric inpatient in the late 1960s, specifically 1967–1969, the biological understandings of mental illness that were already under way during this period but not formally reflected in the *DSM* until the third edition are evident in Kaysen's narrative of her hospitalization.

Unlike *The Snake Pit* or *Rose Garden*, *Girl, Interrupted* makes no claim to be fiction, instead categorized fully as a memoir and an unapologetic exposé of Kaysen's reality as a psychiatric inpatient. Perhaps the most

striking thing about *Girl* is the narrator's (Kaysen's) somewhat conten-
tious relationship with the reader. Rather than treat the reader as a trusted
confidant to whom she is disclosing a stigmatizing experience, Kaysen
instead seems intent on demonstrating the reader's complicity with the
system that hospitalized her. Kaysen juxtaposes the actual reports by various mental health professionals obtained from her case file with her own
recollections detailing how the reported events occurred, challenging
readers to "pick a side" when her accounts and the case reports do not
match up. Overshadowing Kaysen's credibility is her official psychiatric
diagnosis, which readers are confronted with on the very first page of
Kaysen's memoir, in "Image 1" from her "Case Record Folder":

Diagnostic Impression at Admission

1. Psychoneurotic depressive reaction.
2. Personality pattern disturbance, mixed type. R/O Undifferentiated Schizophrenia [. . .]

32A. Established Diagnosis, Mental Disorder
Borderline Personality.[23]

Kaysen's diagnosis, as well as the diagnoses of her fellow patients, are
conspicuously highlighted in her overall narration, mirroring the *DSM*'s
conversion back to a biological comprehension of mental illness. Kaysen
taints her narrative by making her diagnosis her readers' first impression
of her, then forces readers to acknowledge their biases towards her because
of her diagnosis. Strategically, Kaysen does not challenge her diagnosis
right away, but instead waits until the very end of her recollection, after
she has been discharged from her nearly two-year psychiatric hospitalization. By this point in digesting her story, readers have become acquainted
with Kaysen-as-mental-patient through several vignettes Kaysen provides
of key moments during her stay. Readers may even feel a kind of connection with Kaysen and as a result experience similar feelings of confusion
as to why Kaysen has been hospitalized. The moment of revelation
comes when Kaysen finally reads her diagnosis, what she describes as the
"charges" against her, 25 years after her hospitalization. And then, upon
obtaining her diagnosis, Kaysen "had to locate a copy of the *Diagnostic and
Statistical Manual of Mental Disorders* and look up Borderline Personality
Disorder" to determine what the medical staff "really thought about
[her]."[24] After presenting the *DSM-III-R*'s word-for-word explanation of
the diagnostic criteria for borderline personality disorder, Kaysen system-
atically annotates the diagnosis, comparing and contrasting the diagnostic

criteria descriptors with her own state of mind during the period she was diagnosed. This endeavor ultimately produces an unsettling indictment against the validity of the diagnostic criteria for borderline personality disorder. Overall, the major role comprehending her diagnosis plays in Kaysen's interpretation of her psychiatric inpatient hospitalization stands in stark contrast to both *The Snake Pit* and *Rose Garden*'s portrayals of their mental health care experiences. Kaysen's emphasis on her diagnosis might thus be construed as a representation of the influence of the *DSM*'s transformed epistemology of mental illness.

1994: *DSM-IV*

In 1994, one year after *Girl, Interrupted* was published and seven years after the publication of its predecessor, the *DSM-IV* was published. Started the same year the *DSM-III-R* was published, "work on *DSM-IV* began in 1987 so that 'development could be coordinated with the ongoing development of the 10th revision of the *International Classification of Diseases*',"[25] paralleling a similar motivation to create *DSM-II*. The creation of the *DSM-IV* was also reminiscent of the formation of *DSM-II* in that both, for the most part, "focused primarily on the reorganization of categories and criteria, rather than on any major theoretical shifts."[26] Appreciable changes that did occur were "a greater emphasis on culture-specific aspects of diagnosis—including new discussion of 'cultural variation,' 'culture-bound syndromes,' and ways of reporting 'cultural context.'"[27] Clegg points out that such inclusion of multicultural awareness assumed "the *DSM-IV* must not be culture specific but instead be applicable cross-culturally."[28] Furthermore, in addition to the inclusion of culture-specific aspects of diagnosis, the *DSM-IV* contains "an explicit endorsement of a bio-psycho-social model of disease—that is, a model in which the very notion of 'mental' disorder is 'a reductionist anachronism of mind/ body dualism',," and the clarification that "most, if not all, mental disorders result from a complex and varying interplay of biological, psychological, and environmental risk factors."[29] However, changes to the revision process itself, intended to make the process "more systematic than in previous revisions"[30] through "obtaining and reviewing empirical input through three distinct, but interactive, stages, namely, literature reviews, data reanalyses, and field trials"[31] conducted by "those persons likely to be critical of the conclusions of the review,"[32] cast doubt on the sincerity of the *DSM-IV*'s problematization of the concept of mental illness. Denying understandings of mental illness based on beliefs in mind-body dualism accomplishes little when evidence of a mind-body dualism train of thought is present in actions that equate reviewing empirical input with "more systematic" methods for understanding mental illness.

2015: *DSM-5*

Perhaps in an effort to temper any questions related to the validity of the DSM given the comparatively rapid rate of editions between *DSM-III*, *DSM-III-R*, and *DSM-IV* (seven years between each edition versus 12 years between the *DSM-I*, *DSM-II*, and *DSM-III*), the *DSM-5* was published 21 years after its predecessor. Never one to beat around the bush, Shorter characterizes the *DSM*'s fifth edition as giving the impression of "an identical description of 'depression' [. . .] crop[ping] up on every other page."[33] In doing so, Shorter seems to imply that the next, necessary evolution for psychiatric diagnosis will concern the concept of "depression." Only time will tell.

Concluding Thoughts

I began this chapter speculating on the implications of understanding definitions of mental illness as primarily influenced by consensus rather than presumed knowledge about biological characteristics. In particular, I raised questions as to how comprehending mental illness as primarily defined by consensus might emphasize the influence of representations of mental illness in popular culture on overall concepts of what constitutes mental illness. I traced the evolution of the APA's *DSM* as a way to evaluate changing conceptions of mental illness, comparing these conceptions with popular narrative accounts of those characterized as mentally ill. In general, correlating the *DSM*'s implications of what it means to be "mentally ill" with the specific labels given to authors of popular narratives on mental illness demonstrated the reciprocal relationship between scientific methodology and popular portrayals. Given the interdependency of psychiatric diagnosis with popular representations of mental illness, we would be wise to not dismiss popular representations out of hand, instead recognizing the valuable insight such narratives can provide on conceptualizations of mental illness.

Notes

1. Joshua W. Clegg, "Teaching about Mental Health and Illness through the History of the *DSM*," *History of Psychology* 15, no. 4 (2012): 369.

2. Edward Shorter, "The History of Nosology and the Rise of the *Diagnostic and Statistical Manual of Mental Disorders*," *Dialogues in Clinical Neuroscience* 17, no. 1 (2015): 61.

3. Shorter, 62.

4. Shorter, 62.

5. Granville Hicks, "P-N Fiction," *The English Journal* 35, no. 10 (1946): 529.

6. Mary Jane Ward, *The Snake Pit* (New York: Random House, 1946), 102.

7. Ward, 102–103.

8. Ward, 103.

9. Ward, 103.

10. Shorter, 62.

11. David Dempsey, "Shrinks and the Shrunken in Modern Fiction: The Psychotherapist as Villain," *The Antioch Review* 46, no. 4 (1988): 515.

12. Hannah Green, *I Never Promised You a Rose Garden* (New York: Holt, Rinehart and Winston, 1964), 18.

13. Green, 18–19.

14. Clegg, 365.

15. Clegg, 365–366.

16. Shorter, 63.

17. Clegg, 366.

18. Shorter, 65.

19. Clegg, 366.

20. Clegg, 366.

21. Clegg, 367.

22. Clegg, 367.

23. Susanna Kaysen, *Girl, Interrupted* (New York: Vintage Books, 1993), 1.

24. Kaysen, 150.

25. Clegg, 367.

26. Clegg, 367.

27. Clegg, 367.

28. Clegg, 367.

29. Clegg, 367.

30. Clegg, 367.

31. Clegg, 367.

32. Clegg, 367.

33. Shorter, 66.

CHAPTER TWENTY

Edgar Allan Poe's Unreliable Narrators, or "Madmen Know Nothing"

Caleb Puckett

From his poetry to his fiction, Edgar Allan Poe has consistently drawn readers into his texts with the prospect of entering narratives where the fantastic, aberrant, or horrific expose the tenuousness of the mundane world. The lasting appeal of many of Poe's most popular tales largely lies in their ability to make readers question the stability of the worlds they embrace and the mental and spiritual properties which inform their understanding of them. Poe consciously positions readers to play psychologist and detective—to see the texts before them as a condition to be identified and difficulty to be solved. Poe elicits fascination, skepticism, and finally judgment from his readers by asking that they analyze the veracity of his tales, the sanity and moral fitness of his narrators, and their own proclivities as seemingly rational human beings in a bid to piece together narratives capable of revealing truths about the human experience.

The sensation of instability underpinning or even defining many of Poe's stories has proven to be one of the most piquant, rich, and seductive aspects of his work as a whole. In this respect, Poe's use of the unreliable narrator has proven particularly powerful, for it has allowed sensational-ism to coexist with propriety and the fantastic to coexist with the conven-tional in ironic and illuminating ways. As a student of the Gothic tradition in literature and budding science of psychology (then operating in the guise of phrenology), devotee of crime journalism, lover of puzzles, hoax-ster, and market-minded writer, Poe was keenly aware of the abilities of the strange, macabre, and mysterious to attract readers' attention, and he routinely exploited those very abilities in an effort to secure a devoted readership. Ever the showman, his "narratives are designed to appear too crazy not to be believed" and too disturbing to be ignored.[1] However, Poe was not merely interested in selling stories and securing himself a place as a steadily employed scribbler with a reputation for morbid titilla-tion. Instead, he was interested in exploring the dimensions of identity and the margins of reason, all the while creating a highly participatory art of unmistakable aesthetic merit.

Poe's deliberate effort to develop slippery narratives and make investi-gators of his readers—to consciously pull his audience into the meaning-making process—has far less to do with providing immediate satisfaction to his audience and much more to do with sharpening the observational skills of his readers and inviting them to question what stands in for their reality. At the heart of such an approach is Poe's "desire to stimulate sus-picious reading"—to prompt readers to acknowledge language as a most malleable analytical tool and interpretation as a personally revelatory act.[2] Poe's mission in many cases, then, is to encourage the sort of skepticism necessary for readers to break through the surface-level assurances they are so often used to encountering in fiction and in life. Poe wants us to doubt our own sense of consistency as much we doubt the consistency of others.

Poe makes extensive use of the unreliable narrator in his short fiction. With stories such as "The Black Cat," "The Tell-Tale Heart," "The Cask of Amontillado," "The Fall of the House of Usher," "The Man of the Crowd," and "William Wilson," among others, he employs the figure as a means to induce readers into a host of interrogative acts. As Nicol points out, Poe's stories typically follow a pattern "with the narrator confessing to be in some unusual state of mind, a remark which is the prelude to the strange behavior detailed in the story, and which functions as a warning to the reader about his reliability as interpreter of the fictional world depicted in the tale."[3] This pattern does indeed serve as a warning, but it also func-tions as an invitation for readers to play a role in exposing the tale's irreg-ularities or outright falsehoods and in cobbling together its ostensible actualities. Poe's use of unreliability, then, is a call for readers to think through their conceptions of normalcy and impose some semblance of order on what appears disordered or abnormal in nature.

Throughout Poe's works, as Gruesser explains, this "unreliability should be seen as a matter of degree comparable to the concept of insanity."[4] Indeed, unreliable narration in Poe's writing—whether situated as an intentional or unintentional act on the part of the narrator—is virtually synonymous with some form of mental instability and, by proxy, deviance from social norms. If one associates fidelity and stability with being right and good, Poe's narrators are also universally corrupted and, in some cases, corrupting influences on those who take in their tales. Driven by fear, arrogance, or incomprehension, their delusions and self-serving fabrications can have a curiously seductive rather than repulsive effect on many readers. Indeed, the spectacle and message provoked by their insanity can prove too alluring to resist, yet it can also prove too abnormal for readers to fully accept. Readers find themselves constantly pulled towards acts of reconciliation. They want to square their understanding of the world with a presentation of that world that actively resists easy conformity.

Poe presents some of his unreliable narrators, such as the one in the horror classic "The Black Cat," as patently suspect, while he presents others, including the narrator in "William Wilson," as much more ambiguous in nature. With the former type, even the most casual reader understands that madness is both the cause of the story and the principal code operating throughout the narrative. The narrators of such tales repeatedly give themselves away as madmen and criminals. With the latter type, however, readers encounter articulate, seemingly lucid beings who have purportedly fallen victim to strange or malevolent forces and wish to elicit understanding or even a sense of comradery from their audience. Upon closer reading, though, such narrators also show themselves to be suspect by revealing inconsistencies and gaps in their perception of themselves and the presentation of their stories. Poe's narrators in all cases are creatures suffering through a dissonance between intention and actuality, individuals twisted by self-distorting views. McCoppin, in explaining this self-distortion, observes that "Many of Poe's narrators are so enveloped within false personas that they become unclear of their own realities and their own true identities. [. . .] Poe's depiction of these characters shows their unconscious obsession to unmask themselves, revealing a self that does not adhere to societal expectations."[5] The challenge for these narrators, and indeed readers themselves, is to reconcile the terms of that splintered sense of subjectivity as it manifests itself in thought, word, and deed. The challenge is to derive sensibility from madness.

The narrator in "The Black Cat" lays bare this challenge for reconciliation in the story's opening: "For the most wild, yet most homely narrative which I am about to pen, I neither expect nor solicit belief. Mad indeed would I be to expect it, in a case where my very senses reject their own evidence. Yet, mad am I not—and very surely do I not dream."[6] Readers, immediately alerted to the narrator's potential for unreliability, must approach all subsequent discourse with skepticism and continually make judgments about the verisimilitude of the narrator's actions and expressions. Readers must also judge those actions and expressions in light of the personal and larger social values which they have attached to their identities. Aware of the roles that mental conditioning and ego play in reading, Poe understood that readers could not help but work through the inconsistencies they encounter in a bid to moderate, interpret, and ultimately control the terms of the narrative and its narrator. The desire of readers to overcome the challenges set forth by Poe's tale and avoid being duped by the narrator effectively primes them to complete the story and ensure the success of its various effects.

Poe was certainly no stranger to employing games and provocations to further his aims as an artist or make a larger philosophical point about human nature. If we accept that judgment is never a neutral act, it is clear that an important function of Poe's unreliable narrators is to compel his readers to judge and, through the act of judgment, reveal aspects of themselves in the reading of his texts. Readers cannot help but show the colors of their subjectivity once they construct an interpretation. Indeed, as Nunning observes, "Determining whether a narrator is unreliable is not just an innocent descriptive statement but a subjectively tinged value-judgment or projection governed by the normative presuppositions and moral convictions of the critic."[7] When readers engage in detection and the interpretation of an unreliable text, they inevitably expose their own beliefs and biases—lay bare core components of their identity. Poe uses the instance of such exposure to usher readers into a state where self-reflection and philosophical speculation can take hold. In recognizing Poe's ability to turn the act of investigation back on readers, McCoppin makes a salient point about the function of the author's narrators:

> The reader understands that their invented obsessions define them as insane. Yet the structure of these works also induces readers to question what they believe to be reality; Poe's works reveal that reality is limited by subjective perception. If one's unconscious can force itself to be recognized, and if that 'true' self is not socially acceptable, then Poe's fictional horror comes to life, compelling readers to question their own self-identification.[8]

The very terms of a reader's reality, then, are at stake during the act of interpretation. Even if readers choose to push away what distresses them and slip back into the relative comfort of their long-held paradigms of truth, they are nonetheless aware that their identity and world are not quite as simple and stable as they seem. They are haunted, to a greater or lesser degree, by Poe's inducement to question their reality.

In identifying the narrator of "The Black Cat" as a mad and sadistic agent of his own destruction, readers complete one of Poe's desired effects: they seek out the stabilizing influence of their own values and create a horror story out of the unmistakable dissonance they encounter when working through the narrator's confession. The disquiet they face comes from the recognition of the radical differences between the text and their reading—the presentation of the story and its supposed actualities. Along the way, they are forced to question both the narrator's and their own interpretive susceptibilities. In the end, a story like "The Black Cat" foregrounds madness in an explicit fashion as a means to prompt readers to examine their values and identity, if for no other reason than to seek solace in the frameworks of their own sense of rationality and normalcy. Interestingly, Poe practically inverses this formula in a piece like "William Wilson" by foregrounding the tenuousness of identity—both ours and the narrator's—and leaving questions regarding the narrator's degree of deceptiveness and likelihood of illness almost entirely in the hands of his readers.

Like "The Black Cat," Poe presents "William Wilson" as a confession. Indeed, even though the story prompts readers to solve a mystery involving the existence of the narrator's moral nemesis and apparent double, the narrative chiefly functions as a declaration of guilt. Much of the text consists of the narrator recounting his transgressions in detail and conceding his guilt in a seemingly contrite and forthright manner. Yet it is obvious that the narrator is not simply trying to clear his conscience. Instead, he is making a case for his own victimhood and asking readers to grant him absolution. One might argue that he is seeking accomplices to help soothe his conscience. Wilson uses his introduction to beseech readers to look on his case with kindness:

> I long, in passing through the dim valley, for the sympathy—I had nearly said the pity—of my fellow men. I would fain have them believe that I have been, in some measure, the slave of circumstances beyond human control. I would wish them to seek out for me, in the details I am about to give, some little oasis of *fatality* amid a wilderness of error. I would have them allow—what they cannot refrain from allowing—that, although temptation may have erewhile existed as great, man was never *thus*, at least, tempted before—certainly, never *thus* fell.[9]

Once readers have the narrator's request for sympathy embedded in their consciousness, the principal mystery of the tale involving the identity and function of Wilson's doppelganger engenders another mystery: how much culpability should they ascribe to Wilson for the problems he encountered and crimes he committed? When addressing this question, readers must also determine how much lucidity and sincerity they should rightly ascribe to Wilson before granting or denying him his sought-after sympathy. Through the ensuing text, Poe consistently forces readers to assess the accuracy of Wilson's version of events and his intentions as a narrator. Readers are faced with two potential forms of unreliability to consider during those assessments: the text's intranarrational unreliability, i.e., contradictions within Wilson's narrative, and extratextual unreliability, i.e., contradictions stemming from their own perceptions of truth or personal standards when applied to Wilson's version of events.[10] Added to the question of Wilson's accuracy or reliability as a narrator, readers are also prompted to ask if he is advertently or inadvertently trying to put something over on them—attempting to steal a sentiment for personal gain. In a larger sense, as Hartmann notes, Poe presents readers with the option of taking up a "moralistic" reading, "a fantastic (supernatural)" reading, or "psychological reading" of Wilson's story.[11] Depending on the dispositions of readers and how they choose to receive Wilson's confession, he can be seen as a pitiable and altogether sympathetic man afflicted by forces he could not stop or escape, a culpable but nonetheless forgivable man whose imperfections of character were compounded by strange circumstances, a mentally sound but loathsome manipulator seeking goodwill under false pretenses, a mad criminal reveling in his crime and indicting himself with yet another deception, or a madman whose delusions make him both a frightening and tragic figure.

By orchestrating the aforementioned range of interpretations of Wilson's behavior, Poe effectively outs his readers and prompts them to consider how their judgements are reflections of social conventions and the makeup of their own psyches. Seen from the perspective of Poe's understanding and application of phrenological principles to his fiction, one might easily turn the diagnostic properties of Poe's work back on readers themselves and place them into typologies according to the conclusions they have drawn from their readings. In such a case, the shape of one's reading is tied to the shape of one's mind which, in phrenological terms, is tied to the shape of one's head. Poe presents us, then, with an opportunity to identify our own mental and moral faculties—be they cautious, compassionate, or even murderous in nature.

Ever the ironist and provocateur, Poe may well have intended for the true subject of his texts—the center of inquiry or problem to be untangled—to be his audience itself. At root, as Nygaard writes, Poe consciously cultivated unreliability and "was fascinated by what he called 'mystification,' by duplicity, obfuscation, manipulation" throughout his career.[12] Putting aside the perverse pleasure Poe may have derived from mystifying readers, one of the primary functions of his mystification is to transport his audience beyond the surface of the text and, by proxy, from the veneer of lucidity that covers mundane existence into the shadowy regions of the human mind and heart. The unreliable narrators and motif of insanity his readers encounter throughout his poetry and fiction provide just such a dynamic. In the end, then, those mystifying madmen who, in the words of the narrator in the "The Tale-Tell Heart," ostensibly "know nothing" demonstrate the potent capacity to turn readers onto something truly revelatory about the identities and worlds they have assembled for the sake of navigating their waking lives.[13] Poe constructs the detective and psychologist in order that they may deconstruct themselves through the act of knowing.

Poe's ability to turn the act of textual analysis back on readers has given his writing a nearly inexhaustible richness and prescient quality. Indeed, the mysteries he presents or suggests remain as penetrating and varied as the minds of his readers irrespective of the age they inhabit. Poe's ability to perform such a feat has also proven inspirational for scores of artists over the years, giving rise to numerous works of film and literature which borrow, extend, or reenvision that central interrogative impetus. As McCoppin writes, "Poe's theme of the self-obsessed narrator" continues to remain "popular in contemporary times because of its important ability to compel audiences to question their own identity and reality."[14] One need only look at a popular contemporary work such as *Fight Club*—with its allegiance to the spirit, techniques, and thematic implications of "William Wilson"—to see Poe operating anew. In a postmodern world, we are compelled to take on such questioning, if for no other reason than to test the consistency, rightness, and relevance of the systems which have long regulated our thoughts and behavior. Poe's use of unreliable narrators and madmen will doubtlessly prompt us to face those systems we have constructed and our place in them for the foreseeable future.

Notes

1. Jonathan H. Hartmann, *The Marketing of Edgar Allan Poe* (New York: Routledge, 2008), 82.

2. Bran Nicol, "Reading and Not Reading 'The Man of the Crowd': Poe, the City, and the Gothic Text," *Philological Quarterly* 91, no. 3 (2012): 487.

3. Ibid., 479.

4. John C. Gruesser, "Madmen and Moonbeams: The Narrator in 'The Fall of the House of Usher,'" *The Edgar Allan Poe Review* 5, no. 1 (2004): 86.

5. Rachel McCoppin, "Horrific Obsessions: Poe's Legacy of the Unreliable and Self-Obsessed Narrator," in *Adapting Poe: Re-Imaginings in Popular Culture*, eds. Dennis R. Perry and Carl Hinckley Sederholm (New York: Palgrave Macmillan, 2012), 105.

6. Edgar Allan Poe, *Complete Stories and Poems of Edgar Allan Poe* (New York: Doubleday, 1984), 63.

7. Ansgar Nunning, "Reconceptualizing the Theory, History and Generic Scope of Unreliable Narration: Towards a Synthesis of Cognitive and Rhetorical Approaches," in *Narrative Unreliability in the Twentieth-Century First-Person Novel*, ed. Elke D'hoker and Gunther Martens (Berlin: Walter de Gruyter, 2008), 40.

8. McCoppin, "Horrific Obsessions," 106.

9. Poe, *Complete Stories*, 156.

10. Per Krogh Hansen, "Reconsidering the Unreliable Narrator," *Semiotica* 165 (2007): 242–243.

11. Hartmann, *The Marketing*, 91–92.

12. Loisa Nygaard, "Winning the Game: Inductive Reasoning in Poe's 'Murders in the Rue Morgue,'" *Studies in Romanticism* 33, no. 2 (1994): 223.

13. Poe, *Complete Stories*, 121.

14. McCoppin, "Horrific Obsessions," 109.

CHAPTER TWENTY-ONE

Lovecraft and "An Open Slice of Howling Fear"

Eric Sandberg

H. P. Lovecraft achieved little more than marginal literary success during his lifetime. His work was published in pulp magazines such as *Weird Tales*, or obscure anthologies like *Beware After Dark!*, and he spent a great deal of time and energy on the unglamorous tasks of editing, rewriting, and even ghosting for other writers, including, most famously, celebrity escape artist Harry Houdini.[1] He died in poverty in 1937, mourned only by a small circle of writers and readers, his work largely unrecognized. Indeed, its very survival is due to the dedicated efforts of a few individuals, notably August Derleth, to collect and republish his scattered tales. Yet he is now widely considered to be not just one of the key figures in the development of weird fiction, or indeed of the horror genre, but also as a writer of considerable literary stature and an important contributor to American literary history. The process has been a gradual one. Lovecraft has moved from neglect to the sort of critical disdain exemplified by Edmund Wilson's 1945 assessment of his stories as "hack-work" exemplifying "bad taste and bad art," to the sort of institutional centrality implied by the publication of a volume of his work by the Library of America in 2005.[2] This rise to critical respectability has been accompanied by an extraordinary level and type of popularity. As Stephen King has pointed out, Lovecraft is "not just popular with generation after generation of maturing readers, but viscerally important to an imaginative core group that goes on to write that generation's fantasy and weird tales."[3]

Part of this phenomenal if belated success concerns Lovecraft's relationship to, and literary use of, madness. Throughout his life, Lovecraft dealt with the reality of mental illness, and with the frailty of the mental structures that allow us to participate successfully in social life. When Lovecraft was three, his father was confined to the Butler Hospital, an insane asylum in Providence, Rhode Island, where he remained for five years until his death in 1898 of what was then described as "general paralysis," but was almost certainly neurosyphilis. His early symptoms included bouts of violent aggression, periods of paranoid anxiety, and delusions of grandeur, which developed into convulsions, dementia, and physical degeneration. Soon after his father's committal, the young Lovecraft began to have, in his own words, "nightmares of the most hideous description," and in the year of his father's death he experienced the first of the four nervous breakdowns which, according to S. T. Joshi, "ensured he would never lead a 'normal' life." While details of these events are sketchy, the evidence clearly suggests that Lovecraft's mental state as a child and young man was at best delicate and unstable. After his grandfather's death in 1904, Lovecraft and his mother were forced to leave the family home; the loss of his familiar surroundings left Lovecraft depressed and potentially suicidal.[4] His poor mental condition prevented him from graduating high school or entering university, and led to several years of solitary, unproductive, and unhappy inactivity. He had a fraught and unwholesome relationship with his mother, with whom he lived until she, in turn, was committed to Butler Hospital in 1919, where she remained until her death two years later. Nor was Lovecraft's later life conspicuously successful in terms of conventional social forms; his marriage to Sonia Green was ephemeral (married in 1924, they were living apart by the end of the year and formally divorced in 1929), his attempts to obtain remunerative work fruitless. As Michel Houellebecq puts it, by 1926 "his life had for all intents and purposes ended." What was left was his writing, and given his family background it is unsurprising that madness plays a prominent role in Lovecraft's fiction. He is not alone in using mental illness as both a theme and structuring element in his fiction; many other notable early 20th-century writers, such as Virginia Woolf, Knut Hamsun, William Faulkner, and Franz Kafka, understood insanity as an important mode of response to, and reaction against, modern reality. However, few other writers have been able to articulate more convincingly a state of consciousness that is, in Houellebecq's words, akin to "an open slice of howling fear," or have made the experience of mental illness so central to their vision of reality and to the structure of their fiction.[5]

In some of Lovecraft's stories, this occurs in a personal context in which madness is a response to alienation from self and society, mediated through gothic literary patterns. His 1921 story "The Outsider," for instance, which was clearly written under the influence of Edgar Allan Poe, articulates an extraordinarily intense level of self-alienation and loathing. The nameless narrator, who has grown up in total isolation in an underground castle, escapes from his prison-like home, and wanders until he reaches another castle, which is uncannily, "maddeningly," familiar to him, and at which a festive crowd is assembled. When he presents himself to the company, the crowd flees in a "sudden and unheralded fear of hideous intensity" and he is left alone with the "inconceivable, indescribable, and unmentionable monstrosity" which has caused this horror. What is most appalling is not the unspeakable foulness of the monster he sees, but the "*nearness* of the carrion thing," for the monster is, as he realizes "in one cataclysmic second of cosmic nightmarishness," his own reflection in a mirror. The traumatized narrator is left to the inadequate "balm" of "nepenthe," or forgetfulness, and the consolations of what seems to be an open embrace of insane fantasy: "Now I ride with the mocking and friendly ghouls on the night-wind, and play by day amongst the catacombs of Nephren-Ka in the sealed and unknown valley of Hadoth by the Nile." Madness here is not just the inevitable, but the welcome, response to total social isolation and a self-loathing arising from the recognition of the essential monstrousness of the self. It is a form of "wildness and freedom" that compensates, to some extent, for the "bitterness of alienage."[6]

While this alienation, and the traumatized response of the individual to it, is an important aspect of some of Lovecraft's work, the horror he presents is often externalized, an inherent part of an objective world that is intrinsically terrible. The main manifestation of this in his fiction is what is known as the Cthulhu mythos, a fantastic version of history in which humanity plays a role of vanishingly little importance. Instead of existing, as our delusions indicate, as a meaning-bearing center, we are in fact no more than a trivial epiphenomenon, latecomers to a world already long inhabited, fought over, won and lost by races and species of a radically different order from anything familiar to humans, the Elder Things and Yithians and Great Old Ones of Lovecraft's tales. This mythical representation of Lovecraft's philosophy, which he at times referred to as "Indifferentism," is an imaginative extension of the conceptual decentering of humanity begun by the Copernican revolution, and it results in a radically diminished position for the human race. If a story like "The Outsider" explores individual angst, and locates horror in the recognition of the self as a monstrous and monstrously isolated entity from which madness is the only escape, Lovecraft's broader fictional project extends this to a much wider scale. As Houellebecq writes, few authors "have ever been so impregnated, pierced to the core, by the conviction of the absolute futility of human aspiration."[7] In a universe vastly larger, older, stranger, and more powerful than humanity, Lovecraft's stories tell us, individual or collective effort is equally pointless. And, perhaps unsurprisingly, the typical response of the Lovecraftian protagonist to encountering and assimilating this truth is madness.

This pattern is already in evidence in the first of Lovecraft's so-called Great Texts, the series of tales he wrote between 1926 and 1934 which most clearly and powerfully articulate his vision, "The Call of Cthulhu," which opens with an assertion of the terror of knowledge:

> The most merciful thing in the world, I think, is the inability of the human mind to correlate all its contents. We live on a placid island of ignorance in the midst of black seas of infinity, and it was not meant that we should voyage far. The sciences, each straining in its own direction, have hitherto harmed us little; but some day the piecing together of dissociated knowledge will open up such terrifying vistas of reality, and of our frightful position therein, that we shall either go mad from the revelation or flee from the light into the peace and safety of a new dark age.[8]

The focus here is not on knowledge itself but, as S. T. Joshi has pointed out, on the "feebleness of humanity's psychological state," its inability to cope with the knowledge it gains.[9] "The Call of Cthulhu" illustrates this principle by narrating the gradual discovery of the sort of linkages between seemingly disparate facts that Lovecraft indicates leads inevitably to either denial or madness. The narrator's recently deceased uncle, a professor, has left behind amongst his more conventional notes and papers a box containing "a queer clay bas-relief" sculpted by a local artist, depicting a strange octopus-like monster, and a number of seemingly "disjointed jottings, ramblings, and cuttings" concerning the existence of a "Cthulhu Cult." As the narrator retraces and extends the stages of his uncle's investigations, he discovers that there is nothing disjointed about these notes, which record an interlinked network of mysterious and mysteriously interconnected events. There is, for instance, the seemingly impossible coincidence of the dream-inspired imagery and language of the bas-relief, a global outbreak of "panic, mania, and eccentricity," in March of 1925, and the discovery some 17 years earlier of a very similar cult idol in the swamps of Louisiana. These coincidences and connections lead to others, all of which hint at the existence of a worldwide network of cultic activity. Throughout his investigations the narrator maintains an attitude of what he describes as "absolute materialism," seeking always for rational explanations of apparently inexplicable phenomenon; the very structure of the story mirrors this approach, as it presents its evidence in discrete, incremental units and subjects them to the interpretative and explanatory procedures of science.[10]

However, this attempt to rationalize the irrational breaks down as the investigation progresses. A coincidence gives the narrator access to the story of a Norwegian seaman whose horrific experiences provide the key to the web of mysterious occurrences. So appalling are the results of his discovery that, as in "The Outsider," forgetfulness, "the total effacing" of his unwelcome knowledge, is the only "boon" the narrator craves. The seaman has, according to his tale, experienced at first hand the "cosmic horrors beyond man's power to bear" implied by the narrator's investigations. He has visited, in the depths of the uncharted South Pacific, the "nightmare corpse-city of R'lyeh" and seen "The Thing" that lives there: while the monster can be labeled as Cthulhu, it "cannot be described— there is no language for such abysms of shrieking and immemorial lunacy, such eldritch contradictions of all matter, force, and cosmic order." The result of encountering this manifestation of something utterly beyond human understanding and comprehension is madness: first the madness of the Norwegian sailor's shipmates, then the Norwegian himself and, as the story concludes, of the narrator, whose new knowledge horrifies him: "Loathsomeness waits and dreams in the deep, and decay spreads over the tottering cities of men. A time will come—but I must not and cannot think!"[11] Lovecraft again proposes two alternative responses to knowledge of the so-called real condition of the world: blind denial, or madness. This trope is present throughout Lovecraft's tales: in "At The Mountains of Madness," for instance, the narrator craves an unachievable ignorance, a return to a time "before we had seen what we did see, and before our minds were burned with something that will never let us breathe easily again!"[12] What precisely it is the narrator and his companion see here, and throughout Lovecraft's work, is fundamentally less important than the fact of a horrifying and inescapable knowledge and the psychic damage it causes.

A key point here is the way the Lovecraftian universe resists the sort of analytical, material, scientific analysis which in the early part of the 20th century offered modern humanity such high levels of apparent mastery over the world around them. The failure of the scientific worldview experienced in "The Call of Cthulhu" occurs throughout Lovecraft's tales, which collectively undermine the idea of the reliability of scientific thought and procedures.[13] If on the one hand Lovecraft dramatizes the psychic costs of excess knowledge, on the other he explores the inability to genuinely know the unknowable. In "The Color Out of Space," for instance, professors from Miskatonic University are called in as representatives of the scientific community to study a mysterious extraterrestrial stone that has landed in Nahum Gardner's yard, but despite conducting any number of tests, all described by Lovecraft in a highly technical register, they remain utterly baffled: "It was nothing of this earth, but a piece of the great outside; and as such dowered with outside properties and obedient to outside laws." And while the physical effects of this alien object—a poisoned landscape, and the physical and mental degeneration and death of those who live on it—are terrifying, it is perhaps even more the very resistance of the phenomenon to rational explication that provides the impetus for this terror. The fact that this is "a frightful messenger from the unformed realms of infinity beyond all Nature as we know it" rather than the particular form it takes is what "stuns the brain and numbs us with the black extra-cosmic gulfs it throws open before our frenzied eyes."[14] Human rationality is incapable, Lovecraft's tales imply, of coping with the fundamental nature of the universe, and madness is the result.

A second, and not unrelated, trope that Lovecraft deploys in his evocation of the terrifying nature of existence is the inability of language to adequately express the nature of horrific objects. If science is conceived of as a mode of manipulating and controlling nature, and its inability to cope with a horrific reality leads to mental collapse, the failure of language is an even more fundamental trauma, for language is not just a means of controlling reality, but our primary means of apprehending it. That which surpasses the ability of language to register is truly, and terribly, outside of human experience, and it is here that the monstrosities of Lovecraft's imagination reside. We have seen how Cthulhu himself defies description. Similarly, in "At The Mountains of Madness," the narrator claims that "the words reaching the reader can never even suggest the awfulness" of what he sees in the tunnels beneath the lost city of the Elder Things, although this does not of course stop him from trying to convey his impressions of "the thing that should not be."[15] In "The Shadow Out of Time," Professor Peaslee hears a "whistling sound" which is "beyond any adequate verbal description."[16] These narrators are faced with the impossibility of communicating the nature of their experiences, and examples could be multiplied throughout Lovecraft's oeuvre. There is a great irony here, of course, insofar as Lovecraft's stories are themselves linguistic artifacts that repeatedly express their own inability to convey the truth of their contents, but the basic point is clear. In Lovecraft's imaginative world, the genuine sources of terror and madness exist beyond the reach of language. Faced with the ultimate terror of existence, words fail us.

If Lovecraft's vision of horror can be divided into internal and external forms, arising from alienation and isolation and the awesome indifference of a terrible cosmology respectively, with both leading to insanity, his work also explores the way the two can coincide. As Joyce Carol Oates has argued, "in Lovecraft's cosmos, some tragic conjunction of the human and the non-human has contaminated what should have been natural life," and this collision between the human and the non-human, interiority and exteriority, is of major importance in Lovecraft's work.[17] The pattern here is one in which the narrator (always male) of a story first encounters an external horror, usually some manifestation of the Cthulhu mythos, often by piecing together a fragmentary body of evidence. He unsuccessfully applies the rigorous methodologies of some branch of science in an effort to comprehend the incomprehensible, and strains the resources of language to explain the inexplicable; he then undergoes a terrifying transformation as the external source of horror is internalized. In "The Shadow Out of Time," for example, Professor Peaslee gradually recovers from a five-year spell of amnesiac personality displacement, only to experience a "profound and inexplicable horror concerning myself."[18] Despite constant attempts to rationalize and scientifically master his condition, he is eventually forced to accept the story's concluding revelation (for which the reader is perhaps too well-prepared, a rather ponderous approach to a culminating revelation being something of a flaw in Lovecraft's technique) that his missing years have been spent time travelling in an era of the earth's remote past when it was inhabited by a monstrously alien race, of which he has been one. In "The Shadow over Innsmouth" the narrator applies his expertise in antiquarianism and genealogy to unraveling the dreadful occurrences of a small New England town. His discovery of "the daemonic, blasphemous reality" of the town's occupation by the monstrous, aquatic Deep Ones, the "flopping, hopping, croaking, bleating" creatures he has witnessed "surging inhumanly through the spectral moonlight in a grotesque, malignant saraband of fantastic nightmare," is "the end [. . .] of every vestige of mental peace and confidence in the integrity of Nature and of the human mind." But worse than this is the revelation that these monsters are not an external threat, an abomination of the outside world, but are in fact part of his own identity; he is linked by blood ties to the Deep Ones, and as the story concludes his own identity is gradually submerged by his ancestral taint: he is "queerly drawn toward the unknown sea-deeps" and plans his escape from the world of humanity to the ocean depths, where he shall "dwell amidst wonder and glory forever."[19] Like the narrator of "The Outsider," the discovery of his own fundamental monstrosity has led to a delirium of madness.

Lovecraft claimed that "a basic element of horror" is a "mysterious and irresistible march towards doom," and this is certainly true of his own writings.[20] There is in Lovecraft's fiction no escape from the terror of a vast and indifferent universe, and the collision between the impersonal monstrosities of his mythos and the personal fallibility of his narrators and characters is always disastrous. The world's terror overwhelms individuals with incomprehensible force, and, as if this were not enough, it simultaneously compromises them from within. Throughout Lovecraft's work madness is seen as an almost inevitable, and at times salutary, response to the horrors, external and internal, of existence; ignorance and insanity are presented as the only viable alternatives in a world that is figured as literally unbearable.

It is perhaps this understanding of madness as a central response to the world that has accounted for Lovecraft's rise to prominence in the years since his death. At the very cusp of the twentieth century, Joseph Conrad's *Heart of Darkness* delineated the fallen state of the modern individual in the modern world in ways that resonate strongly, if perhaps unexpectedly, with Lovecraft's imaginative universe: "I assure you that never, never before, did this land, this river, this jungle, the very arch of this blazing sky, appear to me so hopeless and so dark, so impenetrable to human thought, so pitiless to human weakness."[21] Kurtz's insanity arises to just this apprehension of an indifferent universe and a degraded self, and while Lovecraft clearly relies on a very different set of literary tropes, and works within a very different genre, his fundamental vision of an indifferent and thus horrifying universe which contaminates the self and to which madness is the natural, inevitable, response is similar. It is a response that seems to make as much, if not more, sense to readers in the early 21st century as it did to their predecessors a century ago.

Notes

1. S. T. Joshi, *H. P. Lovecraft: A Life* (West Warwick, RI: Necronomicon Press, 1996), 452.

2. Edmund Wilson, "Tales of the Marvellous and the Ridiculous," in *H. P. Lovecraft: Four Decades of Criticism*, ed. S. T. Joshi (Athens: Ohio State University Press, 1980), 47.

3. Stephen King, "Lovecraft's Pillow," introduction to *H. P. Lovecraft: Against the World, Against Life*, by Michel Houellebecq (San Francisco: Believer Books, 2005), 14.

4. Joshi, *H. P. Lovecraft: A Life*, 14, 20, 60, 80.

5. Michel Houellebecq, *H. P. Lovecraft: Against the World, Against Life* (San Francisco: Believer Books, 2005), 103, 53.

6. H. P. Lovecraft, "The Outsider," in *Tales of H. P. Lovecraft*, ed. Joyce Carol Oates (New York: Harper Perennial, 2007), 4–6.

7. Houellebecq, *H. P. Lovecraft*, 32.

8. H. P. Lovecraft, "The Call of Cthulhu," in *Tales of H. P. Lovecraft*, ed. Joyce Carol Oates (New York: Harper Perennial, 2007), 52.

9. S. T. Joshi, "'Reality' and Knowledge," in *Lovecraft and a World in Transition: Collected Essays on H. P. Lovecraft* (New York: Hippocampus Press, 2014), 113.

10. Lovecraft, "The Call of Cthulhu," 53–54, 57, 67.

11. Ibid., 68, 70, 72, 74, 76.

12. H. P. Lovecraft, "At the Mountains of Madness," in *Tales of H. P. Lovecraft*, ed. Joyce Carol Oates (New York: Harper Perennial, 2007), 211.

13. Gerry Carlin and Nicola Allen, "Lovecraft in the Time of Modernism," in *New Critical Essays on H. P. Lovecraft*, ed. David Simmons (New York: Palgrave Macmillan, 2013), 79.

14. H. P. Lovecraft, "The Color Out of Space," in *Tales of H. P. Lovecraft*, ed. Joyce Carol Oates (New York: Harper Perennial, 2007), 82, 99.

15. H. P. Lovecraft, "At the Mountains of Madness," in *Tales of H. P. Lovecraft*, ed. Joyce Carol Oates (New York: Harper Perennial, 2007), 216.

16. H. P. Lovecraft, "The Shadow Out of Time," in *Tales of H. P. Lovecraft*, ed. Joyce Carol Oates (New York: Harper Perennial, 2007), 325.

17. Joyce Carol Oates, "H. P. Lovecraft: An Introduction," in *Tales of H. P. Lovecraft*, ed. Joyce Carol Oates (New York: Harper Perennial, 2007), xv.

18. Lovecraft, "The Shadow Out of Time," 284.

19. H. P. Lovecraft, "The Shadow Over Innsmouth," in *Tales of H. P. Lovecraft*, ed. Joyce Carol Oates (New York: Harper Perennial, 2007), 269, 274.

20. Quoted in Houellebecq, *H. P. Lovecraft*, 48.

21. Joseph Conrad, "Heart of Darkness," in *Heart of Darkness and Other Tales*, ed. Cedric Watts (Oxford: Oxford University Press, 2002), 162.

PART IV

Comics, Art, Graphic Novels, and Video Games

CHAPTER TWENTY-TWO

Mind Games: Representations of Madness in Video Games

Shawn Edrei

An enduring challenge for cinematic media such as film and television is the visual portrayal of internal cognitive processes; where a novel may describe, in detail, a character's state of mind via descriptive language, the eye of the camera is limited to externalized markers. Consequently, early attempts to depict madness or mental instability often required direct audiovisual cues (i.e., discordant music, facial or verbal tics, or filming at odd angles). In the absence of textual descriptors, such techniques are meant to inform the viewer that a given character may be suffering from some form of psychological affliction. Over time, these tools have become refined to the point where, according to Robyn R. Warhol, even their limitations provide valuable insight: "Film makes literally graphic the changes and developments in its form, and sometimes a particular film's experiments with widening the boundaries of the narratable can make us conscious of unnarratability we hadn't realized was previously there."[1] However, even films such as 2004's *Eternal Sunshine of the Spotless Mind* (in which the protagonist journeys into his own memories as they are being actively deleted and rearranged) or 2010's *Inception* (most of which takes place within a nested sequence of artificial dream-worlds) are bound by the medium's reliance on symbolism, suggestion, and allegory in order to render visual simulations of the human mind.

With the advent of video games as a technologically innovative narrative platform, new possibilities emerge. Unlike its filmic and textual counterparts, video games require active participation on the part of the player, who is embodied within the fictional world by an avatar—in narrative terms, this is typically the protagonist of the story in question. Karin Kukkonen's definition of metalepsis aptly serves to encapsulate this process:

> In terms of the narrative roles of fiction, an author explicitly interfering with the events befalling the characters, like Diderot suggests for Jacques' master, ends up leaving the narrative level of the teller and puts himself on the narrative level of the story itself, because otherwise he could only report it but not interfere with it. In terms of the world creating function of fiction, such a metalepsis is described as the author entering the fictional world.[2]

What does it mean, then, to play a game in which the primary actant—the player's self-projection into diegetic[3] space—may be suffering from mental illness? What forms might an unhealthy virtual mind take? And how do the player's exploratory powers factor into the experience? This chapter will examine three games which attempt to depict mental illness in ways that are singularly exclusive to the medium in question: Square-Enix's *Final Fantasy VII* (1997), Ubisoft's *Prince of Persia: The Two Thrones* (2005) and Ben "Yahtzee" Croshaw's *The Consuming Shadow* (2015). Each applies different tactics to represent damaged psyches as well as possible routes for recovery that are wholly dependent on action, rather than passive reception of the text.

This is not to suggest that video game narratives are wholly unique and share no overlap or intersection with other media; Evan Skolnick's *Video Game Storytelling* points to foundational similarities shared by games, films, and novels in relation to basic storytelling conceits: "At this core level, stories and games are in blissful agreement. The driving force behind both experiences is the core conflict of a character wanting something, but needing to overcome challenges in order to get it."[4] The key difference is that video games create diegetic spaces in which the player is not just a spectator, but an active participant and explorer whose absolute control over the virtual avatar positions them in an interstitial space between storyworld and reality. According to Grant Tavinor, such spaces are perceived and treated as mimetic analogues of reality while the player is engaged with the game:

> A virtual representation such as a 3D model of a city can be treated like the real city because it replicates features of the city (such as geography, street

layout and addresses, and so on) in a symbolic form. As such, it is as good as the real city—or even better than it, in some respects—for learning the city's layout: practically, one might treat the representation like the thing it represents to achieve some goal (orientating oneself, or learning where to go to find a given street address).[5]

Thus, if a player encounters a fictionalized representation of mental illness, or is embodied by a character who suffers from such an illness, the experience is both cinematic (informed via direct audiovisual cues) and participatory (as the avatar's illness does not prevent the player from assuming total control of the character in question).

The Japanese role-playing game *Final Fantasy VII* demonstrates one such experience through the use of specific techniques that draw players closer to an unstable psyche. The game's protagonist (and initial player avatar) Cloud Strife suffers from a form of amnesia due to unspecified past traumas. The story's first act only hints at this, during an interactive cutscene in which Cloud recounts the fateful and violent demise of his home village, an event also witnessed by his childhood friend Tifa Lockhart. Tellingly, Tifa—who is present during this scene—displays visible signs of discomfort, indicating that something is wrong with Cloud's recollection of the event. As the player progresses, they encounter more hints that their avatar's mental health is questionable at best; he suffers from unexplained seizures and flashbacks, and is partially aware that something is wrong with him: "I'm Cloud, ex-SOLDIER, born in Nibelheim. . . . I came here by my own free will. . . . Or so I thought. However, . . . To tell the truth, I'm afraid of myself. There is a part of me that I don't understand."[6] Late in the game's second act, Cloud and Tifa accidentally fall into the Lifestream, a mystical source of energy that flows beneath the Earth's surface. The player's control abruptly switches to Tifa, in a scenario described by the game's official guide thusly: "Tifa awakens to find herself in a seemingly empty void. Voices from the dark question her actions and challenge her to confess; she's quickly overcome with emotion and sinks into the darkness. When she awakens she's in a surreal world with not one, but three, Clouds. His conscious [sp] hangs overhead as if watching and waiting for answers."[7]

As with *Inception* and similar films, this sequence literalizes mental illness by representing a character's psyche as a visible and tangible mindscape, a pseudophysical environment that can be traversed as though it were a room or a city street. The inner mind becomes a setting, a three-dimensional space within the diegetic world. However, where *Final Fantasy VII* differs from this cinematic tradition is in the player's inherent ability to control the manner and method of exploring this space. Cloud's mindscape is a sickly green platform that branches out into three paths, each containing a different sequence of memories. As Tifa, the player must access those memories by walking the paths, navigating the reconstructed accounts of Cloud's past while comparing them to Tifa's own recollections. The truth is only fully revealed when the player has traveled all possible roads, piecing together clues and conflicting accounts until the root cause of Cloud's breakdown is exposed, and his identity crisis is resolved. Both characters return to reality and emerge from the Lifestream, and the player resumes control of Cloud as the game's primary actant and protagonist. This sequence is framed as a literalized healing process, in which the player is tasked with stitching together the broken fragments of the character's mind; while the speed of Cloud's recovery is a matter of narrative expediency rather than an accurate portrayal of recuperation, this investigation into the protagonist's true history serves to solidify the almost-therapeutic bond between player and avatar, per Benjamin Chandler's assessment:

> Cloud's identity crisis partway through the game forces players to reinterpret the game text; his preset signifiers and the players' understanding of them are altered. . . . players are forced to reorder their impressions of Cloud and the way Cloud shaped their experiences in the game world. The extent to which this is necessary will depend on the extent of their identification with Cloud. Gamers will most likely accept it as it comes: "Cloud has an identity crisis that spurs on the next part of the action." Players will need to reassess their interpretation of Cloud's signifiers and alter the way they have produced the text of the game up to this point. The result is a stronger level of identification with Cloud and a shift in perceptions of the game world based on an alteration of signifiers.[8]

The interactive component of this story segment sets it apart from similar examples of mindscapes in other cinematic media—when the role of the audience is limited to that of the passive viewer, any ability to engage this psychological space is curtailed by the eye of the camera and its choice of focalization. *Final Fantasy VII* offers a more complex experience due to its innate interactivity: Cloud's mind is not merely an abstract space rendered visually, but a programmed area of the game similar in function (if not form) to any town, forest, or secret cave the player may visit in the course of their adventure. The act of controlling Tifa, determining where she goes and in what order she accesses Cloud's memories, and deducing the truth of his condition, create a form of active engagement no other narrative medium can generate.

However, spatial representation of a damaged mind is not the only way in which video games may allegorize madness or cognitive impairment. *The Consuming Shadow*, a Lovecraft-inspired horror game, begins with a clear indication of the protagonist's affliction: the introductory scene offers the player a choice between "Begin Journey" and "Kill Myself." This suicidal tendency is a product of the game's premise: a malevolent extra-dimensional god is poised to invade Earth, and the player is given the daunting (if not impossible) task of preventing this incursion by assembling the scattered pieces of a magical ritual. However, per the general themes of Lovecraft's work—particularly what has come to be known as his "Cthulhu Mythos"—exposure to otherworldly forces and entities results in a gradual deterioration of the protagonist's sanity. Where *The Consuming Shadow* differs from *Final Fantasy VII* is its use of mental health as a gameplay mechanic, rather than a purely narrative function; the avatar's sanity is a resource that must be carefully preserved, and encountering certain enemies may cause debilitating damage to the mind rather than the body:

> Many different levels of reality layer upon ours, most of which we have no means of viewing or accessing (and for that we should be grateful). It seems to be possible for certain entities to exist on more than one level at a time. Such creatures have a strange, distorted appearance, madly blurring and vibrating like a poor quality TV picture. While they have the same physical properties, their touch may induce visions of extradimensional planes that could drive a layman raving mad in an instant.[9]

The player's progress is directly tied to a steady accumulation of psychological damage, and the protagonist's decaying mind begins to affect the game in visible ways: static flashes across the screen, hallucinatory enemies manifest and disappear upon contact, and at random intervals the game controls themselves may become reversed, leading to exponential difficulty for the player. The character's prolonged suffering may also result in sudden suicide attempts which the player can attempt to avert—failure to do so will immediately lead to a bad ending and force the player to restart the game.

The Consuming Shadow portrays mental illness in an entirely different fashion from *Final Fantasy VII*: namely, it is a purely ludic function directly tied to gameplay. At any point, the condition of the protagonist's psyche is determined by the actions (or failures to act) of the player; sanity is quantified, a meter that rises or falls in similar fashion to the more ubiquitous health bar seen so frequently in other games. While it is impossible to completely avoid gradual loss of sanity as the extradimensional incursion draws near, the amount of mental damage the protagonist sustains is dependent upon the player's mechanical aptitude with the game system: the more familiar one is with *The Consuming Shadow*'s rules and mechanics, the longer a given avatar may endure. Cloud's breakdown in *Final Fantasy VII* is a narrative event rather than a consequence of poor gameplay—it cannot be averted, and must be experienced in order for the story to continue; conversely, the format and design of *The Consuming Shadow* is such that, per Clive Fencott, the player's enjoyment is directly derived from gameplay: "The ability to intervene, to be able to reconfigure signs, constitutes the basis of the pleasure we gain from playing games; agency, in a word. Intervention signs are principally conventions; they are symbols; we have to learn them anew for each new game."[10]

But while the techniques used by *The Consuming Shadow* and *Final Fantasy VII* fall into the established schism between narrative and gameplay in terms of critical approaches to video games, the use of these games as examples does not imply that depictions of mental illness must exclusively fall into one category or the other. Games such as action-platformer *Prince of Persia: The Two Thrones* illustrate a hybrid approach, combining elements of story and play. As the final installment of the *Sands of Time* trilogy, *The Two Thrones* represents the culmination of the titular protagonist's character arc. At the start of the series, the Prince is portrayed as a noble, somewhat naïve adventurer who is granted a limited ability to manipulate time. The second game, *Warrior Within*, sees the player in control of a hardened, more violent Prince, the result of a seven-year flight from an implacable monster: "The beast, the Dahaka, is the guardian of the Timeline. You were supposed to die, so it will catch you and see to it that you meet your fate."[11] Mentally exhausted by past events—some of which only he remembers, as a result of his many reversals of the timeline—the Prince is nevertheless revitalized upon defeating the Dahaka, only to return home in *The Two Thrones* to find his kingdom under siege. Very early in the game's story, the Prince is infected with the eponymous Sands of Time, a physical trauma with immediate psychological ramifications that initially manifest as a voice only the Prince can hear. This unidentified persona constantly advises the Prince to take harsh, pragmatic actions in pursuit of vengeance rather than attempt any rescue of his people. However, as the player progresses through the story, it becomes clear that the Prince is struggling against a semiautonomous alter ego, the Dark Prince, an entity capable of taking over his body at scripted intervals. This, in turn, forces a gameplay change upon the player, as the Dark Prince must kill in order to sustain its life, and therefore eschews stealth and acrobatics in favor of brutal violence. The internal conflict is depicted as a form of dissociative identity disorder, as the Dark Prince claims to be the product of the cumulative traumas the Prince has suffered over the course of the trilogy. As with most fictional representations of this particular condition, the alter ego seeks to gain total control of the physical form and assert its will entirely, while claiming it acts in the best interests of the Prince himself:

> Do you think you would be here now if not for me? How many times did I save you? How many times did I unblock your path, take down your enemies, remind you of your mission? While all you did was cry about your father and Kaileena and Farah, and how everything bad always happens to you! Boo-hoo, Prince![12]

This struggle plays out as both a gameplay mechanic (the player must master the different tools and tactics employed by both the Prince and the Dark Prince in order to progress, and shifts between the two may occur at inconvenient points in order to heighten the challenge) and a narrative component that is key to the Prince's personal story arc. The personality shifts occur more frequently as the Sands' infection spreads, worsening the protagonist's psychological condition, until a final conflict erupts within the Prince's mind, taking the form of a running battle between the two personalities. As with *Final Fantasy VII*, mental space becomes ontological space: this realm is visually represented as a composite of locations the player has visited throughout the trilogy, while the Dark Prince taunts the protagonist (and by extension, the player) for past failures. Just as *Final Fantasy VII* requires that the player-as-Tifa progress through the fragments of Cloud's psyche in order to knit his mind back together, so too must the player-as-Prince revisit his past in order to gain a clearer understanding of himself. By accepting the Dark Prince as a product of his repressed anger, vanity, and violent urges, the Prince ultimately emerges whole, a unified self once again.

What these three games share as examples (among many others) of video games that deal with mental illness is the heightened value offered by the inherent interactivity of the medium. Film and television may offer visual manifestations of mental illness, and follow focalizers through spatial allegories, but video games demand that players be both active and complicit in the exploration of the avatar's mental state, as well as the possibility of recovery. The ability to investigate and navigate the diegetic space as a basic function of gameplay is a powerful tool through which players may enter broken minds and attempt to heal them. As previously stated, these processes are typically expedited, and are wholly unrealistic insofar as actual psychological health is concerned—but as visualized metaphors, the complex and immersive interactions offer valuable, innovative representations of mental illness that have no direct parallel in any other medium.

Notes

1. Robyn R. Warhol, *Blackwell Companion to Narrative Theory* (Malden/Oxford: Blackwell, 2005), 227.

2. Karin Kukkonen, *Metalepsis in Popular Culture* (Berlin/New York: De Gruyter, 2011), 4–5.

3. The level in which the story occurs; the fictional world projected by the text.

4. Evan Skolnick, *Video Game Storytelling* (New York: Watson-Guptill, 2014), 16.

5. Grant Tavinor, *The Art of Videogames* (West Sussex: Wiley-Blackwell, 2009), 49.

6. Kazushige Nojima and Yoshinori Kitase, *Final Fantasy VII* (Tokyo: Square-Enix, 1997).

7. David Cassady, *Official Final Fantasy VII Strategy Guide* (Indianapolis: Brady Publishing, 1997), 147.

8. Benjamin Chandler, *Final Fantasy and Philosophy: The Ultimate Walkthrough* (New Jersey: John Wiley & Sons, 2009), 18.

9. Ben "Yahtzee" Croshaw, *The Consuming Shadow*, in-game text (Australia, 2015).

10. Clive Fencott, *Game Invaders: The Theory and Understanding of Computer Games* (New Jersey: John Wiley & Sons, 2012), 166.

11. Corey G. May and Michael Wendschuh, *Prince of Persia: Warrior Within* (Montreal: Ubisoft, 2004).

12. Corey G. May and Michael Wendschuh, *Prince of Persia: The Two Thrones* (Montreal: Ubisoft, 2005).

CHAPTER TWENTY-THREE

Graphic Narratives: Bechdel's *Fun Home* and Forney's *Marbles*

Nicole Eugene

Graphic narratives that feature invisible disabilities must grapple with the dilemmas of representation. This means illustrators, authors, and readers approach narrative ready to wrestle with the interconnected nature of knowledge and visual culture. In her essay about the role of vision in culture, Haraway argues that "struggles over what will count as rational accounts of the world are struggles over *how* to see."[1] This chapter explores how two graphic narrative authors choose to render their invisible mental illness in a visual language and argues that the partial depiction of their lives are examples of feminist embodied knowledge that resists fixed and universalist knowledge claims about the nature of vision and bodies. I conclude that these depictions of mental illness offer two different modes of relating to mental illness and both reflect how mental illness can be visually imagined.

Alison Bechdel's graphic narrative, *Fun Home: A Family Tragicomic*, is a groundbreaking graphic nonfiction book that developed a vocabulary for translating identities that lurk in the shadows of stigma and shame into opportunities to see and be seen on their terms—in comic form.[2] This essay focuses on how Bechdel's book depicts her experience with obsessive-compulsive disorder (OCD) before turning to Ellen Forney's graphic memoir, *Marbles: Mania, Depression, Michelangelo & Me*, to trace how Forney's narrative presents an account of her bipolar disorder.[3] I claim that Forney's work is situated in the author's experience in a way that validates the experiences and perceptions of the mentally ill. The essay concludes by reflecting on how people with invisible disabilities still crave a sense of belonging and suggests graphic narratives appear to be in a position to fulfill this longing to be seen. Additionally, different graphic depictions of mental illness require a concomitant multitude of ways of seeing disability and impairment. Graphic narratives, and the books I discuss here, highlight how the process of seeing determines who can be seen.

Feminist Approaches to the Act of Seeing and Being Seen

Many people with invisible disabilities like mental illness slowly learn to navigate a world that relies on visual culture and visual modes of communication. Accordingly, some people have endeavored to make their invisible impairments more visible to get access to the social assistance and empathy that seem available to those with more apparent impairments.[4] Others focus on the simplified visual symbols used to communicate about disability. For example, one woman created a handicap sign that resembles the iconic wheelchair placard for handicapped parking but instead of denoting a specific type of disability the new sign signals towards disabilities that may not be visible.[5] Since the invisible nature of mental illness is a barrier to accessing understanding and empathy, graphic narratives offer a unique gift because they cultivate empathy while also laboring to render invisible impairments and hidden deficiencies in visual terms.

Graphic body studies refer to a theoretically grounded analysis of graphic representations of embodied experiences and social identities.[6] Feminist commitments to embodied knowledge situate the politics of seeing and being seen prominently in scholarship, praxis, and activism. For example, the critique of the medical gaze, the male gaze, and the Western gaze are not about the perceptual process of observation; rather these critiques posit that seeing and being seen exist within a visual culture and epistemological system that is committed to allocating resources and power to the universal Western male subject. As Haraway explains, "positioning implies responsibility for our enabling practices."[7] To explore what Haraway means this chapter will examine the position from which each author speaks when they illustrate their invisible illness.

The medium of graphic narrative allows authors to present their experiences with mental illness in terms that both depart from as well as rely on conventional depictions of mental illness. Haraway refers to the visual as a type of prosthesis because it is an extension of an individual's perspective and agency.[8] This is a type of violence because it overpowers other ways of interpreting and experiencing the world in exchange for a particular view, a particular interpretation, and a particular position. Based on this understanding of vision and feminism, let me propose that an author's ability to narrate their own experience with a mental illness relies on the violence implicit in the visualization process. This is the God-trick of objective omniscient knowledge that professes to know the psychological subject better than they know themselves. To place one's inner life and inner thoughts in the hands of a trained professional creates a subject position that is forever tied to an institution to access a language to describe one's experiences. To *see* his or her own mental illness, the author's stories must be entangled in a universalist position while also working as a departure from generic visual systems. In other words, rather than speaking about all people with OCD or all people with bipolar disorder, this picture of their lives and their mental illness is decidedly partial and based on local knowledge. These partial depictions of a particular experience with mental illness are powerful antidotes to stigmatizing ideas about mental illness that isolate and silence those who come to know it.

The graphic narratives I focus on extend feminist embodiment research in two ways: (a) because the authors are both self-described queer feminists,[9] and (b) because of how the texts highlight the centrality of the body in everyday life.[10] I focus on politics of seeing and being seen as it pertains to feminist accounts of disability, mental illness, and embodiment. How a mental illness is illustrated communicates a relationship to mental illness. Therefore, depictions of mental illness reflect multiple ways of understanding mental illness regardless of the particular position the illustrator/author speaks from.

To illustrate my argument, I will consider moments in Bechdel's book, *Fun Home*, before turning to Forney's *Marbles*. Bechdel's depiction of OCD is foregrounded by an account of her family that highlights the role perfection played in her childhood family. Later in the book we encounter OCD wedged within the pages of her book taking on a visual and written form but the condition remains in the background of a larger narrative. Alternatively, Forney's depiction of bipolar disorder is central to her book. By drawing bipolar disorder, Forney makes the subjective and perceptual dimensions of the condition visible while resisting the position of an omniscient objective author. Both authors present partial accounts of their experience with mental illness that preserve the semiotic context that give their lives and their conditions meaning.

Seeing Bechdel and What Bechdel Sees

Bechdel's book, *Fun Home*, is half autobiography and half biography of her father, who she depicts as a secretly queer man who subscribed to het- eronormativity while privately adoring Roy, the family's babysitter.[11] In many regards, Bechdel's book is a typical coming-out narrative in that it chronicles the emergence of the protagonist as a queer identity and in doing so features themes of liberation and loss intertwined with navigation of social rejection, fear of familial misappropriation, and the eventual embrace of gay or queer culture as one's own.[12] *Fun Home* is the nickname of the funeral home that her father inherited and ran part-time with the help of Allison and her siblings. Similarly, the memoir puts contrary ideas in juxtaposition via the literary trope of a mistrust of surface appearances.

In the first few pages of the book, Bechdel reminisces about the first years in their antique home that required a number of renovations to restore the gothic structure to its original grandeur.[13] The children proved to be a great source of help in maintaining such a large antique house. This is significant because it is how her father instills in her an attention to details and love of perfection, which reappears later in the book recon- figured as an obsessive idealization of truth that undermines Bechdel's memories as she tries to write about how her day went. Bechdel recreates her personal journals including evidence of her bout with OCD and also illustrates the calendar used to manage her self-recovery. Her inclusion of OCD is simultaneously marginal and yet central to understanding Bechdel as an author and as a character in the book. OCD also is another example of the book's theme of bodies behaving outside of scripted norms.

In an interview, Bechdel admits that she had OCD as a child, but as an adult, she just has compulsive tendencies that help her do the work required to make comic books that aspire to a level of fidelity that few strive for.[14] Bechdel's creative process of authoring the graphic narrative includes ample use of archival material as a way to register the truth of a panel or page. In other words, each panel is a product of long meticulous studies of photographs and artifacts that are eventually transformed into a drawing. Chute says that for Bechdel, "comics is a way for Bechdel to touch the subjects on whom her work focuses and insert herself into their past."[15] Bechdel believes in the visual medium as an arbiter of truth yet she is reti- cent to embrace a subjectivity that might yield a heteroglossia of truths and perspectives. As a child, teenager, and young adult, Bechdel changes, but as the author who pens the story she is an unchanging figure. Throughout the book she maintains authorial control as the person who has the final say on what can be included in a story that features a stable "I," an unchanging set of values, and a narrator with a fixed identity.

One might argue that the social and psychological location of the author is absent in the book. Instead of situating her subjectivity within the story, Bechdel's presence is via the prosthesis of the eye. Her meticulous study of visual scenes inevitably undermines the subjectivity of her story. For example, Bechdel is depicted as queer throughout the book and towards the end of the book she is able to see her father as a fellow queer subject and this reconciles the incongruity between how her father appeared and who he was. However, her father viewed Allison, the child, as cis-female, yet this understanding is not given space. Readers can only see Bechdel's queer self-portrait and only can access her belief that she was born queer— Bechdel misses an opportunity to put her self-perceptions beside the perceptions others have of her. The chastened authority of her authorial voice might be a useful way to approach mental illness and queer identities but it also silences alternative truths in much the same way.

Bechdel is a leader in queer circles and has the rare distinction of also being a meme: the Bechdel test, an evaluation criterion to quickly see if a creative work, such as a movie, comic book, or TV series has a minimal quantity of females who exist as self-determined individuals independent of men.[16] A recipient of the MacArthur genius grant, Bechdel's influence on the world of comics and graphic narratives cannot be overstated. Therefore, it is important to take her depiction of OCD seriously.

In *Fun Home*, Bechdel depicts OCD in layman terms and does not indicate any engagement with the medical system or rehabilitation experts— rather, OCD is a memory from an era of her childhood and it is a condition that debilitates people close to her.[17] The absence of a medical authority in her story simultaneously forces the reader to trust Bechdel's account as an expert of her own past while also warranting skepticism regarding her choice to include depictions of OCD as quirky and funny memories. Her OCD resembles so many postadolescent accounts of puberty—horrible while it lasted, but necessary. In many interviews, she never fails to attribute her success as a comics artist/author to her obsessive-compulsive tendencies.[18] She admits that she has a son who lives on disability assistance because of OCD and as well as a partner who also has the condition. With this in mind, let us return to her depiction of OCD in *Fun Home* and the question of her position. Her portrayal of OCD naturalizes the psychological condition. Rather than casting OCD as aberrant or as abnormal psychology, she shows OCD as a spectrum of behaviors and tendencies. Therefore, readers are presented with a depiction of a child who was closer to one end of the spectrum alongside accounts of an adult who has a different relationship to OCD. Bechdel's inclusion of OCD appears to cast hidden disabilities in relationship terms. This requires that she *not* turn to the abstract psychological concepts of the *DSM-IV* that tend to alienate people not immersed in this world. Bechdel's unwillingness to pathologize OCD in her narrative is very different from Forney's approach to mental illness, which relies on psychology and pathology for a sense of perspective.

How Forney Sees Bipolar and How She Sees with Bipolar

In *Marbles*, the plot is guided by Forney's struggle to personally, historically, and artistically understand bipolar disorder. Discovery of the "Van Gogh club" causes Forney to wonder if unmedicated madness is needed to be a successful artist and writer.[19] This manic brainstorm motivates a dismissal of her therapist's help only to be eventually pummeled by depression. There is little visual continuity as she shifts from depictions of manic periods to episodes of depression—and that is the point. The images change because her perceptions of the world change in relationship to the swinging pendulum of bipolar disorder.

Forney's decision to incorporate subjective intrapersonal dialogue as a major aspect of her experience of bipolar disorder invites the reader into the mind of a person dealing with mental illness. Forney's rendering of subjectivity is informed by feminist sensibilities and by the extensive research she did on the experience of living with bipolar disorder. As mentioned earlier, Haraway's call for feminist partial objectivity, or situated knowledge, draws on metaphors of seeing that have particular relevance to the task of analyzing Forney's graphic memoir.[20] I will argue in this section that Forney's approach to visualizing mental illness draws attention to how seeing involves a neural processing of sensory stimuli that is influenced by her psychological state. Her memoir testifies to how no image or experience is unmediated; there are only highly specific possibilities, each presenting its own wonderfully detailed, partial, active way of organizing the world. Forney's depiction of perception as mediated by the mind is a type of radical situatedness that allows readers to *see* visual systems at work.

Forney makes explicit overtures to perceptual processes by sandwiching her book between a front-page and end-page that are optical illusions: like *Magic Eye* books, the words "Let's take a look at these symptoms" are repeated and placed in a way that hides the secret "YOU ARE CRAZY."[21] Forney approaches the medium disregarding its conventions, endeavoring to overcome the limits of books by creating an awareness of the process of perception. The book, as an object and the story it contains, recognizes that perceptual processes not only buttress explicit events—indeed, they buttress everything.

Another dimension of the subjective experience of living with bipolar disorder is the presence of mood-specific memories. As Martin suggests, the act of being treated and the process of managing bipolar disorder change a person's subjectivity.[22] The constant charting of one's mood in relation to an unchanging instrument of measurement transforms a patient who wonders, as Forney did, "what is too happy?" into a patient who can answer this question based on a meticulous charting of her previous mood cycles. Forney communicates her past from the position of a person who has been managing bipolar disorder for several years now. In other words, the currently stable Forney is writing about a previously depressed or manic Forney by doing what Spector-Mersel calls appropriate meaning attribution: a technique in which a storyteller changes the meaning of an event to fit the purpose of the story.[23] This is necessary because often the gap between the meaning that the event carried at the time of occurrence and the meaning at the time of telling is noted.[24] Forney communicates the difference between the original meaning and the appropriated meaning by repeatedly remarking on the role of mood in creating memories and understandings.[25] Memories are physiological processes that are inextricably tied to the very cognitive processes that make perception possible. These often-silent processes are most visible when they malfunction, as in the case of bipolar disorder.

Depression has many forms in Forney's narrative. Rather than having a sound the way mania did, depression looks like round spheres that threaten to fall and compress Forney.[26] The silence, inactivity, and hyper-solitude of depression are poetically described when her first depression episode occurs. The subjective act of perceiving and interpreting stimuli is a part of the experience of the mental illness, and more importantly, it is a part of the management of the condition. Refaie points out how consciousness is usually directed outside of the self so much that the body disappears, yet when our body seizes our attention it is a dys-appearance: it appears by malfunctioning.[27] Similar to the cancer narratives that Refaie examined, Forney's work in *Marbles* makes several moments of dys-appearance visible, and in doing so the work calls attention to the relays between the self and the body in lived experience of having mental illness.

Unlike Bechdel's book, which does not include a role for health professionals, Forney seems to actively orchestrate treatment, initiate intermissions, and persuade her therapist. Forney's nondisclosures, confessions, reservations, and fears portray an active agent and not a passive recipient of medical care. When Forney later returns to the question of her membership in the "Van Gogh club" and refers to the people in the club as "company," she shows how managing the solitary experience of mental illness requires community and a sense of belonging. Mental illness challenges the connections that bind people together, and accordingly, management of mental illness requires extra attention to these interpersonal aspects of the condition. In her memoir and in interviews Forney has encouraged people to "embrace their illness."[28] This call is not solely directed to the people who have mental illness but includes everyone who might ever be directly or indirectly touched by fire.

Conclusion: Multiple Ways of Seeing Mental Illness

Both narratives, *Fun Home* and *Marbles*, help readers imagine a life with mental illness in ways that recognize that stigma and shame are not a major part of everyone's experience with mental illness.[29] Bechdel approaches the task of seeing as a straightforward process from a position of an author who determines what can and cannot be seen. Forney, on the other hand, renders the subjective and at times isolating experience of mental illness in terms that recognizes how mental illness affects perceptual processes—which is often a delegitimizing position to speak from. Rather than devaluing the position of being in the midst of a manic episode or depressive episode, Forney's rendering validates people who view the world through the tinted lenses of mental illness. Although they each present distinct dilemmas of seeing and being seen, both Bechdel's position as a friend of people with OCD and Forney's position as a person with mental illness are useful feminist techniques for situating one's position as they approach the task of turning an invisible condition like mental illness into a visual story.

Notes

1. Donna Haraway, "The Persistence of Vision," in *The Visual Culture Reader*, ed. Nicholas Mirzoeff (New York: Routledge, 1998), 196.

2. Alison Bechdel, *Fun Home: A Family Tragicomic* (Boston, MA: Houghton Mifflin, 2006).

3. Ellen Forney, *Marbles: Mania, Depression, Michelangelo, and Me* (New York: Gotham Books, 2012); Bechdel, *Fun Home.*

4. Natalya N. Bazarova and Yoon Hyung Choi, "Self-Disclosure in Social Media: Extending the Functional Approach to Disclosure Motivations and Characteristics on Social Network Sites," *Journal of Communication* 64, no. 4 (August 1, 2014): 635–57, doi:10.1111/jcom.12106.

5. Andrea Gordon, "Hidden Disability Symbol May Be the Key to Raising Brain Injury Awareness," Life, *Toronto Star*, March 1, 2015, Sunday edition http://www.thestar.com/life/2015/03/01/hidden-disability-symbol-may-be-the-key-to-raising-brain-injury-awareness.html.

6. Martha Stoddard Holmes, "Cancer Comics: Narrating Cancer through Sequential Art," *Tulsa Studies in Women's Literature* 33, no. 1 (2013): 147–162.

7. Haraway, "The Persistence of Vision," 195.

8. Donna Haraway, "Situated Knowledges: The Science Question in Feminism and the Privilege of Partial Perspective," *Feminist Studies* 14, no. 3 (1988); Haraway, "The Persistence of Vision."

9. S. McBean, "Seeing in Alison Bechdel's *Fun Home,*" *Camera Obscura: Feminism, Culture, and Media Studies* 28, no. 3 84 (January 1, 2013): 103–123, doi:10.1215/02705346-2352167; Tom Spurgeon, "Holiday Interview with Ellen Forney," blog, *The Comics Reporter*, (December 21, 2012), http://www.comicsreporter.com/index.php/cr_holiday_interview_4_ellen_forney/.

10. Courtney Donovan, "Representations of Health, Embodiment, and Experience in Graphic Memoir," *Configurations* 22, no. 2 (2014): 237–253, doi:10.1353/con.2014.0013.

11. Bechdel, *Fun Home,* 79, 211.

12. Monica B. Pearl, "Graphic Language," *Prose Studies* 30, no. 3 (December 2008): 286–304.

13. Bechdel, *Fun Home,* 3–17.

14. Tim Teeman, "Alison Bechdel: Genius to Watch Out For," *The Daily Beast*, September 18, 2014, http://www.thedailybeast.com/articles/2014/09/18/alison-bechdel-genius-to-watch-out-for.html.

15. Hillary Chute, "Comics Form and Narrating Lives," *Profession*, 2011, 113.

16. Andi Zeisler, *We Were Feminists Once: From Riot Grrrl to Covergirl®, the Buying and Selling of a Political Movement*, 1st ed. (New York: PublicAffairs, 2016).

17. Teeman, "Alison Bechdel"; Judith Thurman, "Drawn from Life," *The New Yorker*, April 23, 2012, http://www.newyorker.com/magazine/2012/04/23/drawn-from-life.

18. Anna Gross, "Interview with Alison Bechdel," *AV Club*, October 10, 2011, http://www.avclub.com/article/alison-bechdel-63105; Teeman, "Alison Bechdel."

19. Forney, *Marbles,* 22.

20. Haraway, "Situated Knowledges."

21. Forney, *Marbles,* 241.

22. Emily Martin, *Bipolar Expeditions: Mania and Depression in American Culture* (Princeton, NJ: Woodstock: Princeton University Press, 2009).

23. Gabriela Spector-Mersel, "Mechanisms of Selection in Claiming Narrative Identities: A Model for Interpreting Narratives," *Qualitative Inquiry* 17, no. 2 (February 1, 2011): 172–185, doi:10.1177/1077800410393885.

24. Ibid.

25. Forney, *Marbles*, 30, 77, 153.

26. Ibid., 124–126.

27. Elisabeth El Refaie, "Appearances and Dis/dys-Appearances," *Metaphor and the Social World* 4, no. 1 (March 2014): 109–125.

28. Grace Bello, "Page Turner: Ellen Forney," *Curve Magazine*, November 7, 2012, http://www.curvemag.com/Curve-Magazine/Web-Articles-2012/Page-Turners -Ellen-Forney/; Forney, *Marbles*; Spurgeon, "Holiday Interview with Ellen Forney."

29. Bechdel, *Fun Home*; Forney, *Marbles*.

CHAPTER TWENTY-FOUR

The X-Men as Metaphors: When Gayness Was Illness

Mariel Freeman Lifschutz

Superheroes and mythical role models have existed as long as civilization has. They survive through bedtime stories, literature, art, film, and even comic books. Based on real situations or anxieties in the world, these stories can be used as a window into the issues plaguing society. Deciding who is or is not "mentally ill" is a common concern.

Superhero stories, specifically those focusing on "mutants," shine a light on struggles in our society, mainly those of second-class citizenry. Although some societies have venerated psychosis and valued psychotic insights above ordinary insights, and expected their priests or their shamans to replicate behaviors that we would deem to need treatment for "mental illness," contemporary American society typically assigns lower status to the mentally ill and limits their rights to freedom and occasionally financial independence, among other things. Classifying certain groups as mentally ill, therefore, casts them out of mainstream society.

Superhero stories take the in-group/out-group phenomenon, as found in social psychology, and amplify it tenfold. By having a portion of society designated as "mutants," due to genetic or environmental factors, these stories and comics can depict the problems of discrimination, xenophobia, and exclusion through specific distinctions: "Human" and "Mutant." Marvel's X-Men universe is one that is defined by and heavily depicts the mutant struggle as metaphor for modern in-group and out-group conflict. For this reason, the X-Men franchise, comics and films alike, can be seen as a metaphor for the modern struggle for LGBT+ acceptance, which was impeded when LGBT+ individuals were deemed to be "mentally ill."

The X-Men universe has multiple parallels in the fight for acceptance from both society and the medical community, primarily the fight to remove homosexuality from the *DSM* (*Diagnostic and Statistical Manual of Mental Disorders*), published by the American Psychiatric Association and revised many times. The early years of the AIDS crisis turned up the volume of this discrimination. The fictional mutants of X-Men face discrimination every day for something they cannot change, as the LGBT+ community did and still does.

Discrimination was not a foreign concept for the series' two creators. The original X-Men comic series began in 1963 with the publication of *X-Men #1*, later renamed *Uncanny X-Men #1*, by Marvel Comics. X-Men's creators were Stan Lee (née Stanley Lieber) and Jack Kirby (née Jacob Kutzberg).[1] Both men were first-generation Jewish-Americans who grew up during World War II and the atrocities of the Holocaust. Stan Lee was born to Romanian Jewish immigrants in New York around 1923, and the first hero he created for Marvel's predecessor, Timely Comics, was one designed to defeat the Nazis. He went on to enlist in the U.S. Army in 1942, where he helped create training movies. Stan Lee returned to Marvel Comics in 1945.[2] Jack Kirby was born in 1917 to Austrian Jews on Manhattan's Lower East Side. Once he began writing comic strips, he would sign his work with non-Jewish pen names. Kirby was a co-creator of Captain America in 1941 before he was drafted into the U.S. Army in 1943. While overseas, Kirby saw firsthand the effects of the Third Reich on European Jewry when he saw imprisoned Polish Jews who were horrifyingly emaciated; years later, he would still remember the encounter.[3] Kirby and Lee began working together after the war to create superheroes for Marvel Comics. Together, the two devised and wrote the X-Men partially inspired by their marginalized past.

To focus on marginalization and the feeling of otherness in the mainstream, many of the mutants in the X-Men series are young people who must grapple with the backlash toward and lack of control over their mutations while struggling with other aspects of young adulthood. At the beginning, the first team of X-Men is made up of five young mutants (Cyclops, Phoenix, Beast, Iceman, and Angel) and Professor Charles Xavier. Xavier recruits these younger mutants for enrollment at his school for "gifted" children, which is a school where they can hone their skills and learn to control their abilities. These abilities vary from mutant to mutant; for example, Angel (Warren Worthington III) sprouted wings during puberty while Iceman (Bobby Drake) discovered he could lower temperatures and create ice out of nowhere.[4] Throughout the comics and the films, most of the mutants who come to Xavier's school are young people who seem to be entering or experiencing puberty, like any average high school student.[5] These mutants usually have been chased out of their hometowns or alienated by friends, or have hurt loved ones due to their lack of control. By representing pubescent teens, Kirby, Lee, and Marvel could draw a specific demographic to the adventures of the X-Men and other mutants, making the marginalization of being an outsider relatable to younger demographics.[6]

Since the series' publication, the franchise has come a long way and has continued to win over fans young and old. Over the years, the X-Men as a team of characters has appeared in about 10,764 issues of comic books the world over. Currently, three comic book series in the franchise are running simultaneously.[7] They have appeared in eight to nine blockbuster feature films.[8] To critics, most of the films have been popular and faithful to the comics. The first blockbuster X-Men film, *X-Men* (2000, dir. Bryan Singer), received an 81 percent Tomato Score on Rotten Tomatoes—praise for a superhero and action film.[9] In addition, there have also been five television series between 1992 and 2009, all of which were animated.[10] Like any other popular comic series, the franchise has spawned action figures, Halloween costumes, and video games. Even now, 20th Century Fox has released a new trailer for an upcoming film in the franchise slated for release in 2017: the last film to feature Hugh Jackman as Wolverine, a popular member of the X-Men team.[11] The X-Men series has become deeply entrenched in the current media canon, in part due to its exploration of contemporary issues at its inception which is continued today. *X-Men* was the first comic book series to have a major openly gay superhero with the coming out of a member of the X-Men team, Northstar.[12]

Because the X-Men universe has been growing and evolving since 1963, its writers have could depicte allegories for various major social issues, starting with anti-Semitism. The series' main mutant antagonist is Magneto (also known as Erik Lehnsherr or Max Eisenhardt), a Jewish Holocaust survivor. In both the films and comic books, Magneto's origins are in Eastern Europe—he lived with his family in Germany before being moved to the Warsaw ghetto. While escaping, he and his family are caught by the Nazis, and his family is either shot (in the comic books)[13] or they are taken to Auschwitz (the films). No matter which end his parents come to, Max Eisenhardt, as he is known at this point in his origin story, ends up in Auschwitz. Because of Magneto's experience with human cruelty and extermination in the Holocaust, he is wary of trusting humans and believes that the mutant community will be rejected and exterminated in the same way the Jews and Romani were during World War II. This belief of Magneto's causes him to hate and fear humans, to believe that mutants are superior, and to fight to destroy humankind.

Magneto's fears were not unfounded. Throughout the series, humans display fear, repulsion, and disdain towards the burgeoning race of mutants. There is an island in the comics, Genosha, where mutants are second-class citizens who are property of the government.[14] In the *Days of Future Past* storyline, there is a not-so-distant future in which mutants are so reviled that they are documented and placed in internment camps, just like during the Holocaust and the internment of the Japanese during World War II.[15] This future, thankfully, is narrowly avoided. Senator Kelly spearheads the move towards internment camps and various other discriminatory actions of the U. S. government, including a mandate for registering mutants. The Mutant Registration Act is first mentioned in *Uncanny X-Men #181* (published in 1984 and written by Chris Claremont)[16] but also appears in the first major feature film- *X-Men* (dir. Bryan Singer, 2000).[17] Senator Kelly is a staunchly antimutant human who is eerily reminiscent of Senator McCarthy during the "Red Scare" in the United States during the Cold War. Kelly raves about requiring mutants to register and encouraging humans to turn in those who they suspect of being mutants as well. In *X-Men*, he is even seen brandishing a list of confirmed mutants, most likely written to resemble McCarthy's blacklist. Kelly's actions and vocal rejections are merely amplifications of what the series suggests most of human society already thinks: mutants are unnatural and wrong.

In addition to the fear and rejection from the U. S. government and Senator Kelly, the mutants in the series are met with fear and avoidance every day when they walk down the street simply because they have the X-gene, the gene that separates mutants from the rest of the human population. For the mutants, there is no choice to be human; they are born with their own unique mutations, and no matter how much they are rejected by their society, there is nothing they can do about it. This repulsion, based on the presence of the X-gene and its mutations, a natural, uncontrollable occurrence, can be seen as an allegory for discrimination against LGBT individuals in modern society.

This is incredibly like the effect that the *DSM-I* and *DSM-II*'s classification of homosexuality had on public perception. As Jack Drescher discusses in his article, *Out of DSM: Depathologizing Homosexuality*, most psychoanalysts saw homosexuality as a pathological problem after 1939.[18] Because of this, the *DSM-I*, released in 1952, listed homosexuality as a "sociopathic personality disturbance."[19] This phrasing automatically labeled anyone considered homosexual as disturbed—they weren't normal to the medical community and were therefore abnormal to the rest of society. This continued with the classification listed in the *DSM-II*, released in 1968, which listed homosexuality as "sexual deviation."[20] Yet again, homosexuality is classified as something shameful and abnormal, even though it is generally deemed to arise outside of individual volition and is therefore not controllable. Drescher also mentions the fact that most studies which led to the *DSM*'s classification of homosexuality were biased—the sample was made up of those already seeking psychiatric treatment or those in prison.[21] Not only was the *DSM* classifying homosexuality as a mental illness, but homosexuality was also studied ineffectively. The psychiatric community chose to ignore the work of those such as Alfred Kinsey, which contradicted their findings, in favor of perpetuating the cycle of medical alienation and judgment.

This tension between the APA and the contradictory studies of sex researchers came to a head with the events at the Stonewall Inn in 1969, after which the potential damage could no longer be ignored. Because of the perceived impact of the *DSM*'s classification of homosexuality, activists protested at meetings of the APA in 1970 and 1971, urging for a change to the labeling of homosexuality.[22] Their protests led to various talks about homosexuality meant to educate the APA, such as one in 1971 led by activists Frank Kameny and Barbara Gittings.[23] These panels were meant to show the APA the effect that the *DSM*'s classification had on the lives of homosexual Americans, forcing them to hide who they were for fear of being considered deviant. With some education and redefining, the APA voted to remove homosexuality from the *DSM* in 1973. Drescher describes the APA's conclusion as to the definition of a "mental disorder," ". . .except for homosexuality and perhaps some of the other 'sexual deviations', they all regularly caused subjective distress or were associated with generalized impairment in social effectiveness of functioning."[24] Variations of the classification, however, were not fully removed until 1987. Sexual orientation disturbance (SOD) was listed in the *DSM-II* after 1973, and then there was "Ego Dystonic Homosexuality" in *DSM-III* before it was removed entirely in 1987.[25] The APA was so married to the idea of nonheterosexuality being "unnatural" or "abnormal" that it continued to consider variations on the original classification to keep homosexuality in the *DSM*. Even in 1973, there was pushback against the vote to remove the listing by the psychoanalytic community. This all reinforced the stigma around homosexuality; if the medical community thinks one's identity is an illness, so will the rest of society. Where else would the idea of conversion therapy come from but the belief that a cure is required? Drescher sees that the APA's full removal of homosexuality from the *DSM* in 1987 allows for the medical community to move from a position of prejudice to one of appropriate assistance—homosexuality is no longer pathological, therefore homosexual patients can be adequately helped.[26] When viewed through the lens of the X-Men, these activists were right. By classifying homosexuality (alternatively the X-gene) as an illness, anyone identifying as homosexual or not strictly heterosexual is suspect.

After sales dwindled and the original comic stopped being published in 1975, Marvel reinvented the series.[27] This new and improved series continued through the 1970s and 1980s, so it was in production during the AIDS crisis. During the AIDS crisis, wariness of queer individuals, particularly gay men, was almost a cultural norm. This same wariness is seen in reference to Marvel's mutants. The writers of *X-Men* take the parallels even further with the creation of the Legacy Virus, a virus that at its outset only affects and kills mutants.[28] The virus is designed to only latch on and multiply when the X-gene is present, so if the virus were to infect a normal human, it would simply die out. This storyline first appears in the early 1990s and becomes a major focus for the X-Men series. Hundreds upon hundreds of mutants die from the virus before it can be cured, like the tragedy of the early years of the AIDS crisis. Sean Guynes explains the connection in his essay, "Fatal Attraction: AIDS and American Superhero Comics, 1988–1994." Regarding the Legacy Virus, he writes it was a "heavily and implicitly politicized means for the X-Men's creators to explain why mutants were different from, and feared by, non-mutant humans."[29] The Legacy Virus thus serves as another outlet to connect with the world of homophobia. Although the virus in the comics is released by a villain as a weapon, it still resembles AIDS and HIV. The Legacy Virus evolves into multiple strains, the second of which comes with lesions on the skin and other symptoms similar to those of HIV/AIDS.[30] The Legacy Virus eventually mutates so that it begins to attack humans without the X-gene as well, though it does end up being eradicated at the story line's end.

Much like the Legacy Virus was considered a mutant virus, HIV and Kaposi's sarcoma (the first signs of the burgeoning AIDS crisis) were referred to as "gay-related immune deficiency" and "gay cancer" respectively in 1981 by various outlets. This caused individuals to assume that HIV and AIDS, although without those names, were strictly diseases caught by homosexual men. In 1982, the CDC listed risk factors as "male homosexuality, intravenous drug use, Haitian origin, and hemophilia A."[31] These two years at the dawn of the AIDS crisis primed Americans to believe that gay men would likely have AIDS or HIV and would likely pass it on. In the early to mid-1980s, the U. S. government ignored the need for protection and research for AIDS patients, many of whom were gay men. The FDA allowed condoms to advertise that they would prevent HIV in 1987, the same year that the government chose to ban all HIV-positive foreigners from entering the United States.[32] This ban was not lifted until 2009, meaning that for 20 years the U.S. government discriminated against HIV-positive travelers. As the AIDS crisis grew, the pool of sufferers grew as well. It was no longer "gay-related," but the damage was done. In 1993, the CDC found an increase in new cases of HIV and AIDS in women and added more infections to their definition of AIDS.[33] After years of discrimination for being unnatural, homosexual men were now at risk for even more discrimination due to the fear that they would infect someone with AIDS. By the 1990s, HIV/AIDS was far more widespread with numbers of HIV-positive individuals reaching 22.6 million, per the UN.[34] Even though by this time, and by 2016, HIV and AIDS are no longer restricted to gay men, the prejudice still stands. Although some policy changes are currently underway, the CDC's blood donation ban prevented gay men or women who have slept with gay men from donating blood even if they were HIV-negative.[35] This restriction reflects uncertainty surrounding laboratory detection of very recently-acquired infections.

By deciding that mutations are things that need to be cured or suppressed, the society in the X-Men universe is reaffirming that mutants are "other" or are unnatural, making sure that they remain the out-group in their society, much like the role of the *DSM's* classification mentioned earlier. These dynamics form when a group sees significant differences between themselves and another group of people. Eidelson and Eidelson talk about four beliefs that would drive nations towards violence: superiority, injustice, vulnerability, and distrust. The superior group, the in-group, will retain a large amount of privilege while the inferior group, the out-group, will suffer and be ignored. With the belief of injustice, the in-group will feel particularly mistreated by the out-group even if the slights or actions committed against them are much smaller than they believe. This fear of victimization goes hand in hand with the third belief, vulnerability. When the in-group feels vulnerable to attack by the out-group, no matter if the out-group is a minority or majority group, they tend to jump to the worst conclusion and prepare for extremes.

According to the Eidelsons, distrust is a key feeling of the in-group towards out-groups.[36] This pervasive distrust and paranoid fear helps perpetuate incorrect ideas and stereotypes of the out-group in addition to facilitating various forms of discrimination against the out-group. Both the mutants and the normal humans can be seen as the in-group when it comes to these beliefs depending on the situation. Human society's vulnerability to distrust should be expected, given that humans represent the ultimate in-group. Normal humans are so afraid of the dangerous potential they believe exists in the mutant population that they are willing to go to any means necessary to contain it. This same perception of vulnerability and distrust leads Magneto and his followers to act out against humankind. These behaviors, beliefs, and fears as they manifest in the X-Men universe directly parallel the way they appear in the real world.

What makes X-Men so relatable is that it portrays an exaggerated version of the adolescent struggle. Superheroes often find themselves unable to fit in, struggling to understand and control new abilities, and experiencing the fear of rejection. One of the things about the X-Men franchise that makes it so appealing, in addition to the idea of the teen struggle, is the idea of the outsider and the desire for a functional family—chosen or otherwise. It explores and inhabits the space of finding a family of one's own choosing that is accepting and worthwhile. Many find that their families at home are not necessarily where they feel most comfortable and so end up with families of their own construction made up of close friends, similar to how the team of X-Men found each other. This is a major issue for LGBT+ youth who may find themselves kicked out of their homes or around family who cannot understand them.[37] The *X-Men* is about finding a community and being a part of something good in response to the alienation and discrimination at the hands of others.

The well-framed allegory for discrimination in the X-Men provides a strong mirror for the treatment of the LGBT+ community and how its members were dismissed as suffering from "mental illness" and a variant of sociopathy. Through the years, the mutant struggle has been an allegory for marginalization in society and its many forms; one of the clearest examples is the connection to the LGBT+ community. The struggle for mutants to be seen as "normal" parallels that of the struggle for nonheterosexuality to no longer be considered a mental illness. With the introduction of the Legacy Virus, the franchise wrestles with the issue of visibility and fear during the AIDS crisis, as well as the misguided notion that a virus could be restricted to just one group.

The X-Men franchise skillfully illustrates the weight of these issues and the emotions they bring with them in a more "all-ages friendly" fashion. The franchise consists of a handful of feature films, a handful of animated series, and the long-running comic book series that is still being published to this day. Its facility with this allegory has not only made the franchise more successful, but it has also given the world a metaphor by which to understand the struggle that a group like the American LGBT+ population faced in the 1970s and 1980s, and even today with various efforts to delegitimize their rights. Using the words of the X-Men themselves, the series teaches how to be "mutant and proud"[38]—and not to be "mentally ill" and marginalized.

Notes

1. Lawrence Baron, "'X-Men' as J Men: The Jewish Subtext of a Comic Book Movie," *Shofar* 22, no. 1 (October 1, 2003): 43, doi:10.1353/sho.2003.0075.

2. Ibid.

3. Ibid.

4. Stan Lee and Jack Kirby, *Uncanny X-Men #1* (New York: Marvel Comics, 1963).

5. Joseph J. Darowski, *X-Men and the Mutant Metaphor: Race and Gender in the Comic Books* (Lanham, MD: Rowman & Littlefield, 2014), 8–9.

6. Ibid.

7. Comic Vine, "X-Men (Team)," last modified August 28, 2016, http://comicvine.gamespot.com/x-men/4060-3173/.

8. Rotten Tomatoes, "X-Men," accessed October 28, 2016, https://www.rottentomatoes.com/franchise/x_men.

9. Ibid.

10. Internet Movie Database, accessed October 28, 2016, http://www.imdb.com/.

11. Internet Movie Database (IMDb), "Logan (2017)," accessed October 28, 2016, http://www.imdb.com/title/tt3315342/?ref_=fn_tt_tt_1.

12. *New York Times*, "The Comics Break New Ground Again," Opinion, January 24, 1992, accessed October 28, 2016, http://www.nytimes.com/1992/01/24/opinion/the-comics-break-new-ground-again.html.

13. Greg Pak, *X-Men: Magneto Testament*, vols. 1–5 (New York: Marvel Comics, 2009).

14. Marvel, "Genosha," Marvel Universe Wiki, accessed October 18, 2016, http://marvel.com/universe/Genosha.

15. Clancy Smith, "Days of Future Past: Segregation, Oppression and Technology in X-Men and America," in *The Ages of the X-Men*, ed. Joseph J. Darowski (Jefferson, NC: McFarland, 2014), 70.

16. Comic Vine, "Mutant Registration Act," accessed October 29, 2016, http://comicvine.gamespot.com/mutant-registration-act/4015-43657/.

17. Comic Vine, "Robert Kelly," last modified April 18, 2016, http://comicvine.gamespot.com/robert-kelly/4005-15026/.

18. Jack Drescher, "Out of *DSM*: Depathologizing Homosexuality," *Behavioral Sciences* 5, no. 4 (2015): 569, doi:10.3390/bs5040565.

19. Ibid.

20. Ibid.

21. Ibid.

22. Ibid., 570.

23. Ibid.

24. Ibid., 570–571.

25. Ibid., 571.

26. Ibid., 571–572.

27. Darowski, *X-Men and the Mutant Metaphor*, 1.

28. Ibid., 107–108.

29. Sean A. Guynes, "Fatal Attraction: AIDS and American Superhero Comics, 1988–1994," *International Journal of Comic Art* 17, no. 2 (2015): 191. https://www.academia.edu/24034864/Fatal_Attractions_AIDS_and_American_Superhero_Comics_1988-1994. Many thanks to Sean Guynes for his willingness to talk about this topic and for providing this article.

30. Marvel, "Legacy Virus," Marvel Universe Wiki, accessed October 19, 2016, http://marvel.com/universe/Legacy_Virus.

31. amfAR, "Thirty Years of HIV/AIDS: Snapshots of an Epidemic," accessed Oct 17, 2016, http://www.amfar.org/thirty-years-of-hiv/aids-snapshots-of-an-epidemic/.

32. Ibid.

33. Ibid.

34. Ibid.

35. Andrew Wheeler, "Do You Know What Your Children Are? Mutants as Queer Pariahs [Mutant & Proud Part II]," Comics Alliance, June 23, 2014, accessed October 18, 2016, http://comicsalliance.com/mutant-proud-xmen-lgbt-rights-persecution-discrimination/.

36. Roy J. Eidelson and Judy I. Eidelson, "Dangerous Ideas: Five Beliefs that Propel Groups Toward Conflict," *American Psychologist* 58, no. 3 (March 2003): 187, doi:10.1037/0003-066X.58.3.182.

37. Andrew Wheeler, "House of Xavier: How the X-Men Represent Queer Togetherness [Mutant & Proud Part I]," Comics Alliance, June 16, 2014, accessed October 2, 2016, http://comicsalliance.com/mutant-proud-xmen-lgbt-rights-family-community-identity/.

38. *X-Men: First Class*, dir. Matthew Vaughn (2011, 20th Century Fox).

CHAPTER TWENTY-FIVE

Arkham Asylum's Criminally Insane Inmates and Psychotic Psychiatrists

Sharon Packer

Batman's Arkham Asylum—in any of its many media representations—is a force to be reckoned with, if for no other reason than its popularity in *Batman*'s fictional universe. Batman himself is extremely popular in his own right and is one of the three longest-surviving superheroes since the superhero genre started in the late 1930s. Historically, he has been the preferred superhero because he also functions as a detective. Arkham Asylum, the horrific mental institution, stands in stark contrast to the opulent Wayne Manor in Gotham City.

Besides being a colorful and entertaining form of speculative fiction, *Arkham Asylum* in its many manifestations makes important albeit tacit statements about the public's attitudes toward mental illness. It traces shifts in the ways that psychiatry explains mental illness. It also alludes to many more medically related controversies that are outside of our scope here.

There are many ways to interpret *Arkham Asylum* and its representations of mental illness—and of those who treat such illnesses. Some readings are opposite of others. Yet no one disputes that negative images of mental illness abound in the Arkham universe.[1]

On the upside, Arkham Asylum for the Criminally Insane, as an institution, showcases progressive views that distinguish the clinically mentally ill or legally insane from the "generic" criminal class. The graphic novel's narrator—Dr. Amadeus Arkham—laments that the greatest "crime" of so many institutional inmates is the "crime" of suffering from mental illness. "True" criminals include sociopaths who have no conscience or remorse. They commit crimes of their own volition, with full awareness, even if they are reacting to uncontrollable impulses. They do not have a clouded consciousness or cognitive impairment that obscures their ability to distinguish between right and wrong, which is the current standard for the "insanity defense." Insanity defenses are not new at all and date back as far as the Code of Hammurabi.

Antisocial offenders who do not meet Arkham's criteria for "insanity" go to Blackgate Penitentiary, which is an ordinary (albeit fictional) prison, and *not* a treatment facility, as is the equally fictional Arkham Asylum for the Criminally Insane. Consequently, inmates with serious psychiatric disorders are segregated from the general prison population—unless there is a prison break, when Blackgate inmates storm Arkham, as occasionally occurs.

This magnanimous reading conforms to current psychiatric concerns about the conflation of mental illness with criminality—a view that was standard before reformer Dorothea Dix catalyzed the 19th century mental hygiene movement. Dix campaigned against housing persons with psychosis with common criminals. She won—at the time. To this day, Dix's achievements are admired by both historians of psychiatry and practitioners of psychiatry. However, her cause was upended when economic changes as well as clinical advances closed most of those asylums.

Sentiment toward psychiatric hospitalization was not always so favorable. During the heyday of the counterculture, from the mid-1960s to the mid-1970s, many members of the youth culture, as well as some established academicians, campaigned against excessive and oppressive psychiatric hospitalization. Researchers such as David Rosenhan published persuasive studies on "being sane in insane places."[2] Using exemplary experimental psychology techniques that merited publication in the esteemed journal *Science,* Rosenhan essentially proved how easily shills acting as patients can feign mental illness and dupe trained psychiatrists into diagnosing them and admitting them to hospitals. The fact that psychiatric diagnoses had so little consistency from one psychiatrist to another fortified the contentions of "anti-psychiatrists."

Erving Goffman's often-cited sociological study *Asylums: Essays on the Social Situation of Mental Patients and Other Inmates*[3] also comes to mind.

The book title alone proclaims the parallels between psychiatric hospitals and prisons; the text amplifies his conclusions. Goffman contended that society is simply an insane asylum run by its inmates. Considering that the first mention of Arkham Asylum (the institution) appears in an October 1974 *Batman* comic, it is entirely possible that the original authors intentionally conflated prisons and asylums. But Arkham Asylum has a far more convoluted history than that simple reference from 1974. Arkham evolved and mutated over the decades, as so often happens with comic book stories.

If we view *Arkham* from the lens of contemporary culture, we can make very different inferences. Without saying so directly, the *Arkham* franchise casts shadows on the current state of psychiatric hospitalization, or, rather, on the lack of psychiatric hospitalization, which has led to mass incarceration of persons with mental illness in jails and prisons rather than in treatment facilities. Presently, New York City's Rikers Island houses more mentally ill than the entire country's state hospitals. L.A. County and Chicago's Cook County jails come a close second and third. Veteran psychiatrist Alan Frances, who chaired the American Psychiatric Association's (APA) task force on the *DSM-IV*, addresses this unrelenting problem in a 2016 issue of *Psychiatric Times*.[4] He is hardly the first or only psychiatrist to condemn this situation. Almost all popular "psychiatric tabloids" include articles about the criminalization of the mentally ill.

The closing of asylums, begun in earnest in the 1950s, left many seriously mentally ill persons without supervision and without any housing at all. True, there was a time when persons were committed on shaky grounds, sometimes on the word of rapacious relatives, as dramatized in Tennessee William's Southern Gothic novel, *Suddenly Last Summer* (1959), which made it to stage and screen. Some persons even underwent unnecessary lobotomies.

Some scholars retrospectively impute financial motives to the deinstitutionalization movement, while others insist that it was intended as a humanitarian gesture. Either way, the results were the same. Premature deinstitutionalization allowed some seriously ill persons to fall prey to the criminal milieu. Many adopt criminal behavior simply to survive—or to appropriate illicit drugs. Such activities lead to arrests and incarceration, not in now-defunct state hospitals, but in dangerous jails and prisons. Some scholars call this unintended consequence "transinstitutionalization," to emphasis that one institution is substituted for another.[5]

With the advent of managed care around 1990, even acute care psychiatric stays were shortened dramatically, with emergency rooms often triaging out seriously ill and sometimes dangerous persons, as demonstrated by the tragic example of David Bernstein. Bernstein had a long history of schizophrenia. He had repeated hospital stays—but apparently not enough. In Bernstein's case, his father pleaded with psychiatric staff to admit his son to an in-patient unit. Father and son visited not one but several New York area hospitals. The elder Bernstein alerted staff of his son's deterioration and voiced concern about David's delusions. Despite his father's best efforts, Bernstein was not rehospitalized before his final fatal act. Obsessed with blonde women, he eventually pushed a blonde-haired tourist named Kendra off a New York City subway platform. Kendra fell to her death. This act led to New York's implementation of Kendra's Law, which permits involuntary commitment to outpatient (not inpatient or hospital-based) psychiatric treatment. This treatment provision persists, and is known as AOT (assisted outpatient treatment) and includes over 1,000 patients in New York City as of 2016 (per Bronx AOT Medical Director).[6]

Ironically, Bernstein's NGRI (not guilty by reason of insanity) plea failed at trial, to the surprise of many psychiatrists. Prosecutors argued that his choice of a blonde woman in particular was premeditated and indicated that he had the foreknowledge to stop his act. He was sentenced to a prison term rather than to the treatment facility requested by the defense. This is but one of the more dramatic examples of the push and pull between incarceration and treatment.

Since the institution of Kendra's Law and Bernstein's conviction, America has witnessed many more brushes between murder and mental illness, enough to fill an entire chapter, if not also a whole book. The subsequent surge of mass murders perpetrated by persons with serious psychiatric diagnoses eclipsed attention from this single tragic—yet potentially preventable—act.

Arkham Asylum, Its History, and Its Present

Arkham Asylum has had many incarnations, even though this construct did not exist from the start. *Batman: Arkham Asylum* (2009), the video game, became so popular so quickly—and so financially successful—that it is difficult to imagine a *Batman* universe without Arkham Asylum. Yet the fictional Arkham was late to the party, although it swiftly made up for lost time. The game inspired a string of successors: *Arkham City* (2011), *Arkham Origins* (2013), and *Batman: Arkham Knight* (2015). *Suicide Squad*, a big-screen production about Arkham Asylum, with its array of sundry characters and psychotic psychiatrists, was released in summer 2016. In the midst of this, an animated film, *Batman: Assault on Arkham*, appeared in 2014. A 2005 *Batman* film, starring Cillian Murphy as the diabolical mind doctor, Dr. Jonathan Crane (a.k.a Scarecrow), alludes to Arkham Asylum. Arkham also figures prominently in a popular prime-time television show, *Gotham,* which began in 2014 and continues to the present (Fall 2016).

So far, *Arkham Asylum* has outsold all other video games—and video games as a medium sell well, reaping three times the profits of films.[7] Not that *Batman* movies do badly at the box office. Quite the contrary. Christopher Nolan's *The Dark Knight Rises* (2012) ranks among the top ten grossing films ever. *The Dark Knight Rises* (2012) was released just after *Arkham Asylum*'s first video sequel, *Arkham City* (2013).

The *Arkham* video games changed the landscape of video games to come. That accomplishment is especially impressive, considering that the *Arkham* video games came by way of a comparatively obscure studio. Historians of video games will someday shower attention on this matter—but let us focus on the graphic novel responsible for the *Arkham* craze—and also mention the comic books that hinted about Arkham before the elaborate story arc launched.

Arkham Asylum (the institution) first appears in the Batman universe in October of 1974, a creation of Dennis O'Neil and Irv Novick. It merits only an anemic mention when it premieres in issue #258 and where it is identified as "Arkham Hospital." Even that modest debut was long delayed, considering that Detective Comics introduced *Batman* in 1939. In the 1980s, yet another writer, Len Wein, author of *Who's Who: The Definitive Directory of the DC Universe #1* (1985), expands on the backstory of Elizabeth Arkham and her descendants. Elizabeth is the namesake of the asylum and the matriarch who passed on her neurodegenerative gene to her progressively more impaired progeny—who coincidentally (or probably not so coincidentally) became psychiatrists.

Over time, we learn more about Elizabeth Arkham and the other Arkhams who followed. In 1989, 15 years after Arkham's initial appearance, writer Grant Morrison and artist Dave McKean collaborated on a graphic novel, *Arkham Asylum: A Serious House on Serious Earth.* McKean's hand-painted artwork set a trend for graphic novels that followed. Fans' infatuation with Arkham Asylum skyrocketed after that graphic novel. The literary-artistic collaboration brought conflicts between the creators as well as successes. The author has since spoken out against the artist— yet the book became a best seller and inspired annotated editions and set precedents in graphic art in general. The subtitle derives from a poem, "Church Going," by Philip Larkin.

Arkham Asylum: A Serious House on Serious Earth capitalized on the public's growing affection for graphic novels—and reflects the serious critical recognition accorded to graphic novels.[8] The main motif of *Arkham Asylum: A Serious House on Serious Earth* concerns a plot to bait Batman to Arkham Asylum while asylum inmates hold hostages. We later learn that the asylum superintendent, Dr. Cavendish, engineered the "inmate uprising." Cavendish follows the leads of Norman Bates in *Psycho* (1960) and the transvestite psychiatrist in *Dressed to Kill* (1980), and perhaps also the ritualistic killer of the early *Hannibal* novels of the 1980s, who sewed his own clothes from flayed women's skins. For Dr. Cavendish also cross-dresses as he plots murder. Dr. Cavendish joins a long line of psychotic psychiatrists at Arkham Asylum.[9]

The Elizabeth Arkham Asylum for the Criminally Insane (better known as Arkham Asylum or sometimes simply as "Arkham") memorializes the matriarch (or the "founder," to use genetic terminology) who carried the destructive neurodegenerative and psychotogenic gene. As often happens in comic book story arcs, the backstory leaks out in drips and drabs over time. By the 1980s, *Batman* fans learn that the asylum's namesake, Elizabeth Arkham, developed delusions and then dementia as an adult, after inadvertently passing on the presumably autosomal dominant gene for this unnamed neurodegenerative disorder. Later, she came to believe that the spirit of a bat hovered over her, and hence developed an antipathy for Batman himself.

The asylum was the site of one horrific event after another and was headed by one horrific psychiatrist after another, many of them members of the Arkham clan, rendered psychotic by this immutable genetic predisposition. Arkham Asylum publications do not debate ideas about psychogenic sources of psychosis, which had become passé by 1989, when the graphic novel cemented the legend of Arkham. The 1980s were a time of tremendous change in psychiatric theory and practice, when the highly publicized *Osheroff v. Chestnut Lodge* case convinced psychiatrists—as well as their patients—that psychiatric treatment must be based on fact rather than on belief. Freudian "beliefs" lost ground to the scientifically proven neuropsychiatry.[10] Previously popular concepts about "refrigerator mothers" or "schizophrenogenic mothers" faded to grey, although recognition of the role of environment and nurturing in personality disorders (which are distinct from psychotic disorders suffered by the Arkhams) has never faded away. Interestingly, more contemporary research into schizophrenia shows the importance of familial support in shaping the prognosis of persons with first schizophrenic breaks—even though this research does not override data about basic biological predispositions to such severe illness.[11]

Arkham Asylum's emphasis on the biological basis of mental illness is striking, especially in the face of so many dramatic "family romances" (to borrow a term from psychoanalytic lore). This attitude is also a sign of the times: the mid- to late-1980s. Like the legally insane inmates at Arkham who are not held culpable for their crimes, the Arkham clan members also evade punishment for diabolical deeds performed in the throes of their psychoses. Because of their biological inheritance, the Arkhams lack agency, and have not chosen their fates. Their acts are sinister, to be sure, but they do not act solely of their own volition. In fact, they initially try to aid other mentally ill persons—but fall short of those goals early on.

Elizabeth's son grows up to become a psychiatrist named Dr. Amadeus Arkham. After his mother's mental state has deteriorated and she becomes too preoccupied with the occult and with the phantasmagorical bat figure, Amadeus euthanizes his mother. Initially, Amadeus represses the memory of his mother's murder and comes to believe that she suicided instead. This excuse is entirely plausible, given the dire circumstances related to her psychosis. Amadeus then transforms the family mansion into a sanitarium, hoping to save others from suffering as much as his late mother did. With that, Arkham Asylum becomes a landmark on the landscape of Gotham City.

The "adventures" of Dr. Amadeus Arkham do not stop there—for if they did, there would be no reason for endless versions of video games, superhero stories, graphic novels, or animated shorts. As time passes, Dr. Amadeus Arkham's attitude changes. He shows little compassion for his patients. He experiments on them and tortures some with ECT (electroconvulsive therapy) to retaliate against one patient in particular, Martin "Mad Dog" Hawkins. "Mad Dog" murders Amadeus's family members in the graphic novel.

Having raped and killed his doctor's wife and daughter, "Mad Dog" is admitted to Arkham and treated by Dr. Amadeus Arkham for six months before Amadeus arranges Mad Dog's "death sentence." Dr. Amadeus straps Mad Dog to an electroshock couch and intentionally electrocutes him. Thus begins Amadeus's descent into the same madness that befell his mother. He, too, becomes engrossed in the occult and he also hallucinates bats and other apparitions. Dr. Amadeus Arkham later becomes a patient in his own asylum, the first of several Arkham psychiatrists to be admitted into the very institution where they practice psychiatry. Once again, the fox is guarding the henhouse and the madmen run the asylum.

Other Arkham family members carry on the family tradition of "caring" for inmates of the asylum, even though the same gene twists their minds in the way that it afflicted their forbearers. The advanced education acquired before the onset of the disease cannot override the mental effects induced by their genetic inheritance. The Arkhams are examples of "determinism" at its best (or worst). Their mental landscapes are metaphorically "set in stone," immutable, in their cerebral cortex.

Deprived of his children or other direct heirs, Dr. Amadeus Arkham passes the mantel to his nephew, Dr. Jeremiah Arkham, who is also saddled with this same destructive neurodegenerative gene. Dr. Jeremiah Arkham proves to be even more evil that his uncle and mentor. In addition to heading this ignominious institution for the "criminally insane," Dr. Jeremiah Arkham has a secret side. In contrast to superheroes who live ordinary daily lives and hide their identities behind masks so that they can fight crime, rescue the helpless, and help society's weaker ones, the Black Mask cloaks his face so that he can perform more heinous acts.

Some successors at Arkham Asylum have no genetic ties to the Arkham clan but prove to be no better than direct descendants who carry Elizabeth Arkham's tainted bloodline. Dr. Hugo Strange and then Dr. Crane (also known as "Scarecrow") take over, as does Dr. Alyse Sinner, the one-time medical student who befriends and is presumably bedded by Dr. Jeremiah Arkham. We later learn that she, too, murdered her own family, much in the tradition of Amadeus Arkham. Each of these deranged doctors is admitted to Arkham at some point.

It may sound as if Arkham Asylum exists to house its own psychotic psychiatrists and no one else, but that was hardly its purpose. The original Arkham Asylum housed villains who were deemed criminally insane. Many of the most interesting characters from the Batman comics make their way into Arkham. Patients include the Joker, the Penguin, Poison Ivy, the Riddler, Two-Face, Scarecrow, Bane, Killer Croc, and Harley Quinn. Quinn starts as a resident psychiatrist before going rogue.

The Joker, for one, is in and out of Arkham Asylum, where he is treated by the equally colorful and occasionally criminal psychiatrist, when she is still known as Dr. Harlene Quinzel. Quinzel sheds her white coat, assumes the name of "Harley Quinn," and becomes Joker's accomplice—as well as his paramour and the person who springs him from the jail cell. The comic-tragic tale of Harley Quinn and the Joker are discussed in detail elsewhere.[12]

The Connection between *Batman*'s Arkham and Lovecraft's Arkham

Admittedly, the fictional Arkham Asylum did not exist in the early Batman universe or even in Gotham City, where most of the Batman action takes place. Yet another fictional city named Arkham merits mention. Arkham, Massachusetts exists in H. P. Lovecraft's universe, and dates to

Lovecraft's short story "The Unnamable" (1923). A different mental institution—run by Miskatonic University and its medical school—hovers over the landscape of Lovecraft's Arkham. Lovecraft's institution bears important parallels to insane asylums in *Batman* while it recollects landmark German expressionist films about the charlatan asylum superintendent, Dr. Caligari, from 1919, and the self-proclaimed psychoanalyst, Dr. Mabuse, who starred in dozens of films, starting with Fritz Lang's silent Weimar cinema of 1923.

Batman writers and editors had good reason to appropriate the Lovecraftian term—and not solely because of the content of Lovecraft's story but also because of Lovecraft's family history. Both parents died in mental asylums. His father went first, when Lovecraft was still a child. His father's death certificate attributed his demise to neurosyphilis. Neurosyphilis patients occupied 10 to 15 percent of psychiatric beds in those years.

Lovecraft's mother became psychotic enough to enter the same institution many years later, when H. P. was already an adult. Nonmedical biographers considered the possibility that his mother acquired psychosis-inducing neurosyphilis from his father, given that syphilis is sexually transmitted. Since there is a 10- to 20-year lag time between initial infection and the evolution of debilitating neuropsychiatric symptoms of tertiary syphilis, such speculation was within the realm of possibility, even though later authors eventually discounted those theories.

Lovecraft's personal and creative histories are interesting—but for now, let us simply say that naming the Gotham City asylum that houses—and is hosted by—persons with varying degrees of "neurodegeneration" was fitting homage to a horror/science fiction/fantasy writer who was reared under the shadows of real life psychosis, degenerative disease, and actual asylums. Lovecraft's works often revolved around inheritable evil or bizarre mutations, such as "Shadow over Innsmouth" (1931) and "The Case of Charles Dexter Ward" (1927; published in 1941).

Perhaps *Batman*'s Arkham was anticipated or indirectly influenced by Lovecraft's life and the settings of his short stories. Perhaps *Arkham Asylum* incorporates aspects of Edgar A. Poe's much earlier work about familial degeneration, "The Fall of the House of Usher" (1839), as well as Poe's short story "The System of Doctor Tarr and Professor Fether" [sic]. "Doctor Tarr and Professor Fether" introduces the meme about psychotic psychiatrists and inmates running the asylum, a meme that reaches its zenith in *The Cabinet of Dr. Caligari* (1919) and that continues in popular culture to this day. Len Wein's *Batman: Nevermore*, written in 2003 for DC Elseworlds, hints at the link between *Batman* and Poe.

In *The Fall of the House of Usher,* Poe chronicles the lives and deaths of two siblings stricken with an unnamed inheritable insanity. The sister, Madeline, is prone to "catalepsy" while her brother hallucinates. Poe wrote nearly a century before Lovecraft, well before America's Civil War. Lovecraft was aware of Poe's work, so much so that he devotes an entire chapter to Poe's oeuvre in his much-quoted 1929 essay "Supernatural Horror in Literature."

The physical structure of the actual Arkham Asylum cannot compare to Usher's crumbling gothic mansion, which came to life—and died its own death—as its last remaining heir died. Roderick Usher identified himself as "the last of the line." Poe plays on the double-meaning of the word "house," which can refer to an actual home or to the family line, or to the family that occupies the house. Rather than focusing on the Arkham Asylum edifice itself (to date), the story of the family that owns and operates Arkham Asylum takes center stage and is arguably even more convoluted than the doomed Usher clan in Poe's short story by that name.

We could go on and on about Arkham and its associations with psychiatry and mental illness and even "hereditary degeneration" and antipsychiatry were it not for space constraints. We could write an entire essay about *Arkham Asylum* as an antipsychiatry text and as a parody of the psychiatric profession. The presence of Mr. Zsasz (a play on the name of Thomas Szasz, MD, who gained fame for writings such as *The Myth of Mental Illness* (1960) and his staunch antipsychiatry attitude) reinforces this interpretation, which deserves further exploration.[13] In the end, it becomes clear that the mythos of Arkham Asylum is rich enough to make it a Rorschach test that reflects the interests and inclinations of the reader/viewer/player.

Notes

1. Travis Langley, *Batman and Psychology: A Dark and Stormy Night* (New York: Wiley, 2012).

2. D. L. Rosenhan, "On Being Sane in Insane Places," *Science* 179.4070 (January 1973): 250–58, accessed October 13, 2014, doi:10.1126/science.179.4070.250, PMID 4683124.

3. Erving Goffman, *Asylums, Essays on the Social Situation of Mental Patients and Other Inmates* (Garden City, NY: Anchor Books, 1961).

4. Allen Frances, "Psychiatry and Anti-Psychiatry," *Psychiatric Times.* February 26, 2016.

5. Howard Forman et al., "Orange is the New Color of Mental Illness," in *Mental Illness and Popular Culture* (Santa Barbara, CA: Praeger, in press).

6. My thanks to psychiatrist MB for firsthand insights into the operations of New York City's Assisted Outpatient Treatment Program (AOT).

7. Matthew K. Manning, *Arkham Universe: The Ultimate Visual Guide* (New York: DK, 2015).

8. See Sharon Packer, Book Review, *Graphic Women* by Hilary Chute, *Metapsychology,* August 23, 2011; see also Sharon Packer, "Comics and Medicine: A Conference—or a Movement?" *Psychiatric Times,* August 26, 2014.

9. Sharon Packer, *Cinema's Sinister Psychiatrists* (Jefferson, NC: McFarland, 2012); see also John Watson, *Cinemania: A Brief History of Psychiatry in Cinema,* May 4, 2016, accessed November 20, 2016, http:www.medscape.com/features /slideshow/psychiatry-in-film.

10. See Sharon Packer, "A Belated Obituary: Raphael J. Osheroff, MD," *Psychiatric Times,* June 28, 2013.

11. Benedict Carey, "New Approach Advised to Treat Schizophrenia," *New York Times,* October 20, 2015.

12. M. Keith Booker, ed., *Comics through Time: A History of Icons, Idols, and Ideas,* 4 vols. (Santa Barbara, CA: Greenwood, 2015); Justin Edwards and Agnieszka Soltysik Monnet, eds. *The Gothic in Contemporary Literature and Popular Culture: Pop Goth* (UK: Routledge, 2014); See also Lawrence C. Rubin, *Mental Illness in Popular Media: Essays on the Representation of Disorders* (Jefferson, NC: McFarland, 2012).

13. My thanks to professor and department chair Lisa Hermsen for opening this dialogue.

CHAPTER TWENTY-SIX

Halfworld's Loonies in *Rocket Raccoon* Comics— Serious or Satire?

Sharon Packer

Few terms for the mentally ill are more irreverent than the appellation "Loonie." It reminds us of yet another outdated derogation about the "loonie bin" that housed so-called loonies. The words derive from "lunatic" or "lunacy," which owes its origins to *luna,* or moon, because many people of the past associated psychosis and seizures (and various other ailments) with phases of the moon. The error in scientific understanding is excusable, but the abbreviated form loses its clinical meaning and generally intends to offend and undermine the mentally ill.

Yet the chronically psychotic inhabitants of Halfworld's "Cuckoo's Nest" [sic] in *Rocket Raccoon* comics self-identify as "Loonies." They show no signs of the shame or stigma that the term carries elsewhere. For them, it is a neutral, descriptive term. Moreover, they celebrate their outsider psychiatric status and ritualize their treatments in colorful ways.

The "Loonies" don sacramental straightjackets for ritual worship at their holy temple, known as "The Asylum." They sanctify their departed psychiatrists' Logbook, calling it Gideon's Bible (and recollecting the Beatles' comedic cowboy song about Rocky Raccoon as well as bedside Gideon's Bible). Men in white coats—called "Good Humor Men" here—give gifts to the Loonies and so are welcomed, rather than reviled, in contrast to the proverbial "men in white coats" who cart unwilling people away to institutions.

Despite their segregated status in Halfworld's "Cuckoo's Nest," and despite Halfworld's hierarchies, the Loonies seem happy with their lot in life. They sing, they dance, they pray, and produce dramas. They play with toys and companion animals (which include Rocket Raccoon). If we take the farcical story seriously, we suspect that the Loonies' contentment reflects the concern and compassion showered on them by their "shrinks," who find a safe haven for "Loonies" in Halfworld, and who delegate care-taking tasks to equally committed robots and sentient companion animals after the "shrinks" are forced to depart.

When a cure comes their way, via the "Wonder Toy," the Loonies are equally happy to embrace sanity and dispose of other toys that amused them while ill. In the end, they collaborate with the companion animals who cared for them in Cuckoo's Nest. It sounds like paradise, and maybe it is, were it not for the fact that the theme song, "I am the Walrus," written by John Lennon, was a parody.

Making Lennon's parodic—but memorable—melody so central to the text makes us wonder if the comic book story itself was produced as satire, rather than as a solution. For Lennon wrote his nonsensical *Walrus* lyrics to satirize music critics who read meaning and nuance into every word of the Beatles' songs, even when no meaning was intended. Perhaps *Rocket* is making a mockery of a sorry state of affairs or presenting a tongue-in-cheek commentary derived from countercultural disdain for mental hospitals and institutionalization. This colorful comic book may be black humor, intended to denounce mental health care more and to poke fun at those who expect to find relief from psychiatric services. Or it may represent a "wish-fulfillment" fantasy on the part of the authors . . . or audience.

Before we speculate further, let us look at *Rocket Raccoon* comics mini-series from 1985, which inspired *Guardians of the Galaxy*, the 2014 block-buster film that made us take a second look at this short-lived cult comic published nearly 30 years earlier.

Guardians of the Galaxy (2014), the Film Version

Guardians of the Galaxy conquered the box office in 2014.[1] Based on a four-issue comics miniseries *Rocket Raccoon* (1985),[2] *Guardians of the Galaxy* skyrocketed in popularity in the summer, when the best action-adventure films usually premiere. It remained the year's top-grossing movie. In response to its success on the big screen, it became an animated Disney Channel TV show.[3,4] Another *Guardians of the Galaxy* is on its way.

The film's broad appeal to adults and children alike surprised everyone, for it stars a talking raccoon (Bradley Cooper) and a sentient tree voiced by Vin Diesel, an actor otherwise known for tough-talking, street-smart roles in more standard action-adventure films. With its cast of improbable characters and a human-like animal star, Marvel's film could be billed as "Disney meets *Wizard of Oz*" (which is not so far-fetched, considering that Disney bought Marvel Comics and now owns Marvel Cinematic Universe and *The Wizard of Oz*).

Yet the *Guardians of the Galaxy* film moves in a decidedly different direction from the *Rocket Raccoon* comics original. Rather than elaborating on Rocket's relationship to the Loonies of Halfworld, the film focuses on Rocket's space travels after he leaves Halfworld and after he has fulfilled his obligations to Halfworld's Loonies. It avoids mention of Rocket's mission as a companion animal and sentient pet for "Loonie incarcerates" of the planet's psychotic society. By choosing this starting point, spectators miss out on Rocket (Rocky) Raccoon's immutable connections to mental illness and pop culture's commentary on mental illness in the mid-1980s, when psychiatric standards were shifting, and moving forward as fast as Rocket's rocket ship.

Rocket Raccoon (1985), the Comics Original

Marvel's cult comic book classic *Rocket Raccoon* (1985) is mostly attributed to Mike Mignola (penciller), Bill Mantlo (writer), and Bill Potts (editor). Mignola has since gained fame for his *Hellboy* series, which moved away from this early contribution to comics. The career of his collaborator, Bill Mantlo, in contrast, plunged a few years later, and headed in a direction that eerily—and sadly—parallels the comics' theme. We will elaborate on those tragic events later.

Rocket Raccoon comics function as a superhero story, complete with death-defying Toy Wars waged by competing tyrants and a kidnapped damsel-in-distress who waits for rescue by her intended, Rocket Raccoon. Killer clowns combat sentient animals. With its strange asylum and its even stranger inhabitants, *Rocket Raccoon* stretches far beyond the standard mythic "hero's journey." *Guardians of the Galaxy* the film begins after the Wonder Toy cures the Loonies of insanity and increases the intelligence of animals like Rocket. On-screen, we never see scenes of the Wonder Toy and are never treated to images of the Loonies' strange rituals.

The film's abbreviated approach to the Rocket Raccoon origin story deprives us of Rocket's "real story" of how and why he acquired speech, technological enhancements, and a supra-human sense of responsibility. In contrast, the comics illuminate the era's attitudes toward long-term care of incurable psychiatric patients. It forces us to question contemporary (1985) trends toward the "integration" of the mentally ill into society—and makes us ponder the value of setting seriously ill persons (who cannot care for their own needs) apart for their own safety and not because of stigma, as happened in Halfworld. In hindsight, the *Raccoon* comics also remind us of the seismic shift in psychiatric theories about odd behavior or perceptions, circa 1985.

By 1985, reigning psychoanalytic explanations for psychosis were largely laid to rest and the standard of practice shifted in favor of neuropsychiatry. The groundbreaking *Osheroff v. Chestnut Lodge* case of the 1980s cemented that shift. *Rocket Raccoon* comics show no doubt about the biological basis of serious mental illness. The comics acknowledge the genetic contributions to psychosis, without undermining the added contribution of environmental, parental, or societal factors.

In the real world of 1985, the deinstitutionalization movement freed psychiatric patients from back wards of state hospitals and scattered them into the "community," resulting in the near-extinction of state hospitals, the virtual disappearance of so-called funny farms, the emergence of squalid squatter communities in city streets, and "transinstitutionalization," whereby former asylum inmates become prison inmates after their arrests for vagrancy, disorderly conduct, or various petty (or sometimes serious) crimes or drug-related offenses.

Rocket Raccoon, also known as "Ranger Rocket" or Rocky, witnesses a very different approach to mental illness on Halfworld. On Halfworld, talking animals like Rocket care for patients while an advanced, industrialized, robot-controlled sector exists on the other half—hence the name "Halfworld." Those robots genetically enhance the animals, enabling them to function as "psychiatric aids" and companion animals for patients. Surgical modifications enable the animals to jet-propel. In the film, Rocket *hints* that something extreme happened in his past. When we see surgical scars on his back, we (wrongly) suspect that animal rights violations and unethical animal experimentation are at issue. But surgery is only a small part of Rocket's back story.

This futuristic story arc starts hundreds of years in the past, when space-traveling humanoids searched for a place to conduct scientific research and to provide a safe place for chronic psychiatric patients who could not survive in general society. Their host society cast these patients out, but their psychiatrists retained hopes of a cure. Importantly, no one argues about the validity of psychiatric diagnoses or whether some patients are detained inappropriately or involuntarily—even though anti-psychiatry activists, as well as some civil libertarians plus many academi-cians, would ask such questions at the start of the story arc.

Without debating about the diagnoses—but disagreeing with their superiors about their patients' grim prognoses—the space-traveling psychiatrists chance upon Keystone Quadrant in the outer reaches of the galaxy. They turn it into an "Insane Asylum." The quadrant's name references the bungling "Keystone Cops" of silent cinema. The first issue of the four-book miniseries warns, "You are about to enter a strange and not always rational galaxy . . . a sector of space called Keystone Quadrant." The comic book frames the story by quoting the words of the psychiatrists: "We psychiatrists were determined to prove that those poor souls deemed hopelessly insane could be cured." The comic book explains that the "shrinks" [sic] "administered to them from our headquarters in 'Asylum,'" where they "studied and experimented, expanding our knowledge of the functioning—and dysfunctioning—of the human mind . . . while animals were brought along for the purposes of entertainment and companionship."

In the Marvel comic book, space-traveling psychiatrists make robots to aid their patients and to assist their own quest to learn how and why some people become psychotic. The robots also manufacture toys to entertain the patients. Compared to horrific reports about mid-20th-century state hospitals and some contemporary "adult homes" for persons with "serious and persistent mental illness" (SPMI), the imaginary arrangement of Halfworld sounds idyllic—even if patients are segregated from society and even if they are infantilized and treated like children, albeit cherished children who receive Santa-like toy deliveries, every day.

Rocket Raccoon's psychiatrists and psychiatric robots recorded their observations in "Gideon's Logbook," playing upon the term, "Gideon's Bible," which recollects holy books stored in hotel dresser drawers. It directly references the Beatles' cowboy song parody, "Rocky Raccoon," where Rocky plans to "shoot off the legs of his rival . . . only to find Gideon's Bible." Other touches, such as references to *Alice in Wonderland* characters, amplify the comics' parodic approach to psychosis and connect it to the drug culture and counterculture of the 1960s and 1970s.

In the comics miniseries, the home planet eventually cuts research funding and forces psychiatrists to return home—but not before devising ways to care for patients after their departure. In their Log/Bible, the psychiatrists defend their actions and document their reasoning: "It having been decreed by the council that certain forms of insanity are incurable, we have been ordered to transport our planet's insane to a world of their own, where they may be cared for by robots and kept amused by pets for the rest of their natural lives."[5]

To protect patients from potentially harmful intruders (rather than the other way around, where locked wards protect society from presumably harmful patients), the psychiatrists created a force field around the star system, known as the "Galacian Wall." This protective attitude is intriguing, even more so today than it was in 1985, because the *Raccoon* comics portray Halfworld's Loonies as potential victims of predators rather than as future perpetrators. Indeed, statistics show that persons with serious psychiatric disorders are more likely to fall victim to criminals rather than victimize others, despite relatively rare high-profile crimes committed by persons with untreated mental disease. That sympathetic portrayal suggests that Halfworld's shrinks knew that unsuspecting psychotics make easy targets for the unscrupulous.

After the shrinks leave, the robots stay behind to meet the immediate needs of the planet's patients and to continue their advanced research. Life in Halfworld grows more complicated when patients produce progeny who become psychotic, both because of genetic influences and because of the effects of living in an insane environment with psychotic parents.

The patients appear to be unperturbed by their outcast status. They call themselves "The Loonies" and even begin a religion of their own, devising rituals which worship the ancient "shrinks" as gods. In keeping with the entertainment theme, they call their priests "The Good Humor Men." This appellation reminds us of the childlike antics of the Loonies. The white garb of the Good Humor Men recollects the proverbial "men in white coats" who work in psychiatric institutions and who come to "take people away" and perhaps tie patients in straightjackets.

Instead, Halfworld's Good Humor Men wear white straightjackets as ritual "priestly" garb. They practice an elaborate rite. Each ties the straightjacket of another priest, while reciting sacred hymns about the "Cuckoo's Nest." They chant, "One flew east, one flew west, and one flew over the cuckoo's nest." Those verses originated in a popular children's poem that predated Kesey's novel and Forman's influential film version about the "cuckoo's nest"—but most fans are far more familiar with Milos Forman's rabidly antipsychiatry film, *One Flew Over the Cuckoo's Nest* (1975), which he based on Ken Kesey's best-selling novel from 1962. The benevolent "cuckoo's nest" on Halfworld stands in stark contrast to these pop culture icons.

The Loonies call the old Asylum logbook their "Bible" and store it in a sacred place known as the "Admissions Ward" of the ASYLUM. The comics note that "ASYLUM was the most sacred shrine of the Loonies on Halfworld, and the focal point of their annual pilgrimage and celebration," when they wear costumes of their own choosing. The comic books capitalize the letters of the word "ASYLUM," presumably as a sign of respect or religious reverence.

The comics say, "On the night of the Great Masquerade on Halfworld, each Loonie Incarcerate of Cuckoo's Nest can act out his or her fantasies."[6] This phantasmagorical touch alludes to historical facts about "Lunatic Balls" of the past,[7] which attracted curious onlookers as well as confined "lunatics." This peculiar practice merited mention by no less a source than Charles Dickens.[8] Halfworld, however, has no gawking spectators peering into the Lunatic Ball to amuse themselves, after paying admission, as happened in 19th-century Europe and America.

Reciting their Bible, the Loonies affirm that, "The acting out of fantasies is therapeutic, so sayeth the ancient lore of the shrinks, which we must all obey." They are describing psychodrama, a form of therapy that was in vogue through the 1970s and that is resurfacing today.[9] Their arcane jargon, with words such as "sayeth," recollects the King James Bible.

The patients' deification of long-departed psychiatrists seems preposterous to readers and yet it reflects a certain truth. This deification and idealization goes far beyond garden-variety "positive transference," which, in psychoanalytic parlance, refers to the analysand's reactions toward the analyst. "Transference" represents displaced reactions to real-life relationships that are "transferred" onto the anonymous analyst. ("Positive transference" refers to the analysand's positive feelings toward the analyst; "negative transference" is the opposite.)

For the Loonies, their psychiatric care has become their religion—not surprisingly, considering that many critics deride the "Cult of St. Sigmund" and accuse psychoanalysts of functioning as shamans (rather than scientists) by making unprovable proclamations that carry near-canonical authority. We laugh at the slapstick-like rituals of the Loonies, where chorus lines of straightjacketed patients chant incantations and quote "sacred" writings of their long-departed shrinks as if they were reciting Scripture. This scene recollects Philip Rieff's influential sociological book, *The Triumph of the Therapeutic* (1966), which explains how psychotherapy usurped religion's authority in post-World War II America. As they say, many a truth is said in jest.

According to the comics, Halfworld's patients remain stable, but "As the ages passed the robots exceeded their original programming—perhaps caused by radiation from a nova, affecting their inner workings. Anyhow, they developed an artificial intelligence . . . and yet they still faithfully looked after the generations of loonies who, if not congenitally insane as their ancestors had been . . . were born into and affected by parents' insane environment. Here, insanity was normal." The comic book continues, stating that, "the robots—supremely logical—began to chafe at the illogic of the humans in their care. They sought a way out . . . and found one." The robots "played around with genetics and enhanced the intelligence of the *animals,* enabled them to *talk,* gave them prosthetics that mimicked *human* movement . . . and set [Rocket Raccoon's] ancestors to the task of tending to the Loonies' needs."[10] At this point, fans have an "aha moment" as they recall Rocket's offhanded reference to "unethical experiments" performed on animals. Rocket's glib explanation in the film suddenly makes sense.

Rocky Raccoon continues to listen intently to his elders. He learns that "the robots retreated to their own industrial side of Halfworld . . ." and there "they have manufactured machines for us and toys for the Loonies, while they have labored on their huge humanoid *Starship* ever since." Rocky seems shocked to hear of his origin story. He stammers when he responds, confirming that, "T-then we animals started out as . . . as pets for mentally deranged humans?!?" A community elder—a walrus—speaks, (in keeping with the walrus theme of the Beatles' nonsensical song). Wal-rus concurs with Rocket's conclusion, but Rocket grows more perplexed and retorts, "B-but that means that I've spent my whole life searching for *sanity* in a universe established to house the *insane!*"

The comics do not quote R. D. Laing but parallels to Laingian antipsychiatry ideas are obvious.[11] Laing, the radical psychiatrist, claimed that society is insane, so the mentally ill are merely mirroring their surroundings or reacting to those insane situations. We can identify tacit references to Erving Goffman's often-cited sociological study, *Asylums: Essays on the Social Situation of Mental Patients and Other Inmates.*[12] Goffman contended that society is simply an insane asylum run by its inmates. The seminal 1973 studies of Stanford social psychology professor, David Rosenhan, "On being sane in insane places,"[13] are equally apparent. Rosenhan sent supposedly "sane" shills to psychiatric hospitals, tutored his shills on what to say to admitting psychiatrists, and found that his shills received serious psychiatric diagnoses based on the unsubstantiated histories they relayed, even though they showed no superficial signs and symptoms of psychosis. Rosenhan proved that it is easy to fake psychiatric symptoms and even easier to confuse psychiatrists. Rocket's comments to Wal-rus reify Rosenhan's conclusions.

Surprisingly, the Loonies do not question their diagnoses, whatever the specifics may be. They do not argue that they were unfairly declared insane or incarcerated against their will, as many antipsychiatry advocates would claim. For them, their state of "insanity" is a given fact—just as the curative Wonder Toy Helmut of the future is also a given, and is welcomed by all who acquire it, without resentment or recriminations for all that they endured before its invention.

The comic book story grows more complicated. In the comics, Rocky and fellow animals regard their work with the Loonies as a mission, just as doctors are trained to do. Then a comic-book villain and toy tycoon who supplies toys for the "loonie incarcerates" challenges Rocket's altruistic attitude, saying, "If the Loonies want their laughs, they're going to have to *buy* them from *me*!" Rocket objects and says, "Buy? It's every animal's *duty* to entertain the incarcerates of Cuckoo's Nest—*free* of charge!" Rocket's philosophy of life and purpose for living is polar opposite of the for-profit approach of the malicious owner of Mayhem Mekaniks.

Eventually, Mayhem Mekaniks and competitors engage in the Toy Wars, which are essentially Trade Wars. The Toy Wars turn into a complete story arc that is beyond our scope here, except to say that during the Toy Wars, the Loonies' Bible—the one-time logbook of the departed shrinks—falls into the wrong hands. Rocket heroically retrieves the Bible and gives it to the robots, hoping that they can decipher the data contained within. And that indeed happens!

The robots consume the sacred tome in a very concrete fashion. They literally "digest" its contents and follow its instructions to make a "Wonder Toy." This Wonder Toy helmet cures the Loonies instantaneously. It looks like the helmet used in TCMS (transcutaneous magnetic stimulation), which was not commercially available in 1985. Unlike contemporary medications, which require weeks of exposure, and unlike the much-maligned ECT (electroconvulsive therapy), which takes 8–12 sessions, the Wonder Toy literally works wonders in a single wearing. Even companion animals benefit from "Wonder Toy" because "it works on imbeciles as well as on those who are just plain looney!" Low IQ animals become as intelligent as humans. The comics mention that Rocket, for one, had an unusually low "A.I.Q." (animal intelligence quotient).

Optimism abounds. Someone announces, "Soon, they'll [Loonies] be as normal as the ancient shrinks who left them on Halfworld eons ago!" "Soon they'll become *productive people* instead of *passive patients*—and they'll no longer have the need to be entertained by . . . toys."[14]

With the Loonies cured and freed from psychosis and no longer in need of the toys, the Toy Wars end. Animals and Loonies elect former Loonies to refashion their world. At that point, Rocket chooses to accompany robots that leave the planet via *Starship* and seek adventure in the company of the *Guardians of the Galaxy*. The blockbuster film begins here, minus the origin story.

Reality Intervenes

Readers could rejoice in this happy ending, and that is probably what they did for a few years. Sadly, the issues raised by the miniseries became eerily relevant to the life of its writer, Bill Mantlo, who suffered grievous injuries from a hit and run driver in 1992, just a few years after *Rocket's* 1985 publication.

Mantlo had already left comics when he had his accident. He had become an attorney and public defender, having studied law at night while working for Marvel. According to online blurbs, this choice was in keeping with his character; he was always socially and politically committed and the role of public defender allowed him to exercise that part of his personality.

After the accident, he was unable to practice law, collaborate on comics, or even remain in an ordinary rehabilitation facility that did not offer extensive psychiatric staff. Mantlo's closed head injury stripped him of the ability to care for himself. He could not move independently from bed to wheelchair, maintain his balance, articulate clearly, or control his emotions. So Mantlo traveled from treatment center to treatment center, before settling into an "adult home" that serves persons whose mental or physical conditions require 24/7 nursing assistance as well as psychiatric care. His brother has carried the torch since that time, enlisting the support of fans and reminding the public (and corporate controllers) of his brother Bill's contribution to the original *Rocket Raccoon* story.[15] Where is Halfworld when you need it?

Notes

1. Ray Subers, "Weekend Report: 'Guardians' Holds Top Spot on Slowest Weekend in Two Years," Box Office Mojo, September 7, 2014, http://www.box officemojo.com/news/?id=3902&p=.htm.

2. Mike Mignola, Dave Stewart, and Scottie Young (Editor-in-Chief Alex Alonso); Series Editor Mark D. Beazley, *Rocket Raccoon and Groot* (Salem, VA: R.R. Donnelly, 2013). Originally published by Marvel Worldwide, Inc., 1960, 1976, 1982, 1985, 2011, and 2012.

3. Brook Barnes, "Disney Pins Hopes on 'Guardians of the Galaxy' Show," *New York Times,* October 10, 2014.

4. Marvel's *Guardians of the Galaxy* (2015-). www.Imdb.com, accessed February 19, 2017.

5. Mignola, 88.

6. Mignola, 79.

7. Lynn Gamwell and Nancy Tomes, *Madness in America: Cultural and Medical Perceptions of Mental Illness before 1914* (Ithaca, NY: Cornell University Press, 1995).

8. Sharon Packer, review of *Encyclopedia of Asylum Therapeutics, 1750–1950s* by Mary de Young, *Metapsychology* 19, no. 24 (June 10, 2015), http://metapsychology.mentalhelp.net/poc/view_doc.php?type=book&id=7411&cn=139.

9. Sharon Packer, "Using Psychodrama to Teach CBT," *Psychiatric Times* (April 29, 2015), accessed April 29, 2015.

10. Mignola, 115.

11. R.D. Laing, *The Divided Self: An Existential Study in Sanity and Madness* (Harmondsworth, Middlesex: Penguin, 1960).

12. Erving Goffman, *Asylums: Essays on the Social Situation of Mental Patients and Other Inmates* (Garden City, NY: Anchor Books, 1961).

13. D. L. Rosenhan, "On Being Sane in Insane Places," *Science* 179.4070 (January 1973): 250–258, accessed October 13, 2014, doi:10.1126/science.179.4070.250, PMID 4683124.

14. Mignola, 137; See also Bill Mantlo, *Rocket Raccoon* #1–4 (1985 miniseries), Marvel Comics, May-August 1985.

15. Sharon Packer, "The Secret Psychiatric Origins of Rocket Raccoon," *Psychiatric Times,* October 24, 2014; Dave Itzkoff, "Armed Animals Don't Invent Themselves: *Guardians of the Galaxy* Character Creators Eight for Cash and Credit," *New York Times*, August 6, 2014.

CHAPTER TWENTY-SEVEN

Van Gogh and the Changing Perceptions of Mental Illness and Art

E. Deidre Pribram

This chapter explores interconnections among conceptualizations of mental illness, artistic genius, and emotional suffering.[1] It does so through the extended example of Vincent van Gogh from 1890, the year of his death, to the 1990s, a period of record-breaking sales of his work. My intention is to assess, first, how popular culture in contrast to modernist high art circles regards the place of emotionality in aesthetic activity. Second, I examine the role of emotions and emotional disorders in public perceptions of mental illness when applied to 20th century art. Emotional disorders, as I use the term, encompass mood, anxiety, and significant aspects of personality disorders.[2] The two preceding concerns link together in that modernism's artistic persona attempts to unite madness, troubled emotionality, and aesthetic brilliance in one figure. However, as we will see in the case of van Gogh, attempts to integrate such vastly different, complex aspects of human existence have created more controversy than clarity.

Modernism's artist as mad genius is often depicted as a struggling, misunderstood figure, a martyr to the cause of art through his or her isolation, imposed by a troubled but inspired brilliance. As a cultural influence,

van Gogh has captured popular imagination on a global scale, which culminated in a series of blockbuster exhibits in the 1980s and 1990s that
broke attendance records. The same two decades witnessed the zenith of
van Gogh's economic impact, when his work sold repeatedly for record-
breaking prices.[3] His persona endures as the epitome of simultaneous
insanity and inspired brilliance, in which mental illness plays a key role
in this cultural legacy.

The Van Gogh Legacy

In a 1998 article in *Newsweek* titled "Tortured Souls" with the subhead-
ing, "Do Artists Really Have to Suffer Greatly to Make Art?" critic Peter
Plagens reviews major exhibits of the work of Vincent van Gogh and
Jackson Pollock that both took place in autumn of that year.[4] Although
Plagens, citing the work of Warhol, ultimately concludes that not all artists need be tortured souls, the article makes clear an intimate link
between artists' psychiatric disorders, their artwork, and their capacity to
feel intensely. In the case of van Gogh, Plagens describes his only "natural
qualification" as an artist to be "the lack of a psychological shield to protect him from the pain of feeling everything—*everything*—right down to
the quick."[5]

In this view, it is precisely their intense capacity to feel that makes great
artists first, exceptional, and second, mentally ill. Additionally, their ability
to translate their powerful emotional sensibilities onto the canvas expli-
cates their popular reception. A front page article in *USA Today*, similarly
using "Tortured Artist" as part of its title, reviews the same 1998 van Gogh
exhibit.[6] Describing him as "the exemplar of the crazy, starving, tragic artist," the author attributes the artist's enormous popularity to his emotionality and, specifically, to the way museum-goers are able to recognize and
respond to the work's affective intensity.[7] The paintings, crafted by and
saturated with emotion, cause their viewers, in turn, to feel—a positive,
desired outcome. Yet it remains a sought-after effect with clear limitations,
as exemplified by the artist-figure with his/her perilously excessive emotionality. A boundary exists in which enhanced emotional capacity is safe
and highly valued as long as it falls short of the dangerously acute emotional sensibilities, leading to mental illness, embodied by such artists.
The capacity to feel, and to chronicle those feelings in one's artwork, draws
viewers to certain artists. Simultaneously, this same quality sets the artist
apart, marking him or her as exceptional in a troubling way.

In contrast, in professional artistic circles many of the most highly
valued attributes of 20th-century modernism reject inner turmoil and

emotionality in favor of formal, aesthetic, or intellectual properties. As a result, contestation within modernism occurs between an emotion-based aesthetics of the popular versus a pure aesthetics of "high art." Both high formalism and high emotionality exist as features of modernist artistic practices; however, they usually have been structured as contradictory, competing impulses. Van Gogh is a significant figure in this conflict because his legacy brings struggles surrounding emotionality versus pure art into high relief.

A century before the reviews of his 1998 exhibition in Washington, D.C., similar observations about van Gogh's excessive emotionality were already being made. In her study of the early reception of van Gogh's work, *The Formation of a Legend,* Carol Zemel examines responses to the artist in four European countries (the Netherlands, France, Germany, and England), in the period from 1890 to the 1920s, by which time many art historians, including Zemel, believe van Gogh's legendary status is entrenched.[8] In those early decades, van Gogh's critical fate—whether he is lauded, reviled, or ignored by art experts—varies from nation to nation. However, in *all* cases, discussion centers on the place of emotionality in art, based on the prominence of passion and disturbance, whether "anguished or ecstatic" in van Gogh's work and life.[9]

From the outset, in art circles van Gogh's paintings and persona elicited mixed reviews, garnering little consensus concerning his rightful place in the pantheon of modernism. In the Netherlands, emotionality was accepted as key to the critical understanding of van Gogh's work and, thus, central to his elevation as an artistic master in his country of origin. In Germany, he was hailed as a harbinger for the expressionist movement. Drawn by his story of madness and suicide, that movement perceived a "liberating and visionary sensibility" in his paintings.[10] In Germany and the Netherlands, van Gogh was a tragic figure who struggled heroically and, as such, is already the tortured soul of accounts a century later.

In contrast, in France, the country in which he created his most famous paintings, critical opinion had difficulty reconciling the emotionality of van Gogh's work with the aesthetic standards of the day. By the first decade of the 20th century, French commentators, under the influence of modernist aesthetics that stressed "balance, order, stability," found van Gogh's work wanting and many art experts "simply doubted his lucidity."[11] As a result, in France it wasn't his art that took hold, but rather the narrative of van Gogh's life. The story of his difficult, impassioned nature, his madness, his social isolation, and despite all, his determination to keep creating fit well with the dominant conceptualization of the modern artistic genius. Thus, in the early years of the 20th century, van Gogh's art went into decline in France, while the legend of his person flourished.

In England, van Gogh met with the harshest response of the four countries studied by Zemel. For Roger Fry and other influential English critics, emotionality and mental illness could not be integrated with the dominantly formalist aesthetics they espoused. In England, his work was seldom shown in the decade after 1913, and both his paintings and his life story were consigned to playing "a marginal part [in] Post-Impressionist and modernist history."[12]

Despite a lack of critical consensus about the aesthetic merit of van Gogh's work in Europe and, indeed, some heated opposition to him, Zemel contends that by 1920 "the presence of his paintings in public collections [and] their growing market value . . . testified to his international success."[13] Yet his mixed reviews from members of the art world well into the 1920s fail to explain his "international success" by 1920. As the title of her book suggests, Zemel never doubts van Gogh's early legendary status. However, focusing primarily on experts in the art field leaves some element unaccounted for in the leap from mixed reviews to legendary status. In emphasizing the perspectives of the specialized art world, Zemel's account neglects the impact van Gogh has had on a general public: that is, his place in popular culture, based on the intense emotionality of his work, as the 1998 reviews pinpoint.

In contrast to Zemel, Cynthia Saltzman's account traces van Gogh's growing reputation over the course of the 20th century through the provenance of a single painting, *Portrait of Dr. Gachet* (1890), which sold in 1990 for the then-record sum of $82.5 million. Turning to the development of van Gogh's standing in the United States, she argues popular reactions were so enthusiastic that by the late 1940s he "was probably the most well-known artist in America."[14] However, his rise in popularity came with a simultaneous decline in his status as a painter among some art authorities, who cast doubt on his technical and formal skills. For example, the very influential Clement Greenberg raised questions about van Gogh's "craft competence" and whether he could even be considered a great painter.[15] Saltzman contends that the negative recalibration of van Gogh's reputation in the United States replicated a similar occurrence in Europe in the 1920s among art critics, as a result of the artist's accelerating popular reception. She links the reassessment of van Gogh's artistic skills specifically to his popularity beyond the art world: "the success of the van Gogh legend in America's mass market culture unsettled art professionals."[16]

Yet, despite critical denigration and an absence of museum exhibitions of his work, "the price of his pictures rose with his public popularity."[17]

Thus, regardless of critical word or action, van Gogh's attractiveness to a broader public beyond art professionals strengthened. At the same time, critical resistance continued around the intense emotionality of van Gogh's work, viewed as a reflection of his "troubled psyche."[18] Effectively, the paintings could not be simultaneously emotional and intellectual, the product of measured consideration and intense feeling, or of mental illness along with the clarity of aesthetic concerns.

Ultimately, the problem for members of the art field who advocated against van Gogh's formal and technical skills is that their position could not be maintained. By the 1980s, in the face of van Gogh's seemingly ever-ascending popularity and the accompanying rise in prices for his work, and in an era that encompassed "blockbuster exhibits" devoted to him in Europe, North America, and Japan,[19] which museums depend upon to sustain them economically, the art world simply could not afford to dismiss him.

Thus arose the constitution of what Saltzman dubs "the new van Gogh," although clearly neither van Gogh nor his work had changed.[20] Instead, members of the art world worked to reappropriate van Gogh on their own terms. Saltzman reports that analyses by art experts altered drastically between 1984 and 1990, in an effort to reclaim van Gogh for high art by reinventing him. She regards his reinvention as "part of an effort by art historians to dismantle the persistent van Gogh legend and replace it with more accurately drawn historical information," including the conclusion that his mental illness "had little to do with his accomplishments as a painter."[21] Here Saltzman states, in accordance with scholarly reevaluation, the accurate account lies in the fact that van Gogh's illness had little, if anything, to do with his artistic output or subsequent success. For example, Saltzman quotes from a 1984 catalog exhibit: "In van Gogh's case, there was what has been seen as a preordained progression from asylum (with the implied assumption of madness) to suicide, which has fueled the myth of the mad genius. But whatever his illness may have been . . . the fact [is] that it did not directly affect his work."[22] Critical recuperation by the art world necessitated that van Gogh's legacy be distanced from both excessive emotionality and madness. "Freed" from the limitations of his emotional and disordered psyche, van Gogh became suitably fit for reinstatement in the pantheon of modern art, as "an intellectual leader of the Postimpressionist generation" and "a consummate craftsman and a cerebral painter."[23]

While I certainly do not wish to quarrel with assessments of van Gogh as a consummate professional in formal and intellectual terms, evidence remains that he also was always emotionally troubled. To omit this surely is to neglect an important aspect of his work and life and, therefore, to ignore a significant source of the meanings and value he, and other artists, hold for audiences. From Saltzman:

> In the course of the 1980s, van Gogh not only withstood the demanding inquiry of historians, but emerged as a painter of far greater intellectual substance than before. . . . in a way that would convince a skeptical late-20th-century audience of his true stature.[24]

The late-20th-century skeptics she references were certainly not the broader, art-viewing public, such as those who attended the 1998 "blockbuster" exhibition with which I began my discussion of van Gogh. Such attendees weren't skeptics but avid fans. And they weren't fans because suddenly the veil of historical misinformation had been lifted to reveal van Gogh's greater than previously believed "intellectual substance." None of the reevaluation that occurred within the art world altered van Gogh's already extensive popularity among a broader public. Nor did reassessment by art experts change the reasons for the widespread popularity of van Gogh's paintings. Those reasons remained attributable to the emotionality of his work, coupled with his life story. Instead, adjustment was made within the art world, working to synchronize itself with a much wider-held popular view. However, art professionals sought—and largely failed—to reconstruct the collectively held meanings of van Gogh's work. As discussion surrounding the 1998 exhibition reveals, van Gogh's public value remains vested in him as a painter of emotion.

Troubling Emotion

In the case of van Gogh, while the popular imagination of a general public largely succeeded in preserving the importance of emotionality for artistic activity, a similar struggle was enacted over the place of emotions in conceptualizations of his mental illness.

The most intense period of van Gogh's difficulties began in Arles, in the south of France, in December 1888. With its onset signaled by the famous act of cutting off a portion of his left ear, van Gogh experienced, over a period of a year and a half, hallucinations, disorientation, severe agitation and anxiety, and intervals of amnesia that required three periods of hospitalization as well as a year-long stay in an asylum (May 1889 to May 1890). During these attacks, he moved "in and out of coherence" for stretches at a time.[25] He "lashed out violently," "trusted no one, recognized no one . . . took no food, could not sleep, would not write, and refused to talk," or if he did, his "words came out in an incoherent bab-ble."[26] Additionally, in the midst of these bouts, he could not paint or draw. His biographers, Naifeh and Smith, describe six instances of attacks that, progressively, became more intense, persisting for a month or a month and a half instead of a week. These psychotic episodes are the ones most closely associated with van Gogh's madness, although much current opinion believes these were manifestations of a form of epilepsy.[27]

In determining that his illness manifested only in a limited manner, in both episodic duration and time period in his life, art scholars have felt justified in maintaining that "whatever his illness may have been . . . the fact [is] that it did not directly affect his work."[28] Art historian Griselda Pollock characterizes the critical distance put between van Gogh's art and his madness—enabling his recalibration to a cerebral, consummate professional—as a "sanitized" event, in the dual sense of cleansing and rendering sane.[29] The process of sanitization enables Zemel to interpret a painting such as *Self-Portrait (Dedicated to Paul Gauguin),* painted in Sep-tember 1888, three months before wounding his ear, as predating "the record of any destabilizing episode."[30] However, Zemel's claim, as with any scholar who maintains van Gogh's illness did not affect his art, rests on a selective understanding of what constituted his "madness."

According to Naifeh and Smith, already in his childhood van Gogh was "a boy of inexplicable fierceness" who, throughout his life, pursued all his activities "in a fury," that is, with extreme urgency, rapidity, and fervent single-mindedness.[31] Although often interpreted as a sign of the psychotic/epileptic behavior that plagued his final two years, the frenzy with which van Gogh painted was not indicative of his latter-day illness but part of a lifelong pattern.

Well before he determined, in 1880, to become an artist, van Gogh lived through significant periods of anger, despair, and what Naifeh and Smith describe as "bizarre excesses of behavior."[32] His bizarre behaviors included extended lengths of time during which he failed to eat or sleep, maintained a disheveled appearance in both hygiene and clothing, engaged in frequent combative encounters with other people, and pursued physi-cally punitive activities such as walking extraordinarily long distances, despite the availability of inexpensive transportation.[33]

His biographers record "breakdowns" everywhere he lived.[34] And throughout his life, he demonstrates social ineptitude resulting in isola-tion. His relations with acquaintances, friends, and family, including his brother Theo, were typified by prolonged arguments and habitual upheaval. On one occasion of many, Naifeh and Smith characterize the tone of contact between Vincent and Theo as suffused with "acrimony," during which Vincent, in his letters, "unleashed a torrent of abuse" on his brother.[35] Throughout his life, people regarded him as odd and eccentric or, equally often, as "crazy," treating him—or shunning him—as mad.[36]

An alternate way to understand van Gogh's madness other than episodic and confined to his mid-30s, is to consider his difficulties constitutive of "a life of struggle, poverty, and psychological pain."[37] This is the position Saltzman attributes to numerous art critics, from the period immediately following the artist's death until the reformulation of his image in the 1980s as "the new van Gogh." Regarding van Gogh as subject to lifelong psychological troubles entails viewing some form of mental illness as part of his existence prior to the onset, in the last year and a half of his life, of psychosis possibly associated with epilepsy.

If we accept this alternate view, it becomes questionable to maintain, as Saltzman does, that the 1980s art history revision of van Gogh served to "sweep away" the romanticized view of him as "an emotionally volatile, gifted amateur" in favor of a more accurate image of the artist as a "consummate professional."[38] What cannot be so easily swept away is the emotional volatility he experienced for much of his life and expressed in his work.

Yet, after itemizing a lifetime of difficulties and disorder ("In the princely Hague they spat on him; in Neunen, they banished him; in Arles, they threw stones at him"), Naifeh and Smith summarize van Gogh's existence as "years of failure, penury, guilt, loneliness, and finally madness."[39] Compiling his life difficulties in this sequence suggests he was mad only at the end ("finally") and that his madness occurs as a result of other events in his life, including failure, penury, guilt, and loneliness.

Psychoses, of course, have intense emotional aspects. They are not circumstances in which issues of rationality can be neatly excised from emotionality. In van Gogh's instance, his psychotic episodes encompassed severe anxiety, agitation, "outbursts of temper," "brooding silence," paranoia, panic, and other mood swings.[40] Further, symptoms of temporal lobe epilepsy may well include irritation, anger, rage, "easy excitability, furious work habits," apathy, depression, impulsiveness, aggression, and other forms of "profound mental suffering" and labile moods.[41]

Yet, van Gogh's legacy represents an attempt in which, if madness as psychoses can be dismissed, then the need to address any emotional disorders attached to his temperamental volatility, can be minimized as well. The effort to explain away van Gogh's madness as sporadic and occurring only in the last year and a half of his life assumes that once the issue of mental illness as psychosis presumably is put to rest, concerns about his emotional volatility also disappear as if satisfactorily resolved. Emotional volatility is recognized as disturbing when it exists in conjunction with a failure of lucidity, but often treated as a minor vicissitude when appearing in stand-alone fashion.[42]

The emotionality that holds such a prominent position in the legend of van Gogh's life and art in the popular imagination becomes subjected to attempts at recuperation at least twice. First, a bid to eliminate emotionality occurs in efforts to render him a worthy modernist figure, in which he resurfaces as a consummate professional, a painter befitting the echelons of high art. In this first attempted reinvention, instead of exhibiting a style driven by emotional intensity, he is refigured as a painter of formal and intellectual substance in the cause of a pure aesthetic. In the second attempted rejection of emotionality, his mental illness is dismissed as barely a factor in his creativity or aesthetic successes. In arguing that his madness is limited to episodic psychosis only, his emotional disorders presumably can safely be ignored. In the process of sanitizing his reputation, his emotional volatility is marginalized in order to make the claim that no form of disorder directly affects the pure quality of his work.

Notes

1. An earlier, expanded version of this chapter appeared in E. Deidre Pribram, *A Cultural Approach to Emotional Disorders: Psychological and Aesthetic Interpretations* (New York: Routledge, 2016).

2. For a detailed discussion of emotional disorders, see E. Deidre Pribram, *A Cultural Approach to Emotional Disorders: Psychological and Aesthetic Interpretations* (New York: Routledge, 2016).

3. For example, *Vase with Fifteen Sunflowers* and *Irises* sold in 1987 for $39.9 million and $53.9 million, respectively; 1990 saw the sale of *Self-Portrait (Dedicated to Charles Laval)* for $26.4 million and *Portrait of Dr. Gachet* for $82.5 million. The record for *Portrait of Dr. Gachet* was not surpassed until 2004 with the sale of Picasso's *Garçon à la pipe* for $104.2 million.

4. Peter Plagens, "Tortured Souls," *Newsweek,* October 12, 1998, 78–80.

5. Plagens, "Tortured Souls," 78, italics in original. As for Jackson Pollock, "letting the paint leap off the end of a stick . . . allowed his deepest feelings to go directly into his pictures"; Plagens, "Tortured Souls," 80.

6. Maria Puente, "Tortured Artist Would Never Have Understood His Appeal," *USA Today,* October 2–4, 1998, 1A–2A.

7. Puente, "Tortured Artist," 2A.

8. Carol Zemel, *The Formation of a Legend: Van Gogh Criticism, 1980–1920* (Ann Arbor, MI: UMI Research Press, 1980).

9. Zemel, *Formation of a Legend,* 94.

10. Ibid., 105.

11. Ibid., 94, 103.

12. Ibid., 148.

13. Ibid., 149.

14. Cynthia Saltzman, *Portrait of Dr. Gachet: The Story of a Van Gogh Masterpiece* (New York: Viking, 1998), 234.

15. Greenberg quoted in Saltzman, *Portrait of Dr. Gachet*, 237.

16. Ibid.

17. Ibid., 239.

18. Ibid., 237.

19. Puente, "Tortured Artist," 1A.

20. Saltzman, *Portrait of Dr. Gachet,* 260.

21. Ibid., 254.

22. Ibid.

23. Ibid., 254, 255, 265.

24. Ibid., 271.

25. Steven Naifeh and Gregory White Smith, *Van Gogh: The Life* (New York: Random House, 2011), 707.

26. Ibid., 708, 725.

27. For example, Naifeh and Smith, *Van Gogh,* 749–751, 762–763; Griselda Pollock, "Artists' Mythologies and Media Genius: Madness and Art History," *Screen* 21.3 (1980): 74. Turning to psychiatric accounts for elucidation on the nature of van Gogh's illness remains precarious given the extensive number of differing diagnoses that have been made. Blumer, in 2002, indicates more than 150 physicians have written on the subject and 30 distinct diagnoses have been conjectured. Dietrich Blumer, "The Illness of Vincent van Gogh," *The American Journal of Psychiatry* 159.4 (April 2002): 519, 522.

28. Exhibit catalog quoted in Saltzman, *Portrait of Dr. Gachet,* 254.

29. Griselda Pollock, "Crows, Blossoms and Lust for Death: Cinema and the Myth of Van Gogh the Modern Artist," *Mythologies*, ed. Tsukasa Kōdera (Amsterdam: John Benjamins, 1993): 219.

30. Carol Zemel, *Van Gogh's Progress: Utopia, Modernity, and Late-Nineteenth-Century Art* (Berkeley: University of California Press, 1997): 158.

31. Naifeh and Smith, *Van Gogh,* 4.

32. Ibid., 210.

33. Ibid., 122.

34. Ibid., 434.

35. Ibid., 414.

36. Ibid., 418, 434.

37. Saltzman, *Portrait of Dr. Gachet,* 58.

38. Ibid., 260–261.

39. Naifeh and Smith, *Van Gogh,* 748, 858.

40. Ibid., 701, 708, 749.

41. Ibid., 750, 751, 760–761.

42. For more on this, see Pribram, *A Cultural Approach to Emotional Disorders.*

CHAPTER TWENTY-EIGHT

From the Beats to Jean-Michel Basquiat: Cultural Madness and Mad Art

Morgan Shipley

"Madness" has many etymological meanings, only one of which references the clinical term "mental illness," which is the overarching theme of this book. In popular parlance, madness also refers to an emotive state (e.g., rage or even ecstasy).[1] This chapter emphasizes the madness that is intertwined with ecstatic expression and which recollects an untethered existence, relieved of rational restraints. From that space, artists deconstruct the neuroses driving the modern world in order to construct a response more reflective of and responsible to the lived human experience.

Mad art offers an ecstatic escape. Within that mad art, we uncover a distinct expression of the sacred, which favors unmediated and *sacred* understanding over institutionalized approaches. The coalescence of madness and art, then, is not necessarily a sign of mental breakdown, but rather signals a purposeful move. Mad art functions to release the individual from the malaise of conformist thinking by creating space to reconsider the mental contingencies associated with daily living.

D. H. Lawrence, a luminary of American literature, notes how "art-speech is the only truth . . . art, if it be art, will tell you the truth of [one's] day." Recognizing that art-speech often contains "lies" that nevertheless detail the contingencies of a specific time and place, Lawrence argues that true art is a "subterfuge," an imaginative means to break free from convention in order to provide "an emotional experience" that, in turn, "becomes a mine of practical truth."[2] Lawrence's indictment reveals the very uncomfortable psychological state produced by a nation torn between the expectations of a new social order and the demands this placed on notions of individual worth and self-discovery. Rather than produce a kaleidoscope of cultural identities, American society—particularly following World War II until our present moment—limited expression to how well one fits within the western "machine." As opposed to decades of progress and individual expression, postwar American society, mired as it was in "uneasy conformity . . . flight from conflict . . . political quietism . . . [and] the embrace of class privileges"[3] resulted in a world gone mad.

Such internal inconsistencies mimicked a psychotic state as the American populace struggled to conform, but also sparked a growing recognition that madness allows one to break free from a condition of insanity in order to locate, as Jack Kerouac celebrates, identities "mad to live, mad to talk, mad to be saved."[4] Kerouac's language highlights how one must expand beyond the confines of the modern project in order to be "saved" from a world of blind obedience and systemic control. He implies that one must remain open to the nonrational, ecstatic, and *mad* states suggested by Allen Ginsberg's poetic provocation: "America when will you be angelic?"[5] From "mad" to "saved" to "angelic," Beat authors like Kerouac and Ginsberg capture the intertwining of the artistic and the sacred, as does the religiously infused art of Jean-Michel Basquiat, who acts as the concluding case study for this chapter. The art of each of these three guides western culture toward a holy reality that liberates the individual from stifling conventions to find space for imaginative reconstruction.

Within the poetic language of figures like Kerouac and Ginsberg, or through the juxtaposition of religious symbols and cultural/economic motifs in the work of Basquiat, art contains the capacity to rescue madness as the true nature of modern American subjectivity, a perspective that connects the Beats and Basquiat to a broad American tradition of searching for identity (and the divine) outside the walls of traditional institutions and normative structures. In madness, which Basquiat symbolizes through the often-grotesque juxtaposition of angelic, skeletal, and oppressed bodies with religious and profane symbols, one finds the doorway to authentic identity. Yet because such a statement might sound "crazy," visual and poetic art becomes a means to both uncover this sensibility of locating coherency outside mental rationality, while also creating the condition to overcome the reification of (false) spiritual belief and ersatz cultural living. In this sense, the intertwining of lived bodies, religious iconography, and perspectives of madness highlights the apocalyptic aspect of modern American living—and specifically the associated existential angst presented by questions of mortality—and, in so doing, presents us with an intimate portrait of the nature and reality of sanity in contemporary America. Ultimately, these artists direct us back to the demands, expectations, and potentialities found within the self-reliant ideal of the American project.

Mad Generation(s)

The myth of post-World War II America presupposes an idealism marked by affluence and familial bliss.[6] Fortified in the dual narratives of self-determination and economic opportunity, the romanticism of American exceptionalism shaped a growing belief that liberal democracy and capitalism offered the pinnacle of human progress. From Levittowns to a growth in consumerism, the baby boomer generation came of age believing that the world was at its fingertips[7]—a reality come to life in today's instant access to everyday materials via tools like Amazon Prime, entertainment using the Internet, and knowledge via smartphones.

Liberalism and capitalism promised postwar youth the capacity for personal fulfillment unknown to an adult generation raised during the Great Depression; yet it also produced a paradox of dependency and alienation, a condition captured, for instance, in Betty Friedan's study of the "feminine mystique" or in Robert Putnam's recognition that more and more Americans are "bowling alone."[8] Today, this paradox translates through material ideologies, expressed in a general cultural narrative that 1) prioritizes technological capability, 2) commoditizes success through purchasing power, and 3) mediates daily realities by structuring relationships through technology dependency via platforms like Twitter and Facebook.[9]

In other words, modern Western culture routinized existence, producing an individual whose sanity, by being constituted through technological and economic adherence, becomes marked by a broad disconnect from any felt notion of selfhood and community.[10] Within this modern imperative—an imperative pushed to its extreme in today's world of standardized testing—to be sane means to assume one's role within the social machinery; to step outside one's identity markers, or to challenge the coherency of one's societally-sanctioned trajectory, is to appear mad, a condition requiring greater social intervention, which has ranged from the coddling gratification of Dr. Benjamin Spock to the competitive fire of tiger moms.[11] Yet by equating socialization and education with the ability to exist in and produce for the external world, individuals "grow up absurd"[12] in a "modern civilization [which] fails to satisfy profound needs"[13] in people, resulting in a culture gone mad by making sanity a measure of how well one integrates into and is dominated by one's social worlds and their conformist contingencies.

Why though? In decades of economic growth and social development, what compelled individuals toward an expression of life seemingly cut off from authentic relationships and devoid of personalized dreams? Although promised much, those who grew up after World War II in America "could set little in store regarding the future"—with death seemingly around every corner, turning to the instant gratification presented by consumerism and materialism *made sense*.[14] With the "exterminating angel of nuclear holocaust" and the "colossal slaughter and devastation wrought by global war" hovering in America's public imagination,[15] an image fortified in the 1950s and 1960s by the proliferation[?] of bomb shelters and the daily school survival chore of practicing "duck and cover," and mirrored today in America's mediated obsession with terrorist attacks and rumors of nuclear proliferation, the postwar pursuit of happiness devolved into ordered insanity.

Rather than decades of progress, equality, and opportunity, postwar America continues to struggle with its own internal failings: the base truths of poverty, systemized racism, enculturated misogyny, entrenched patriarchy, and the prevalence of violently divisive international relations (epitomized in postwar decades by the Cold War, and exemplified today in rhetoric surrounding terrorism) reveal the root hypocrisies that disconnect the desires and needs of individuals from themselves, from each other, and from their government. As Allen Ginsberg witnessed so honestly, "I saw the best minds of my generation destroyed by madness, starving hysterical naked."[16] Ginsberg's "Howl" grasped prophetically the first meaning of madness within this chapter—that is, the psychological state of insanity that came to define American society in the age of postindustrialization, an age of increased wealth and educational opportunity, but also one designed around social control and contrived connectedness. It is no accident that Ginsberg's own mother (whom he memorialized in "Kaddish") was diagnosed with schizophrenia and confined to state hospitals, or that Ginsberg himself had a court-ordered stay in Columbia-Presbyterian Hospital's psychiatric ward as a young man.

Ginsberg identified the system of control as "Moloch," a religiously appropriated symbol from the Hebrew Bible denoting an idolatrous god to whom children were ritually sacrificed through fire. Ginsberg appropriates such material idolatry in order to associate Moloch with war, government, and capitalism, positioning Moloch as a symbol of the cultural insanity that reduces humanity to functional cogs driving the Western "machine." Visualizing an inhuman monster consuming America's soul, negating expressions of love by fortifying the world externally, Ginsberg bemoans: "Nightmare of Moloch . . . Moloch whose mind is pure machinery! Moloch whose blood is running money."[17] Within such a world, people find themselves bound to an identity beyond their making, a constructed reality in which one has no choice but to go "Crazy in Moloch!" exactly because, as Ginsberg continues, "Moloch who entered my soul early! Moloch in whom I am a consciousness without a body! Moloch who frightened me out of my natural ecstasy!"[18]

Yet in beginning with the "best minds" driven "mad" who ultimately go "Crazy in Moloch" because the system deprives them of their "natural ecstasy," Ginsberg reverses the source for true identity and the meaning(s) of sanity and madness within contemporary American society. Dehumanized and disfigured by a modern system, Ginsberg identifies a way beyond the machinery of western culture, highlighting the ecstatic states—vis-à-vis religion, drugs, and community (e.g., sex)—that allow for both a point of reflection (for Ginsberg, art and poetry produce this condition exactly because "the poem is holy the voice is holy the hearers are holy the ecstasy is holy")[19] and, as a direct result, space to break free. In other words, insane states of being result from staying within the strictures of modern society; one is driven to this state by the compulsive expectation of fitting within normative states of being.

The "madman," however, is freed from this condition—she finds herself within the realm of the ecstatic, which etymologically denotes a state of *ex-stasis*, or a radical disjoining of subjectivity from fixed identities and stagnant realities. A true moment of *mysterium tremendum et fascinans*, to understand madness within the ecstatic (and the ecstatic within madness) shakes the very ontological foundations of western culture, resulting in an experience, as R. D. Laing proposes, where "mundane time becomes merely anecdotal, only the Eternal matters."[20] As with Ginsberg's mad response to the insanity produced by Moloch, Laing laments against a modern world predicated on a basic psychological sacrifice that, in order to "live in a secular world," the "child abdicates its ecstasy," leaving one "unconscious of our minds . . . it is we who are out of our minds." However, as Laing ultimately suggests, "we need not be unaware of the inner world."[21]

Mirroring Laing's caveat, Ginsberg, when howling "Breakthroughs! over the rivers! . . . Highs! Epiphanies! Despairs! . . . Minds! New loves!

Mad generation! down on the rocks of Time!" invokes this second meaning of madness as the desire to become aware of one's "inner world" in order to see how "only the Eternal matters."[22] Within such an autonomous zone of awareness, in which epiphanies bring both despair and newness, Ginsberg ultimately highlights madness as sacred: "The world is holy! The soul is holy! . . . Everything is holy! everybody's holy! . . . everyday is in eternity! Everyman's an angel! The bum's as holy as the seraphim! *The madman* is holy as you my soul are holy!"[23] In understanding a reality in which "everyman" is an "angel," Ginsberg fully positions madness as a divine condition, a point of and for holy reflection against the mad state produced by Moloch. To see the "madman" as "holy," and then to make this all about the sacred nature of one's own "soul," removes sanity from the modern game of assuming the roles and masks expected by society in order to reconstruct "true sanity" as entailing subjective madness.

A Mad Vision(ary)

As Gilles Deleuze and Félix Guattari develop, within a western culture mediated and governed by economic principles that blindly bind individuals to their social herd, madness becomes the sphere for individuality in the purest sense exactly because such space remains untethered and—by nature—isolated from society.[24] Jean-Michel Basquiat lived and embodied this space as a willful act, as a consequence of the abuse he experienced at the end of a heroin needle, and at the hands of an art industry all too quick to exploit him (he completed nearly 2,000 works before his death at the age of 27). Using a collage of images, symbols, and words as a means for self-actualization and as a process to represent ecstasy in a world bound by self-deception, Basquiat played with meaning, using his art to express both disdain for a world *gone mad* as a consequence of liberal capitalism and the need to *go mad* to break free from the condition this produced. Emerging onto an East Village, New York art scene dominated by the Pop Art aesthetics of figures like Roy Lichtenstein and, most significantly in his life, Andy Warhol, Basquiat challenged the homogeneity of an art-world-turned-industry defined increasingly by pastiche, wealth, and repetition, the last a compositional process Basquiat played with and exploited through his disjointed use of photocopied images, which he often placed (and covered) within his paintings, making his art "simultaneously *found* and *made*."[25]

For Basquiat, art created the opportunity to speak back against the norms—cultural, political, and artistic—constricting individual potential and creative expression. And, although Basquiat found himself labeled as the "first black artist to achieve anything close to blue-chip status in the contemporary art market,"[26] his capacity to inhabit two spaces simultaneously—graffiti/gallery artist, high/"primitive" art (the latter, a label he rightly challenged as racist), black/white, rich/poor—left Basquiat in a mad state, an insider and outsider whose work, amidst an art world "less a business than an industry,"[27] remained "concerned with the production of meaning rather than with the isolation of specific icons or texts."[28] Regarding Basquiat's work, art curator Marc Mayer warns against literal interpretations of Basquiat's intertextual images: "I can't help feeling that a painstaking analysis of Basquiat's symbols and signs is a trap that lures us away from the abstract and oneiric purpose of these pictures. They are not sending us coded messages to decipher, so much as confusing us at once with their discursive sleight of hand."[29]

Through an intertwining of black skeletal figures, arms upraised, positioned within religious iconography interspersed with textual signs, symbols, and markers, and referenced by divinely inspired names (for example, *Untitled [Baptism]*, 1982; or *Profit 1*, 1982), Basquiat not only inspired viewers to "decode its [his art's] particular representations," but also, as Jordana Moore Saggese stresses, "to discover the possibilities for representation."[30] As Saggese continues, in subverting "the relationship between artist, object, and viewer by creating a nonlinear narrative of painting,"[31] Basquiat evades the very binary thinking that reifies the consumerism of contemporary culture while creating space, as bell hooks argues, to grapple "with both the pull of a genealogy that is fundamentally 'black' (rooted in African diasporic . . . tradition) and a fascination with white Western traditions."[32] Basquiat's deliberate ambiguity and *madness*—captured through his collage of text, media varieties, compositional methods, and neo-expressionistic painting—thus reflect the realities of living in a materially-contingent world, one that results in racialized bodies, gendered expectations, and class divisions, but also creates the conditions to use art as a point of ecstatic overcoming.

Through images that play with the limitations of formal—and pop—aesthetics, Basquiat's work signals a willingness to locate and expose the violence and boundaries of socio-cultural normativity, pointing the viewer to the complexities of artistic appropriation and construction, as well as the instability of identity within the modern moment. In *Profit I* (1982), which consists of acrylic and spray paint on canvas, the juxtaposition of a skeletal figure with arms upraised, letters standing alone and near one another, scratch-outs and paint-overs, numbers and table graphs, an incomplete clock and roman numerals, and an almost endless train of partially complete symbolic references (from a crown of thorns to the dollar sign), signals an indignant understanding on the part of Basquiat that led to the production of a defiant "sacral exceptionalism" within his work.[33] Basquiat demonstrated an ability, to borrow from Susan Sontag's reflections on interpretation, "to recover our senses . . . to see more, to hear more, to feel more" through the obfuscation of immediate meaning and within the process of constructing, deconstructing, and reconstructing images.[34]

Along with his high school classmate Al Diaz, Basquiat initially sought such recovery from modern America—for himself and others—through street art images produced under the pseudonym SAMO, an acronym for the "same old shit." Tagging poems, jokes, aphorisms, and prophecies in marker and spray paint on subways throughout New York City, the two used SAMO to critique, as Saggese notes, "consumer culture":

SAMO AS AN END 2 NINE-2-FIVE
NONSENSE
WASTIN' YOUR LIFE
2 MAKE ENDS MEET . . . TO GO HOME
AT NIGHT TO YOUR
COLOR T.V. . . .[35]

Such public exhibitionism positioned SAMO "as an alternative to the commercial art world,"[36] an antagonism that Basquiat transitioned into his gallery exhibits through subject matter that, although allowing him entrance into the 1980s high art scene, nevertheless "always separates him [Basquiat] once again, and defamiliarizes him,"[37] leaving the viewer with "paintings and drawings [that] highlight the dynamic process of looking,"[38] both in terms of the works of art under one's gaze and at one's current moment, cultural history, and fabricated identities.

To engage Basquiat's work, then, is to gain access to a culture gone mad in its materiality; it also, however, presents the viewer with insight into the spiritual, physical, and ephemeral nature of modern life. In *Profit I*, through the image of a white-outlined, black body, arms upraised, crowned with a nimbus accentuated by golden rays, Basquiat speaks to the body's eventual degeneration while simultaneously celebrating its sacrality. As with SAMO graffiti, Basquiat forces us to engage an outwardly religiously inspired figure within the contemporary frames of capitalism, playing with words and labels, ubiquitously naming this piece with a phonetic sign that speaks to a sense of foreseeing (prophecy) while remaining bound by an economic system that transforms everything into a "profit," including Basquiat's art. Within this dual sense, Basquiat invokes Christian scripture—"The love of money is the root of all evil" (1 Timothy 6:10)—while fully positioning religion as a source for/of such evil within a world defined by producers and consumers, wealth and profits, the saved and the damned. The main figure thus emerges as martyred, a character whose upturned arms can be read as both lamentation against the insanity of the world and surrender against a system beyond one's control. Through its stark light/dark contrast, the image ultimately captures Basquiat's perception that, amidst the chaos of modern culture, self-actualization can be found within the creative madness of fragmented presentations.

As Cathy Curtis details, "encoded within the seeming randomness of Basquiat's writing and imagery is a bleak lack of trust in systems—however superficially benign—that fuel or reflect power struggles."[39] Basquiat's aphorisms, graffiti, and artworks decenter perspective, forcing the viewer (and reader) to turn off pragmatic thinking and empirical meaning in order to understand how, in the redefinition and reformation of words, signs, and images, we can locate a spark of authentic living. In recognizing the boundaries of linearity and traditional modes of understanding, we come to see the double-bind of madness that drives the aesthetic response and cultural alternative of the Beats and Basquiat. More importantly, through this recognition, these artists invite us to participate in constructive chaos—within prose and imagery that inundate us with meaning only to be canceled by a well-placed brushstroke or symbol of a world gone insane, mad art functions to unveil our individual holiness. Horrified by the decay of subjectivity and spiritual values, Ginsberg, Kerouac, and Basquiat pursue art as a means to challenge the banality and excess of western society by representing the costs of commodity culture. In locating insanity as the consequence of modernity, and madness as the source to imagine anew, these artists purge themselves of structure, syntax, and normative meaning, sharing "a desire to journey inward to the darkest recesses of the human psyche" in order to remember what it means to be human and, through this remembering, revive the capacity for selfhood and community.[40]

Notes

1. See Roy Porter, *Madness: A Brief History* (Oxford: Oxford University Press, 2002).

2. D. H. Lawrence, *Studies in Classic American Literature* (New York: Penguin, 1977), 8.

3. Jonathan Franzen, "The Man in the Gray Flannel Suit (2002)," *Farther Away: Essays* (New York: Farrar, Straus & Giroux, 2012), 309.

4. Jack Kerouac, *On the Road* (New York: Penguin, 1991), 5.

5. Allen Ginsberg, "America," in *Howl and Other Poems* (San Francisco: City Lights, 2002), 39.

6. See Lizabeth Cohen, *A Consumers' Republic: The Politics of Mass Consumption in Postwar America* (New York: Vintage, 2003), and Jessica Weiss, *To Have and to Hold: Marriage, the Baby Boom, and Social Change* (Chicago: University of Chicago Press, 2000).

7. See Karal Ann Marling, *As Seen on TV: The Visual Culture of Everyday Life in the 1950s* (Cambridge, MA: Harvard University Press, 1996).

8. Betty Friedan, *The Feminine Mystique* (New York: W.W. Norton & Company, 2001), and Robert D. Putnam, *Bowling Alone: The Collapse and Revival of American Community* (New York: Touchstone, 2001).

9. See Jose van Dijck, *The Culture of Connectivity: A Critical History of Social Media* (New York: Oxford University Press, 2013).

10. See Robert W. McChesney, *Digital Disconnect* (New York: The New Press, 2014).

11. See Benjamin Spock and Robert Needlman, *Dr. Spock's Baby and Child Care*, 9th ed. (New York: Pocket Books, 2011), and Amy Chua, *Battle Hymn of the Tiger Mother* (New York: Penguin, 2011).

12. See Paul Goodman, *Growing Up Absurd* (New York: Vintage, 1956), 5–10.

13. Erich Fromm, *The Sane Society* (New York: An Owl Book, 1955), 11.

14. Carl A. Raschke, *The Interruption of Eternity: Modern Gnosticism and the Origins of the New Religious Consciousness* (Chicago: Nelson Hall, 1980), 2068.

15. Raschke, *The Interruption of Eternity,* 207.

16. Allen Ginsberg, "Howl," in *Howl and Other Poems* (San Francisco: City Lights, 2002), 9.

17. Ginsberg, "Howl," 20–22.

18. Ginsberg, "Howl," 22.

19. Ginsberg, "Howl," 27.

20. R. D. Laing, "Transcendental Experience in Relation to Religion and Psychosis," in *The Psychedelic Review* 1, no. 6 (1964): 8.

21. Laing, "Transcendental Experience," 11.

22. Ginsberg, "Howl," 23.

23. Ginsberg, "Howl," 27, emphasis added.

24. Gilles Deleuze and Félix Guattari, *Anti-Oedipus: Capitalism and Schizophrenia* (New York: Penguin, 2009).

25. Jordana Moore Saggese, *Reading Basquiat: Exploring Ambivalence in American Art* (Berkeley: University of California Press, 2014), 108.

26. Steven Hager cited by Dick Hebdige, "Welcome to the Terrordome: Jean-Michel Basquiat and the 'Dark' Side of Hybridity," in *Jean-Michel Basquiat*, ed. Richard Marshall (New York: Whitney Museum of American Art, 1992), 62. Basquiat challenged the racialization that accompanied the "tropes and stereotypes

of primitivism," which defined narratives surrounding black artists and, in particular, Basquiat. See Saggese, *Reading Basquiat,* 17–19.

27. Lisbet Nilson, "Making It Neo," *ARTnews* 82 (January 1983): 64.

28. Saggese, *Reading Basquiat,* 7.

29. Marc Mayer, "Basquiat in History," in *Basquiat,* eds. Marc Mayer and Fred Hoffman (New York: Brooklyn Museum of Art, 2005), 49.

30. Saggese, *Reading Basquiat,* 7.

31. Saggese, *Reading Basquiat,* 9.

32. bell hooks, "Altars of Sacrifice: Re-Membering Basquiat," *Art in America* 81, no. 6 (June 1993): 70.

33. Leonard Emmerling, *Jean-Michel Basquiat 1960–1988: The Explosive Force of the Streets* (Taschen, 2006), 32.

34. Susan Sontag, "Against Interpretation," in *Against Interpretation: And Other Essays* (New York: Picador, 2001), 14.

35. Saggese, *Reading Basquiat,* 3.

36. Ibid.

37. hooks, "Altars of Sacrifice: Re-Membering Basquiat," 70.

38. Saggese, *Reading Basquiat,* 7.

39. Cathy Curtis, "A Bit of Basquiat: Meaning More Important Than Style in 11 'Blue Ribbon' Works From '84 at Newport Harbor," *Los Angeles Times*, July 27, 1993, http://articles.latimes.com/1993-07-27/entertainment/ca-17242_1_newport -harbor-art-museum.

40. Saggese, *Reading Basquiat,* 124–125.

CHAPTER TWENTY-NINE

"Autists" and Merchandising "Autistic Art"

Leni Van Goidsenhoven

The fifth and latest edition of the *Diagnostic and Statistical Manual for Mental Disorders* (also known as "the bible of psychiatry") dismisses a number of categories that until recently were frequently used, including Asperger Syndrome, PDD-NOS, and Autism Syndrome. All are now classified under one big common denominator: "autism spectrum disorder." As a result, "autism"[1] is defined as a neurological developmental disorder that covers a broad spectrum.[2] In the course of the 20th century, our knowledge and understanding of autism, deeply embedded in historical, social, cultural, and discursive contexts, underwent a remarkable evolution. Autism grew into a flexible and multivalent signifier, spurred on by continuous interest in circles of academic research and by unceasing attention from popular culture. Controversies about diagnostic criteria, medications or treatments attest to the prominence of this neuropsychiatric condition in public and professional imaginations. Along with deepening of academic research and widening of public debate, an industry arose to guarantee steady popularization of autism studies. It comprised fashionable alternative therapies and self-help books, autobiographies and blogs, adaptations in literature, cinema, and television.

At the start of the 20th century, Eugene Bleuler coined the term "autism" to explain specific behavior among schizophrenic patients, emphasizing the process of aversion from reality through withdrawal into a fantasy world. In the next three decades, the notion occupied a marginal position in psychiatric vocabulary. From the early 1940s on, however, autism managed to manifest itself as a distinctive diagnostic category and pathology, thanks to child psychiatrist Leo Kanner and pediatrician Hans Asperger, among others. The tone of the autism-discourse was set, and the notion lost every connection with fantasy, creativity, or imagination. The opposite aspect, a complete absence of fantasy, creativity, or imagination, became central to the discourse. Nevertheless, over the last ten years, the "autism landscape" has even witnessed a genuine *artistic* revolution. The condition, and the persons who have been diagnosed with it (those who are "living on the spectrum"), became the center of museum exhibitions, theater and dance productions, creative workshops, and artistic health projects. In Europe, and especially in Belgium, the so-called "ateliers" or creative workshops have established a close relationship with well-known museums of art brut and outsider art (notably, Museum Dr. Guislain, MADmusée, Art & Marges). These activities deserve a warm welcome, but have not yet achieved critical integration into the discourse of outsider art. Furthermore, it remains unclear what their influence would be on current thinking about outsider art or art brut, and how exactly such an influence would function.

The artistic "turn" also triggered the emergence of notions such as "autistic art" and "autistic aesthetics." They appeared, and continue to appear, in contexts that have a higher degree of specialization, but also spread through popular media and communication channels. All this raises questions about the meaning and functioning of the notions, and about the status of "the autistic artist" implied in a concept of "autistic art." Perhaps of fundamental importance is the question of whether the notions can form an obstacle to any valuing of autism as a potential enrichment of art and culture.

Ateliers, or Workshops

Workshops (ateliers) and creative courses have made their way into psychiatric buildings and care centers for quite some time now. Expressive therapy, music, dance, and theater are believed to stimulate inclusion, provide (reflexive) insights into the identity of "the other," and help develop talents that lie dormant. This creative therapy frequently serves a larger treatment, is bound by a program, and answers to pedagogical objectives— after all, a trajectory needs to be covered. Apart from these "creative little hours" within the framework of more meaningful therapeutic guidance, there are also contexts created by organizations (so-called ateliers) in which the focus on art and creative expression is completely detached from the pursuit of specific solutions, remedies, or treatments.

One of the first workshops in Belgium that directly addressed persons with an artistic talent and a limitation was Créahm (1979, Liège). The workshop's activities resisted all understanding within the rigid structure of hospital activities or other medical-mental treatments. The primary objective was the creation of a safe environment within which a vulnerable group was challenged artistically and was given the opportunity to develop. The workshop's supervisors were not therapists or caregivers, but persons with an artistic background. They helped to create a clear structure and a relaxed, inspiring atmosphere. A central aspect of the workshops were project-related collaborations with contemporary artists, including authors, playwrights, and visual artists, which gave rise to intense and enriching collaborative relationships. Thanks to this method, Créahm established a solid reputation in Europe, being recognized as a pioneer in the field of inclusive projects. Following in the wake of Créahm, workshops mushroomed across the Belgian map. A few examples are De Zandberg (Harelbeke), La 'S' Grand Atelier (Vielsalm), and Platform K (Gent). A number of workshops, such as (W)onderweg and Aanbeeld Autimistisch Atelier (Puurs), focused specifically on persons with autism. Aanbeeld Autimistisch Atelier, for example, is an atelier *for* and *by* persons with autism. All these workshops were intended for people that have the common property of being vulnerable in society, yet they did not share one univocal method. Each possessed, and continues to develop, its own context, rhythm, method, and artistic discipline(s).

Whenever there is talk of art within a framework of autism (and, by extension, of persons with vulnerabilities or disabilities of a psychiatric nature), the discussion invariably leads to the notion of *art brut* or *outsider art* (the Anglo-Saxon alternative notion). The ateliers, however, form a kind of *Fremdkörper* within the classic story of art brut, as they attempt to disrupt the discourse from the inside out. They raise questions about the initial definition of art brut, formulated by Jean Dubuffet shortly before World War II.[3] It is true that workshops focus on vulnerable persons who, for one or the other reason, lead a life of isolation, yet they also offer a frame of reference, courses, and guidance. People can open up artistically, broaden the horizon, and attend further training, as well as enter into a dialogue with artistic paradigms and traditions. This collides with Dubuffet's initial notions of "authenticity," "naturalness," and "spontaneity." In addition, workshops regularly collaborate with contemporary artists. The exchange is characterized by an understanding of mutual influencing.

Contemporary artists have stopped looking at "outsiders" as a potential source of inspiration for new directions chosen in their own artistic trajectory. The core of the exchange lies in the encounter, in the interaction with each other, and in the dialogues. Collaborations of this kind wipe the floor with the Romantic myth of the authentic, lonesome artist as a creative genius.

Exhibitions resulting from creative workshops are very interesting high-profiled events. In Belgium, museums specialized in art brut such as the Belgian MADmusée (Luik), Museum Dr. Guislain (Gent), Art & Marges (Brussel) and WIT.H (Kortrijk) have shown great expertise and professionalism in setting up productive collaborations with the workshops. Regretfully, there is still very little reflection on this complex practice. In the rare event of attention being paid to the projects, reflections quickly slip into the feeble and uncritical discourse that surrounds social-artistic work.

Autism as a Metaphor for the Creative Process

Creative workshop activities, exhibition projects, and the accompanying shift in focus toward capabilities are now manifest presences in the "autism landscape." Overall, the practice is extremely praiseworthy, deserving support on a permanent basis. Still, the field also shows a trend that raises questions, particularly concerning the interaction with, and designation of, this creative work. In the last few years, for example, there has been a growing use of terms such as "autistic art" and "autistic aesthetics."

Again, this is not the first new development in the conceptual history of autism, nor is it the first time that autism is employed as an adjective or as a metaphor. Since the 1990s, the term has lived its own life. Both in fictional and nonfictional worlds, autism often served an external goal, reducing the condition to the status of a prop or accessory. In the media, for example, the term was abundantly used to refer to unusual, strange, and even dangerous social or political situations and persons. Stuart Murray was right to claim that "the condition has become almost ubiquitous frame of reference for recent notions of difference. . . .] Such usage is the product of a slippage of terminology, a widening of meaning, which displays the manner in which an *idea* of autism has spread through public culture."[4]

"Autistic art" or "autistic aesthetics" initially appeared to be innocent terms, which mainly popped up in online contexts such as blogs, and intended to bring the creative work of persons with autism into the limelight. The existence of Facebook communities should be viewed along the same line (e.g., autistic artist, autistic arts, and autistic art space). These groups also promote the creative work (and by extension, talent) of people with autism, yet are mainly concerned with community building and, by extension, with managing the interests of persons with autism. Of a less innocent nature, however, is the growing frequency with which both art historians and psychiatrists make explicit mention of "autism and art," as if it concerned a separate category. Thus, *Out of Art: Magazine for Contemporary Outsider Art*, one of the few (and therefore leading) journals about outsider art in the Low Countries, has already published two issues about the subject in less than a decade (2006, 2013). In the same way, the exhibition *akku e.V., I See What You Don't See. Art and Autism* (2010), which explicitly and exclusively focuses on autistic art, has been traveling around the world for a number of years now. The exhibition is accompanied by a catalogue of over 300 pages containing essays by experts such as Elsen Volker, Roger Cardinal, and Sabiene Autsch. The volume would be quite a nut to crack, were it not for its frequent and conspicuous use of the term "autistic art" without ever offering an interpretation or throwing some light on what is to be understood with the term. The book also lacks every form of reflection about the discussed (therapeutic) ateliers or about their role within outsider art. Apart from this, the recent years were also marked by a swift rise of small-scale exhibition projects around autism and art that usually promote some form of charity. Because of this, the conceptual pairing of "autism" and "art" acquired a touch of obscurity and the connotation of lack of substance.

There is still more. The examples do not only show that "autistic art"—because of its name or because of the diagnosis?—does not belong to the corpus of outsider art or art brut, but also that plain commercial interest lies in wait (these days, autism seems to hold great attraction for people). Furthermore, there is the clear and present danger of what can be called a "savant rhetoric."

In the context of autism, savant rhetoric implies speaking about autism in terms of "intellectual disability" combined with "very sizeable talent or extreme giftedness" that exceeds "the limits of normality." It also covers the use of the terms "idiot savant," "learned idiot," or "knowledgeable idiot." The idea that persons with autism possess a spectacular talent but otherwise remain completely context-blind and alienated was avidly picked up by popular culture and its fictional worlds. It also occurred in contexts that involved art and autism.[5] Famous examples of "autism celebrities" or "phenomena" are Nadia and Stephen Wiltshire. At the age of three, Nadia was able to draw perfect perspectival drawings, while Stephen, also known as "the living camera," drew cities from a bird's eye view or in panorama. Wiltshire only needs to see the cities for a few seconds to memorize them and to be able to draw them by heart, even in the smallest details. The architectural artist has his own gallery and is prominently present on YouTube, where possible skeptics can become eyewitnesses of this "abnormal talent." Nadia and Wiltshire are never approached as artists per se. As far as their spectacular talent is concerned, the emphasis is always on their condition of autism. Just as the view that focused too heavily on deficit, this approach to the savant disengages autism from every sense of humanity. What's more, the mode of thinking feeds the idea that everyone on the spectrum must possess an outsized talent or extreme giftedness, which in turn reinforces a contradictory inclusion story and adds curious value judgments.

Terms such as "autistic art" and "autistic artist," which regularly pop up in social media, exhibition catalog, and academic texts, implicitly feed the savant discourse. Furthermore, the terminology of "autistic art" is something of an oddity in the context of outsider art, in which there are no other categories based on disorders, conditions, or syndromes of the artists involved. It is as if the designation of autism serves no other purpose than flirting with the popularity (and, by extension, with the commercial dimension) of the condition in popular culture.

Apart from this, the central problem with a term such as "autistic art" is that hardly any clarity exists about its meaning, or the function it fulfills. Thus, "autistic art" could refer to the Romantic idea that art or creative expression is an extraordinary way of getting to see the "true person." The term would then function as a diagnostic category, implying that the disorder or mental condition can be detected and understood through the art. This view, however, was eclipsed long ago. More than likely this is not what is currently meant by the term "autistic art." What seems to be the case, rather, is that "autistic art" is being employed as an aesthetic category. Researchers such as art historian Roger Cardinal (2010) and psychologist Ilona Roth (2014), for instance, are seeking the "typically cognitive autistic style" through fixated aesthetic qualities such as trueness to life and nature, sense of detail, and repetitiveness. Working from a medical perspective, physicians like Kyle Hunter (2012) attempt to connect cognitive elements with aesthetic views, in order to construct a profile of the "autistic artist."[6] These understandings, however, are also not without problems. By creating a category of this sort, autism is watered down to a metaphor of the creative process. Consequently, it detracts from its complexity as a neurological condition, and evidently also from the essence of art and creative expression.

Today, the terms "autistic art" and "autistic artist" still impede any richness and multidimensionality that autism could inject into art and culture. The question of what would be a different way of addressing the matter is difficult to answer. Perhaps artists who are working implicitly or explicitly with or around the matter can shed some light. In this respect, the author of this contribution had the pleasure of making the acquaintance of Schipper Landschip [Skipper Land-Shipe], a Belgian artist who has built a commanding oeuvre. Landschip has autism and does not shy away from communicating this. He often toys with autism in his work, applying the category or label on a meta-level. Contrary to Nadia and Wiltshire, Landschip is not an artist who is the result of some spectacular talent owing to his condition. His autism simply belongs to his identity—nothing more, nothing less. Precisely because of this, it is also part of his artistic practice, which has no place for sensational talents or exceptional gifts.

Since the 1980s, Landschip has exhibited under various pseudonyms, such as Ndizi Zinatosha, Efflux, or The Joseph Boys. He has worked with different materials, and his earliest work is distinctly different from what he would create today. Yet, there is one constant and recognizable element: a raw, ironic, and direct style. One of the recurring elements in Landschip's earlier work was a form of hieroglyphs, which gave evidence of the degree in which an expressive form of communication matters to him. Later, the hieroglyphs disappeared, and the artist started combining text and image. The work, however, never lost its recalcitrant and committed dimension. In 1986, when flamboyant art curator Jan Hoet wrote history with the exhibition *Chambre D'amis*, Landschip set up his own *Antichambre*. Although he was never part of the official exhibition, he expressed his opinion and willful response to the establishment by making a *chambre* on a run-down industrial site. Together with a friend, he also formed the duo The Royal Givers. Raising his voice in protest against the global arms race, he made weekly visits to the Antwerp Museum of Fine Arts, bringing in his own paintings to fill up the vacant spaces of permanent collection works that were removed for restoration or were on loan. In fact, throwing spectators into confusion is a leitmotif in Landschip's art. It is never entirely clear whether his actions are dead serious or ironic. This confusion is heightened by the fact that the artist seems to incarnate a kind of "character." This impression is brought about by the use of pseudonyms, but also by the fact that he is hardly ever or never available for interviews or reflections on his own work. Only a handful of people really know the artist. Undoubtedly, this can be linked to his autism. At the same time, it succeeds in giving a twist to it. The aspect of "character creation" and "inaccessibility" is turned into a critique of the inner workings of an artistic field that sometimes succumbs to commercial motives.

Autism only becomes a theme in Landschip's later work, even then rather "sneaking" inside, instead of "imposing" itself. In 2002, Landschip wrote—or rather drew—the booklet *The Invisible Autist*, in which he proposed an elegant, delicate definition of autism. Now, the artist makes two paintings on a daily basis, usually little self-portraits, and immediately posts these on his blog, thus creating a form of expressive diary. The constant choice of small square canvases is interesting in itself, because it demonstrates his love of details. Using oil on canvas, the self-portraits raise a critical voice in social debates. At the same time, Landschip manages to mock his own autism and certain ways of representation. Slowly but surely, the artist is building a complex oeuvre that addresses issues of self-representation and autism, yet avoids every external label.

The Arts and Their Fascination with Autism

So far, this short contribution has remained silent about a recent and interesting development, which places autism right in the middle of the artistic landscape. Apparently, a group of contemporary artists has grown fascinated with autism. Representations of autism in literature and cinema have been frequent and various, even to such an extent that there is now a small commercial industry dedicated to it. Still, there are artists who have no interest in the representation of autism, but are genuinely fascinated by a form of autistic (and, by extension, neurodiversity) thought. They try to question, and even distrust, their own "language," working with what they do not know. Obviously, the interest of artists in cognitive processes is far from new. A similar movement can be observed in the humanities, where the development is often designated as "the cognitive turn." The interest can originate from a personal experience, or it can be associated with a critical view of a society in which overstimulation has become a matter of course, a theme that has an obvious and strong connection with autism.

Examples of artists who look beyond the representation of autism are, among others, theater stage director and playwright Robert Wilson, painter Yves Velter, dance performers and choreographers Gabriel Schenker and Sonja Jokiniemi, and filmmaker Olivier Smolders. As early as 1989, Smolders codirected with Thierry Knauff the 12-minute short *Seuls*, a controversial film that depicts autistic children in a way that calls to mind the work of Fernand Deligny and Renaud Victor. From the 1960s until his death in 1996, Deligny took care of autistic children who had been given up by psychiatry. In South France, assisted by Victor, he searched for a way of understanding them. He filmed and transcribed their movements, moves, and acts (*lignes d'erre*), without ever focusing on a narrative aspect or any form of telos. Deligny's approach seems to reverberate in the film made by Smolders and Knauff.

In 2015, Sonja Jokiniemi created a dance performance called *Hmm*, which was based on her collaboration with autistic youngsters. The latter taught her how to shuffle and stumble in a world that shows little cohesion, in which objects and sounds do not seem to have any meaning. Autism is never an explicit subject in the performance, yet it is integrated in a larger whole of reflections on Jokiniemi's artistic practice. The artist is primarily fascinated by other forms of meaning-giving and of bodily experience. Specialized literature usually perceives the autistic body in a negative way. Some of the clichés hold that it is a fortress in which the "real person behind autism" is imprisoned, that it reacts as a machine, or that it is deprived of a delicate motor system. Jokiniemi, by contrast, detects poetical aspects in the body and bodily experience of persons with autism.

The works of these artists are of high quality, and the same qualitative excellence is maintained in the ways of integrating autism in their creative practice. Nevertheless, these artists walk a very thin tightrope. The danger of slipping back into the perverse story of inclusion lurks behind every action. At the time that all normality thinking has been terminated, it has become fashionable to focus on differences or otherness. In addition, autism may quickly be reduced to aesthetics or even mobilized for specific aesthetic purposes.

A Multivalent Signifier

The connection between autism, creativity, and art remained unnoticed for a long time, partly because of a medical canon that assumed persons with autism did not possess imagination and that based its actions on a deficit-model. Nevertheless, autism does not exist outside of culture, as was argued by Roy Grinker.[7] Autism enriches the cultural and artistic landscape on various levels. Cultural filters that provide context and representation have a positive effect on the identity building and empowerment of persons with autism. In addition, they contribute to the creation of a broader basis that puts forward autism spectrum as both a multivalent, complex, and extremely interesting multitude, and as a flexible and multivalent signifier. Nevertheless, some caution is warranted when terms such as "autistic art," "autistic aesthetics," and the "autistic artist" are used since these have the potential of curtailing creativity and reducing autism to a univocal and static category of aesthetics combined with diagnostic criteria.

Notes

1. The term "autism" covers the full diversity of autism spectrum disorder. This article is a revised version of a Dutch essay.

2. American Psychiatric Association (APA), *Diagnostic and Statistical Manual of Mental Disorders*, 5th ed. (Washington, DC: APA 2013). The release of the *DSM-V* met with a storm of criticism, see: Stijn Vanheule, *Diagnosis and the DSM: A Critical Review*, (Basingstoke: Palgrave Macmillan, 2014).

3. Leni Van Goidsenhoven and Arnout De Cleene, "Brizzolari's Dismantling of The Romantic Outsider Myth: Inclusive Strategies Seen from a Belgian Perspective," *Elsewhere—The International Journal of Self-Taught and Outsider Art*, 3.1, (2016): 25–39.

4. Stuart Murray, *Representing Autism: Culture, Narrative, Fascination* (Liverpool: Liverpool University Press, 2008), 9.

5. Leni Van Goidsenhoven, "Playing with Autism and Outsider Art," *Psychoanalytische Perspectieven* 32.3, (2014): 263.

6. Roger Cardinal, "Outsider Art and The Autistic Creator," In *Autism and Talent*, eds. Francesca Happé and Uta Frith (Oxford: Oxford University Press, 2010), 181–194; Ilona Roth, "Imagining Differently: The Cognitive Style in Autism," Conference Paper at *Cognitive Futures in the Humanities*, 2nd International Conference University of Durham, (Durham, April 24–26, 2014); Kyle Hunter and Deborah Barnbaum, "Pragmatic Aesthetics and the Autistic Artist," *The Journal of Aesthetic Education*: 46.4, (2012): 48–56.

7. Roy Grinker, *Understanding Minds: Remapping The World of Autism* (New York: Basic Books, 2007).

CHAPTER THIRTY

Slipping into *Silent Hill*: Transnational Trauma

Brenda S. Gardenour Walter

Since its release in 1999, Konami's survival-horror digital game, *Silent Hill*, has become a pop-cultural universe with a dedicated transnational fandom. In *Silent Hill* and each of the eight subsequent games, the player takes on the role of a main character who has experienced some horrific trauma, including the violent death of a loved one, sexual abuse, or PTSD from military service. As the story unfolds, the player-character begins to "slip" from his or her quotidian life into an inverted world of madness personified by the town of Silent Hill, a duplicitous realm of repression and dissociation. At once real and unreal, populated and abandoned, the spatial construction of Silent Hill is a projection of the haunted body, a ruined world of skeletal buildings that appear to be dead but whose basement-bowels and fetid hallways are alive with nightmarish beings, writhing in the dark.[1] Through the lens of the main character, the player explores this slippery mindscape of animated corpses, entering into these decaying body-buildings to discover repressed fragments of the forgotten self, all while being stalked and tormented by traumatic memories in the shape of monsters who attack without warning. Thinking only of survival, the character must act in the moment to defeat each monster-memory and collect clues, shining like fragmented mirrors in the gloom, that facilitate a narrative of self disclosure.

The therapeutic process that unfolds during gameplay in *Silent Hill* is multivalent, in part because "the player inhabits a twilight zone where he/she is both an empirical subject outside the game *and* undertakes a role inside the game."[2] The player not only witnesses the traumatic past and present of the main character, but also experiences the shocking recovery of those memories *as* the main character. The player's interpretation of this dual experience is shaped not only by personal history but also by the often-slippery construction of mental illness and its treatment within his or her culture. For example, an American player might find slipping in and out of *Silent Hill 2* (2001) and *Silent Hill: Shattered Memories* (2009) to be fluid and uncanny. Located somewhere in the American Northeast, Silent Hill's architecture and signifiers, as well as the tropes of haunted asylums, "madness," and therapy, are familiar narratives in American popular culture. These themes are woven like a thread through H. P. Lovecraft's weird tales, films such as *Session 9* (2001), the television series *American Horror Story: Asylum* (2012), and "reality" shows focused on pop-psychology, such as *My Strange Addiction* (2010) and *Hoarders* (2009). While individuals suffering from mental illness, especially those who manifest unpredictable or violent behaviors, continue to be stigmatized in daily life, the narratives of mental illness and its myriad treatments are prolific and very public discourses in American culture, and the processes of psychotherapy are well-known. In Japanese culture, on the other hand, mental illness and its treatment remain taboo subjects. Despite horrifying rates of depression and suicide, hospitals rarely have psychiatric wards, and mental institutions are sparse and often located in remote and unmarked buildings. Those who suffer from mental illnesses are expected to do so in silence, lest they lose their jobs and bring dishonor to their families.Because of this, the terrifying experience of slipping in and out of *Silent Hill* might prove far more complex for the Japanese player. In Japan, to play *Silent Hill* is to take on the "sick" role of the main character, to enter into a world of "madness" and asylums, and to risk abject contamination by the "other," permanent stigmatization, and loss of identity. Western models of psychotherapy that demand direct confrontation with the past and a willingness to openly "own" one's mental illness are likewise problematic for the Japanese player. The gameplay narrative of *Silent Hill 4: The Room* (2004) speaks to Japanese cultural concerns with mental illness and its treatment, offering a different and distinctively Japanese approach to posttraumatic care, known as Morita Therapy, which focuses not on remembering the past but on transcending it through mindfulness in the present.

Confronting the Past: Western Therapies in *Silent Hill: Shattered Memories*

To slip into *Silent Hill* is to cross a sacred boundary, to enter into a "magic circle," a playground with "forbidden spots, isolated, hedged around, hallowed, within which special rules obtain."[3] "Temporary worlds within the ordinary world," digital games serve as warped mirrors with the power to reflect deep cultural concerns, such as mental illness, back out to the player and beyond.[4] To cross *Silent Hill's* magic threshold is to dissociate from the present-self and to associate with a delusional and terrified other, to wander through a digital hardscape that reflects that character's mental state.[5] For the Western player, the exploration of the game's physical ruins, including abandoned homes and hospitals, is an autopsy-like journey into the corpse-bodies that harbor monstrous secrets in their darkest recesses. As the building-bodies are excavated and the monsters revealed, so are the game's narrative and the character's memories. This process of discovering locked chambers long hidden in the mind and opening them to release forgotten memories, known as cryptonomy, serves as the narrative foundation of *Silent Hill 2* (2001).[6] In this game, the player identifies with James Sunderland, an at-first sympathetic character, who arrives in Silent Hill after receiving a letter from his dead wife, Mary, who tells him to meet her in their "special place." For James, the town of Silent Hill acts as a memory theater; as he moves from space to place, he uncovers painful memories buried in his own mindscape. James navigates much of the ruined town in isolation, with the exception of a suicidal young woman searching for her mother in a graveyard—an allusion to James's hopeless search for Mary among corpses—and a psychopathic teen, who represents James's repressed rage. Another recurring character is Maria, a more promiscuous version of Mary, who leads him to slowly uncover the clues that ultimately expose his horrible and half-forgotten secret, that he killed his wife. The only other character in the game is a little girl named Laura, who doesn't think that there is anything wrong with Silent Hill and doesn't see any of its monsters. Laura, who acts as a sort of control in the gameplay experiment, confronts the player with the possibility that Silent Hill's nightmares exist only as delusions in James's mind, and that the player has been battling those delusions from behind the eyes of a madman.

The informal therapeutic process of cryptonomy in *Silent Hill 2* is formalized as clinical psychotherapy in *Silent Hill Shattered Memories* (2009). Unlike James, who journeys to Silent Hill of his own volition, the main character in *Shattered Memories*, who is not revealed until the game's ending, is drawn back to the town under the guidance of a therapist. The game begins in first person perspective, with the player in a clinician's office awaiting a therapy session. Upon entering the room, the therapist looks directly at the player, saying "I'm glad you came. Just showing up shows your commitment to the process . . . we take this at your pace. No notes. No drugs. No theories. We go back to the start. Understand what happened." In this first session, the player is required to fill out a basic personality inventory; in subsequent sessions, he or she must color a picture, sort images, fill out forms, and answer the therapist's probing questions. All of the responses provided by the player are used to shape the physical environment, events, and recovered memories within the game, as well as the ultimate ending of the narrative itself. In *Shattered Memories*, the character slips into Silent Hill as flashbacks; gameplay takes place in the patient's memory theater and in a distant past. In this respect, the game being played has already ended; it is a haunted magic circle. The flashback sequences follow Harry Mason as he searches for his young daughter, Cheryl, in the ruins of Silent Hill. Unlike James in *Silent Hill 2*, Harry has no weapons and cannot fight any of the monsters that assail him as he attempts to solve the puzzles of the past. He can only wander helplessly through a nightmare of frozen madness, hiding from monstrous memories and waiting for them to crawl back into their crypts. Again and again, the player slips out of Silent Hill and back into the therapist's office in an attempt to piece together the shattered memories of game's the title. The game ends with the psychiatrist enraged at his patient's lack of progress, throwing his glass against the wall and yelling, "I'm spelling it all out for you . . . eighteen years of repression . . . blind children clutching photos in the dark . . . the dad walking around in your head isn't even a ghost. He never existed!" In this chilling moment, the player realizes that he or she has not been playing the character of Harry in Silent Hill, but of Cheryl's haunted memories of her father that exist only in her own mind. For the first time, we see the patient, Cheryl, a delusional teenager on the edge of adulthood, trying to cope with a lifetime of abuse and loss. Looking at her father's ghost, she reaches out to him, "You've been with me so long." The moment is cathartic for both player and character, a hard ending to an arduous process.

As both James in *Silent Hill 2* and Cheryl in *Silent Hill: Shattered Memories*, the player slips into a Silent Hill shaped by the mental illness of the main character. In this role, the player explores the ruined pasts and shattered psyches of the protagonists as they seek to uncover lost memories, and with them, clues to their identities in the present. In both games, "reality" and "delusion" are fluid categories, allowing the player to identify with the isolation, confusion, and terror of dissociation, if only for a time. *Shattered Memories* intensifies this experience, introducing the player to psychotherapy, the power of clinicians, and the distrust of that power on the part of some patients. The game comes with a "psychology warning" stating that "the game psychologically profiles you" and uses this "knowledge against you, creating your own personal nightmare. The game plays you as much as you play it." For many players, it is their first experience being closely analyzed and feeling as though their every thought and action is being judged. It is likewise terrifying because it expands the magic circle outward; the rules of the game are *no longer bound to the game*, but slip into the player's world and back again.Despite its potential for emotional trauma, the narrative of therapy is a familiar one to the Western player; surviving mental illness means directly confronting the past and openly acknowledging dysfunction in an attempt to find closure. In the words of James Sunderland, "I don't care if it's dangerous. I'm going to town either way."

Suffering in Silence: *Silent Hill 4*, Mental Illness, and Therapeutic Experience in Japan

The narratives of mental illness and the therapeutic processes that shape the digital magic circle of *Silent Hill* are experienced differently across cultures. While the American player might find such discourses to be delightfully dangerous and perhaps strangely comforting, the Japanese player might find the experience of slipping into *Silent Hill* to be one of abject horror. In Japan, the very discussion of mental illness is taboo, and psychiatric care is never discussed openly.[7] Treatment facilities are often located in remote areas in unmarked buildings; patients are seen on a walk-in basis, assessed by a physician, prescribed medication, and dismissed without lengthy conversations, let alone psychotherapy. This invisibility of mental illness and its treatment in Japanese culture is bound to ideals of self-control and self-cultivation. Any external signs of depression or psychosis suggest that the sufferer has neither sufficient self-control nor the discipline required to develop it. Because of this, an individual who experiences mental illness is expected to suffer in silence, maintaining an outside face, or *tatemae*, of quiet confidence while hiding an inside face, or *honne* of despair and dissolution. This denial of mental anguish complicates Western approaches to psychotherapy; for the Japanese patient, confronting the past or recovering lost memories serves no practical purpose, and the very act of remembering might cause significant suffering in the present. From a Japanese perspective, then, the ghosts buried in the mind-crypt are best left undisturbed, as awakening them might curse the patient and further stigmatize his or her family by revealing the truth behind their collective *tatemae.*

Confronting and remembering a long-buried past are the very foundations of gameplay in *Silent Hill*. For the Japanese player, the dangers inherent in these therapeutic processes are intensified by *Silent Hill's* setting in a ruined American town, a truly foreign place where things are not what they seem. Swallowed by the town of Silent Hill, the Japanese player makes a terrifying journey not only into his or her own haunted mindscape to recover lost personal memories, but also into his or her cultural past, excavating the horrors of nuclear holocaust and the American occupation, as well as the present traumas of a global economic crisis that has deeply wounded Japanese masculine culture.[8] Since the mid-20th century, Japanese cultural expectations of success have demanded that young men endure an intense educational process with grueling exams in order to be admitted to the best universities and procure high-paying jobs in business as *sararimen*. Economic decline in the 1990s followed by the economic crash of 2008 have made high-paying jobs increasingly scarce and the attainment of previous levels of financial success almost impossible. In recent years, many individuals who have lost their positions have chosen to disappear into Aokigahara, the Suicide Forest outside of Tokyo; for some, dying in anonymity is preferable to facing public failure, enduring the onset of shameful depression, and bringing dishonor upon their families. A concomitant phenomenon is that of the *hikikomori*, typically young men between the ages of 15 and 30, who see no hope of employment or future success and have chosen to withdraw into their bedrooms to live a virtual life of digital gaming and electronic communication, never to emerge.[9] Supported by their parents, the *hikikomori* live between worlds; both alive and dead, they haunt the family home like ghosts, strange presences with no future, hidden away from public view.

The Japanese construction of mental illness as shameful, the dangers of remembering, and the phenomenon of hidden suffering, particularly in the form of *hikikomori*, are all evident in *Silent Hill 4: The Room* (2004). The game's narrative centers on Henry Townsend, a painfully shy 20-something who lives alone in a rundown apartment in Ashfield, a town adjacent to Silent Hill. The player slips into Henry's world in first-person perspective, awakening in bed blurry and disoriented. An investigation of the apartment reveals that the character-player is locked in, isolated from the outside world and several neighbors who know that Henry is missing but are unable to or uninterested in connecting with him. At first, the apartment feels safe, like a cocoon; through Henry's eyes, the player sees other people through the window, a peephole, and a crack in the wall, but no one—not even the player—can see Henry himself, who remains invisible. Despite this initial sense of insular isolation, Henry discovers that this apartment is not a safe haven. Following a fetid tunnel that erupts in his bathroom wall, Henry slips into the nightmarish world of Silent Hill, where gameplay is experienced in the third person. There, he uncovers the secret history of his apartment, which was once occupied by a serial killer named Walter Sullivan, all while being attacked by monstrous beings and engaging with people who may or may not exist. After each revelatory journey through Silent Hill, Henry awakens in his bed, only to discover that his apartment is now haunted, infected by a past that is actively destroying the present.[10] With each return, the apartment, which features the game's only "save point," becomes increasingly dangerous. The duality that marks gameplay across the Silent Hill franchise takes on new meaning in *Silent Hill 4*. The player-character is torn between two horrible choices: either remain isolated in first-person perspective in the now-toxic room and suffer madness in silence or escape into a dangerous third-person world of vicious monsters and unpredictable people. Withdrawal or engagement are both fraught with the risk of failure and potential death—a conundrum faced in modern Japan by the *hikikomori* and those who suffer from anxiety in perpetual silence while painting a placid "outside face." For the Japanese player of *Silent Hill 4*, stepping into Henry's character means taking on the sick role and entering into the isolating and slippery experience of mental illness—a process fraught with risks of contamination by association.

Silent Hill 4 not only illuminates issues surrounding mental illness in Japan, but also suggests a therapeutic approach different from the memory-obsessed western models of psychotherapy that dominate gameplay in *Silent Hill 2* and *Silent Hill: Shattered Memories*. The therapeutic experience in *Silent Hill 4* is rooted in a Zen Buddhist-based therapy, pioneered by Shoma Morita in the early 20th century, which entails a rejection of the past and a focus on the present. Morita therapy is divided into four phases, the first of which requires that the patient be kept on absolute bedrest and remain silent for about a week. In the second phase, the patient engages in physical activity while remaining mostly silent; the third phase continues with increased physical activity while allowing for conversation. While having been granted permission to communicate with others, the patient "should not explore his fears, worries, doubts and anxious feelings, but leave them as they are."[11] In the fourth phase, the patient is integrated back into society, but is "not allowed to talk of his internal problems" and "encouraged to talk only of external conditions."[12] Unlike western psychotherapies, which require continual discussion and an obsessive examination of past events, Morita therapy ignores the past in order to focus on mindful activity and to transcend anxiety in the present. In *Silent Hill 4*, Henry is stalked by events in his own and, by extension, his apartment's past; the more he learns about that past, the further he is drawn into Silent Hill's maddening maw. His only hope of survival is to focus on myriad seemingly menial tasks that will ultimately allow him to kill Walter's ghost (a literal destruction of the past) and escape from the haunted room that holds him captive. For the Japanese player—as for the *hikikomori*—each task accomplished might be viewed as a discrete event, a single step on the stairway away from isolated anxiety and into the integrated and active present.[13]

A Shared World

Like an unfolding lotus, the complexities of *Silent Hill*, including its construction of mental illness and the myriad cultural experiences of its therapeutic dynamics, persist beyond the magic circle of digital gaming and into the world of transmedial and transnational storytelling. *Silent Hill* has not only inspired two feature-length horror films, but also created a dedicated global fandom who interact through social media such as message boards, YouTube, Reddit, and Tumblr, as well as local and international cosplay conventions. Through interactive role playing, fans slip into myriad transnational interpretations of *Silent Hill* over and over again; in the process, they act out individual and collective traumatic memories, bringing them to life, confronting them, and ultimately experiencing a shared therapeutic transcendence that defies categorical boundaries. In the virtual and physical Silent Hill fandom, individuals from around the globe participate in an active dialogue about mental illness—including the experiences of dissociation, isolation, and stigma—from multiple narrative perspectives.[14] In the freedom of the magic circle, the culturally-imposed boundaries of "internal-self" and "external-other" become blurred, allowing for increased empathy and compassion, as well as connection, healing, and transcendence.

Notes

1. Consider the nature of mental illness itself; the sufferer might seem "fine" on the outside, but his/her calm veneer belies the pain and suffering roiling just below the surface. In Japan, this duality manifests as the "inside face" and the "outside face."

2. Jesper Juul, "Games Telling Stories?" *Game Studies: The International Journal of Game Research* 1:1 (2001). Retrieved at: http://www.gamestudies.org/0101/juul-gts/.

3. Johann Huizinga, *Homo Ludens: A Study of the Play Element in Culture* (Boston: The Beacon Press, 1985), 10; For digital game as magic circle, see Jan H. G. Klabbers, *The Magic Circle: Principles of Gaming and Simulation* (Dordrecht: Sense Publishing, 2006).

4. Huizinga, *Homo Ludens*, 10.

5. In "Ruin, Gender, and Digital Games," Evan Watts argues that ruined structures and degraded environments represent a destruction of the present and greater freedom from cultural restraints. *Women's Studies Quarterly* 39 (2011): 3–4.

6. On the archaeology of memory in forgotten places, also known as cryptonomy, see David Punter, "Spectral Criticism" in *Introducing Criticism at the 21st Century*, ed. Julian Woffreys, (Edinburgh: Edinburgh University Press, 2002).

7. Shuntaro Ando, Sosei Yamaguchi, Yuta Aoki, Graham Thornicroft, "Review of Mental Health Related Stigma in Japan," *Psychiatry and Clinical Neurosciences* 67 (2013), 471–482.

8. John W. Dower, *Embracing Defeat: Japan in the Wake of World War II* (New York: Norton Publishing, 2000).

9. Maggie Jones, "Shutting Themselves In," *New York Times*, January 15, 2006.

10. Upon awakening, the first-person blurriness intensifies, an experience shared by those suffering from acute mental illness in Japan. On his near overwork to desperation, depression, and near-suicide, a man named Karaoshi recalled, "I couldn't tell what day it was or which season. I could not register the scenery around me. Everything was blurred." Syota Nakahara https://www.youtube.com/watch?v=zKjgta8RDeQ.

11. Ken Takeda, "Morita Therapy," *Journal of Religion and Health* 3:4 (1964), 335–344 [340].

12. Takeda, 343.

13. Fumiko Maeda and Jeffrey H. Nathan, "Understanding *Taijin Kyofusho* through its Treatment, Morita Therapy," Journal of Psychosomatic Research, 46:6 (1999), 525–530.

14. Kai Mikkonen, "Graphic Narratives as a Challenge to Transmedial Narratology: The Question of Focalization," *American Studies* 56:4 (2011), 637–652.

PART 5

Music, Musicians, and Musical Theater

CHAPTER THIRTY-ONE

Kurt Cobain, Nirvana, and Generation X's Suicide Symbol

*Robert L. Bryant, Daniel Schwartz, and
Howard L. Forman*

Among the most iconic 1990s rock-and-roll posters was a portrait of Kurt Cobain's face, a plain white border, and the words, "Kurt Cobain 1967–1994" beneath his face. Viewers could interpret those facts as they chose. Kurt Cobain, the popular, beloved, admired face in the picture, lived until 1994 when he shot himself in the mouth with a shotgun at age 27. The generation's poet laureate died a death consistent with the painful existence and hopeless future depicted in songs he wrote and performed worldwide. What did it mean that he had killed himself? Was there a lesson? Was there a proper emotional response? Who were Nirvana, and what did they represent?

Nirvana, Popular and Defining Popularity

Nirvana's breakout album *Nevermind* displaced Michael Jackson's *Dangerous* as the week's best-selling album on the Billboard charts,[1] yet Nirvana's cultural significance cannot be conveyed through record sales alone. Nirvana was not only popular but also drastically and abruptly changed the face of music for years to come. It is no accident that, 25 years following the release of *Nevermind*, Pearl Jam, emerging from the same

Seattle music scene as Nirvana, remains one of the most pursued concert tickets in the United States. Nirvana's drummer Dave Grohl fronts one of today's most popular and politically active rock bands, The Foo Fighters. Nirvana's influence has been cited by a wide variety of artists. Lana Del Rey called them her most important musical inspiration.[2] Kanye West has been seen wearing a Nirvana T-shirt,[3] and Jay-Z quoted Nirvana's "Smells Like Teen Spirit" lyrics in his 2013 song "Holy Grail," rapping the famous chorus lyrics nearly verbatim, when he said, "And we all just entertainers, and we stupid, and we famous!"

Nirvana made most contemporaneous popular rock music sound laughable. It paved the way for stylistically similar musicians to achieve mainstream success with a new genre the media dubbed "grunge."[4] Almost overnight, the blowhard, hypermasculine, skirt-chasing "hair-metal" bands of the 1980s (Poison, Mötley Crüe, Quiet Riot, etc.), could no longer be taken seriously. Hair-metal bands, for all their spandex-leopard print, lipstick, leather pants, and pyrotechnic-fueled debauchery, were not rebels. They weren't out to change the world in the political or philosophical sense; they just wanted to party as hard as they could. Few were defended by critics as genuine artists, apart from Guns N' Roses. Musically and visually, the hair-metal sound drew influence from glam rock of the 1970s and highly costumed/choreographed hard rock bands such as KISS. Central to the hair-metal look and sound was theatricality and a competitiveness: Who had the most outrageously poufy long hair? The tightest leather or spandex pants? The biggest stage explosions? The most women? The fiercest/fastest guitar solo? With this summer-blockbuster mentality, most hair metal bands played what many critics considered uninspired, formulaic, shallow songs about sex, drugs, and rock and roll—indifferent to the claims that the 1960s- and 1970s-era sex, drugs, and rock and roll was originally a revolutionary mission, not simply a medium for partying, womanizing, and living out male fantasies. Grunge, by contrast, countered this paradigm by presenting a sound that did not attempt to be flashy at all. Stereotypically, grunge artists performed in drab flannel, thrift-store T-shirts, or whatever they might wear normally on the street. The guitars were still heavy, but the tempo slowed down, and overly flashy musicianship removed. Thematically, songs were more introspective and melancholy. For example, compare the hair-metal song "Girls, Girls, Girls" (1987) by Mötley Crüe and Soundgarden's popular grunge song "Black Hole Sun" (1994). The video for "Girls, Girls, Girls" shows muscle-bound bandmates in leather vests riding motorcycles to strip clubs, ogling dancers while singing lyrics as, "Trick or treat, sweet to eat . . . Yankee girls you just can't be beat / but you're the best when you're off your feet." Compare this to the video for

"Black Hole Sun," where the band wears faded, dingy jeans and T-shirts while playing in a field near a suburban development for deranged, creepily stylized 1950s families. A bizarre burning black orb from outer space slowly engulfs and destroys the planet—band included—as they sing the chorus lyrics, "Black hole sun / won't you come / and wash away the pain." In summary, there is a sharp stylistic divide between these genres. Why did Nirvana's music resonate so widely?

Cobain as Exemplar of a Generation's Struggle

Teenagers of the early 1990s lived in a different social reality from those before them. When the Berlin Wall fell in 1989 and the Soviet Union followed in domino fashion, the specter of nuclear war that hovered over American life during the post–World War II/Cold War years suddenly evaporated into thin air. Especially for teenagers who were constructing their identities, the question of purpose soon set in. With Communism defeated, what was the purpose of this young American generation? What did it mean to be American in a unipolar world?

Other massive changes in the social structure of America, planted in the late 1960s, were coming to fruition in the early 1990s as the children born from this newly liberated society approached adolescence and early adulthood. These children, the generation that followed the baby boomers, came to be known as generation X. Pew Research defines gen X as those born from approximately 1965 to 1980.[5] This generation grew up in an era demographically different from the baby boomers in two major ways. First, the family structures in which the children of gen X grew up differed from the family structures common to the baby boomer generation. Second, the fertility rate decreased significantly. Several historic causes for this abrupt change in family structure and fertility rate have been identified. In the late 1960s, more women entered the workforce. For example, the percentage of married women in the workforce rose to 50 percent by 1979.[6] Divorce rates reached unprecedented levels.[7] Improved contraceptive methods, including birth control pills, became available. *Roe v. Wade* legalized abortion. The U.S. economy shifted from postwar boom to 1970s stagflation. Because of these and other changes, more children grew up with divorced parents or single parent households. Furthermore, decreased fertility rates meant that *fewer* children were born each year, compared to the years following World War II's end. Pew Research estimates that 55 million gen Xers were born, as opposed to 75 million Baby Boomers.[8] Thus, in the democratic politics and market-driven culture of the United States, baby boomers had the numbers to call the shots and garner attention in popular culture.[9]

When the early 1990s arrived, just as the Cold War narrative was ending, the children of gen X were becoming teenagers and arbiters of youth culture. Seemingly overnight, as quickly or quicker than the American family structure changed in the late 1960s/early 1970s, the popular culture 20 years later shifted drastically and abruptly, going from glamorous, glittery, spandex-laden forms of hair metal to gritty, raw, grungy, and *real* (in the eyes of this new generation). Musicians such as Kurt Cobain, a "regular" guy from a broken home in an obscure part of the country, performed on stage in thrift-store clothes that seemed to say, "no, the life you've been showing us is not how we've lived it." The goals of American life were not so clear to this generation.

Cobain's adolescence, as documented in the HBO documentary *Kurt Cobain: Montage of Heck*[10] and in his personal journals,[11] was defined by his parents' divorce, which shattered his worldview. Per his mother's interview in this documentary, Cobain had been this happy, gregarious, energetic, creative young kid who had an unnatural magnetism and spark that drew people to him. (So energetic, in fact, she admits to taking him to see a doctor to be prescribed a pill for hyperactivity—"something like Ritalin"). After his parents' divorce, however, he was embarrassed by his family's transformation, compared to peers' "normal" families in his typical American small hometown of Aberdeen, Washington. "No one got divorced in those days," as his mother said. He began to act out at home and school, becoming an increasingly angry and depressive person. His father remarried, which angered him further. His antipathy to authority grew, and his angry, irritable mood became so unmanageable that he was eventually kicked out of his father's house. He spent years bouncing around between houses of family members and friends. Meanwhile, Aberdeen's economic fate, like many other small towns, mirrored and validated his decaying worldview. His published journal tells of feeling isolated in high school to the point of an actual suicide attempt. He claims to have decided to sit on the tracks at night and wait for death. As the headlight approached in the dark from the distance, he sat and accepted his fate, but when the train finally arrived, he felt the whoosh of a gust of wind and he realized he had sat on the wrong track of the two tracks. He never graduated high school.

Why Did Nirvana Resonate Psychologically?

Revisiting Cobain's creative output 25 years later, the first thought to come to mind from the mental health perspective is, "how could music this *depressing* be so hugely *popular*?" Could one imagine a contemporary musician coming out with a top-of-the-charts song called, "Rape Me" (a single on Nirvana's album, *In Utero*)? Perhaps the dim vision offered by Nirvana's music gained traction through tapping into the top A. H. Maslow's famous pyramidal hierarchy of needs, i.e., self-actualization. In brief, Maslow's "pyramid" explains human motivation to perform one behavior before another. Humans are motivated to perform actions to fulfill needs. The base of the pyramid includes survival needs: food, water, clothing, shelter, etc. If/when these physiologic needs are not met, all behavior focuses on obtaining them. When this basic level of necessity is attained, motivation is directed toward higher and more abstract needs: safety, then love (familial or otherwise), then esteem (feeling of self-worth and competence), and then the highest level, self-actualization, which is the state of a unified psyche, when a person becomes what they believed they could be. If we consider the drive to feel psychologically unified, to feel accepted as we are, whether our baseline mood is euphoric or dysphoric, then perhaps the idea of enjoying angry, sad, even suicidal music might not seem so far-fetched, for the enjoyment of validation may temper the ill effects of dysphoria.[12]

Like the Maslowian explanation of Nirvana's rapid embrace by U.S. popular culture, philosophers such as Ortega y Gasset postulated that motivation springs from *belief*. Much of what motivates us in life springs from the belief that we are unlikely to participate in an activity unless we *believe* it is worthwhile and true. When the average person boards an airplane, for example, this person boards based on beliefs about what will happen on the trip. This person doesn't know for a fact that the place will be safe, that the pilot will fly the plane to the correct location, or that the plane won't be hijacked. The average person simply believes these things based on former experience flying, the reputation of the airline, the number of times this person has personally experienced violent crime, etc. In this view, psyches can be considered as a collection of beliefs about the world, stories we tell ourselves about what is real and what is not real, stories about what the world is like and what the world is not like.[13]

With the music video for the band's breakout song, "Smells Like Teen Spirit," Nirvana confronted head-on the myth of what life was supposed to be like versus the actual experience for many adolescents. The video takes place in the dead of the night at a dystopian American high school pep rally, with the band playing in a dimly lit and dingy brown gym. Cheerleaders sport gothic black uniforms with unmistakable red anarchy "A" symbols on their shirts, and they perform in a cloud of dust before a crowd of disheveled, sloppily dressed, and disaffected teenagers. For added effect, a creepy, elderly night janitor gets prominent screen time as he dances to the side of the rally with his pathetic dance partner, a mop handle. This is a pep rally for rebellion, and in this way, the music captures this feeling of defiance-together. It is a collective recognition that this notion that the idyllic American life as presented over and over on television—that high school years are the best years of your life, that America is the most colorful, happy, best place in the world—was far-removed from the firsthand experience of many teenagers. The song ends with a catchy, repetitive hook that has been belted out countless times at parties. Oddly enough, it became the anthemic sing-along line: "A denial! A denial! A denial!"

Nirvana and the grunge sound of Seattle bands, more than any genre of rock and roll before or after, were associated with "teen angst." Why are teenagers and angst so often associated? Using developmental theorist Erik Erikson's stages of psychosocial development as a lens, it seems that the adolescent developmental stage is perhaps necessarily comprised of rebellion and discontent as youth enter a shape-shifting, limbo-like stage of identity selection. They take stock of childhood accomplishments and interests, experimenting with new roles and ideologies as they select who they will be as they pass from childhood into the final adult stage. Past roles and assumptions assigned to a person as a child may not correspond with what that person as an adolescent desires to continue as an adult, thus resulting in rebellious behaviors towards adults. Adults have already passed through adolescence and have, in general, already chosen what they believe about themselves and the world. But history marches forward, and thus teenagers always form their identities in a societal context separated in time (and increasingly, space) from the societal context of the preceding generation. Furthermore, especially in the rapidly changing technological and demographic context of the United States, roles that parents envision for their children may not *still exist* in the current society as they did when the parents were young.[14] Thus, as the children of generation X developed into teenagers in the early 1990s, their unique demographic viewpoint coincided with global cultural shifts that occurred at the exact moment in their personal development where they were exploring who they were, who they wanted to be, and what they believed.

Mere Teen Angst?

The problem with explaining the popularity of Nirvana's depressive music by ascribing it to teen angst is that one can so easily write it off as an expression of *mere* teen angst, i.e., something not to be taken seriously. It is possible so many have identified with Cobain because, simply, a lot of people, especially the young, experience mental illness. It is somewhat astounding to know that suicide is the 10th most common cause of death of people of all ages in the United States, per a 2013 study of deaths published online by the Centers for Disease Control and Prevention (CDC) as "Suicide: Facts at a Glance 2015" (www.cdc.gov). Suicide is the third leading cause of death for those between 10 and 14 years, and the second leading cause of death among people aged 15 to 34.[15] Considering the stigma of suicide, it is possible the real rates are even higher. In a National Institutes of Health (NIH) epidemiological study of high school students in grades 9–12, 14.5 percent (more than 1 in 7 people) had experienced suicidal ideation during the past year. Additionally, among that same group of students, 6.9 percent reported at least one suicide *attempt* during that past year. It is likely that the average high school student knew someone who either attempted or contemplated suicide. To punctuate the findings of this study, considering Cobain's demise, firearms were the number one method of completed suicide among this group.[16] Another study found the 12-month prevalence of suicidal ideation among adolescents to be as high as 17 percent, with 22.4 percent of females and 11.6 percent of males.[17]

Among adolescents diagnosed with major depressive disorder (MDD), suicidal thoughts and acts are even higher. Up to 85 percent of adolescents who were clinically followed for MDD or dysthymia presented with suicidal ideation. Of that number, 32 percent would attempt suicide during adolescence or young adulthood, 20 percent would make multiple attempts, and between 2.5 percent and 7.5 percent would complete suicide before or during young adulthood.[18]

Considering Nirvana's success among teens and young adults, it is interesting to consider the prevalence of major depressive disorder in the young. Studies from 2010 and 2011 show that 8 percent to 11 percent of teens aged 12 to 17 years and young adults aged 19 to 34 met criteria for MDD during that 12-month interval.[19]

Intertwined with manifestations of mental pathologies—e.g., generalized anxiety disorder, major depression, mood dysregulation, personality disorders, PTSD, etc.—is self-medication through substance abuse, used as a coping strategy. Such attempts to counter the effects of one mental disorder can lead to an additional mental disorder, specifically, the various substance use disorders. It was well known during his life that Cobain had recurring problems with heroin use. The media coverage even prompted an intervention from Child Protective Services. His wife Courtney Love admitted years later that they used heroin even while she was pregnant with their child, Frances Bean Cobain. The autopsy report after Cobain's death reported a blood heroin level of 1.52 mg/mL, triple the level that is fatal to some people.[20] Heroin users are fourteen times more likely to commit suicide. Heavy alcohol users have a fivefold increased risk.[21]

Increased suicidal tendencies occur not only with depression or drug use, but also with other mental illnesses, such as bipolar disorder[22] or schizophrenia. Without attempting to diagnose Cobain with a specific mental illness, we can see that the theme of mental illness in general was prevalent in Cobain's oeuvre. For example, on *Nevermind*, the song "Lithium" most likely refers to lithium as a psychiatric medication, a "mood stabilizer" most often used to treat bipolar I or II disorder, schizoaffective disorder, and borderline personality disorder. When he sings lines such as, "And I'm not scared / . . . / in a daze 'cause I found God," or, likewise, "I'm so excited / I can't wait to meet you there . . . I'm so horny," he arguably is evoking the manic phase of bipolar I disorder. Broadly speaking, bipolar I disorder (the more severe form of the disorder, formerly and colloquially known as manic depression) includes intermittent "manic episodes" that last at least a week, during which the person shows a euphoric mood, increased energy, and goal-directed behavior, starting new projects, with decreased need for sleep (as little as one or two hours per night), delusions of grandeur, hyperreligiosity (e.g., thinking oneself as a deity), hypersexuality, irritability, rapid rate of speech (think of someone speaking *much* faster than the average person, jumping from one loosely-related subject to another, unable to stop their flow of thoughts), and more. Problematically, this increased energy, productivity, and self-confidence are not necessarily directly toward completion of healthy or reality-based goals and often lead to self-destructive, risky behavior or shirking of one's work, school, or familial responsibilities (such as suddenly acting on the urge to drive cross-country, without alerting anyone). Other bipolar disorder symptoms include long periods of major depression between manic episodes, as well as emotional lability, i.e., rapidly shifting, intense mood swings.[23] The bridge verses of "Lithium" evoke this emotional lability of bipolar disorder; Cobain sings, "I love you, I'm not gonna crack / I killed you, I'm not gonna crack." Young members of generation X who already felt alienated and misunderstood by the baby-boomer-driven culture found a potent rallying cry in expressions of alienation from society uttered by such a talented popular culture artist. However, when Cobain ultimately committed suicide, the notion of Cobain as spokesman for the generation clashed with reality and implied that he was not simply a national icon but was perhaps an individual with his own personal mental crises. Perhaps this is one reason he was so reticent to accept the label of the voice of a generation.

Peace, Love, and Empathy

When trying to make sense of Cobain's suicide, Nirvana bassist and friend to Cobain since adolescence Krist Novoselik said, "You see the art, a lot of his messages are as plain as day [. . .]. In 20/20 hindsight you're like, why didn't I see that, I should have said something."[24] Cobain sang candidly about his anger, his sadness, and his most disturbing inner thoughts. He became the most famous man in music for a short time, and his words and music have resonated far beyond his rise to fame in the early 1990s. Yet even with near-universal acclaim for his ability to articulate his emotion and vision in ways that connected with so many, he was unable to feel that he was understood. Depression, suicide, mental illness . . . all remain stigmatized beyond Cobain's death, and probably will remain so for some time to come. Cobain did leave the world a final letter before his suicide. For all the dark imagery of his music, the closing lines of his farewell to the world are as instructive and succinct as any available approach to attempting to understanding mental illness: "Peace, Love, Empathy. [signed] Kurt Cobain."[25]

Notes

1. Billboard, "Billboard 200: 1992 Archive," accessed November 6, 2016, http://www.billboard.com/archive/charts/1992/billboard-200.

2. NME, "Lana Del Rey: 'I Was Inspired by Nirvana's Kurt Cobain,'" December 9, 2011, accessed November 6, 2016, http://www.nme.com/news/music/lana-del-rey-225-1286566.

3. Sarah Jones, "Rap Star Goes Rocker! Kanye West Pays Tribute to Nirvana Wearing a Vintage Sweatshirt from the 90s Grunge Band," *Mail Online,* November 19, 2015, accessed November 6, 2016, http://www.dailymail.co.uk/tvshowbiz/article-3326321/Rap-star-goes-rocker-Kanye-West-pays-tribute-Nirvana-wearing-vintage-sweatshirt-90s-grunge-band.html.

4. David Fricke, "Kurt Cobain, The Rolling Stone Interview: Success Doesn't Suck," *Rolling Stone,* January 27, 1994, accessed November 6, 2016, http://www.rollingstone.com/music/news/kurt-cobain-the-rolling-stone-interview-19940127.

5. Richard Fry, "Millennials Overtake Baby Boomers as America's Largest Generation," Pew Research Center, April 25, 2016, accessed November 6, 2016, http://www.pewresearch.org/fact-tank/2016/04/25/millennials-overtake-baby-boomers/.

6. U.S. Department of Labor, "Facts Over Time," Women's Bureau, accessed November 6, 2016, https://www.dol.gov/wb/stats/facts_over_time.htm.

7. Patricia H. Shiono and Linda Sandham Quinn, "Epidemiology of Divorce," *The Future of Children,* 4, no. 1 (1994): 18–23.

8. Fry, "Millennials Overtake Baby Boomers."

9. Shiono and Quinn, "Epidemiology of Divorce."

10. *Kurt Cobain: Montage of Heck*, dir. Brett Morgen, Hollywood, CA: Universal Pictures, 2015.

11. Kurt Cobain, *Journals*. New York: Riverhead Books, 2002.

12. A. H. Maslow, "A Theory of Human Motivation," *Psychological Review* 50, no. 4 (July 1943): 370–396.

13. Pascual Gargiulo and Humberto Luis Mesones-Arroyo, eds., *Psychiatry and Neuroscience Update: Bridging the Divide* (New York: Springer International Publishing, 2015), 49–62.

14. Erik H. Erikson, *Childhood and Society*. New York: Norton, 1964.

15. Centers for Disease Control and Prevention (CDC), "Injury Prevention & Control: Data & Statistics (WISQARS™)," last modified May 4, 2016, http://www.cdc.gov/injury/wisqars/index.html.

16. Scottye J. Cash and Jeffrey A. Bridge, "Epidemiology of Youth Suicide and Suicidal Behavior," *Current Opinion in Pediatrics*, 21, no. 5 (2009): 613–619.

17. CDC, "Understanding Suicide: 2015 Factsheet," accessed November 6, 2016, http://www.cdc.gov/violenceprevention/pdf/suicide_factsheet-a.pdf.

18. Ibid.

19. Ruth Perou et al., "Mental Health Surveillance Among Children: United States, 2005–2011," CDC, May 17, 2013, http://www.cdc.gov/mmwr/preview/mmwrhtml/su6202a1.htm; R. C. Kessler et al., "Age Differences in Major Depression: Results from the National Comorbidity Survey Replication (NCS-R)," *Psychological Medicine,* 40, no. 02 (June 17, 2009): 225–237.

20. Seattle Post-Intelligencer, "Nirvana's Kurt Cobain Was High When He Shot Himself," *Baltimore Sun*, April 15, 1994, accessed November 6, 2016. http://articles.baltimoresun.com/1994-04-15/features/1994105028_1_kurt-cobain-cobain-suicide-heroin.

21. Holly C. Wilcox, Kenneth R. Conner, and Eric D. Caine, "Association of Alcohol and Drug Use Disorders and Completed Suicide: An Empirical Review of Cohort Studies," *Drug and Alcohol Dependence* 76 (December 7, 2004): S11–S19.

22. Ross J. Baldessarini et al., "Decreased Risk of Suicides and Attempts during Long-Term Lithium Treatment: A Meta-analytic Review," *Bipolar Disorders* (October 2006): 625–639.

23. American Psychiatric Association, *Diagnostic and Statistical Manual of Mental Disorders (DSM-5)*. (Washington, DC): American Psychiatric Association, 2013.

24. *Kurt Cobain: Montage of Heck.*

25. Isaiah Rendorio, "Kurt Cobain's Suicide Note," *Seattle Television History*, last accessed November 6, 2016, http://depts.washington.edu/sthp/items/show/264.

CHAPTER THIRTY-TWO

Metallica, Heavy Metal, and "Suicide Music"

Adam W. Darlage and Paul "Hoagy" Burton

Jump in The Fire

In 1985, Tipper Gore and the Parents Music Resource Center (PMRC) convinced the U.S. Senate to hear testimony that rock music was dangerous for kids because lyrics about sex, drugs, and violence supposedly influenced them to engage in risky behaviors. At the same time, Ozzy Osbourne's "Suicide Solution," Metallica's "Fade to Black," and the alleged subliminal messages of Judas Priest's album *Stained Class* (1978) were held accountable for the tragic suicides of several young people in the mid-1980s. Metallica's protagonist is pretty clear about what he has in mind: "I have lost the will to live / Simply nothing more to give." At the Senate hearing, opposing witnesses Frank Zappa, John Denver, and Dee Snyder railed against Parental Advisory stickers, which they considered a form of censorship. It wasn't just about heavy metal, of course, but glam rock and hair bands too; nine of the dreaded "Filthy 15," the songs deemed most offensive by the PMRC, were by bands such as Def Leppard and Mötley Crüe in addition to heavier acts like Black Sabbath, AC/DC, and W.A.S.P.

Black Sabbath, AC/DC, and W.A.S.P.[1]

Heavy metal music bore the brunt of this criticism because many of its lyrics reference sex, drugs, and violence. As sociologist Deena Weinstein has pointed out, the lyrical and performative themes of heavy metal music represent both "Dionysian" and "chaotic" impulses within ordered society—sex, drugs, evil, death, abandonment, trauma, insanity, war, and the devil.[2] According to Weinstein, "the devil is frequently mentioned in heavy metal lyrics because he serves as shorthand for the forces of disorder."[3] Metallica's "Devil's Dance" is indicative of this trope, as it plays on biblical imagery from the perspective of the snake in the Garden of Eden: "Snake, I am the snake / Tempting, that bite you take." "Jump in the Fire" takes the devil's perspective as well: "The summons bell will chime / to join our sinful kind." The devil beckons you to "Jump in the fire!"

Many heavy metal artists write their own lyrics, and their own struggles with these forces of disorder make their music intensely personal. Metallica's lead singer James Hetfield has either written or cowritten all of the band's songs, and he has been very forthcoming about his trauma after his parents' divorce and his mother's death.[4] A Christian Scientist, she rejected traditional medicine on the basis of her faith; the lyrics of "The God That Failed" lament that choice: "The healing hand held back by the deepened nail / Follow the god that failed." Moreover, in 1986 the band lost their bassist Cliff Burton in a tragic bus accident while touring through Sweden during their Damage Inc. Tour. Metallica was also known as "Alcoholica" throughout their early years because of their heavy drinking, and lead guitarist Kirk Hammett notes that the name "became part of our legend."[5]

The band has been open about their internal issues as well. The documentary *Some Kind Of Monster* recounts Metallica's near implosion between 2001 and 2003 after the departure of bassist Jason Newsted and James Hetfield's time in rehab. The band hired therapist/life coach Phil Towle to help facilitate communication between band members, most notably Hetfield and his fellow cofounder, drummer Lars Ulrich. The movie portrays a raw band searching to rediscover itself despite personality conflicts and differences over creative control. The album *St. Anger* (2003) emerged from these dark days in the Metallica camp, and the band also found a new bassist, Robert Trujillo, formerly of Suicidal Tendencies and Ozzy Osbourne.[6]

Heavy metal concerts represent the physical, ritualistic expression of these Dionysian and chaotic impulses. Thunderous volume and pyrotechnics as well as alcohol and drug use fuel the aggressive behaviors typical of young (mostly male) crowd members looking for a "release" from the inhibited and routinized behaviors of respectable social interaction.[7] Many attendees whip themselves into a frenzy as they bang their heads in unison to their favorite songs, while others jump into "mosh pits" or go "crowd surfing." Both the personal lyrics and the Dionysian and chaotic themes of the music cannot be separated from their ritual performance at concerts and other venues.

Like heavy metal concerts, mental illness can be considered a form of social chaos. The "forces of disorder" within the culture of heavy metal certainly reflect mental health issues that society finds uncontrollable and threatening. These issues include addiction, depression, anxiety, paranoid schizophrenia, borderline personality disorder, and suicidal ideation. Violence is a chaotic theme in heavy metal culture as well, and like the young male "head-bangers" at heavy metal concerts, those who suffer from mental illness are more likely to be identified as aggressive or violent. The stereotype of the "madman" or "deranged lunatic" persists in American pop culture despite corrective efforts by the mental health community.[8] Band names such as Suicidal Tendencies, album titles like Ozzy Osbourne's *Diary of a Madman*, and song titles like Slayer's "Criminally Insane" play to this common stereotype.

The Recording Industry Association of America's (RIAA) decision to implement Parental Advisory stickers in 1985 only inspired heavy metal bands to play to these negative stereotypes about morality and mental health even more, as shock value—and identifying stickers of explicit content—certainly helped album sales. Today, death metal, black metal, and other subgenres of heavy metal have taken that logic to disturbing extremes.[9] As such, heavy metal music and mental illness suffer from an image problem exacerbated by groups like the PMRC who contend that correlation (listening to heavy metal and engaging in risky behaviors) invariably means causation (heavy metal causes these behaviors). Scholars have tested these claims scientifically with respect to mental health and explored whether those who listen to heavy metal music are more likely to have these kinds of issues compared to their peers who do not listen to heavy metal. Most studies end with some variant of the claim that "more research needs to be done in this area," although there has been promising new research on the potential benefits of heavy metal as a way for listeners to process their anger in healthy ways.[10]

This essay addresses the connection between heavy metal and mental health by examining the music of perhaps the biggest heavy metal band of all time, Metallica. Rather than focus on the elusive question of causation noted above, I examine what Metallica's music says about mental health issues such as post-traumatic stress disorder (PTSD), addiction, paranoia, and suicidal ideation. While the band's sound has changed over time, there is nonetheless a core ethic that pervades its music. Insofar as my analysis resonates with the experiences and expectations of others who listen to Metallica, I hope that it sheds light on the issue of mental illness within American pop culture.

Some Kind of Monster

Metallica is one of the most influential heavy metal bands all time, with sales of over 50 million albums in the United States and over 90 million worldwide since their debut album in 1983. With fellow American bands Anthrax, Megadeth, and Slayer, the band is considered one of the "big four" of thrash metal, heavy metal's largest subgenre. Thrash is aggressive and fast, with driving beats and lengthy guitar solos. The lyrics address personal and social issues such as addiction, institutional greed, and personal trauma. For many die-hard Metallica fans, their first four albums—*Kill 'Em All* (1983), *Ride the Lightning* (1984), *Master of Puppets* (1986), and . . . *And Justice For All* (1988)—represent the "canon" of Metallica's music. Despite its departure from thrash, the band's self-titled release *Metallica* (better known as the "Black Album") from 1991 is responsible for over 16 million domestic album sales alone.

Metallica has proven resilient to the changing musical tastes of America's youth, and retains a fandom of loyal "head-bangers" dominated by young men between the ages of 12 and 25. The most hard-core listeners of this genre reject the "softer" music favored by the majority of their peers (Top 40, hip-hop, country). Metallica's rigorous touring schedule has certainly helped them maintain fans despite charges that they have "sold out" to mainstream American culture. Few bands can rival the number of live shows that Metallica has performed. New generations of fans can hear classics such as "Seek and Destroy," "Master of Puppets," and "One" alongside newer tracks such as "St. Anger" and "Cyanide." Radio stations across America have instituted segments known as "Mandatory Metallica," during which only songs by Metallica are played.

Metallica's ability to adapt to changing musical tastes has also contributed to their staying power. During the commercial success of the 1990s grunge scene, Metallica survived in part by cutting their hair and incorporating elements of grunge, Southern rock, and country music into *Load* (1996) and *Reload* (1997). Some fans decried these moves as "selling out," but these albums both displayed the band's versatility and ability to bring in new audiences. The "new wave of American heavy metal" (NWOAHM) rose to prominence in the early 2000s through bands like Slipknot and Korn. Instead of rejecting these new acts, Metallica embraced them. Metallica's Summer Sanitarium tours of 2000 and 2003 featured Korn, System of A Down, Kid Rock, and Limp Bizkit and Linkin Park, respectively. Metallica was inducted into the Rock and Roll Hall of Fame in 2009, and only four other bands in the Hall represent the heavy metal genre as it emerged from the 1970s "new wave of British heavy metal" (NWOBHM): Led Zeppelin, Deep Purple, Black Sabbath, and AC/DC. Along the way, Metallica has released *Death Magnetic* (2008) and the EP *Beyond Magnetic* (2011). Both represent a return to the band's roots in thrash metal.

Disposable Heroes

Driven by Hetfield's distinctive downpicking (or "chugging") on rhythm guitar, Metallica's music revels in unbridled masculinity and energy. Metallica's lyrics tell stories of young men who are tested to the limits of human endurance through forces of disorder that include war, imprisonment, mental illness, or addiction. The victim in "Trapped Under Ice" fights his desperate condition: "I am dying to live . . . I'm trapped under ice." "The Judas Kiss" speaks of the chaos of addiction, encouraged by the devil: "Venom of a life insane / Bites into your fragile vein." The aggressive thrash tempo only heightens the sense of chaos in the lyrics.

Metallica may channel the Greek gods of Dionysus and Chaos, but the band does so through an existentialist ethic modeled on the Homeric virtue of arête. In the *Iliad* and *Odyssey*, "arête" means "excellence," especially with respect to bravery, and it is measured by the hero's effectiveness in a martial world of chaos. Metallica's arête, however, is the existential excellence of willpower and solitary endurance of suffering in the midst of horrific circumstances. The "whipping boy" of "The Unforgiven" decides "That never from this day / His will they'll take away." Similarly, "Broken, Beat & Scarred" recounts one who endures abuse and keeps getting back up despite the fact that "They cut and rape me," because "What don't kill ya make ya more strong." In "Eye of the Beholder," the protagonist takes pride in his ability to endure: "Endurance is the word / Moving back instead of forward seems to me absurd." These protagonists may not be Greek heroes, but they nonetheless achieve a kind of excellence through their willpower. These young men gain a measure of autonomy, if only through their ability to endure visceral suffering in a world beyond their control.

Unlike the world of Homer's *Iliad*, Metallica's arête of endurance speaks to the absurdity of wars and the consequences for the men who fight them, and their lyrics include elements that speak to PTSD. Both "For Whom the Bell Tolls" and "Disposable Heroes" lament the futility of war and excoriate government policy makers. Yet both also present the soldiers in a positive, if tragic, light. In "Disposable Heroes," the hero who must go "back to the front" realizes the ruse in a haunting lament and accepts his fate: "I was born for dying!" "For Whom the Bell Tolls" makes both the cynicism and heroism palpable. The soldiers described in the song should not have to experience this trauma and suffering, and yet they do. "Hero of the Day" recounts the PTSD of a soldier who comes back wholly different. His symptoms include the nightmares born of his experiences: "But now the dreams and waking screams." True to Metallica's arête of endurance, the soldier claims that while others try to "break" them, they go on. "One" recounts the plight of a wounded soldier, a mind trapped in his own body and cut off from the world, begging to be killed. The landmine he stepped on has left him with "life in hell." He will never be the same, and the trauma is his alone to bear.

Metallica's heroes campaign through battlefields of Dionysian addiction as well. Willpower is paramount, as these lyrics from "Frantic" demonstrate: "My lifestyle determines my deathstyle." "Master of Puppets" points to the crippling power of addiction from the perspective of the substance itself: "Come crawling faster / Obey your master." Addiction destroys everyone around the addict, as expressed in the dark "Harvester of Sorrow," which chronicles an addict's treatment of his family. "The House Jack Built" tells of the temptation of escape into Jack Daniels. "Sad But True" and "Sweet Amber" speak to the power of addiction that completely takes over the life of the addict: "I'm your only true friend now." True to the band's arête, the addict must conquer the addiction alone or be defeated by it. The substance in "Master of Puppets" claims that "I will occupy / I will help you die," a solution alluded to at the end of "The House Jack Built." There is no one to help the Homeric protagonist of a Metallica song; he stands alone to vanquish his demons or to fall deeper into addiction.

Frayed Ends of Sanity

Chaos of the mind may be precipitated by war and addiction, but also by experiences of fear, anger, or hopelessness. Like other heavy metal artists, Metallica often lumps different diagnoses of mental illness together under the terms "madness," "insanity," or "lunacy." The aptly titled "The Unnamed Feeling" may reference anxiety or panic or something else with lines such as, "Can't you help me be uncrazy?" and "I'm frantic in your soothing arms." In the space of three lines, "The Shortest Straw" mentions hysteria, megalomania, and dementia. In both cases, the connection to mental illness is there, but it is amorphous. One of Metallica's most haunting songs, "The Thing That Should Not Be," takes up the Cthulhu mythos of H. P. Lovecraft. Following the plot of *The Shadow Over Innsmouth* (1936), the song depicts a man's descent into madness through the "thing that should not be," an ancient immortal monster that "drains you of your sanity." The song ends by reminding the listener that, "in madness you dwell." This "madness" is inchoate and terrifying.

True to its testosterone-fueled thrash tempo, the band often connects mental illness to acts of violence. The refrain of "Whiplash" is "Acting like a maniac," and the song implores concertgoers to bang their heads against the stage "In a frenzied madness." Members of the "Metal Militia" exude "Metal madness." "Welcome Home (Sanitarium)" is the story of one who claims that he is wrongly locked up because he is "labeled mentally deranged." The patient claims that his captors toy with him by continually telling him that he is indeed insane. To escape his prison, he decides that he must kill, perhaps warranting his placement there in the first place. In addition, one of Metallica's most popular songs, "Battery," is a veritable anthem of anger and aggression.

Certain songs deal more explicitly with specific diagnoses. "Frayed Ends of Sanity" recounts the protagonist's struggle with what the lyrics suggest is paranoid schizophrenia. Schizophrenia, however, is also referenced alongside dementia in the space of two verses: "Twisting under schizophrenia / Falling deep into dementia." The song mentions depression as well. Mental health professionals treat schizophrenia, dementia, and depression as different, if sometimes related, forms of mental illness. The band uses these diagnoses to portray a man descending into mental chaos. True to the arête of endurance and masculine willpower, he must face his own fear because, as he admits at the end of the song, "Myself is after me."

Metallica's arête of endurance does not always mean that the hero wins the day. Songs about suicidal ideation suggest that sometimes the pain is just too much to endure. In "Just a Bullet Away," the protagonist contemplates suicide, perhaps because of a relationship gone wrong. Here, suicidal thoughts are juxtaposed with auditory hallucinations, the "voices" in his head. There is no resolution, as the listener is left to his or her imagination. Suicidal ideation appears most prominently in "Fade to Black." Grounded by late bassist Cliff Burton's deep driving riff, the lyrics deal expressly with suicidal ideation through the protagonist's feelings of worthlessness. As the song continues and becomes progressively heavier, our hero stands forth on the lonely precipice of suicide. A failed hero; if only he could have saved himself.

St. Anger

The lyrics of much of Metallica's music suggest that addiction and mental illness are forms of chaos that must be endured through will-power. Metallica's protagonists stand against absurd physical, mental, and emotional forces and exert the only control that they can. Through this, they attain a kind of excellence, or arête, that honors their sacrifices. Still, a few songs hint at alternate coping mechanisms. "My Friend of Misery" suggests that those who wallow in their misery, those "smothered in trag-edy," need to get over themselves. Here, dwelling on the pain is a fool-hardy strategy, not an opportunity to prove oneself. "St. Anger," which references Hetfield's alcohol addiction, holds out hope that anger can be channeled in a positive way. Here, the arête of endurance is replaced by a desire to channel his anger in a positive way.

Despite these exceptions, much of Metallica's music is about disposable heroes of the day besieged by the forces of disorder. This is precisely what makes the band's music so powerful. Fans are drawn to Metallica's music because they can identify and empathize with the protagonists of songs like "For Whom the Bell Tolls," "Frayed Ends of Sanity," "Hero of the Day," "Welcome Home (Sanitarium)," "Fade to Black," "Disposable Heroes," and "One," and fight alongside them in their minds as they listen to the music. For those fleeting moments, listeners become a part of the "Metal Militia": "We are as one as we all are the same / fighting for one cause."

Within the music of Metallica, the struggle for wholeness, mental health, and even life itself is both a solitary quest and a communal endeavor born of the relationship between the music and the listener. This heroic quest, defined by the cultivation of an arête of endurance, inspires an emotional release that can be witnessed at any heavy metal concert by observing the frenzy of the "head-bangers." Drawing upon the concept of "tragic pleasure," or "catharsis," as articulated by Aristotle in the *Poetics*, Robert Fudge adds that "we are instinctively drawn to such music, because of the emotion it elicits. By arousing our anger, our anguish, or our resentment, music helps us deal with our emotions and get over them sooner."[11]

Metallica's exalted place in American pop culture compared to other heavy metal bands is in no small measure due to the band's ability to inspire this kind of emotion through the combination of an aggressive musical style and quasi-Homeric lyrics that speak of tragic heroes fighting against forces beyond their control. People are drawn to the music because they can relate to issues of addiction, psychological trauma, war, and death, the forces of chaos they desperately want to control in their own lives.

Notes

1. On the PMRC and continued concerns about media violence, see Steven J. Kirsh, *Children, Adolescents, and Media Violence: A Critical Look at the Research* (Thousand Oaks, CA: Sage Publications, 2012).

2. Deena Weinstein, *Heavy Metal: The Music and Its Culture* (New York: Da Capo Press, 2000), pp. 35–43.

3. Weinstein, *Heavy Metal*, 41.

4. For an account of Hetfield's early days, see esp. Mark Eglinton, *James Hetfield: The Wolf at Metallica's Door* (Church Stretton: Independent Music, 2010).

5. MTV Icon interview, May 2003, cited in William Irwin, ed., *Metallica and Philosophy: A Crash Course in Brain Surgery* (Malden, MA: Blackwell, 2007), 30.

6. Director Joe Berlinger wrote about this process with Greg Milner in *Metallica: This Monster Lives: The Inside Story of* Some Kind of Monster (New York: St. Martin's Press, 2004).

7. On masculinity and heavy metal, see Robert Walser, *Running with the Devil: Power, Gender, and Madness in Heavy Metal Music* (Hanover, NH: University Press of New England, 1993), and Glenn T. Pillsbury, *Damage Incorporated: Metallica and the Production of Musical Identity* (New York: Routledge, 2012).

8. On this stereotype, see esp. Otto F. Wahl, *Media Madness: Public Images of Mental Illness* (New Brunswick, NJ: Rutgers University Press, 1995).

9. See Gavin Baddeley, *Lucifer Rising* (London: Plexus, 1999), and Michael Moynihan and Didrik Søderlind, *Lords of Chaos: The Bloody Rise of the Satanic Metal Underground* (Los Angeles, CA: Feral House, 2003).

10. Leah Sharman and Genevieve A. Dingle, "Extreme Metal Music and Anger Processing," *Frontiers in Human Neuroscience* 9, no. 272 (May 2015), doi: 10.3389/fnhum.2015.00272.

11. Robert Fudge, "Whisper Things into My Brain: Metallica, Emotion, and Morality," in *Metallica and Philosophy, A Crash Course in Brain Surgery*, ed. William Irwin (Malden, MA: Wiley-Blackwell, 2007).

About the Editor and Contributors

About the Editor

Sharon Packer, MD, is a New York-based physician, psychiatrist, and assistant clinical professor at Icahn School of Medicine at Mount Sinai (New York). She has authored six books on the interface between popular culture, film, comics, and psychiatry, as well as several book chapters on psychiatry, religion, and race, and has published academic articles on the history of medicine and psychopharmacology. She writes a column called "Why Psychiatrists Are Physicians First" for *Psychiatric Times.* For more info see http://psychiatryinpopularculture.com.

About the Contributors

Aaron Barlow teaches English at New York City College of Technology of the City University of New York.

Rosa JH Berland is a curator and historian of modern and contemporary art. Her research interests include the intersection of modern psychiatry and visual culture. She holds an MA in Art History from the University of Toronto and serves as the honorary director and curator of the Edward E. Boccia Artist Trust.

Alexis Briggie received her PhD in clinical psychology from the Derner Institute of Adelphi University. She is currently an attending psychologist in the Addiction Psychiatry Consult Service at Montefiore Medical Center, Bronx, NY. Her areas of professional interest include psychosomatic medicine, substance use disorders, and mindfulness-based psychotherapies.

Robert L. Bryant, MD, is a psychiatry resident at Montefiore Hospital/Albert Einstein College of Medicine, Bronx, NY. At Tulane University he earned an English major, wrote about music for an alternative news weekly, played in a local rock band, and drove delivery service for a poboy shop.

Jeffrey Bullins is an assistant professor of communications at Plattsburgh State University of New York. His research interests include sound design for film and television as well as genre studies, particularly horror. Jeffrey is also a freelance sound designer and audio engineer.

Paul "Hoagy" Burton has been involved in writing, recording, and performing music in one form or another since 1997. In 2010, he cofounded Crusader, a Chicago-based heavy metal band.

Mary L. Colavita, MD, is the chief resident at Bronx Psychiatric Center in the Department of Psychiatry, Montefiore Medical Center/Albert Einstein College of Medicine. She completed her BA in English at Columbia University and her medical school training at New Jersey Medical School, UMDNJ.

Laura E. Colmenero-Chilberg is professor of sociology, Black Hills State University, and has focused her scholarly interests on inequality and popular culture. Her recent research analyzes society through the lens of the apocalyptic novel, an interest that began with Nevil Shute's *On the Beach* and continues with our present-day obsession with zombies.

Adam W. Darlage is an instructor in the Humanities and Philosophy Department at Oakton Community College in Des Plaines, Illinois. He teaches courses in world religions and world mythologies.

Jocelyn Dupont is associate professor in American studies at Perpignan University, France. His current research focuses on the cinematographic representation of psychopathology in the American feature film from 1945 to the present day. In 2016, he edited an issue of the film journal *CinemAction* about cinema and mental illness.

Shawn Edrei recently completed his doctoral studies at Tel-Aviv University and continues to pursue research in the fields of digital narratology and interactive fiction. He has taught courses on contemporary American fantasy, superheroes in American mythology, and narratology in the digital age at TAU's Department of English and American Studies.

Nicole Eugene is a doctoral candidate in communication studies at Ohio University. As an interdisciplinary scholar she focuses on hidden disabilities, narratives, and feminist theory. Her work has been published in *Howard Journal of Communications* (forthcoming) and *Anthropology of Consciousness* and *Callaloo: A Journal of African Diaspora Arts and Letters.*

Howard L. Forman is assistant professor of psychiatry at Albert Einstein College of Medicine. He is director of the Addiction Consultation Service at Montefiore Medical Center and is frequently sought out to opine on the intersections of addiction, mental health, and popular culture.

Daniel R. Fredrick is an assistant professor at the American University of Sharjah, where he has taught writing since 2008. His primary interests are in Greek and Roman rhetoric and literature. In his spare time, he travels to key places in the history of rhetoric, including Athens, Rome, Syracuse, and Leontini.

Haley Gienow-McConnell is affiliated with the Department of History, York University (Toronto). She is a specialist in U.S. disability history. Her academic work is bolstered by her personal life, as her husband is deaf. She is a fluent ASL user and ally to the deaf community.

Sonal Harneja is a psychiatry resident at Montefiore Medical Center in the Bronx, NY. Her interests within psychiatry include understanding the relationship between mental illness and society, and working to be an advocate for patients with mental illness along with their families.

Kristi Rowan Humphreys is editor and senior writer for the University of Mary Hardin-Baylor in Belton, Texas. Recent publications include the monograph *Housework and Gender in American Television: Coming Clean* (2015).

Jessica N. Lee received her PhD in rhetoric, composition, and the teaching of English from the University of Arizona. She is currently an instructor at Portland Community College's Rock Creek campus, where she teaches composition and technical writing. Her approach to teaching writing is informed, in part, by her research interests, which include medical rhetoric, particularly with regard to self-disclosure and psychiatric stigma.

Kate Lieb is a third-year psychiatry resident at Montefiore Medical Center. She graduated from the Sackler School of Medicine of Tel Aviv University. Her main interest is in perinatal psychiatry, but she also has an interest in community resources and advocacy for the severely mentally ill.

Mariel Freeman Lifschutz is a fourth-year student at Oberlin College, graduating in May 2017. She is studying English with a concentration in creative writing, and French. Her areas of interest are Shakespeare, popular media, and the connection between early literature and contemporary entertainment.

Vincent LoBrutto is the author of 11 books on the cinema including *Stanley Kubrick: A Biography* (1997), *The Encyclopedia of American Independent Filmmaking* (Greenwood Press, 2000), and *Becoming Film Literate* (Praeger, 2003).

Martin J. Manning is a research librarian in the United States Diplomacy Center, U.S. Department of State, Washington, D.C., and curator of the Public Diplomacy Historical Collection. His areas of research and expertise include popular culture, world's fairs, propaganda, and library history. He has a BS from Boston College and an MSLS from Catholic University of America.

Michael Markus holds a PhD in history from Washington University in St. Louis. His research focuses mainly on 19th-century British political history and on the history of British imperialism.

Sean Moreland is a writer, editor, and educator, much of whose research concerns Gothic and horror fiction in its literary, sequential art, and cinematic guises. He teaches in the English department at the University of Ottawa.

Mark O'Hara, PhD, is an educator, poet, and filmgoer who teaches at Stephen T. Badin High School and Miami University (Ohio).

W. Scott Poole is a professor of history at the College of Charleston. He has authored *Monsters in America* (2011), an award-winning study of monstrosity and American history, as well as *Vampira: Dark Goddess of Horror* and *In the Mountains of Madness: The Life and Extraordinary Afterlife of H.P. Lovecraft*.

E. Deidre Pribram is professor in the communications department of Molloy College, Long Island, New York. She writes on cultural emotion studies, film and television studies, gender, and popular culture. Her most recent book is *A Cultural Approach to Emotional Disorders: Psychological and Aesthetic Interpretations* (2016).

Caleb Puckett is a writer, editor, instructional designer, and independent researcher. His work has appeared in a host of small, large, and academic press publications for well over a decade.

Eric Sandberg teaches literature at the University of Oulu, Finland. His research interests include modernism, 20th- and 21st-century literature, and genre fiction. His monograph, *Virginia Woolf: Experiments in Character*, was published in 2014.

Daniel Schwartz is a medical student at Albert Einstein College of Medicine, class of 2018, and an alumnus of the University of Vermont, where he studied psychology.

Morgan Shipley is a visiting assistant professor and academic advisor, Department of Religious Studies, Michigan State University.

Lisa Spieker is a third-year PhD candidate at Tübingen University. Her thesis, "Writing Madness: Confession and Stigma in Contemporary Mental Illness Memoirs," is about the literary strategies authors use to negotiate stigma and regimes of truth. Further research interests include medical humanities, popular culture, and sexuality studies.

Eric J. Sterling, PhD, Indiana University, is distinguished research professor of English at Auburn University Montgomery, where he has taught for 23 years. He has authored four books and 70 refereed articles.

Leni Van Goidsenhoven is a doctoral researcher of the FWO Flanders at KU Leuven (Belgium), connected to the research unit Literary and Cultural Studies. Currently, she is preparing a PhD on autism and self-representation.

Brenda S. Gardenour Walter is associate professor of history at the Saint Louis College of Pharmacy. Her most recent publications examine the multivalent relationships between popular cultural constructions of the body, architectural theory, and the natural world.

Index